The New World Guide To

BEER

MICHAEL JACKSON

THE NEW WORLD GUIDE TO

BEER

MICHAEL JACKSON

RUNNING PRESS
PHILADELPHIA, PENNSYLVANIA

D E D I C A T I O N
To Sam Gunningham
On my travels, I miss you

A QUARTO BOOK

Text copyright © 1988 Michael Jackson

First published in the USA in 1988 by
Running Press Book Publishers
125 South Twenty-second Street
Philadelphia
Pennsylvania 19103

Canadian representatives: General Publishing Co. Ltd.
30 Lesmill Road, Don Mills, Ontario M3B 2T6.

Reprinted 1989

ISBN: 0 89471 649 2

This book was designed and produced by
Quarto Publishing plc
The Old Brewery, 6 Blundell Street
London N7 9BH

SENIOR EDITOR Maria Pal
PROJECT EDITOR Paul Barnett
EDITORIAL Lydia Darbyshire
Eleanor Van Zandt
Malcolm Couch

DESIGNER John Grain
DESIGN ASSISTANCE Richard Slater
ADDITIONAL PICTURE RESEARCH Joanna Wiese
EDITORIAL DIRECTOR Carolyn King
ART DIRECTOR Moira Clinch

Typeset by Burbeck Associates Ltd
Manufactured in Hong Kong by Regent Publishing
Services Ltd.
Printed by Leefung-Asco Printers Ltd, Hong Kong.

This book may be ordered directly from the publisher.
Please add $2.00 for postage. But try your bookstore
first! Running Press Book Publishers, 125 South Twenty-
second Street, Philadelphia, Pennsylvania 19103.

TO TASTE OTHER LANDS is a sociable experience, even if the traveler has to remember the notebook and camera in his pocket. As all writers know, the long lonely haul comes later, at the keyboard. At this stage, a little encouragement goes a long way. When I began to explore in earnest, 15 years ago, not everyone understood my preoccupations and intentions, but I have been sustained by the encouragement of my fellow writers. For this, I especially thank members of the wine-writing community on both sides of the Atlantic, and the pioneers who are now my colleagues in the British Guild of Beer Writers.

In the earliest days, I was greatly encouraged by words of praise from Professor Doctor Ludwig Narziss, at the Weihenstephan Faculty of Brewing, Munich University. More recently, I have come to know Dr Hans Günter Schultze-Berndt, of the University of Berlin, whose kind helpfulness I also greatly appreciate. In Britain, I have been helped by Dr John Hammond and others at the Brewing Research Foundation, Nutfield. In the United States, I have enjoyed exchanging opinions (and beers) with the principals of the Siebel Institute, Chicago, and Dr Michael Lewis, of the University of California, Davis.

The bodies that represent the brewing industry in different countries know I cannot praise all of their members, and may criticise some, but they have always done their even-handed best to help me. My special thanks to Ulrich Opherk, of the Deutscher Brauer-Bund; Michel Brichet, of the Confederation of Brewers, in Belgium; Michael Ripley and David Long at the Brewers' Society, in Britain; Charlie Papazian, Daniel Bradford, Jeff Mendel and all friends at the Association of Brewers, in Boulder, Colorado.

When I began writing on this subject, there was only one consumerist organization for beer-lovers, and that still thrives: The Campaign for Real Ale, 34 Alma Road, St Albans, England AL1 3BW. Several others have been formed since, and I have especially enjoyed the assistance of The Objective Beer-Tasters, Post Office Box 32, 2600 Berchem 5, Antwerp, Belgium; and PINT, Post Box 3757, 1001 AN Amsterdam, The Netherlands.

I owe a special debt of gratitude to beer-lovers everywhere, especially Jaroslav Koran, Johannes Schulters, Mr and Mrs Klaus Emmerman, Antoine Denooze, Nico van Dijk, Derek Walsh, the journalistic community of Helsinki, the management and staff of The Northern Brewer (Toronto, Canada), Karl von Knoblauch, Philip Kralovec (of the National Restaurant Association, Chicago), Alan Dikty, George Makris, Mark Kessenich, Michael Howe, the American Homebrewers Association, Vince Cottone, Fred Eckhardt, Brad Gordon, Ken Vermes and Larry Popelka. They helped me find my way.

I have visited more breweries than anyone, and I thank their proprietors for their patience, and for helpfulness far beyond self-interest. Many beer-importers and retailers have also been of great assistance to me, and I very much appreciate their help.

For the love of good beer, I hope it was all worthwhile.

CONTENTS

The Beer Renaissance

THE WORLD ALWAYS KNEW that beer was a noble and complex drink, but, for a moment in history, that was forgotten. Now it is being remembered. In every country that can afford such luxuries, traditional styles of beer are being revived and new ones are being created.

Some are being produced in tiny, new breweries adjoining pubs or restaurants, and serving only the one outlet. This type of establishment, often known as a brew-pub, is itself a tradition revived. So is the new generation of very small, craft breweries. These new micro-breweries are in general far smaller than the old-established local and regional independents, and they in turn are dwarfed by the national and, increasingly, international, giants.

The smaller the brewery, the more easily it can devote itself to specialty styles of beer. The size of a batch, and the number of consumers required to appreciate it, permit individuality in the product. Not every brew-pub takes this opportunity, but many do. The best of the micro-breweries certainly do. A good few old-established independents have rediscovered the confidence to assert their heritage. Even some of the national and international giants have found time to produce a few specialty beers, despite their greater commitment to the uniformity of their principal, mass-market brands.

In volume, sales of these "boutique beers" are tiny, but that is of no concern to those consumers who seek character in what they eat and drink: whether it be beer or wine, bread or pasta, cheese . . . any of the basic, honest pleasures that span the elemental and the gastronomic. Château Latour or Freemark Abbey are a drop in the Gironde or the Pacific as compared to Gallo, but no less fine for that.

What the revivalists and new brewers offer is a variety, not just of names and packages, but of classic beer-styles. That is why many of them dislike the term "boutique beer": it is descriptive, but perhaps suggests that their products might be "designer" whims, fashionable but ephemeral.

Beer and wine are both as old as civilization. Beer may be the older of these two great fermented beverages, and perhaps even pre-dates bread. There may have been beer more than ten thousand years ago, and there is specific evidence of its having been enjoyed in Mesopotamia as early as 4000 BC. Not until the civilizations of modern Europe — and the 1700s — did either drink begin to assume the styles that we know today, but that is pedigree enough.

The oldest styles of beer still in production are the Lambic family, of Belgium, traditionally fermented with wild yeasts, matured in wood from Bordeaux, Oporto, and occasionally Jerez, and emerging with the apéritif sharpness of a Manzanilla *fino*. The Weisse Wheat Beers of Berlin, with their acidic sparkle, are still the "Champagnes of the North," as Napoleon's troops dubbed them. Britain's fruity ales, at their finest cask-conditioned, suit a nation with a taste for the wines of Bordeaux. Ireland's famous Stouts might be summed up as being "dry and almost stingingly powerful of flavor, with a dark, fat, rich tang", just as Hugh Johnson has described a true Amontillado. The Munich Dark and amber-red Märzen beers of Bavaria have the spiciness of a Gewürztraminer. A true Pilsener, pale, dry and fragrant, is the beer world's Meursault or Montrachet. There are around 20 principal styles of beer, and as many sub-categories, the differences between each as great as those that distinguish a Chardonnay from a Pinot Noir. Each style of beer has its own time of day, or place at the dinner table. No one style is better than another; they are merely different.

Some breweries produce beer in only one style, whereas others may have as many as a dozen in their portfolio. There are about 5,000 breweries in the world, producing around 15,000 brands of beer.

By far the largest proportion of these beers are distant derivatives of the Pilsener style. Outside the most traditional brewing nations, these represent the only style of beer with which many drinkers are familiar. Small wonder that such unfortunates may be puzzled, or even shocked, when they are confronted with a beer of more character. A drinker accustomed only to an American generic Chablis might detest the Burgundian product, and consider a Sauternes to resemble cough medicine.

As the principal types of fermented drink, wine and beer are companions of honor: a part of the gastronomic heritage of the warm and cool climates which respectively grow fermentable fruits (especially the grape) and grains (notably malting barley).

The two shared their celebrity in the 1700s and early 1800s, and in some parts of Europe beer never lost this respect. Perhaps wine became more precious in the late 1800s, when in Europe it was threatened with extinction by the pest *Phylloxera*. At the same time, a better understanding of yeast behavior, and of refrigeration, was making the most celebrated beers more consistently and widely available.

The first beer made with the intention that it be a mass-market product was the American Budweiser, launched in 1876 and still growing in sales. Almost a century later, Dr E. F. Schumacher's book *Small Is Beautiful* captured a new mood in Western society. One manifestation of this was a new generation of micro-breweries. They first emerged in Britain, and spread with astonishing speed. The movement gained momentum against a background of other social changes: more leisure and travel, a more widespread interest in the everyday culture of other countries, including their food and drink, a desire to conserve the best of Britain's heritage, and a more eclectic attitude toward behaviour and status. In 1976, the first micro-brewery in the United States fired its kettle. That was New Albion, in Sonoma, Northern California. Sad to say, New Albion did not survive — but in both Europe and the New World the memory of small-scale craft brewing had been roused from its slumbers. It is now wide awake.

Why Beers Differ

LIKE THE BIGGEST-SELLING wines, many mass-market beers are made to appeal to as broad an audience as possible. This means they have to be produced at a highly competitive price, and that their character must offend no one. They are not exciting because they are not meant to be.

If a beer is to have character, it must be because the brewer deliberately gives it one. That is the first requirement. Some brewing companies try to accommodate both approaches. They make a bland product as a basic, quenching alcoholic drink, and one or two more interesting specialties for the beer-lover.

Yet ambition is not enough. A brewer can do everything right, and still produce a disappointing beer. Another may seem casual, but make a classic. The study of different brewers' methods does not diminish this mystery, but heightens it. However great their knowledge, experience, and care, some people are intuitively good brewers; others are not. Brewing remains an art as well as a science.

The varieties of barley (or sometimes wheat) used; the place and season in which they were grown; the procedure of malting, especially at the kilning stage; the number of different malts employed; the method of their infusion or decoction; the use of less traditional grains (corn or rice, for example) or other brewing sugars as "adjuncts" to the main mash; the way in which the solution of fermentable sugars (known as wort) is run off; the character of the water (it can always be softened or hardened, but the less it has to be treated, the better); the length of the boil in the brew kettle; the way in which the kettle is heated; the varieties of hops added; the stages at which they are used; the type of yeast; the temperature and duration of fermentation; the further maturation and conditioning; the type of (or absence of) filtration and pasteurization: all of these elements shape the beer. Among them, and especially in the temperature and duration of various processes, the permutations are infinite.

If a beer is dark, sweet or cloudy, that is not because the brewer did not know how to make a pale, dry, clear beer. An Abbey Ale does not represent a failed attempt to brew a Miller Lite.

There is a recognized basic method for the production of each classic style. Certain malts are characteristically used to produce beers of a particular palate and color; certain varieties of hops are favored for this classic style or that; the yeast strain, fermentation, and maturation represent a major divide. These are to the brewer what a recipe is to a chef. With the same ingredients and methods, no two brewers make exactly the same beer, any more than two chefs produce identical soufflés.

Even with the same brewer, no two batches are identical. Any sizable brewery blends batches to improve consistency. A company that tries to brew exactly the same beer in more than one place can never achieve a perfect match. In these instances, some beer-lovers will claim they can distinguish

Vents, cowls, pagodas and pyramids (*left*) are the signs of a building in which barley is or once was malted. Many breweries used to do this themselves, and some still do. *Bottom:* Traditional "floor maltings" in Bohemia. Malt is turned and dried on the stone floor.

between the products of different locations; it is doubtful whether the differences are that great.

"Only recently have we begun to understand what a remarkable art brewing really is," wrote Professor Anthony Rose in the *Scientific American* in 1959. "The brewmaster has been manipulating some of the subtlest processes of life."

When Pasteur studied the mysteries of yeast for wine- and beer-makers, he laid the basis for brewing science, microbiology and biochemistry. These sciences continue to share their foundations. In Japan, Suntory has established, separate from its brewing and distilling operations, an institute to work on DNA recombination and synthesis. There are other, less dramatic, examples of the proximity of these sciences. In practice, the mechanics of brewing are the same for the artist or the scientist (or the combination of both), in the French farmhouse or what appears to be a Japanese spacecraft.

MALTINESS

What grapes (or other fruits) are to wine, grain (usually barley) is to beer. Wine is easier to make than beer. Before barley, or sometimes wheat, can be fermented, it has to be turned into malt. This metamorphosis renders its starches soluble, and is the first step toward their release as fermentable sugars.

Malt is the fermentable material. Hops are the seasoning. Yeast is the agent of fermentation. These are the three central elements in the character of all beer. Their balance is different in each classic style of beer, but they are always there: in bouquet, palate, and finish.

Barley or wheat grains are turned into malt by first being steeped in water, then allowed partly to germinate. This is arrested by the grains being dried, in a kiln, over hot air. Different characteristics can be imparted to the malt (and ultimately to the beer) by the way in which it is dried. Its moisture content at the time of drying, the temperature and the duration of the process — all create differences.

The most lightly kilned, palest malts are used in Pilsener beers. A slightly longer kilning, but a "curing" and definitely not a toasting, is used to produce what the British call Pale Ale Malt and the Continental Europeans sometimes refer to as being in the Vienna style. A moister kilning, almost a stewing, produces what the Americans call Caramel Malt, the British call Crystal and the Continental Europeans call the Munich style. Further degrees of kilning produce Chocolate Malt (named because of its resemblance in color and taste to the bean) and Black Malt (which has almost the character of burnt toast). There are several other variations and names; some beers contain as many as eight different styles of malt, and that is just the beginning of their complexity.

The place in which these procedures are carried out is called a maltings. There are many independent maltings, but others are owned by breweries (or whiskey distilleries), and are sometimes on the same site.

At the brewery, the malt gives up its fermentable sugars in an infusion or decoction in hot water, in a vessel known as a mash tun. The maltiness of the beer will be influenced by the cycle of temperatures and the method used.

The infusion method, which is not unlike the making of tea, has traditionally been favored by British brewers. It might be carried out at a temperature of 65-68°C (149-154°F) for one, two, or three hours. The decoction method, traditionally used in Continental Europe, is more complicated, but brings about a more exhaustive conversion of starches. The British say their malt is so sweet and clean that they do not need to go to such trouble. Protagonists of the decoction method take pride in their traditionalism and craftsmanship, especially if they carry it out in a sequence of two or three operations per brew. A decoction starts at a lower temperature, perhaps 35°C (95°F), and can last for five to six hours. Portions of the mash are periodically removed, heated to a higher temperature, then replaced, gradually increasing the temperature of the whole until it reaches perhaps 76°C (169°F). A method that combines elements of both techniques is known as step infusion.

The sweet liquid formed in the mash is filtered either through a false bottom in the tun or through a separate vessel; this liquid is known as wort. After the first run, water is sprayed over the bed of the mash to extract more wort. The first run is, naturally, the maltiest and sweetest.

HOPPINESS

The actual process of brewing is a boiling of the wort for at least an hour, usually 90 minutes, and sometimes longer. During this time, the principal addition of hops is made. What is variously known as the cone, blossom or flower of the hop is used. It may be employed in its natural form, or compacted into pellets (for ease of airtight storage), or in the form of a liquid extract.

Some brewers feel that the blossom best retains its natural resins and oils if it is not pelletized. Others argue that the blossom is vulnerable to oxidation, while the pellet is protected from the atmosphere by being so tightly packed. Hop extract is used for convenience. Although it is an extract solely of hops, the process of production does alter its nature.

Hops may be added only once during the boil, or two or three times. The earlier the addition, the drier or more bitter the end result. Most brewmasters, if they were producing the beer solely for their own consumption, would make it more bitter than they do for their customers. The later the addition of hops, the more they impart aroma, which is equally valued. If blossoms are used, the brewed wort may be run through a strainer, to remove their residue, on its way to being cooled and fermented. Some brewers place a bed of fresh hop blossoms in the strainer to add yet more aroma.

Different varieties of hops may be used for each addition. Or there may be a different blend of varieties each time. The varieties that best confer bitterness are regarded as workaday hops. Those that impart aroma are the aristocrats. Even among bittering hops, there are differences of character between, for example, the softness of Fuggles or the dryness of Northern Brewer. Among classic aroma hops, the American Cascade has variously been described as having minty, geraniol, and citric notes; the English Golding has a delightful rounded pungency; the German Hallertau, Hersbruck, and Tettnang and the Czech Saaz are fresh and delicate. There are more varieties, and new ones are constantly being introduced.

FRUITINESS

Before the workings of fermentation were understood, it was always allowed to take place at natural temperatures, in its own fevered way. When that happens, the yeast rises to the top of the vessel. This old method, top-fermentation, produces beer with a natural fruitiness.

Top-fermentation is used to make all Wheat Beers, true Ales, Stouts, and Porters, and as a result they should always have some definite fruity notes in their character.

Top-fermentation takes place at 15-20°C (59-68°F), and products made in this way will express their palate fully only if they are served at a moderate temperature. Their fermentation may take only three or four days, though traditional brewers like them to spend eight (two sabbaths) in the vessels. In traditional top-fermentation, the yeast is then skimmed from the vessels, and the fermented wort transferred either to casks or to conditioning tanks. The beer may then be matured at a natural or cellar temperature, often for only a few days, sometimes for a month, only occasionally longer. This is known as warm conditioning.

Some top-fermenting beers also have a period of colder maturation. In top-fermentation, neither long nor cold maturation is necessary, but the method used depends upon the result the brewer is seeking. He may add these stages to restrain the fruitiness a little (arguably at risk to its overall character), to stabilize the beer further, or to enable it to be served cooler.

During the conditioning period, more hops may be added to further enhance aroma. This is known as dry-hopping. Although many brewers feel that dry-hopping imparts only aroma and not flavor, this is arguable. Some brewers, notably in Belgium and the south of Germany, add a fresh dosage of yeast, and condition the beer in the bottle. The British tradition is to add a priming of sugar to the cask to create a secondary fermentation. Both methods cause a build-up of natural carbonation.

The traditional difficulty with top-fermentation was the susceptibility of the yeast to breed with

Below: Our beautiful brewery ... This 1938 copper, from a defunct brewery in West Germany, was restored and set to work in Minnesota in 1986. Mark Stutrud (far left), a former social worker, was 34 when he founded the new Summit micro-brewery with his wife Margaret. Supervising Master Brewer Fred Thomasser (second left), 70 at the time, had become accustomed more to closures than to openings. He began work as a cooper in the 1930s, at a New York brewery that made top-fermenting dry-hopped ales.

naturally occurring yeasts in the atmosphere. Wild fermentations rendered brewing impossible in summer. The first solution to this was to develop yeasts that would sink to the bottom of the vessel, out of harm's way. This was first achieved empirically by Bavarian brewers, who observed that their beer became progressively more stable when it was stored in icy Alpine caves during the summer. That observation led them to seek colder and longer fermentation periods, followed by several months' maturation in almost freezing conditions.

While more conservative brewers stayed with top-fermentation, most of the world switched to the bottom yeasts and the cold storage (lagering) method during the late 1800s and early 1900s. The last to take up lager-brewing on a widespread scale were the British, in the late 1970s and early 1980s. By then, top-fermentation was enjoying a small revival elsewhere.

Today, refrigeration and atmospheric control enable brewers to work with top yeasts all year round, but bottom-fermentation has become the convention, and consumers in most countries are accustomed to lager beers. Although either method can be used to produce dark or pale beers, the division between them is reminiscent of that between red and white wines. In general, top-fermenting beers have a more expressive, complex palate, while lagers are cleaner, often softer, and rounder.

While fruitiness is a defining characteristic in top-fermenting beers, it should be barely evident, if at all, in a well-made traditional lager. The classic way of fermenting lagers is to begin at about 5°C (41°F), and allow the temperature to rise to about 9°C (48°F), before returning to the starting point. Today, many brewers use warmer cycles. The fermentation can last for as long as two weeks, and be followed by anything from three weeks' to the classic three months' lagering at, or around, 0°C (32°F).

During lagering, a secondary fermentation and natural carbonation may be stimulated by the addition of a proportion of partly-fermented wort. This is known as *kräusening*.

After a long journey through variations in brewing methods, the decision to *kräusen* or not is one of the last. Like all of the others, it will make its own contribution of character and finesse to the final product.

The Brewery

No two breweries are alike. Although the basic principles of brewing are the same everywhere, the actual appearance and working of the equipment varies according to the preferences of the brewer and the designs which were available at the time of its installation. Most breweries have a mixture of old and new equipment. Traditionally, breweries were often built to a "tower" layout. The raw materials could then be stored at the top, and flow down through the building as they were transformed into the finished product.

1 The basic raw material of brewing is malt, first fed via sieves into a mill.

2 The mill grinds the malt, and the resultant material is called grist.

3 The grist is fed into the mash-tun, along with hot water. A porridge-like mash is formed in this vessel. If the infusion method is used, only one vessel is required, but many breweries employ the decoction system, in which the mash is passed between two vessels. A stirring device aids the mashing process.

4 If the decoction system is used, a further vessel is employed to clarify the mash. This is known as a lauter tun. Rotating blades thin out the mash, so that the maximum amount of liquid can be passed through the holes in the base. The clarified liquid, known as wort, goes to the brew-kettle.

5 Hops are added to the wort in the brew-kettle, and it is then boiled. This is the brewing process.

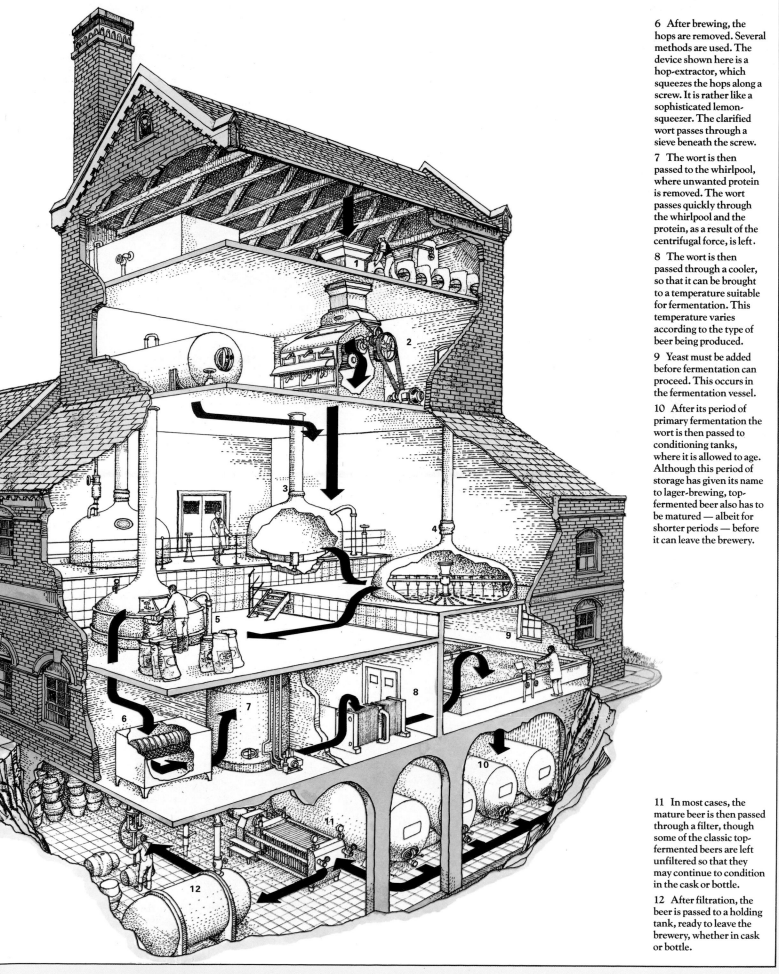

6 After brewing, the hops are removed. Several methods are used. The device shown here is a hop-extractor, which squeezes the hops along a screw. It is rather like a sophisticated lemon-squeezer. The clarified wort passes through a sieve beneath the screw.

7 The wort is then passed to the whirlpool, where unwanted protein is removed. The wort passes quickly through the whirlpool and the protein, as a result of the centrifugal force, is left.

8 The wort is then passed through a cooler, so that it can be brought to a temperature suitable for fermentation. This temperature varies according to the type of beer being produced.

9 Yeast must be added before fermentation can proceed. This occurs in the fermentation vessel.

10 After its period of primary fermentation the wort is then passed to conditioning tanks, where it is allowed to age. Although this period of storage has given its name to lager-brewing, top-fermented beer also has to be matured — albeit for shorter periods — before it can leave the brewery.

11 In most cases, the mature beer is then passed through a filter, though some of the classic top-fermented beers are left unfiltered so that they may continue to condition in the cask or bottle.

12 After filtration, the beer is passed to a holding tank, ready to leave the brewery, whether in cask or bottle.

The Best Beer: The Choice, and How to Choose

A MAN WHO DOES NOT CARE about the beer he drinks may as well not care about the bread he eats. Neither should a woman be so careless. The wealthy lady Pu-Abi used a pure gold straw with which to drink her beer at the banquets of ancient Mesopotamia. Her golden beer-straw can be seen in the Museum of the University of Pennsylvania, in Philadelphia.

Beer can be taken simply as a refreshing drink, or as a balm at the end of a hard day. These are worthwhile functions, but beer offers much more to those with the time to appreciate it. Drink, food and sex can all provide quick satisfaction or a more relaxed enjoyment. Some people take their pleasures quickly, and swear loyalty to the same beer every day, but they miss much. The search for the perfect pint should last a lifetime.

In the meantime, there is a classic style of beer for every mood and moment. Each can be judged only according to the characteristics of its style. To say that a Pilsener is better than a Stout is like arguing that a Chardonnay is more worthwhile than a sherry, or apples more important than oranges.

Abbey Beer Fruity strong ale made by secular brewers in Belgium, but modeled on the product of the Trappist abbeys. *See* Trappist.

Ale Fruity accent comes from relatively quick, warm fermentation, with a variety of yeast that rises during the process. This procedure, known as top-fermentation, classically defines an ale. Color and strength vary, and there are many types. *See* Bitter, Brown Ale, Cream Ale, India Pale Ale, Mild, Pale Ale, Scotch Ale.

Alt German word for "old." Altbier usually means a copper-colored, clean-tasting German ale of the style especially associated with the city of Düsseldorf. (*See* page 71.) For sociable drinking, or with appetizers of strong cheese or coarse sausage. The German glass is similar to that used for a highball. Ideal serving temperature just under 10°C (50°F).

Barley Wine English term for a very strong ale. (*See* page 174.) Serve at room temperature as an after-dinner drink. Or as a nightcap, to be enjoyed with a good book.

Beer Any fermented drink made primarily from malted grain and seasoned with hops. Lagers, ales, Stouts and other styles are all beers. Americans wrongly associate the term "beer" only with lager. The British embrace an opposite misunderstanding by applying it only to ale.

Berliner Weisse Acidic, refreshing, light-bodied style of Wheat Beer made in Berlin. (*See* page 61.) Low in alcohol. Serve in a Champagne saucer as an elegant summer quencher, laced with a dash of raspberry syrup. Chill lightly (7-10°C; 45-50°F).

Bière de Garde Style made in France, especially the northwest. (*See* page 183.) Broadly of the ale type. Medium-to-strong in alcohol. Fruity. Good with soft, sharp, or herb cheeses. Serve at a natural cellar temperature (10-13°C; 50-55°F).

Bitter British-style dry ale, often served on draft. (*See* page 165.) A sociable drink, ideally enjoyed in a pub from a plain pint glass. Should be served at around 12-13°C (54-5°F).

Bock Strong lager served as a warming beer in late winter, early spring, or autumn, depending upon the part of the world. (*See* page 51.) Color varies. Classically served at not less than 9°C (48°F), from a stoneware mug. Sometimes with the seasoned veal sausage Weisswurst.

Brown Ale In Britain there are two styles, of varying degrees of sweetness. (*See* page 170.) Both go well with desserts or nuts. Belgium has a sweet-sour type, made around the town of Oudenaarde. (*See* page 126.) This is more often served as an apéritif. Serve at 13°C (55°F).

Cream Ale A very mild, sweetish, golden style of ale made in the United States. A sociable brew. Serve at 7-10°C (45-50°F).

Dark Beer This term usually refers to the Munich Dark type. Beyond that, it is too general to have any useful meaning.

Diät Pils Made for diabetics, not dieters. An unusually thorough fermentation eats up the carbohydrates, but in the process creates alcohol (which is full of calories). This procedure makes for a strongish, very dry beer. It could be applied to any style of beer, but the best known examples are adaptations of the Pilsener type.

Doppelbock "Double" Bock. (*See* page 51.) Extra-strong style of lager, especially associated with Bavaria. Very rich. Offered in late winter as a warming beer. Serve at 10°C (50°F).

Dort Abbreviation indicating a beer affecting the Dortmunder Export style. Used in the Netherlands and Belgium.

Dortmunder Any beer brewed in Dortmund. However, the city is especially associated with the Export style. *See* Export.

Dunkel "Dark," in German.

Export In Germany, pale lager that is drier than the Munich type but less hoppy than a Pilsener, and slightly stronger than either. (*See* page 68.) Good with salads, fish, or chicken. Serve at 8-9°C (48°F). Elsewhere the term means simply "premium."

Faro Sweet version of Belgian Lambic. (*See* page 120.) A mid-afternoon or early-evening restorative. Serve at natural cellar temperature.

Framboise/Frambozen Raspberry Lambic. (*See* page 119.) An elegant drink with which to welcome guests. Serve lightly chilled, in Champagne flutes.

Gueuze Blended Lambic. (*See* page 118.) Sparkling, winy, and sharp, sometimes with rhubarb notes. In its native Belgium, served at natural cellar temperature in a fluted tumbler. Favored with Sunday lunch, or an appetizer of blood sausage.

Hefe- German prefix meaning "yeast". Indicates a sedimented beer.

Hell/Helles "Pale" (ie golden), in German.

Imperial ("Russian") Stout Strong, rich Stout, with fruity, "burnt currant" character. (*See* page 174.) A festive drink for winter holidays or as a nightcap. Serve at room temperature.

India Pale Ale Fruity, hoppy, super-premium pale ale. Serve at 13°C (55°F). Good with red meat, Cheddar cheese.

Kölsch Delicate, dry, lightly fruity golden ale made in the Cologne area of Germany. (*See* page 64.) A good apéritif or digestif. In Cologne, often served with an appetizer of Mettwurst made from raw minced beef. The German glass is similar to that used for a Tom Collins. Serve at 8-9°C (48°F).

Kriek Cherry Lambic (*see* page 119), with some almondy dryness. Elegant welcoming drink or apéritif. Serve lightly chilled, in Champagne flutes.

Lager In some countries, the term "lager" is applied only to the most basic beers. In general, any bottom-fermenting beer is a lager.

Lambic In palate, sometimes reminiscent of a Chardonnay, a Manzanilla, or even a dry vermouth. Spontaneously-fermenting beer from Belgium. (*See* page 114.) Serve at natural cellar temperature with sharp-tasting cheese, radishes, coarse bread.

Light Ale In England, an alternative term for a bottled Bitter. In Scotland, a dark ale of low gravity. Not intended to imply a low-calorie brew. For sociable drinking.

Light Beer American low-calorie beer in a watery interpretation of the Pilsener style. Serve at 7°C (45°F) as a refreshing drink.

Maibock Bock beer made to celebrate Spring. Usually pale and of super-premium quality. (*See* page 52.)

Malt Liquor American term for a strong lager. American versions are usually cheaply made, sometimes with a high proportion of sugar. Not very malty, and not liquor. Often consumed for a quick "high". Serve at 7°C (45°F).

Märzen Medium-strong, full-colored, malt-accented lager. (*See* page 47.) Especially associated with late September and the Oktoberfest. Serve at 9°C (48°F). Good with chicken, pork, or spicy foods.

Mild English term for a lightly-hopped ale, usually of low strength, and sometimes dark. Normally served on draft in the pub, at a natural cellar temperature. A sociable beer.

Munich Dark/Pale The Munich brewers traditionally produced dark lagers, with a spicy malty-coffeeish palate. The term "Münchener" is generally taken to mean this type of beer, which can go well with chicken or pasta dishes. Today, the city also extensively produces pale lagers, but with a distinctively malty accent. Sociable beers. Serve at 9°C (48°F).

Oktoberfest *See* Märzen.

Old Ale In Britain, this term is sometimes used to indicate a medium-strong dark ale most often consumed in winter. (*See* page 172.) In Australia, any dark ale may be identified as "Old."

Pale Ale Fruity, copper-colored style of ale originating in England. (*See* page 160.) Serve at 13°C (55°F). Good with red meat, Cheddar cheese.

Pilsener/Pilsner/Pils Classically, a super-premium pale lager with a fragrant, flowery bouquet, a soft palate and an elegantly dry, hoppy finish. Modeled on the original from Pilsen. (*See* page 32.) Serve at 9°C (48°F). Good as an apéritif or with fish dishes. The term is more broadly applied to any ostensibly dry pale lager of conventional gravity. *See* Diät Pils.

Porter A dark, almost black, fruity-dry, top-fermenting style, originally from London. (*See* page 157.) Serve at 13°C (55°F). Good with oysters, other shellfish, and crustaceans or salt-cured fish.

Rauchbier Smoked lager, produced especially around Bamberg and elsewhere in Franconia. Good with smoked meats and sausages.

Saison Sharply refreshing, faintly sour summer ale from Belgium. Sometimes seasoned with spices or herbs. Medium strong.

Scotch Ale Scotland's ales are generally malty. (*See* page 177.) Elsewhere in the world Scottish brewers are especially known for strong examples. Serve at 13°C (55°F) after a meal or as a nightcap.

It is said that King David of the Jews was a brewer, but the six-pointed star often seen on engravings of brewers is the symbol of alchemy... an allusion to the brewer's art. With fire and water, the brewer can still blend a wide variety of magical mixtures.

Steam Beer Name trademarked in the United States and some other countries by the Anchor brewery of San Francisco for its unique hybrid of ale and lager. Serve at not less than 7°C (45°F). A sociable beer or apéritif. In countries where the name has not been protected other brewers have launched "Steam" Beers, but not made by the same method.

Stout Almost black, roasty brew made by top-fermentation. English Stout (see page 171) is often sweet, and is a good mid-afternoon restorative. The more famous Irish style (see page 179) is dry, intense, sociable, and wonderful with oysters. Best not chilled. See Imperial Stout.

Trappist Strong, fruity, sedimented ales made by Trappist monks in Belgium (see page 129) and the Netherlands (see page 142). Some have a port-like character. Serve with reverence, at room temperature, in a goblet. Do not store chilled. Good with blue cheeses.

Ur-/Urquell "Original source of," in German.

Vienna Reddish-amber, sweetish, malt-accented lager, originally brewed in Vienna (see page 192) but the inspiration of the German Märzenbier. Good with pork, chicken and spicy dishes such as Mexican food.

Weisse/Weissbier/Weizenbier German words for "white" or Wheat Beers. For northern German style, see Berliner Weisse. Southern examples, served in a tall, vase-shaped glass (see page 59), have notes of apple, plum, perhaps clove. Sharply fruity, refreshing summer beers. Sometimes offered with elderberry fritters. Serve lightly chilled. A slice of lemon as a garnish is optional.

White Beer General term for Wheat Beers. Apart from the German styles, Belgium has Muscat-like white beers. (See page 122). Serve lightly chilled as a dessert beer.

Ideal serving temperatures

Well chilled (7°C; 45°F)
 "Light" beers; American and Australian lagers

Chilled (8°C; 47°F)
 Berliner Weisse

Lightly chilled (9°C; 48°F)
 European lagers; all Dark Lagers; Altbiers; German Wheat Beers

Cellar temperature (13°C; 55°F)
 Regular ales and Stouts in the styles of the British Isles; most Belgian specialties

Room temperature (15.5°C; 60°F)
 Strong Dark Ales (especially of the Trappist type); Barley Wines

Such fine distinctions are not always possible. In general, the "chilled" categories should be served from the refrigerator, which should be set at as gentle a temperature as is possible. The other categories should be kept in a place that is not refrigerated, but naturally cool and dark.

The Family Tree of Beer Styles

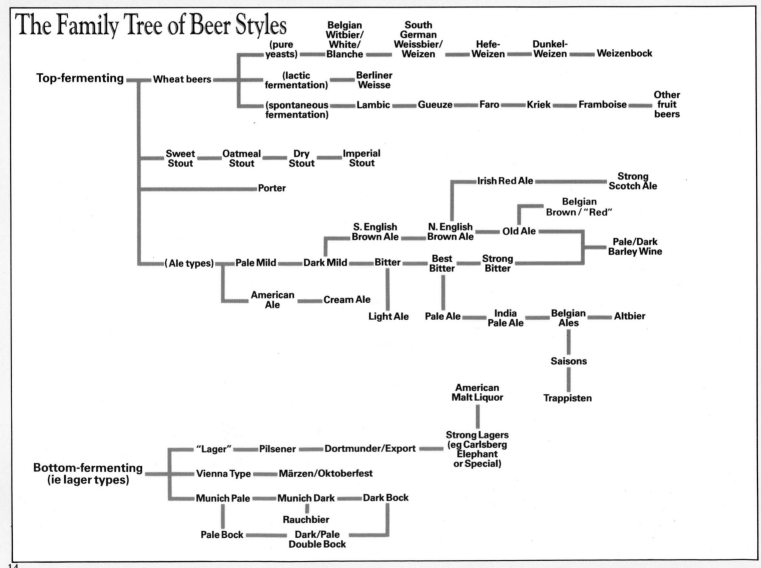

How to Taste and Judge Beer

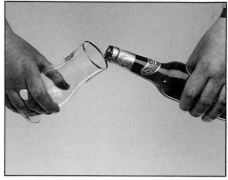

TO STARE TOO INTENTLY at a glass of beer, or sniff it too obviously, in a bar or pub can be a questionable enterprise, but those are the first steps in appreciation. All food and drink is enjoyed with the eyes and nose as well as the mouth, and beer is no exception.

A glass of beer should look good. Some drinkers look for a deep, dense, uneven head on their beer. The Germans, who know something about beer, call it a "beautiful flower." If the flower is sufficiently beautiful, it will not quickly fade. As the beer is enjoyed, each swallow will leave behind what brewers call "Brussels lace." The bubbles in the beer will be small and sustained, and there will be no "carbonic bite." In most styles of beer, these are easily recognizable signs of a fresh, natural brew, though some of the finest English Bitter ales do not have a big head.

Therein lies the difficulty: every style of beer has its own balance of characteristics. They can be very different from one style to the next. Every beer is intended by the brewer to be in one style or another. It can be judged only according to the style it affects.

Every style has its own typical range of *color*, but within that some interpretations are more subtle, complex, even beautiful, than others. A bright, clear, golden Pilsener can look especially appetizing, but so can an opaque, ebony Stout. In their blend of malts, brewers aim for certain levels of color in their beer. They express these according to a scale agreed by the European Brewery Convention. A single brewery may make a Pilsener with six E.B.C. units of color and a Porter with 80 or far more. These figures are a useful guide, but they cannot tell us what the eye sees: whether a beer has an earthy, autumnal, russet color or the richness of mahogany.

Nor does *clarity* count for much in a style of beer that is meant to be sedimented, or even hazy. The question is: which presentation is appropriate to the style?

All beers should have a *bouquet*, but this is more important in some styles than in others. It is most central to the Pilsener type. In all beers, the bouquet should be pleasant and appetizing. In a Pilsener, it should be fragrant, flowery, herbal, hoppy. In the Bavarian styles, there should also be some maltiness in the bouquet. In a Wheat Beer or ale, there should be some fruit.

In all styles, there should be a complex of these elements. Every time the glass is raised, new notes should be noticed in the bouquet, and the same goes for the *palate*. The accent of hop, malt, and fruit in the palate should vary according to the style. So should the character of the hoppiness (fragrant, herbal, bitter?), maltiness (sweet, drier, spicy, coffeeish, roasty?), and fruitiness (subtle or assertive, citric, apple-like, a hint of banana?). Many lager brewers would worry about the apple notes, even more about the banana, but these are part of the character of some styles. In whatever style, the elements should find their own balance. A hoppy

Top: Aroma. This glass was selected by The Objective Beer-Tasters, a Belgian consumer campaign, as the perfect vessel in which to nose beer. *Above*: Appearance. A simple straight glass seems to have the best tactile quality for the British pint-drinker. In general, the British like their pint poured fairly flat, but it still has a "collar" of foam. *Right-hand column*: Presentation. A Czech or German Pilsener should form a good head naturally, without being bullied into it. First, pour the beer gently into a tilted glass. Straighten the glass as a final flourish. The beer needs two "fingers" of foam.

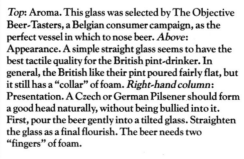

beer should not simply be harshly bitter. A malty one should not merely be sweet and sticky. A fruity one should not be all acidity and nothing else.

More than 120 descriptions for flavor elements in beer have been jointly agreed by the European Brewery Convention, the Master Brewers' Association of the Americas, and the American Society of Brewing Chemists. Hundreds more have been identified by flavor specialists. The recognition of these elements gives some measure of beer's complexity of character. To the drinker, the same can be evident in one mouthful of a truly wonderful beer: the senses are aroused; the appetite quickens; and the subtleties of flavor, like all pleasures, defy captivity. They are the beer's soul.

In body, a Berliner Weisse should be light, but not thin. An ale might be light-bodied or full. A Märzen or a Bock should certainly have some malty "mouth-feel." Again, it is a question of style. Carbonation may vary, too. Continental European brewers measure this in grams per liter. English-speakers talk of volumes. One volume equals just under two grams per liter. The range can extend from 0.75 volumes to more than 3.0.

After it has been swallowed, no beer should altogether vanish. As the glass is put down for a moment, the pleasure of the beer should linger. There should be some *finish*. All the elements contribute to the finish, but the dryness of the hop is most important in several styles, especially English Bitter and Pilsener. The hop offers aroma and flavor as well as bitterness, but that is what the brewer can most readily measure, again according to a scale agreed by the European Brewery Convention. A beer with 10-15 European Units of Bitterness will be bland; one with 40 or more will be packed with flavor.

Inexperienced lovers can be intimidated. Untrained eaters can dislike oysters. Unaccustomed drinkers can pronounce: "That beer tasted funny. Sort of bitter." They have probably just encountered a classic.

ORGANIZING A TASTING

IN ALMOST EVERY brewery of any size, a group of workers from different departments gathers at 11 o'clock each morning to check the latest batch of beer, often alongside its immediate competitors. They sample at this time because the immediate flavor of breakfast has gone, and hunger is beginning to arouse the palate. Mid-morning is the best time to sample, but not the most convenient if the tasting is to be among friends at home, or in a restaurant or club. For a sociable tasting, the time before the evening meal is ideal.

The daily tasters are not all brewers. They are picked not for their knowledge but because they have shown that they have sensitive palates. Special knowledge is not necessary: anyone can taste, and perhaps discover some surprising sensitivities to flavors. The tasters at the brewery often use opaque mugs, so that they will not be prejudiced by the color, or perhaps recognize the beer by its hue. For the sociable taster, the opposite is required: the color is a part of the pleasure. Glasses that are not colored, engraved, or otherwise decorated should be used. Wine glasses are best, because their curve helps to retain the aroma.

A sample of two or three ounces of each beer is enough, and will look more than adequate in a small, narrow wine glass. This will also be sufficient for the taster to judge head formation and lacework. Five or six beers is plenty, ten or a dozen the maximum. If different styles are being compared, the lightest in overall character should be sampled first.

In breweries, the tasters often sample the beer at room temperature, because its flavor will be most fully expressed that way, defects and all. In a sociable tasting, the beer should be served at its appropriate temperature: it is being judged as it is normally consumed.

Professional tasters may be required to score a beer on 25 or even 50 points. Sociable tasters should have a simple score-sheet, awarding points on bouquet, palate, finish and fidelity to style. If that is thought too basic, appearance and body (or "mouth feel") can be added. Some tasters like to clean their palate with bread or crackers between beers, but this can leave the floury taste of stale beer. Plain water, and lots of it, is better. It also guards against hangovers if the tasting becomes excessively rigorous.

STORING BEER

MOST BEER IS BREWED to be consumed immediately, not to be stored. It may not deteriorate, but it is vulnerable from the moment it leaves the brewery. Some brewers recover their beers from the trade after three months, whatever the "sell-by" date says.

Only a handful of beers, always strong and usually sedimented with living yeast, are made to be laid down, and they are usually vintage-dated. Many Belgian specialties, some Imperial Stouts and Old Ales, and one or two Barley Wines are examples. Most reach a peak within 18 months to five years, though some will evolve for 25 years.

All beer should be stored in the dark. Conventional beers should be kept upright, so that the beer is not in contact with the crown bottle-top. Beer in wine bottles should always be stored on its side, so that the cork is kept moist.

Sedimented beers should never be kept in a refrigerator; the yeast will not work, and the beer will "die." They should be kept at a consistent temperature, preferably in a cool cellar. A sedimented ale should not be brought home from a store and served immediately. It will need several hours, possibly a day, to settle. German Wheat Beers *mit Hefe* are normally served with the yeast in suspension. Lager beers should be kept in a refrigerator, but ideally not at too cold a temperature setting. In very cold temperatures, a high-quality, all-malt, lager may become hazy. Once it is removed from the refrigerator, this "chill haze" will gradually vanish, but no beer likes extremes of temperature.

DEFECTS

THE MOST COMMON DEFECT in bottled or canned beers is staleness caused by oxygen. This imparts a floury, papery, damp-cardboard aroma and taste. If the beer has been newly-purchased, it should be returned to the retailer. He is probably not rotating his stock on the proper basis of "first in, first out." New bottles should not be stacked in front of old ones.

A very common defect in bottled beer is "skunkiness." This aroma, less graphically compared with over-cooked cabbage, is caused by sunlight or supermarket lighting. Bottles should not be kept in store windows or other places where they are exposed to direct light.

CANS VERSUS BOTTLES

THE STRONGEST ARGUMENT against cans is that they are aesthetically unpleasant. Deep in their hearts, most brewers also still harbor misgivings about the lengthy contact of beer and metal. When a batch of beer is not quite up to par, as inevitably happens in even the best-run establishments, some brewers will send it to the canning line. The theory is that consumers are less likely to return cans than bottles.

BOTTLES VERSUS DRAFT

SOME STYLES OF BEER are by nature draft products. The classic example is British cask-conditioned ale. Most beer-lovers prefer draft because it is less often pasteurized (though practice varies from one country to another) and more likely to be fresh. Brewers do not install draft systems in outlets with a slow turnover. A pub owner who does not clean his lines will ruin his beer. In that respect, bottled beer is less vulnerable — but it, too, has to be well kept.

ADDITIVES

LIKE THE FOOD AND WINE INDUSTRIES, the beer business has occasional scandals over additives. In all three areas, additives are perhaps less fashionable among producers than they were.

Many brewers say they use no additives whatever, and some indicate this on their labels. One difficulty is to define an additive. Tannic acid, for example, occurs naturally in brewing, but may also be added to clarify beer. Most additives are used to clarify or preserve beer, or improve head retention. At best, they are "beauty aids" where none should be needed. At worst, they may be used clumsily, there is no such thing as "chemical beer."

No additive currently used has been proven to be harmful, though some could trigger allergies or other health problems. This is the strongest argument for ingredient labeling, which would also discourage the use of additives and allay public fears.

Actual size

Strobile {

Seed
*The hop as used in
brewing is the female
plant. In the wild, its
seeds are fertilized by
wind-borne pollen
from the male plant.
In most countries, the
male has been
eradicated, so that the
female is not fertilized.*

Resin glands

Bracteoles

Humulus lupulus

THE COMMON HOP

The Hop

Barley

ALL ALCOHOLIC DRINKS were originally seasoned with herbs, spices, berries, fruits, or tree-barks. A vermouth is a seasoned wine. Most gins and some traditional aquavits or vodkas are flavored spirits. Liqueurs such as Chartreuse are made by the maceration of herbs in alcohol. If seasonings are not used, the wood of the barrel is often employed to add a balancing note to the original character of the wine or spirit.

Juniper berries, coriander, and Curaçao orange peels are still used in a handful of specialty beers, but the hop eventually became the accepted seasoning.

Hops were known to the early civilizations, and Pliny's study of natural history mentions them as a garden plant. He knew the hop as a plant whose young shoots were eaten in spring — like asparagus — and this custom is still sometimes observed in areas where it is grown. Apparently the hop grew wild among willows "like a wolf among sheep," and thus the Romans called it *Lupus salictarius*. This was the origin of its botanical name, *Humulus lupulus*. The ancients may have used hops in beer. Records of the Jews' captivity in Babylon refer to a *sicera* (strong drink) *ex lupulis confectam* ("made from hops"). This drink alleviated leprosy.

More persistent references to the cultivation of hops do not appear until the eighth and ninth centuries AD, when gardens are mentioned in Bohemia, the Hallertau district of Bavaria, and various parts of Charlemagne's Europe. It is not clear whether the hops thus grown were employed in brewing, though documents from the year 822 suggest that monks from Picardy certainly brought this technique with them when they established the abbey of Corbay on the upper Weser, in northern Germany.

The use of hops presented an unfamiliar challenge to established brewers and to people whose livelihood depended upon the cultivation and sale of other plants employed in the making of beer. The Flemings exported hopped beer across the Channel in the very early 1400s, but the use of the plant by English brewers was viewed with horror. Even after Flemings settled in Kent and cultivated the plant there a century later, it took many years for its merits to be generally accepted.

The cultivation of hops was introduced into North America in the very early 1600s, and it was later reported that they grew "fair and large" and thrived well in the New Netherlands and Virginia. Today, the United States is second only to Germany in the volume of its hop-growing, and production is centered in Washington State. Wild hops from Manitoba were interbred with Kent hops in the early part of this century to improve the vigor of the British varieties. Hops are also grown on a large scale in the Soviet Union, and in Japan and Tasmania.

In Europe, a certain amount of international tension has been caused by the sex-life of the hop. Only the female, with its cone-like flower, is used in brewing. Being a perennial, it can be propagated from cuttings, and seeds are not needed. Therefore, the male is at best redundant and at worst a nuisance. It is not cultivated, but it can still manifest itself in the wild. It disseminates wind-borne pollen, which fertilizes the seed in the female, adding weight to the cone without doing anything to improve the beer. In fact, the fertilized seeds cause problems in the clarification of bottom-fermented beer.

In Continental Europe, the wild male hop has been exterminated. In Britain, however, seeded hops never presented a problem in the method used to produce ales. Furthermore, some of the British hop varieties ripen more quickly, fully and evenly if they have been fertilized. The two classic British varieties of ale hop, the splendidly-named Fuggles and Goldings, now find their future threatened by the popularity of lager in their home country. If Fuggles and Goldings are to continue their libertine behavior, how can British growers cultivate the unseeded varieties needed for lager? One possible solution is for Fuggles and Goldings to be restricted to their favorite territory, East Kent, and for seedless varieties to be grown elsewhere. A better answer would be for the British to remain faithful to their great ales and let permissiveness flourish.

The flower of the female hop is popularly known as a cone, and technically described as a strobile. Each strobile is made up of overlapping bracteoles, the "petals." At the base of each bracteole is the seed. Both the base of the bracteole and the seed bear sticky yellow glands containing the chemical compounds that the brewer needs. The glands produce resins and essential oils, which provide aroma and bitterness, and the bracteoles contain tannin, which helps clarify the brew. Although the chemistry of the hop is immensely complicated, the alpha acids within it, also known as humulones, are of particular importance. They provide the bitterness, while also having a rather secondary role as an antiseptic and preservative.

The hop itself is preserved by being dried with hot air. In Britain, this was once done in picturesque oast-houses, but these have largely given way to less individualistic buildings, even in the most tradition-conscious hop-growing areas.

Hop-picking, from a growers' guide produced in England during the 1500s.

A WILD GRASS called *Hordeum spontaneum* seems to have been the principal ancestor of barley, but it is likely that man learned to cultivate the cereal long before he was able to write. His first purpose in doing this may well have been to brew beer. By the time man had the ability to record his history, about 3,000 years before Christ, brewing was already a sophisticated industry. Early Babylonian texts actually discuss the suitability of different barleys for different types of beer. Man had decided that raw grain was not especially palatable, and had somehow developed the process of malting in order to remedy this defect. The Ancient Egyptians recorded that they first baked the grain into loaves, which they then crumbled in water to make a brewing mash. The process was described in 23 scenes depicted in reliefs on graves, and pieced together in *Bier und Bierbereitung bei den Volkernder Urzeit*, by Dr E. Huber, published in 1926. The question *Did man once live by beer alone?* was subsequently raised in a paper compiled by several experts for the *American Anthropologist* in 1953. Inspired by this study, Professor Solomon Katz and Dr Mary Voigt, of the University of Pennsylvania, did more work on the topic. In 1986 they produced a paper taking the theory considerably further.

The following year a study was published suggesting that barley, oats, and herbs had been used to make a fermented beverage on the Inner Hebridean island of Rhum in about 2000 BC.

The idea that beer may have pre-dated bread is not unreasonable. It is difficult to make acceptable bread with barley, because the gluten content of the grain is low, and the loaves do not hold together very well. Clearly, this didn't matter if they were to be crumbled, anyway, for the purpose of brewing. Barley's unsuitability for baking is one factor in its long and continuous history as a brewing grain. Beer can be brewed, though less easily, with wheat, but that grain makes excellent bread. Thus the brewer and the baker have been able to pursue their crafts in a perfectly complementary way.

Barley is also the grain most suitable for malting. When germination begins, the shoot of the developing plant travels inside the grain and is protected by it for several days until it emerges at the far end. In wheat and rye, the shoot sprouts straight out of the grain and can easily be damaged or broken during malting. An even greater advantage is barley's ready response to warmth, which makes malting a simpler operation than it is when other cereals are used.

Without having been malted, the grain cannot be fermented. Its starches must first be broken down into their component sugars. The corn, or seed, of the barley is a spindle-shaped structure with a protective outer husk. Compared with huskless cereals such as wheat, germinating barley is normally reasonably free from mold growth, and this characteristic is another advantage offered by the grain. The husk also provides a useful filter aid

Below: Barley was used in brewing in the third millennium BC, according to studies made at the University of Pennsylvania of Sumerian pictograms. These studies identify the world's first known recipe as having been for beer. Tablets like the one shown here have been found in Mesopotamia and Egypt.

during traditional methods of wort-separation. Inside the husk is the tiny embryo of the plant, supporting itself from food reserves in the form of a relatively much larger endosperm. It is these food reserves that the brewer needs. They include large polysaccharide molecules, which are broken down by the action of enzymes produced during malting into maltose and dextrin. It is principally the maltose that is later converted by fermentation into alcohol and carbon dioxide, while the dextrins are important in supplying fullness of flavor to the beer.

These biochemical processes are extremely complex. Their ability to proceed properly depends upon the skills of the plant-breeder, the farmer, the maltster, the microbiologist and the brewer. The task of all concerned is made no less difficult by the fact that the chemical composition of both barley and hops varies significantly according to the soil and season.

Good malting barley must be free from excessive moisture, which can be caused by premature harvesting; it should be sweet-smelling, and not musty; it should have a low proportion of skinned or broken grains, which attract fungoid infection; and it should have a high proportion of starch to protein. This last, and most important, requirement can be established if the grain is mealy and opaque, rather than translucent.

Only the best barley is employed in brewing, while about nine-tenths of production finds other uses, mainly in cattle-foods. There are three principal races of barley, distinguished according to the number of rows of grain in each ear. Two-rowed barley is the most widely grown, especially in Central and Western Europe. In warm climates, six-rowed barley is also found. Good malting samples are produced in the west of the United States, in Chile, Australia, and the Mediterranean region. Four-rowed barley is grown in cold northern climates, but its high protein content makes it less suitable for brewing.

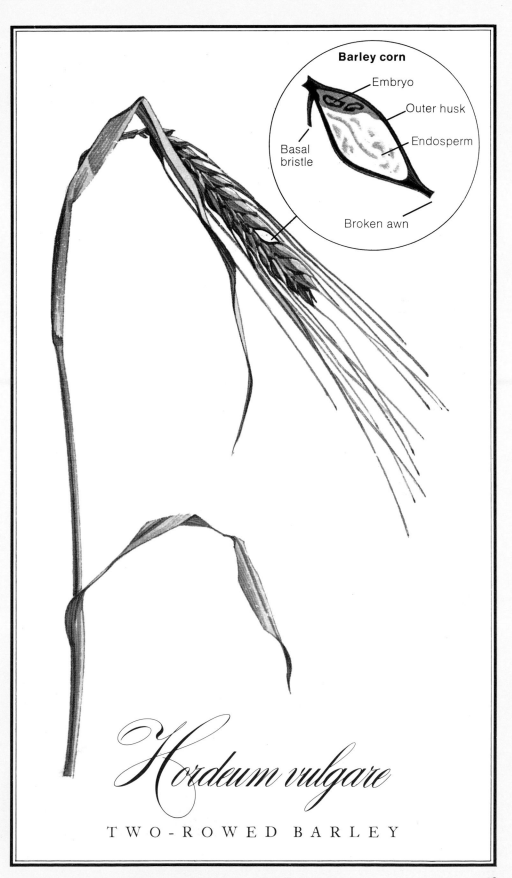

Barley corn

Embryo

Outer husk

Endosperm

Basal bristle

Broken awn

Hordeum vulgare

T W O - R O W E D B A R L E Y

Brewing Nations

The classic styles of beer originate from five nations that stand side by side across Europe: Czechoslovakia (where Bohemia gave birth to Pilsener beer); Germany (where Bavaria, Berlin, and the Rhineland have their own various styles); Belgium (where Flanders contributed the Lambic family, among others); Britain (the greatest home of ale) and Ireland (the land of Dry Stout).

In their contribution to the tradition and character of beer, these are the greatest brewing nations.

To their immediate south lie Austria (home of the Vienna style), Switzerland (where St Gall's abbey pioneered brewing after the Dark Ages), and northern France (with the Bières de Garde of French Flanders). To the immediate north are the Baltic cities (guardians of Imperial Stout), Denmark (which popularized lager beer), and the Netherlands (which has the most international of brewers). This is the heartland of brewing in the Old World.

In the New World, the United States makes a greater volume of beer than any other country. In their liveliness, California, Oregon, and Washington are beginning to assume in the world of beer a position similar to the one they enjoy in the milieu of wine. Latin America has large brewing industries. Japan is a sizable brewing nation. So are Australia and New Zealand. There are some nations in the world that do not have breweries, but they are an unlucky few.

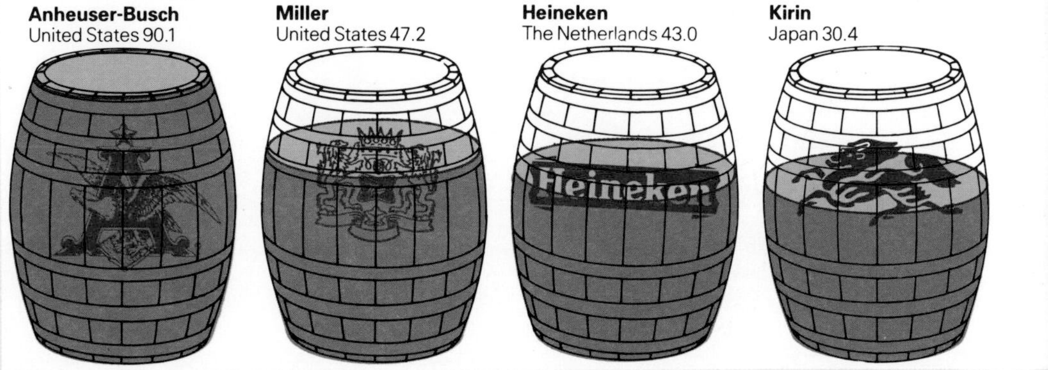

Right: Some of the world's best-known brewers do not feature in this "top ten" for volume production. Carlsberg enters at number 13, with 16.3 million hectoliters; Bass at 18, with 13.8; Guinness at 20, with 11.4; Allied at 24, with 9.0. No German brewer figures, because each has to compete with 1,200 others in its home market.

The Top Twenty Beer-drinking Nations
Consumption per head, per year, in litres

One liter = 1.76 Imperial pints = 2.11 US pints
One hectoliter = 100 liters

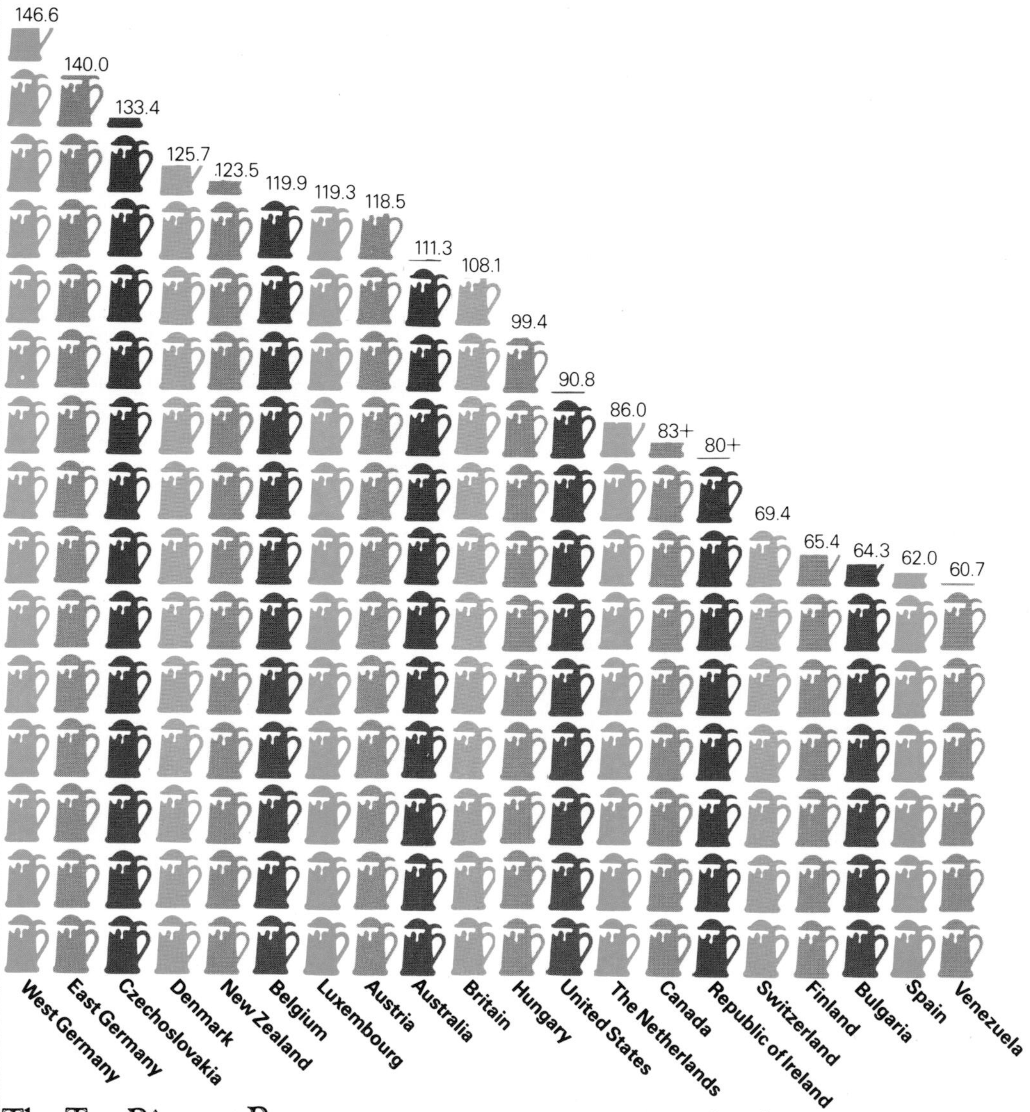

146.6 West Germany
140.0 East Germany
133.4 Czechoslovakia
125.7 Denmark
123.5 New Zealand
119.9 Belgium
119.3 Luxembourg
118.5 Austria
111.3 Australia
108.1 Britain
99.4 Hungary
90.8 United States
86.0 The Netherlands
83+ Canada
80+ Republic of Ireland
69.4 Switzerland
65.4 Finland
64.3 Bulgaria
62.0 Spain
60.7 Venezuela

The Ten Biggest Brewers (Figures in millions of hectoliters)

Anheuser-Busch
United States 90.1

Miller
United States 47.2

Heineken
The Netherlands 43.0

Kirin
Japan 30.4

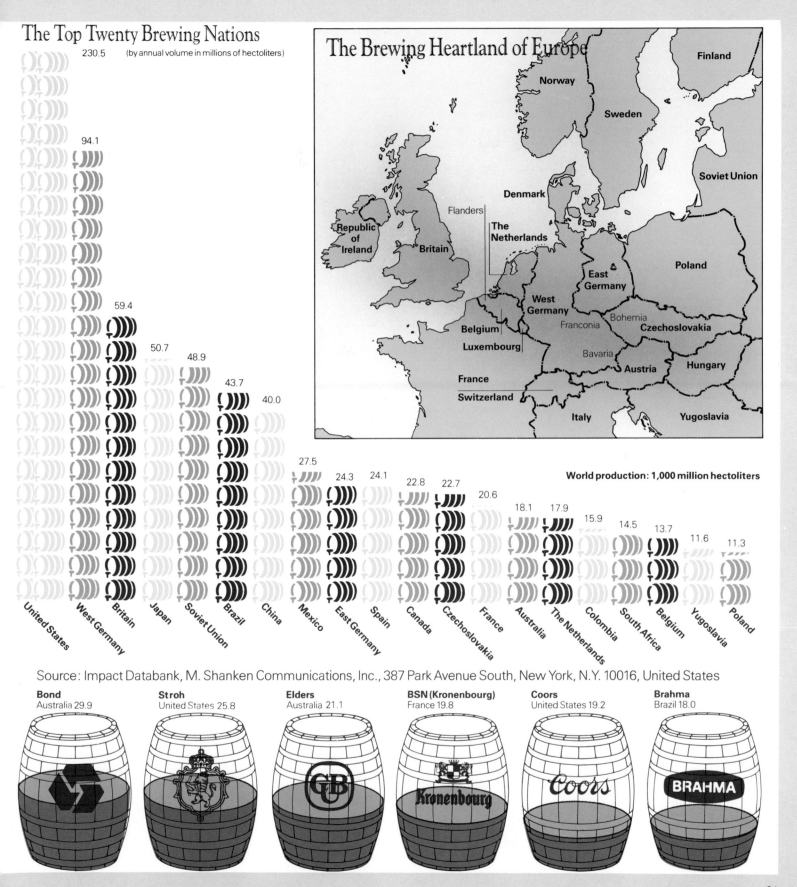

The Top Twenty Brewing Nations

230.5 (by annual volume in millions of hectoliters)

94.1
59.4
50.7 48.9
43.7
40.0
27.5
24.3 24.1
22.8 22.7
20.6
18.1 17.9
15.9
14.5
13.7
11.6 11.3

United States · West Germany · Britain · Japan · Soviet Union · Brazil · China · Mexico · East Germany · Spain · Canada · Czechoslovakia · France · Australia · The Netherlands · Colombia · South Africa · Belgium · Yugoslavia · Poland

The Brewing Heartland of Europe

Norway · Finland · Sweden · Soviet Union · Denmark · Flanders · Republic of Ireland · Britain · The Netherlands · Poland · East Germany · West Germany · Bohemia · Czechoslovakia · Belgium · Franconia · Luxembourg · Bavaria · Austria · Hungary · France · Switzerland · Italy · Yugoslavia

World production: 1,000 million hectoliters

Source: Impact Databank, M. Shanken Communications, Inc., 387 Park Avenue South, New York, N.Y. 10016, United States

Bond	Stroh	Elders	BSN (Kronenbourg)	Coors	Brahma
Australia 29.9	United States 25.8	Australia 21.1	France 19.8	United States 19.2	Brazil 18.0

Yeast

Strength

TO THE NAKED EYE, yeast is a cheesy, viscous substance, familiar to people who bake or brew at home. Under the microscope, a sample of yeast is a clump or chain of tiny fungus organisms which can convert sugars into alcohol. If the skin of a fallen fruit is broken, the yeast in the air will immediately set to work on it, and the pulp will start to ferment. Since ancient times, man has observed that this process of fermentation can be made to produce a potable drink from almost anything. Wild yeasts flourish on the skins of grapes, and thus lie in wait for the process of wine-making. Once barley has gone through the processes which liberate its sugars, it too is receptive to yeast.

The earliest brewers merely permitted this to happen naturally, and hoped that this extremely unpredictable process would produce a drinkable brew. There is, though, evidence from early pictograms that they knew that an outside agent was at work in the fermenting vessels, and that this substance could be recovered from the dregs of the brew. At least one archaeologist has claimed that some primitive form of yeast-selection was being carried out in 1440 BC.

Medieval brewers knew the substance by a variety of names, and recognized that it was required to insure fermentation, but they did not know how it worked. Yeast was first viewed under a microscope in 1680 by the Dutch scientist Anton van Leeuwenhoek. In the 1700s and 1800s, the work of French chemists Lavoisier and Gay-Lussac furthered knowledge in this area, but it was not until 1857 that Pasteur began to develop some real understanding of yeasts. By then, it was known that some brewers' yeast rose to the top of the fermentation vessel while others sank to the bottom, but no one was sure why this happened. Liebig talked about "ordinary frothy yeast" and the "precipitated yeast of Bavarian beer".

Eventually, the Bavarian type of yeast was successfully broken down to a single strain by Emil Hansen at Carlsberg, in Denmark. It was established that, by isolating the right strain, brewers could get a dependable result.

Nearly all the yeasts used in the production of fermented drinks belong to the genus *Saccharomyces*. Traditionally, to honor Hansen's work, bottom-fermenting yeasts have been known as *Saccharomyces carlsbergensis*. This name is still widely used, though in recent years taxonomists have decided that bottom and top yeasts should be categorized as the same species, *Saccharomyces cerevisiae*. The distinction has been further blurred in that top-fermenting yeasts are now often cropped from the bottom, by the use of conical fermenting vessels. However, they still ferment sugars in different ways, producing their own distinct alcohols and palates. In Continental Europe, especially Germany and Belgium, brewers make a clear distinction in the use of the terms top- and bottom-fermentation. In the English-speaking world, some prefer to talk simply of "ale" and "lager" yeasts.

THE MYTHS THAT SURROUND the potency of beer are fostered by the many different ways in which it is measured and expressed, most of them confusing.

In the United States, the system used is alcohol by weight. As alcohol is lighter than water, this system produces figures that sound very low. If the same percentage is measured by volume, the figure is higher. In some states, a bar or supermarket is permitted to sell only beers of 3.2 per cent alcohol by weight. Such a beer has 4.0 per cent alcohol if it is measured by volume. Alcohol by volume is used to measure the strength of beer in Canada, the Netherlands, and some other countries. It is also commonly used on wine labels, and increasingly for liquors. It is certainly the easiest system to understand and it will soon be universal in Europe.

In the oldest brewing nations, the first measurements taken were those of raw materials. How much malt did the brewer put into the water in his mash tun? How "dense" was his beer? This measurement was made in the days when beer continued to ferment in the cask (as it still does to some extent in the case of British "real ale"). The density, or "original gravity," could be established to the satisfaction of both the brewer and the tax-collector, but the alcohol content could not be predicted with precision.

These systems are confusing for the consumer. Britain has a system based on a scale of 1,000. The beer of 3.2 per cent alcohol by weight and 4.0 by volume might in Britain be described as having an "original gravity" of 1040. If the last two figures, the 40, are divided by four, the resultant 10 would, more or less, be the gravity under the Plato system used in Germany. The Plato scale is a perfected version of the Balling system, which originated in Czechoslovakia, and the two provide similar figures. There are also a number of other systems, but these are falling out of use.

Conversions between alcohol content and gravity can only be approximate, because they are governed by the degree of fermentation. If a beer is very thoroughly fermented, a high proportion of its malt is turned into alcohol. If it is not so well attenuated, less alcohol is created.

Alcoholic strength is not a measure of quality. The great brewing nations all make beers of very low strengths as well as extremely potent ones. People who like to drink large volumes of beer do not look for the kick of a billy-goat in every glass. A Czech draft beer of seven or eight degrees Balling, a Berliner Weisse or an English Mild are all weaker than an American 3.2 beer. American brewers will make the same beer to 3.2 standard for "control states" and to 3.6 or 3.9 in other markets. In many states, they are required by law to stay under 4.0 per cent by weight unless they are producing an ale or Malt Liquor.

Internationally, ales are made at all gravities and strengths. The unofficial, but recognized, international standard for a true Pilsener-type beer is around 4.0 by weight; 5.0 by volume; 1048; 12. In some countries, the figure 12, representing degrees Plato or Balling, is printed on the label. Although this is an honest and traditional measure, visitors are often misled into thinking they are drinking a beer of 12 per cent alcohol. In countries where gravity is used in labeling, drinkers do not generally know the alcohol content of their beers, but they recognize which are low, medium, and high.

Measures of drinks vary from one country to another but, by rule of thumb, a bottle of a Pilsener beer of the classic gravity contains about the same amount of alcohol as a reasonable glass of wine or shot of liquor.

Most brewing nations also have much stronger beers, but these are less easy to find in the New World than they are, for example, in Britain, Belgium, or Germany. The strongest beers approach 11 by weight; 15 by volume; and have gravities of 30 Plato (1120) or more. They are extremely heavy. No one would want to drink such a beer regularly, but it is nice to have the choice.

Some typical beer strengths

Alcohol by weight	Alcohol by volume	Original gravity	Degrees Plato
2–2.5	2.5–3	1030–32	7.5–8
Berliner Weisse			
2–3	2.5–3.75	1030–37	7.5–9.25
British Mild			
2.3–3.2	2.8–4	1030–40	7.5–10
US light beers			
2.6–3.2	3.2–3.9	1030–36	7.5–9
Regular British lagers			
2.8–3.2	3.5–4	1035–42	8.75–10.5
British ordinary Bitter; regular Porters and Stouts			
3.2–3.9	4–4.8	1044–50	11–12.5
US lagers; premium British lagers; British special Bitter			
3.7–4.3	4.6–5.6	1044–51	11.2–12.8
European lagers; regular Belgian ales; Lambics			
4	5	1046–47	11.5–11.8
Canadian lagers and ales			
3.9–4.1	5–5.25	1047–52	11.75–13
Most Wheat Beers			
4.25–4.5	5.3–5.6	1047-56	11.75–13.25
Many ales in the United States; premium Pale Ales			
4.4–4.6	5.5–5.7	1054–55	13.6–13.7
German Märzenbier			
4.4–5.9	5.5–7.4	1058–75	14.5–18.75
Some Malt Liquors; some export Stouts; British Old Ales; specialty ales			
5.3–5.5	6.7–7.25	1065–67	16.25–16.6
German Bock beer			
5.4–7	6.8–8.75	1073–88	18.25–22
Regular German Double Bock; Extra-strong lagers			
4.8–8.8	6.0–11	1065–98+	16.25–24.5
Regular Barley Wines; Baltic Porters/Imperial and Tropical Stouts			
10–12	12.5–15+	1100–40+	25–35
Specialty brews of various types, including extra-strong interpretations of Old Ales, Barley Wines, Double Bocks			

Legal requirements vary from one country to another, and even between states of the United States. These bands of alcohol content and gravity are based on analyses of typical products in their country of origin. They are intended as only a general guide.

THE
WORLD'S BEERS

Brews and Drinking Styles, Nation by Nation

CZECHOSLOVAKIA

Top: The Czech folk hero, the Good Soldier Schweik, gives his name to a restaurant in Prague and features on its beer-mats. Its house beer is Pilsner Urquell. *Above*: This cavalier guards the Krušovice brewery. *Left*: Pale for the men and dark for the women?

EVEN THE KEENEST of beer-lovers is often unaware of the prime position occupied by Czechoslovakia as a brewing nation. Things become clearer when it is appreciated that Czechoslovakia grew out of the old nation Bohemia. All over the world, there are beers with the word "Bohemia" in their name or description. Or "Bohemian." Or "Bohemian-style." When those names were coined, the brewers were trying to associate their products with one of the greatest brewing regions in the world. It was then, and it still is.

Within the region still known as Bohemia are the Czech capital, Prague, and two great brewing towns: Pilsen (Plzeň) and the former Budweis, now known as České Budějovice. The town of Pilsen gave its name to the world's most widely produced style of beer. The spelling may vary, but the allusion is the same: Pilsner, or Pilsener or simply Pils. It became an internationally used description of a style of beer before anyone could register it as a brand-name. The town of Budweis is not associated outside Czechoslovakia with a style, but does find itself in two famous, trademarked brand-names, one Bohemian and the other American.

Bohemia today grows the world's most prized hops, renowned for their delicacy of fragrance, and widely exported. There are records of hop-growing in the region as early as AD 859, so it is possible there was brewing in Bohemia at that time. From 1101,

hops were shipped down the river Elbe to the famous Hamburg hop market, the Forum Humuli. The first record of a brewery in Bohemia is at Čerhenice, in 1118. Brewing in Pilsen and Budweis dates from the 1200s. In the 1500s, Budweis began to supply beer to the Bohemian royal court. Its brews are said to have been known since then as "The Beer of Kings."

Bohemia was best known at that time for Wheat Beers, but in more recent centuries this part of the world has gained a reputation for the cultivation of sweet, clean-tasting malting barley. Oats were also used as a fermentable material in the distant past, and beer was seasoned with berries, oak leaves and spices. Today, only hops are added.

While the country's main hop-growing areas are around the Bohemian town of Žatec, the region of barley cultivation is in the middle of Moravia, in the Hana district. Czech malting barley is also exported. Czechoslovakia has good brewing water, too. The water is especially soft in Pilsen, where it also has a distinctively alkaline quality.

The proud brewing history of Bohemia reached a peak in 1842, when Pilsen produced the world's first truly golden lager. The fame of this new, golden type of beer from the town of Pilsen spread during the 1850s, 1860s and 1870s. Its availability spread, too, with the building of railroads in Continental Europe, and with a new economic union between the German-speaking countries.

Above: Two classic labels from the town of Pilsen and a beer-mat from "Budweiser" Budvar. *Below*: Hardly a singles bar, but it really is called the old Meat Market.

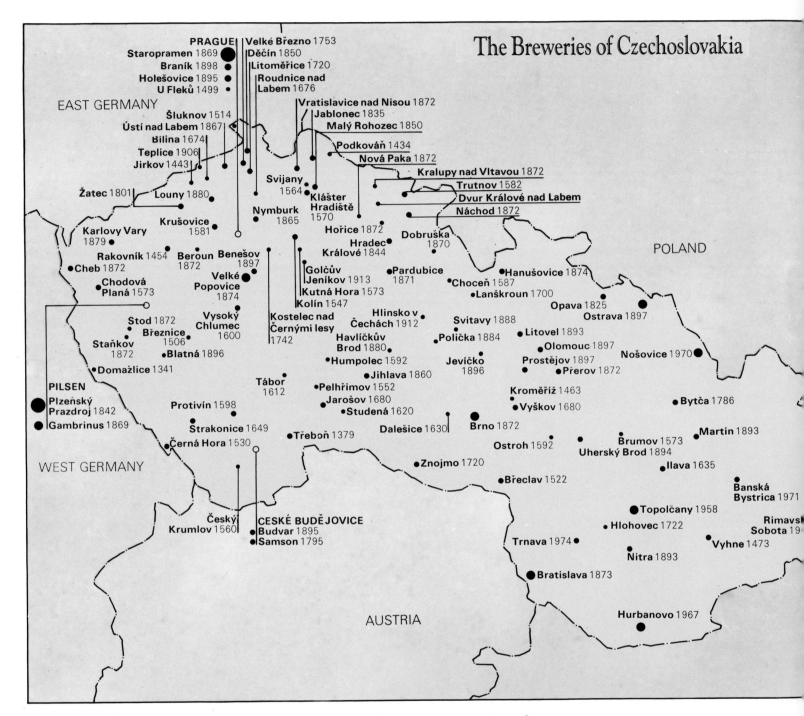

The Breweries of Czechoslovakia

PRAGUE | Velké Březno 1753
Staropramen 1869 | Děčín 1850
Braník 1898 | Litoměřice 1720
Holešovice 1895 | Roudnice nad
U Fleků 1499 | Labem 1676

EAST GERMANY

Vratislavice nad Nisou 1872
Šluknov 1514 | Jablonec 1835
Ústí nad Labem 1867 | Malý Rohozec 1850
Bílina 1674 | Podkováň 1434
Teplice 1906 | Nová Paka 1872
Jirkov 1443 | Kralupy nad Vltavou 1872
Svijany 1564 | Trutnov 1582
Žatec 1801 | Louny 1880 | Dvur Králové nad Labem
Krušovice 1581 | Nymburk 1865 | Klášter Hradiště 1570 | Náchod 1872
Karlovy Vary 1879 | Hořice 1872 | Dobruška 1870
Rakovník 1454 | Beroun 1872 | Benešov 1897 | Hradec Králové 1844 | POLAND
Cheb 1872 | Golčův Jeníkov 1913 | Pardubice 1871 | Hanušovice 1874
Chodová Planá 1573 | Velké Popovice 1874 | Kutná Hora 1573 | Choceň 1587
| Kolín 1547 | Lanškroun 1700
Stod 1872 | Vysoký Chlumec 1600 | Kostelec nad Černými lesy 1742 | Hlinsko v Čechách 1912 | Opava 1825
Březnice 1506 | | Svitavy 1888 | Ostrava 1897
Staňkov 1872 | Blatná 1896 | Havlíčkův Brod 1880 | Polička 1884 | Litovel 1893
Domažlice 1341 | | Humpolec 1592 | Jevíčko 1896 | Olomouc 1897 | Nošovice 1970
| | Jihlava 1860 | Prostějov 1897 | Přerov 1872
PILSEN | Tábor 1612 | Pelhřimov 1552 | Kroměříž 1463 | Bytča 1786
Plzeňský Prazdroj 1842 | Protivín 1598 | Jarošov 1680 | Vyškov 1680 | Martin 1893
Gambrinus 1869 | | Studená 1620 | Brno 1872 | Brumov 1573
| Strakonice 1649 | Třeboň 1379 | Dalešice 1630 | Uherský Brod 1894
Černá Hora 1530 | | Ostroh 1592 | Ilava 1635
WEST GERMANY | | Znojmo 1720 | Banská Bystrica 1971
| | Břeclav 1522 | Topolčany 1958
| Český Krumlov 1560 | CESKÉ BUDĚJOVICE | Hlohovec 1722 | Rimavská Sobota 19
| | Budvar 1895 | Trnava 1974 | Vyhne 1473
| | Samson 1795 | Nitra 1893
| | Bratislava 1873
AUSTRIA
| | Hurbanovo 1967

At the same time, there was a wave of emigration to the New World. Throughout Continental Europe, brewers wanted to proclaim that they, too, had a beer in the "Pilsener style." Or, more generally, in the "Bohemian style." The emigrants to the United States took the idea with them.

Bohemia had in the past been in the German Empire (and at one stage provided an Emperor). At the time of its greatest brewing triumphs, it was in the Austro-Hungarian Empire. The Austrians were at the height of their economic and political influence. Their capital, Vienna, was a world center of culture and sophistication.

"Austrian" and "Vienna" were words that found their way onto beer labels in distant lands during this period, though sometimes as another way of suggesting the Pilsener type. Across the German border, "Bavarian" and "Münchener" (Munich-style) added their contributions, usually indicating a dark-brown lager.

Geographical names have been used to describe styles of beer (and wine, other drinks, and foods) since such products were first traded outside their own home towns, probably in the late Middle Ages. At that time, any brew from the town would have been described as "a Pilsener beer." Only after 1842 did the name begin to indicate a specific style.

At one stage, the High Court of Imperial Germany ruled that the term Pilsener, with no qualification, could be used by only the brewery that originated the style. Other breweries would have to put their name first, followed by the description. This was to lock the stable door after the dray-horse

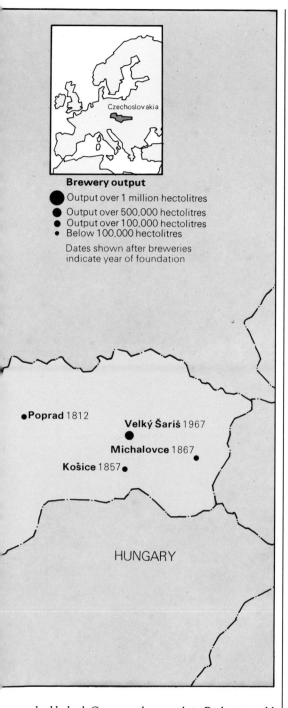

Brewery output

● Output over 1 million hectolitres
● Output over 500,000 hectolitres
● Output over 100,000 hectolitres
• Below 100,000 hectolitres

Dates shown after breweries indicate year of foundation

• **Poprad** 1812

Velký Šariš 1967

Michalovce 1867

Košice 1857 •

HUNGARY

How Bud Became Crystal

Above: These bizarre cabins in a public park were once lagering tanks at the Budvar brewery. Pilsner Urquell still uses this type of vessel. Budvar is sometimes known as "Bud" in Germany. The Czech beer was exported to the United States as Budweiser until 1911, when a legal agreement was made with Anheuser-Busch. For some time after that, the Czechs used the name Crystal on their handsome US label. In Czechoslovakia Crystal is still used as a secondary brand, and continues to be personified by a Bohemian blond.

had bolted. Once, any beer made in Budweis would have also been known by the name of the town. It would have been classified as a *Budweiser* beer. Individual brand-names are a much newer idea, their beginnings having been in the late 1800s.

Today, the best-known beer brewed in České Budějovice has the brand-name Budweiser Budvar. The producers like to call it "The Original Budweiser." The town of Budweis was making beer long before any brewer from elsewhere borrowed its name, although it did not produce pale lagers until the mid-1800s. It was nonetheless the fame of beers from Budweis that led to its name being used as an allusion by brewers in the New World. In a sense, any beer from the town is "original" Budweiser.

The snag in the Budvar claim is that this particular brewery did not open until 1895. By then, the American brewery Anheuser-Busch had already been using Budweiser as a brand-name for 20 years. With one of the largest and most prosperous countries as its domestic market, American Budweiser is the world's biggest-selling beer. Its slogan is "The King of Beers."

There have in the past been various agreements between the two companies as to the use of the name in different territories, and there have been a number of legal disputes in recent years as the distribution of both products becomes wider. Since 1896, Anheuser-Busch has also used the brand-name Michelob, which derives from the name of another Bohemian town once famous for its beer. The Czech (and generally Slavic) word *pivo*, meaning beer, was adapted by Anheuser-Busch as a brand-name for a non-alcoholic drink during Prohibition. It is still carved into the stonework of one of the brewery buildings in St Louis, Missouri. This is not unusual. Words and phrases in Czech and German are still often seen or heard in American breweries. Come to that, the "dollar" was originally a Bohemian coin.

Since the end of World War I and the birth of Czechoslovakia, Budweis has officially been known as České Budějovice. The town has two breweries. So has Pilsen. Prague has four. The number of breweries in the country as a whole has in recent years reached 130, though there are fears that the opening of some new, large plants will cause the closure of smaller ones. The most densely breweried area is the original Czech part of the country,

Left: Czech students pick the famous hops. It could be argued that hand-picking is gentler on the hops' resin glands than mechanical harvesting. *Right*: the Třeboň brewery (founded 1397) has reintroduced its Porter to bring warmth to a snowy afternoon.

comprising Bohemia (which centers on Prague) and Moravia (which centers on the city of Brno). There is, though, also a healthy scatter of breweries in Slovakia (which centers on Bratislava).

Many breweries, even small ones, have their own maltings attached. Often, these are of the traditional type in which the grain, having been steeped, is spread out on the floor to sprout. A handful of similar "floor maltings" are to be found at Scottish whisky distilleries.

Only the Germans regularly drink more beer per head than the Czechs. Only the British consume a higher proportion in pubs (in Czechoslovakia, taverns) on draft. In Czechoslovakia, the term "draft beer" is often used to indicate not just a brew that is on tap but also a low-strength thirst-slaker. The sense is the same as *Schankbier* in Germany.

Cafeterias at coal mines and steel works dispense large quantities of quenching beers at very low gravities, sometimes as modest as 7.0 or, more often these days, 8.0 Balling (around 1028-1032). In alcohol content, these are similar to the Mild Ale favored in some industrial areas of England. Their alcohol content is in the region of 2.6 per cent by weight; 3.2 by volume. The Czech low-gravity beers are mildly hopped and fresh-tasting, and none is especially distinctive.

Beer-drinkers in Czechoslovakia, like those in Germany and Britain, are accustomed to identifying their choice by its gravity. The gravity of bottled beers is usually shown on the label. The system of degrees used is that devised by the internationally-recognized brewing scientist C.J.N. Balling, who was a Czech. Brewers in many other countries, notably the United States, often use the Balling system, though they do not necessarily quote it on their labels.

The most commonly enjoyed beers are the 10-degree brews. At around 1040, with an alcohol content of 3.4 by weight; 4.2 by volume, these are what British brewers would term "session" beers. They are consumed by the half-liter in Czechoslovakia's many taverns. A substantial number will be consumed in an evening's session among a group of friends or family.

The famous beers of Czechoslovakia, including the local versions of Pilsner Urquell and Budweiser Budvar, are in the bracket of 11-12 degrees (1044-48), with an alcohol content in the region of 3.6-4.0 by weight; 4.5-5.0 by volume. Probably because they were the first beers made by bottom-fermentation, they are sometimes identified simply as lager, though this seems a modest description for such fine products. They are much more than everyday lagers, at least by the definition applied in many countries. Their gravity, though, has become something of an international standard for a "premium" beer. The lower-gravity beers may contain up to 30 per cent unmalted barley, wheat starch, sugar or other adjuncts, though figures closer to 10 per cent are more common. The 11-12 products are all-malt. Minimum lagering times are in excess of 21 days, but the premium beers are matured for two to three months. On occasion, beers stay in lagering for six to nine months, but this is unusual.

All over the world there are brewers who like to make exaggerated claims as to the length of their lagering procedure. Czech brewmasters have been known to demonstrate the maturity of their beer in the lagering tank by placing a heavy coin on top of the foam. The head on the beer is so dense that the coin does not sink. "See ~ our beer is so good that it keeps our currency afloat." This demonstration is a favorite in small country breweries.

The 11-12 beers are often served with food, and that is especially true of the famous names. The hoppier Pilsner Urquell makes the better apéritif; the sweeter Budweiser Budvar goes especially well with the ubiquitous pork. In Bohemia, wine is often presented as a lesser drink, in dive-like cellar bars. Beer is the drink of Bohemia; wine belongs to Moravia, where Rieslings and rather acidic reds are grown in an area close to the Austrian vineyard country.

The beer-lover inquiring after a "special" is seeking a stronger beer, of 13-20 degrees (1052-1080). At the lower end, such a beer might have an alcohol content of around 4.5 by weight; 5.6 by volume. At the top, it will have more than 6.0; 7.5.

Although the famous beers of Czechoslovakia are pale, some breweries also have dark lagers. These are available at most gravities, though they are considered to express themselves best at 14 degrees (1056). Some are produced at this gravity for Christmas. Dark (in Czech, *tmavé*) lagers are sometimes identified as being "black" (*černé*), but their actual color varies from garnet red to dark brown. Some are colored with caramel, but the better ones are made with dark malts. A good dark lager in Czechoslovakia may contain as many as four different malts. Some have a splendidly spicy aroma and palate, but they are often dismissed as being "for women." As always, men are the victims of their own sexism.

Bohemia and It's Hops

An ancient oast-house at Duba (*below left*) and a selection of labels from all over the country (*below*). Staropramen ("Old Spring") is in Smíchov, now an industrial district of Prague. It is Czechoslovakia's biggest brewery.

PEOPLE ARE OFTEN SURPRISED that Bohemia really exists; that it is not a mythical homeland of arty nonconformists. The expression "Bohemian" seems to have originally been applied to gypsies, as they came west, via Hungary, from Asia. The people of Bohemia have often displayed political passion, but are otherwise hard-working, forever busy, and at first sight slightly dour. After a few beers, that changes.

Their country is at the meeting point of Teutonic and Slavic peoples, and straddles the frontier between the wine-growing south of Europe and the beer-brewing north. In weather, temperament and drinking habits, the nation faces north. Bohemians, by and large, enjoy watching ice-hockey and drinking beer.

The way in which the term "Bohemian" has been bandied around by brewers elsewhere in the world has perhaps also made Bohemia seem some mythical, idealized place where the beer is wonderful. Much of it is.

Then there is the King Wenceslas factor. "Good" King Wenceslas of the Christmas carol is perhaps perceived as a figure of legend, but he was a popular leader of the Bohemians in the 10th century. He was known as Wenceslas the Holy, and later canonized. The broad thoroughfare in the center of Prague is called Wenceslas Square.

King Wenceslas II granted brewing rights to Pilsen and Budweis. A later Wenceslas of Bohemia became German emperor in the 1300s. He forbade the export of hop cuttings from Bohemia, while also ordering that Burgundy vines be planted in Moravia. He was not a very effective ruler, but he was clearly a friend of the drinker.

SAAZ

Several rulers of Bohemia have issued edicts forbidding, sometimes on pain of death, the export of hop cuttings. The export of the hop cones themselves is a different matter. Brewers all over the world ~ perhaps most notably in Germany, Belgium, Britain, the United States, and Japan ~ use a proportion of Bohemian hops in their beers. They are especially employed, as might be expected, in Pilsener-style beers. Their particular use is in the last stage of hop-addition, which contributes most to the fragrance of the beer.

Bouquet is important in most types of beer but in none is it a more critical feature than in a Pilsener. This style of beer classically takes its aroma from Bohemian hops in the same way that a true Chablis is made from Chardonnay grapes.

Several of the world's classic hop varieties are grown especially for their aroma but none has quite such a reputation in this respect as the Bohemian type. In both fragrance and bitterness, Bohemian hops confer a delicate, fresh, soft character.

The variety cultivated is sometimes known by the name "Bohemian Red," after the amber-gold tinge of the dried cones. More often, it is described Saaz or Saazer. This is a German derivation from the name

Žatec, the town at the heart of the main hop-growing region. In West Germany, some brewers proclaim in the labels of their beer that they use Saazer hops. In Czechoslovakia, local buses going to Žatec display a drawing of a hop on their destination sign.

Žatec is in the northwest of Bohemia, between Prague and Carlsbad (Karlovy Vary). About 125 miles farther west are the Bavarian hop gardens of Hersbruck. In Czechoslovakia, there is a secondary growing area north of Prague, around Mûstek, in the direction of Dresden, East Germany. There are also smaller districts in Moravia (at Tršice) and Slovakia (Piešťany). Although all Czech hops are regarded as being of the same variety, a strain originally cultivated in 1865, only those from the Žatec region are designated as being Saaz.

The Žatec hop-growing area, which includes two other towns (Louny and Rakovník) and many villages, is sheltered from heavy wind and rain by two mountain ranges and a group of hills. The air is dry, and the light rain of the region is conserved in soil that comprises limestone and red clay, especially the latter, with a high iron content. The hops are low in the acids that confer bitterness to beer, but notable for tannins, resins, and certain essential oils.

The hop content is monitored by brewers as a matter of routine, but no amount of analysis can wholly describe properties as subjective as aroma and palate. Some brewers argue that Saaz hops are too dear, but many are ready to pay the price.

There is still some hand-picking of hops in Czechoslovakia, especially by students on working vacations. Patriots and romantics say that Czech hops are so good because so many of them are harvested by the tender hands of young women.

The Country Breweries of Bohemia, Moravia and Slovakia

THERE ARE LOCAL breweries in the hop-growing towns of Žatec, Louny and Rakovník, and some dry, aromatic pale lagers are produced elsewhere in the western part of Bohemia. Good examples at 11 degrees are the Karel beer from Karlovy Vary; Zlatý kůn ("Golden Horse"), from Beroun; and the fresh, firm, hoppy-tasting Platan ("Plane Tree"), the local label of the Protivín brewery, farther south. In some markets, this brewery uses the brand Schwarzenberg, the name of the feudal lords who once ruled part of Bohemia.

Bohemian beer has been made by aristocratic and royal breweries and by commoners. It has been produced by monks in abbeys and by lay brewers. It has been made in individual brew-pubs and in communal breweries. This is the history of beer in the oldest brewing regions of Europe, and in Bohemia there are visible memories of it everywhere. Today, the breweries operate in regional groups and are owned by the state, but their history is not forgotten.

Down an avenue of birch trees, behind a handsome, green-painted iron gate, a decorative wooden barrel, adorned with a malt shovel and mashing fork, symbolically announces the purpose of the mustard-colored brick-trimmed buildings of Protivín. Inside the buildings are a small floor maltings, with the traditional vaulted ceiling, and a black-and-white tiled brew-house, with copper vessels and brass handrails. These are classic designs in Czechoslovakia and in the German-speaking world. Some small Bohemian breweries still have open copper vessels to cool the wort. Most have open stainless-steel fermenters. This one was founded in 1598 and built in its present form in 1876.

None will accept casual guests ~ the idea is unknown ~ but visits can be arranged through official channels. In the smaller ones, the maltsters and brewmasters are pleased to talk about their work, proud, and opinionated.

Near Protivín, the Strakonice brewery has a splendidly aromatic pale lager. Among dark beers, there is a good, roasty-tasting 10-degree from the brewery in Stankov and a sweetish, very malty one from Krušovice, both in western Bohemia. Between these two locations, the Chodová brewery has a good 13-degree dark. These beers are hard to find outside their own districts, but that is true of most local brews.

In the north of Bohemia, the 12-degree Kapučin of the Vratislavice brewery has a deep, reddish-black color, a velvety texture, a sweet start and a dry finish, with some bitterness. In central Bohemia, the Vysoký Chlumec brewery has a sweetish, 12-degree dark. So does Černa Hora, in the south, with its Granát. This means "garnet," an evocation both of the beer's color and of the gem found in Czechoslovakia.

In the 14-degree pale beers, there is inevitably more of a malt accent. A very well-balanced example is the fresh, aromatic Krakonoš from Trutnov, in eastern Bohemia. Another is the very tasty Brnenský Drak ("Dragon"), of Brno, in Moravia. One of the best-regarded 14-degree dark beers is the malty, coffee-ish, sweetish, Kozel ("Billy Goat"), from Velké Popovice, in central Bohemia. Further north, the Litoměřice brewery makes another good example, the bittersweet Konsel.

The mining town of Ostrava, in the north of Moravia, is noted for its interest in beer. When prices went up some years ago, local drinkers organized a one-minute silence in protest. Ostrava is noted for Ondráš, a 16-degree dark beer with a rich, sweet start and a dry finish.

The strongest beer in Bohemia is a 19-degree Porter, bottom-fermenting but both roasty and hoppy, from the brewery in Pardubice, in the eastern part of Bohemia. This is made only at Christmas. It may be tasted at two old taverns in Pardubice: The Stork (U čápa) and the Green Frog (Zelená žába).

The most potent beer in the country comes not from the great brewing region of Bohemia, but from the central Slovak town of Martin. The 20-degree Martinský Porter is a hefty brew with a nice "burnt" character and plenty of hop. It is hard to find outside its home town, but it has been known to appear in the great, multi-story beer hall of Bratislava.

The Krušovice maltings and brewery (*above*, with labels) was founded in 1581, and some of today's buildings date from 1856. It is a well-equipped and proudly run traditionalist brewery. *Left*: Beechwood "aging" at another brewery, in Bohemian forest country. The beechwood chips are used to fine the beer in the lagering tank.

Pilsen and Budweis

OUTSIDE THE GERMAN-SPEAKING WORLD, almost every golden-colored beer in the world is a distant derivation of the product first made in Pilsen in 1842. Until that time, all beer had been either darkish or hazy. The technique of methodical bottom-fermentation was new, and the brewery at Pilsen used it to make its famously golden beer.

Even a lesser golden-colored beer would probably have attracted attention at the time, especially as industrially-produced glass began to replace pewter and stoneware drinking vessels. Bohemia was a leader, too, in the production of glassware (and not just the expensive crystal type).

The Pilsener lager was not only golden and bright; the local water gave it (and still does) a wonderfully soft drinkability; and the hops of Bohemia imparted a seductive fresh bouquet and a long appetizing dryness in the finish. It was (and still is) a beer of light-to-medium body.

When brewers elsewhere began to imitate the style, they tried to replicate these qualities, as well as following the Pilsener gravity of 12 degrees Balling (1048).

Today, some German Pilseners have a slightly lesser gravity (at the lowest, about 11.3) but they may also have more hop character. In that respect, they are trying not only to match, but also to exceed, the original.

Elsewhere, many brewers use the term "Pilsener" for any golden lager. All Pilseners are pale lagers; not all pale lagers are truly Pilseners. Unfortunately, there is no universally accepted term for a lesser lager derived from the Pilsener style. It can only be described as being broadly in the Pilsener style. In the New World, this is what people mean when they say "beer." All their everyday beers are distant derivations of Pilsen's original. A distant derivation indeed: comparing a serious Pilsener from another country with the Czech original is rather like comparing a Californian Chardonnay, with one from Burgundy.

The Czechs do not recognize Pilsener as a style at all. To them, it still means specifically a beer from Pilsen. They reserve it for the original. The brewery of 1842 still operates, and internationally its beer is called Pilsner Urquell (German for "original source of"). In Czech, it is identified as Plzeňský Prazdroj. It has the noteworthy distinction of being the biggest-selling import in Germany, and it is marketed in about 100 countries.

Tasted fresh, it has an astonishingly appetizing bouquet and a lovely, soft body. It can be delicious in export markets, too, but it is very susceptible to deterioration. Its house character of a light, fragrant spiciness can become overwhelmingly buttery if the beer has lain around for too long. Out of a wish to protect its beer, the brewery is inclined to pasteurize it excessively, and that merely exacerbates the problem. No beer-lover can fail to respect Pilsner Urquell, nor to seek it at its freshest and refuse to be satisfied until that pleasure has been experienced.

The Pilsner Urquell brewery has its own floor maltings. It uses a triple decoction mash, has direct-flame kettles of the traditional shape, and adds hops three times. Only Saaz hops are used, as blossoms. (The finished beer has about 35 units of bitterness.) There are two adjoining, smartly-fitted, tiled brew-houses. The most unusual parts of the procedure are the fermentation and lagering, both of which take place in pitch-lined oak vessels. The lagering vessels are of the very old type in the shape of large barrels.

There are six miles of lagering cellars, dug into sandy rock, and said to maintain a sufficiently low natural temperature for the maturation of the beer (0-3.5°C; 32-38.3°F).

When a lagering vessel has to be re-pitched, after perhaps a year, it is manhandled into the brewery yard for the treatment. Two men will manipulate the vessel, which will be taller than either of them. So many of these vessels are required that the process is continuous, and the brewery yard is continually filled with the smoke and aroma of melting pitch.

A Napoleonic-looking double "triumphal arch" stands as the entrance to the brewery, which in parts resembles a church, elsewhere a railroad station, with what seems to be a lighthouse in the middle. Parts date from 1842, more from 1892, and some are post-war. Many of the world's breweries are likewise fine examples of the decorative architecture of what the British remember as the Victorian period. Most big breweries spread into a revealing jumble of architectural styles, each representing the period of a further extension.

Around the corner from Pilsner Urquell, on a street called Ulice Veleslavína, is a very small museum of Bohemia's extensive brewing history.

The world's first encyclopedic work on beer was probably the study made in 1585 by the Bohemian Thaddeus Hájek, personal physician to the German Emperor Rudolf II, who ruled from the Hradčany Castle in Prague. Some pages of his work are in the museum. In the 1700s, the Bohemian František Ondřej Poupě was one of the first brewers anywhere in the world to use a thermometer and other measuring instruments.

Among the nations of Eastern Europe, Czechoslovakia has a considerable tradition of technology and industry. Pilsen itself is a heavy engineering town, with the Škoda works, as well as being a brewing center (and having a distillery that makes, among other products, Czech whiskey).

Its second brewery, Gambrinus, also built in the 1800s, should not be overlooked. It produces a beautifully fresh, aromatic, hoppy, 12-degree pale lager, in much the same style as Pilsner Urquell, and with a better capacity for travel. It also makes a rich, full-bodied, dark lager called Diplomat, at 18 degrees. There are taverns by both breweries, and in the town center.

Farther south, the town of České Budějovice produces its Budweiser Budvar in a considerably modernized brewery. This is a notably well-rounded beer, with a depth of spicy-sweet maltiness, drying out to a good, hoppy finish (just over 30 units of bitterness). Anywhere else in the world, it would be described as being in the Pilsener style, but the Czechs simply regard it as "a Budweiser beer."

The town also has beers of a similar palate, but slightly lighter in body, from the Samson brewery, which was founded in 1795. Today's Samson brewery is a remarkable antique. It presents an excellent example of what was in its day one of the earliest large-scale breweries, and it is to be hoped that some of this character can be preserved.

Although both Pilsen and České Budějovice are heavily industrialized towns, each is set around a very handsome old square. Pilsen has a magnificent 16th-century Renaissance town hall, elaborately gabled and decorated with gilded friezes. It also has an elegant, 14th-century Gothic church. If anything, the square at České Budějovice, with its cloistered shops and central fountain, is even more beautiful.

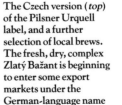

The Czech version (*top*) of the Pilsner Urquell label, and a further selection of local brews. The fresh, dry, complex Zlatý Bažant is beginning to enter some export markets under the German-language name Goldener Fasan.

Prague

Above: Across the heavily ornamented Charles Bridge, the castle and St Vitus' Cathedral dominate the skyline of Prague. This part of the town has revealing walks and thirst-making, hilly streets. The thirst can be dealt with later, back in the Old Town, at the Golden Tiger (U Zlatého Tygra). *Left*: An elaborate system of pressure control makes for a soft fresh half-liter of Pilsner Urquell.

A PERSON AFFLICTED with the inability to appreciate good beer should visit Prague anyway to see an unmatched meeting place of Gothic and Renaissance, Baroque, and Jugendstil architecture, and to walk the mosaic pavements that have felt the footsteps of Kafka and Einstein, Smetana and Dvořák. Neither its beer nor its architecture are as well known as they should be. In the city's renowned taverns, the two go glass-in-hand. Each tavern serves the products of a single brewery. The best-known fill early in the evening, often with "traffic jams" at the (almost compulsory in winter) coat-check.

The most famous, beneath its ornate hanging clock, is U Fleků. This was founded in 1499, and in parts dates from the late 1700s, but nonetheless contrives to be in the quarter known as the New Town, at Křemencová 1. U Fleků, named after its one-time owners the Flekovské family, is one of the world's great beer-taverns, ranking with the Hofbräuhaus in Munich. Like the Hofbräuhaus, it has a number of well-worn interconnecting rooms in a vaulted, "gothic" style and a beer-garden, and can accommodate several hundred drinkers. Unlike the Hofbräuhaus, this Prague counterpart still brews beer on the premises.

U Fleků makes a highly distinctive, yeasty dark beer of 13 degrees which is one of Bohemia's classics. This delightfully earthy brew is similar to some of those found in Franconia, the northern part of Bavaria. In U Fleků's main room, the beer is consumed to the tune of a raucous burlesque show, and the resultant appetite blunted with fried-bread snacks.

In the Lesser Town, a courtyard entrance leads behind the high wall of the former Augustinian monastery of St Thomas, at Letenská 12. Beer was produced there until the 1950s, but no longer is. U Tomáše nonetheless remains a beer restaurant, serving the thinnish 12-degree dark of Branik, smallest of Prague's free-standing breweries. Like most of the taverns, it also serves hot food, generally of the goulash family, with the bread dumplings of Czechoslovakia. In the Old Town, U Supa ("The Vulture"), at Celetná 22, serves Branik's very clean-tasting pale beer, but no longer has the 14-degree dark for which it was once known. U Supa is also known for hot meals.

The soft, sweetish, easily drinkable Smíchov pale

beer, from the larger Prague brewery Staro-Pramen, is widely available. A well-known outlet is U Glaubicu, at Malostranské nám 5, in the Lesser Town. This beer has a lovely dense head and fine hop aroma. The yeasty Pražan pale beer, from Holešovice, yet another Prague brewery, is more easily found in neighborhood bars.

The freshest-tasting Pilsner Urquell in Prague is found behind the unobtrusive exterior of U Zlatého Tygra, a very popular tavern with a loyal clientele, at Jusova 17, in the Old Town. In the Lesser Town, good Pilsner Urquell is served at U Kocoura ("The Tom Cat"), Nerudova 2; and at U Schnellů, at Tomášská 2, near U Tomàsě. U Schnellů is also known for hot food. The main Prague outlet for

Budweiser Budvar is U Medvídků ("The Bears"), Na Perštýně 7, in the Old Town.

Beers from smaller out-of-town breweries can also be found in some neighborhood bars, though these may be subject to change. In Prague 2, at Vinohradská, U Tržnice has traditionally served the hoppy-fruity beer of Velké Popovice. In Prague 5, at S.M. Kirova 1, Rakovnitská Pivnice is the outlet for the beer whose name it bears.

Taxis are terrifyingly fast, and inexpensive. There is an elegant subway, and an extensive streetcar system. Near the streetcar stops in the center of town, there are many sausage stands and beer cafeterias. They, too, are a part of the Bohemian experience.

Above, far left: At street level, the face of the "New Town" — and a heavy hint that it might be time for an evening drink. The vaulted cellars remain well worn, but U Fleků's own backroom brewery (*above left* and *right*) has been completely restored in recent years. Like the old brew-kettle, the new one is in the traditional style. *Top*: U Fleků has capacity to house some 900 drinkers.

GERMANY

THERE ARE OTHER GREAT beer nations, and there is Germany. Most drinkers know that, even if they are not aware what a variety of classic beer-styles Germany has. Regions and even cities have their own styles, and so do seasons.

In a sequence of social rituals, the population of Germany consumes, as often quietly as jovially, almost 150 liters of beer per head each year. In the German state of Bavaria, the figure is closer to 240. The Germans drink more beer than any other nation. West Germany usually tops the international league table in this respect, with East Germany not far behind.

Germany also has far more breweries than any other nation, and in this instance there is simply no contest. Germany has almost 40 per cent of the world's breweries. West Germany has just under 1,200, and the far smaller East Germany has about 200. There were even more — there has been great attrition in recent years — but there are also new micro-breweries opening. For the moment, closures exceed openings, but perhaps that will change. For too long, the Germans have enjoyed their riches a trifle smugly, and shrugged over brewery closures. The British used to take the same view about their architectural heritage.

The number of breweries makes for a great choice, but the availability of different styles is more important. Germany has about a dozen classic styles of beer, some of which can be divided into several categories. The distinctions between the styles are very clear.

Even the most local or seasonal styles can usually be found outside their home town or time of the year,

though they will taste best in the right place at the proper moment. Some styles are national and available all year round.

Elsewhere in the world, it is often assumed that all German beers are lagers. This is far from being the case. Nor is the term "lager" generally used. Insofar as it does occur, it indicates the most basic of bottom-fermenting products. This type of beer is usually ordered simply as a Helles. The word means "clear," "bright," or "brilliant," but is used without the noun to indicate an everyday pale lager beer. The world of brewing might regard all bottom-fermenting beers as lagers, but the German drinker distinguishes each of them by style, of which there are six or seven.

The term "Helles" is used all over the country, but this basic style of beer is to some extent associated with the state of Bavaria. The term Pilsener means a specific style. That, too, is national, though examples show some regional variation of character. Pilseners tend to be driest in the far north, very elegant in the part of the Rhineland known as the Sauerland, soft in the wine country, and on the malty side in Bavaria. The style of beer known as Export is particularly linked with the city of Dortmund. Bock beer is especially associated with the springtime and with the cities of Einbeck, Lower Saxony, and Munich, Bavaria. Double Bock is a Munich and Kulmbach style, especially for late winter. Märzenbier is also a Munich and Kulmbach style for the Oktoberfest. Dunkel, too, is notably a Munich and Kulmbach style. Most of the styles associated with Munich and Bavaria are brewed throughout the south. One of the most distinctive bottom-fermenting styles, Rauchbier, is especially associated with the town of

Opposite: Even in a cosmopolitan city like Munich, *lederhosen* are still sometimes worn in beer-halls — especially at festival times. Bavaria remains deeply rooted in rural tradition, and thrives as one of Europe's most conservative and cohesive societies. *Below*: As elsewhere, even the new can be old. Drinkers in Nürnberg can buy pot-stoppered bottles of an "organic" dark-brown lager from the new "Old Town-house Brewery." Its brewing equipment is that of a working museum. The wooden lauter tun filters the mash. The ridged copper machine is a wort-cooler.

The Brewing Towns of Souther

Bamberg. Germany also has many top-fermenting beers, styles that the English-speaking world might regard broadly as ales. The style that most resembles an ale in the British tradition is Altbier, which is especially associated with the city of Düsseldorf. The Kölsch of Cologne superficially resembles the golden type of ale made in Canada and the east of the United States. However, both of these Rhineland styles are made in a decidedly German fashion.

Wheat Beers are also top-fermenting, and these are an important category in Germany, especially in summer. There are two principal styles of Wheat Beer, one in the north (primarily Berlin), the other in the south (especially Bavaria). The southern style of Wheat Beer divides into several sub-categories. Having once been perceived as an old-fashioned, rustic style, the Wheat Beers of southern Germany enjoyed a revival in the 1980s and became very fashionable among the young. The yeast-sedimented types are especially popular.

Because these classic styles are very clearly defined in Germany, examples from rival breweries are often similar. There is always some variation of interpretation and house character, but it may not be huge. As is often the case in other countries, the very smallest breweries often make the most idiosyncratic beers.

In addition to the classic styles, there are a growing number of beer-types that have each been created by a single brewery. Some of these, though not all of them, are the products of new micro-breweries. These new beer-types are intended to be more localized than most of the established styles. They are 'meant to offer a style for a town or district that has been bumping along without one. This idea — that every town should have its own style of beer — was

A Blossoming Hop Industry

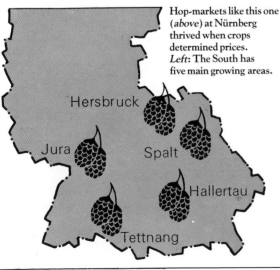

Hop-markets like this one (*above*) at Nürnberg thrived when crops determined prices. *Left*: The South has five main growing areas.

Hersbruck

Jura

Spalt

Hallertau

Tettnang

GERMAN HOPS

The choicest varieties of hops grow well on the soil of Germany. Their reputation covers the whole world. Their aroma and flavour guarantee the brewing of the finest beers

Information in regard to supplies obtainable only through

Ausfuhrgesellschaft
der Deutschen Brauwirtschaft m.b.H.
MÜNCHEN 27
Vilshofenerstraße 8

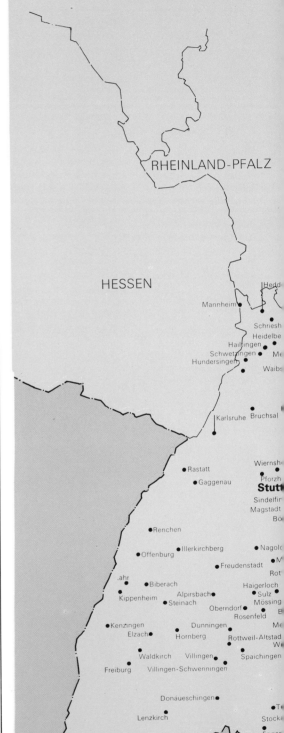

RHEINLAND-PFALZ

HESSEN

Mannheim

Hedd

Schriesh

Heidelbe

Hailfingen

Schwetzingen • Me

Hundersingen • Waibs

Karlsruhe Bruchsal

Rastatt

Wiernsh

Pforzh

Gaggenau Stutt

Sindelfir

Magstadt

Bo

Renchen

Nagol

Offenburg • Illerkirchberg

M

Freudenstadt

Rot

.ahr

Biberach Haigerloch

Alpirsbach • Sulz

Kippenheim

Steinach Mössing

Oberndorf B

Rosenfeld

Kenzingen Dunningen Me

Elzach • Hornberg Rottweil-Altstad

Waldkirch Villingen Spaichingen Wi

Freiburg Villingen-Schwenningen

Donaueschingen T

Lenzkirch Stocka

Enger

Lörrach

once more widespread in Germany and other brewing countries, notably Britain. Today, it is best understood in Belgium, where such brews are known as *streek* (district) beers.

Many of the new beers in Germany are served with yeast in suspension. Some are made from malting barley and hops that are organically grown. Several of the new breweries use equipment that has been custom-made in an almost medieval style. Others have beautifully copper-clad brew-houses operated by state-of-the-art computer systems.

Such design features are devised in part with an eye on the drinker. Many of the old, small breweries, and most of the new ones, are attached to a tavern (usually serving food), and the kettles are often visible to the customer. The older type of small brew-house in Germany usually has a design of classic simplicity, its vessels all copper, trimmed with brass, and set into tiling that often has some mosaic decoration. German brew-houses are almost always as clean as a new pin. (Although that particular measure of beer is British.)

All varieties of yeast, whether for brewing, baking, or whatever, are so promiscuous that cleanliness is an article of more than faith wherever they are handled. Most brewers take this very seriously, but German brewers are especially concerned about it. The Germans would be horrified at the sight of some of the funkier, smaller breweries in Belgium and Britain. They are usually the ones that produce the most idiosyncratic beers, and in their picturesque surroundings the yeasts have acquired their own boldness. That is not the German way.

The sight of a handsome brew-house undoubtedly enhances the experience of eating and drinking. The

brewmaster, in his white overalls and rubber boots, working away behind a window, is like the chef in his toque who bobs in and out of the dining room, his presence reassuring the guests that their *boeuf en croute* did not emerge from a vacuum pack.

Brew-houses that can be seen in this way are beginning to be taken up elsewhere in the world. Many of Germany's bigger and less public brew-houses are of the same design, but with larger kettles and more of them. Some look like theaters (that is not a Wurlitzer; it is a mash filter). Others, with their stained-glass windows, are obviously places of worship. Many are uninviting puzzles of stainless steel. The beer is made in the same way, but the appetite is not aroused. This contrast can be observed elsewhere, but it is especially striking in Germany, where so much of the world's brewing equipment is designed.

What English-speakers call a brew-pub is known in Germany as a Hausbräuerei. It is an institution that has never seemed in danger of dying, but is being revived nonetheless. How many such establishments there are is hard to determine. Even in Britain and the United States there are some that operate primarily as a brew-pub but also sell their beer elsewhere. In Germany this is very common.

In a village, a single building might house a brewery, a tavern, a restaurant, and several guest bedrooms. Such an establishment — an inn in the full, old-fashioned sense of the word — may also supply two or three other taverns in the village. Should this be counted as a brew-pub? Or is it a small brewery with its own "tap"? In Germany the line between the two is hard to set. Confusingly, the term Bräuerei Gasthaus can mean just a tavern. There is a guide published to some of those that have guest bedrooms; they provide a wonderful facility to the beer explorer.

The term "Landbräuerei" is sometimes used to indicate a village brewery. Although these can be found in the north, they are much more common in the south, especially in Bavaria, where some villages may even have a couple of breweries. Bavaria is by European standards a big state, and it has two-thirds of all the breweries in West Germany. Within Bavaria, the region of Franconia is the most heavily-breweried of all.

Like several other countries, Germany entertains a great north-south rivalry. In Germany, the north is taken to include not only cities like Hamburg and Bremen but also the more westerly stretch of the country, embracing Dortmund, Düsseldorf and Cologne. In the whole country, Dortmund is the city making the most beer. From the beer-lover's standpoint, it has become a much more interesting city to visit with the opening of two brew-pubs. It also has a small museum of brewing. No beer-lover would visit workaday Dortmund without also seeing fashionable Düsseldorf, which has four old-established brew-pubs, all producing Altbier. Cologne has more breweries than any other city: a

baker's dozen within its boundaries, and the same number again in the surrounding area. Several of these are brew-pubs.

Despite all this, the north has the less pervasive beer-culture. Perhaps because it is mainly Protestant, the north likes to drink quietly, indoors. Nor do its weather and its industrial setting encourage beer-gardens. Its Protestantism also means that it has a long tradition of secular beer-production. In this climate of commercial competition, fewer small breweries have survived than in the south.

The major brewing groups in Germany are northern, but none has achieved the level of nationwide identity enjoyed by their counterparts in other countries. Thus far, the German beer-drinker has shown a good nose for breweries managed by accountants or marketing men. Some of these have, of course, succeeded, but companies managed by brewers are suspected of making better beer.

The biggest grouping links Dortmunder Union (D.U.B.) with Schultheiss, of Berlin, and owns several breweries in other cities. Dortmunder Actien (D.A.B.) is linked with Germany's largest single brewery, Binding, of Frankfurt, and with Kindl, of Berlin; this group is owned by the food company Oetker. There is some uncertainty over the future composition of a group originally formed by Bavaria-St Pauli (Hamburg), Hannen (Rhineland-Westphalia), Henninger (Frankfurt), Tucher (Nürnberg) and a number of smaller breweries. This enterprise was assembled by the Reemstma cigarette company but Hannen has now been sold to Carlsberg of Denmark, and Henninger and Tucher have joined hands with E.K.U. (Kulmbach), Eichbaum (Mannheim) and others. In the south, property-based interests control Paulaner and Hacker-Pschorr, two of Munich's breweries. Several groups and breweries that operate quite separately are nonetheless backed by the same major banks.

Unlike the Americans, for example, the Germans have shown a commendable loyalty to their local breweries. This is based on the belief that the local beer must surely be best, and perhaps on an appreciation that it is freshest. It is not as detailed and specific an appreciation as a member of the Campaign for Real Ale might apply to a particular product in Britain.

The Catholic south, and especially Bavaria, is the most conservative part of Germany, in all respects. Munich may be the home of BMW cars, but it is still a cultural capital — and of a state that was once a nation. In Franconia, the city of Nürnberg may have some heavy engineering, but it is still a bookish place, a guardian of a culture.

Bavaria is predominantly rural, and its impeccably tidy villages are invariably set around a church (often onion-domed), a brewery (sometimes with its own maltings), and a tavern. In Alpine Bavaria, the snowy winter welcomes the strong, warming seasonal beers. In spring, the sun reflects off the lakes and warms the village beer-gardens.

Every village has a maypole, painted in candy-stripes in the pale blue and white that are the "national" colors of Bavaria, and often decorated with shields depicting the rituals of agriculture and brewing. In summer, there are village festivals: a service of blessing in a meadow, then a beer tent in the next field. There may be three or four thousand people present from the village and surrounding hamlets.

Once again, God has been good. The snow has fallen and melted, and water has laughed its way down the mountainsides to the lakes and breweries. The waters and the sun have set the fields of the Munich Basin sprouting with sweet, clean malting barley. By Lake Constance, and on the road from Munich to Nürnberg and Bayreuth, hop gardens are dense with vines, budding and ready to flower.

The priest has thanked God, and the villagers have sung and intoned their responses. It has been an elaborate service. Now, the priests and nuns sit down to taste the beer with their flock. It was produced, undoubtedly, in a brew-house with a crucifix overlooking the kettles, and with thanks to God set into the stained-glass windows.

The owner of the brewery, an especially respected citizen, mingles with his customers. He wears a Bavarian loden jacket, as he does almost every day. The villagers have dressed in traditional costume, just for the festival. The women wear fetching bodices. On stage, the local bucks show how they can yodel, or race to saw through a tree-trunk. Children give a display of country dancing. The oompah band plays *Ein Prosit*. At every chorus, the entire community raise their glasses, each containing a liter of beer. By the time the verse resumes, another hectoliter will have been added to the balance sheet of the brewery and the official statistics of the state of Bavaria. It is an enviable economic system.

Across the Alps to the south is Italy, whence came Christianity and the monastic tradition. Not far west in Switzerland is the monastery of St Gallen, where brewing was restored after the Dark Ages. Across the Bohemian Forest to the east, there was a monastic tradition, too, and the water of Pilsen and the hops of Žatec.

The monks who came from Italy to Bavaria at first grew wine-grapes, but soon began to brew beer. If wine is the tradition of the warm south and beer of the cool north, then the natural frontier between them in the Old World is either the Alps or the river Danube. Both are washed on each side by the two great fermented beverages, but allegiances are clear. Germany is proud of its wines, but is first and foremost a beer country. Often beer is served before and during a meal, with a glass of a typical sweet German wine presented afterward as though it were a liqueur.

From Central Europe to the North and Baltic seas, Germany is by far the biggest country in land area and population; Teutonic languages are the most extensively spoken, and beer the natural drink.

fchencken/vnd verkauffen. Wir wőllen auch fonderlichen/
das füran allenthalben in vnfern Stetten/Márckthen/vñ
aufff dem Lannde/zů kainem Pier/merer ſtückh/dañ al=
lain Gerſten/Hopffen/vñ waſſer/genomen vñ gepraucht
ſőlle werdñ. Welher aber diſe vnſere Ordnung wiſſentlich
überfaren vnnd nit hallten wurde/dem ſol von ſeiner ge=
richtzőbrigkait/daſſelbig vas Pier/zůſtraff vnnachláß=
lich/ſo offt es geſchicht/genommen werden. Jedoch wo

THE BEER PURITY LAW

The Bavarians were the first to have a Pure Beer law, the *Reinheitsgebot*, in 1516, and insisted upon its retention when they became a part of the Republic of Germany in 1919. It was originally a means to promote the brewing industry (as a source of tax revenues) and in 1987 was deemed by the European Court to be protectionist. German brewers have since insisted that they themselves will continue to brew according to the *Reinheitsgebot*, even if they cannot prevent "impure" beer from being imported.

In Bavaria, the law had always applied also to beers that were brewed for export. In the rest of Germany, it did not. The law insisted that beer be made exclusively from malt, hops, yeast, and water, with no additives. In Bavaria, several brewers were caught in breach of the law while it was being discussed in the European Court. This led to a scandal and a suicide. The scandal hardened the attitudes of German consumers, who insisted that beer must be "pure," but it heightened skepticism in the European Court. The jurors were unconvinced about a law that even some Bavarians broke. The behavior of a few brewers in the north posed an even bigger question. They were willing to use other brewing sugars (for cheapness, or lightness of body) and additives (for shelf-life) in beer made for export. If this sort of beer was bad for Germans, how could it be sold to other countries?

The *Reinheitsgebot* is meant to protect the integrity of the product, and was not framed purely as a health measure. All the same, it is reassuring to think that a beer contains only malt, hops, yeast, and water. In fact, the original legislation did not mention yeast. At the time of its drafting, a form of spontaneous fermentation was used. The law is an antique, and so has its faults, but it does have the merits of being very simple and of being based on a sense of beer as an honest product — pure and wholesome, too.

The law itself could not insure that all brewers would have skill, flair, and sensitivity, but in no corner of the world has as much good beer been made as in Bavaria. No beer routinely tastes as clean and malty as that made in Bavaria. If the law prevented the Bavarians from making Belgian Kriek or British Sweet Stout, for example, nobody seemed to mind.

Now, if the Germans want either of those specialties, they may import them.

Meanwhile, it is to be hoped that they stick to their pledge to maintain their own tradition. The *Reinheitsgebot* may be imperfect, even restrictive, but which is better: to have a law concerning the contents and purity of the beer we brew and drink, or to have no such specific a safeguard?

"Brewed according to the Purity Law." This labeling device was designed by the German Society of Brewers. In the first two years of its availability, 200 brewers sought permission to use it. Others displayed a simple plaque outside their premises.

Munich Dark and Pale

THE CITY OF MUNICH and the state of Bavaria have many claims to be a home of brewing, but it was their development of the lager method that did most to spread their names around the world. The term "lager" means "store."

This is a method not of brewing, but of maturation. The difference is not in the brew-house but in the cellar. In some parts of the world, beers are advertised as being "slow-brewed," but the term really refers to their being stored in tanks at cold temperatures and for supposedly long periods.

The first brewers in the world to practise this technique seem to have been based near Munich. The lagering method is first mentioned in brewing history in 1420, in the minutes of Munich town council. At that time, without the benefit of artificial refrigeration, it was impossible to brew in summer. When brewers tried, their beer was turned sour by wild yeasts. Instead, a supply of beer was stored in casks during summer, to be tapped when it was needed. In Bavaria the brewers had a natural storage place: caves in the foothills of the Alps. They observed that this cold storage not only preserved the beer, but actually enhanced its stability. They did not know why, because the nature of the yeast was not understood at the time.

The lager method was not understood and perfected until much later. From the late 1700s, there was a golden century of innovation in the brewing industry. This was the period when brewing ceased to be empirical and became scientific. From Britain and France to Bavaria and Bohemia, and later Denmark, important discoveries were made, especially concerning the nature and behavior of yeast. For the first time, brewers in different countries exchanged knowledge. Brewing was evolving from trade into industry. In the early 1800s, the innovative Munich brewer Gabriel Sedlmayr the Younger made his company something of a clearing-house for technical knowledge. In the 1830s, a time when beers brewed from barley malt were all dark, Sedlmayr began working to produce lagers by more methodical techniques. His original lager beer was dark brown in color and malty in character.

Today, the term "Munich-style" is taken by brewers in many parts of the world to indicate a dark-brown lager. In some countries, beers of this type are labeled "Bavarian-style." In Germany, they are labeled simply Dunkel, meaning "dark." In the United States, a product labeled "dark beer" is usually a lager in loosely this style. In some other countries, notably Britain, the idea of a dark lager is virtually unknown.

The great brewer Sedlmayr went on to collaborate with his contemporary Dreher, in Vienna, and with Carl von Linde, on the development of the first refrigerator. Sedlmayr's brewery, called Spaten, and still predominantly owned by the family, is today one of Munich's Big Six. It continues to include a dark, "Munich-style" lager in its range, as do many other German breweries.

Whereas their predecessors would have been fruity, and broadly in the style of ales, the early lagers brewed in Munich would have enjoyed the cleaner character that is now known to derive from bottom-fermenting yeasts. This cleanness no doubt also unmasked the maltiness that is typical of bottom-fermenting beers made in Bavaria.

Although all beers were in those days either opaque or cloudy, some brewing historians believe that dark brews survived longer in Munich because the local barley has traditionally been high in protein. In earlier times, the high protein content presented difficulties in the production of pale beers.

This characteristic is imparted by the climate, and is generally true of barleys grown far inland. Maltsters regard these as "Continental" barleys, and those from Denmark or Britain, for example, as "Maritime." Continental barleys produce deliciously malty-tasting beers; the Maritime crop has a lighter touch. Because they have been accustomed to working with high-protein barleys, Continental brewers sometimes use a more intensive mashing method, known as triple decoction. This is especially used in the production of dark beers. In brewing worldwide, the style of malt used to produce a dark lager is often identified as being of the Munich type. It

Below and *left*: The most elegant place devoted to the consumption of beer in Munich is Augustiner's 1890s restaurant on Neuhauser Strasse. It has an extraordinary number of visual references: an interior glass dome fit for an Edwardian English winter garden; mussel-shell patterns that could have strayed from Barcelona cathedral; and a Florentine courtyard at the rear. *Lower right*: "Fairy-tale" castles are a Bavarian specialty. The one at Kaltenberg, 30 miles from Munich, is the residence of Prince Luitpold of Bavaria. Its specialty is a dark lager.

is highly kilned, but does not have a roasted taste.

Spaten's dark lager is brewed to an Export gravity (12.7 Plato; 1051) and has an alcohol content of 4.0 per cent by weight; 5.0 per cent by volume. It has a dark mahogany color, with some translucency (47 E.B.C.); a medium-to-full body; a palate that is malty but not especially sweet; and only a light hop character (20 E.B.U.).

This kind of profile is quite common, though some brewers, especially in Franconia, aim for a marginally higher gravity and more intense character. Despite its name, Spaten Dunkel Export is not widely available in overseas markets. In some countries, the brewery is represented in the dark beer category by its much stronger Optimator, a Double Bock.

Spaten has royal connections in that Sedlmayr's father had been the Bavarian court brewer. Another royal brewery, that run by Prince Luitpold of Bavaria, at the castle of Kaltenberg, not far from Munich, has a dark lager as its principal specialty, even though it is known in some export markets for a "diät" Pilsener. Its specialty dark lager, König Ludwig Dunkel, is malty, coffee-ish, and relatively light-bodied for the style. In 1988, Prince Luitpold began construction of a Hausbräuerei in Munich. He has also acted as an adviser to brew-pubs in other cities. It was not initially clear what style of beer would emerge as Prince Luitpold's specialty in Munich. Dark lagers have for some years been considered old-fashioned,

Spaten is one of several major breweries in Germany and elsewhere that still uses horses for very local deliveries (left). They seem all the more delightfully incongruous against the airport-like exterior of the Spaten brewery. The initials are those of the great Gabriel Sedlmayr. "Spaten" is German for "spade". It was a corruption of the name of Georg Spaeth, who owned the brewery in 1622.

The original Munich Dunkel is Spaten's. Paulaner calls its pale "original." The world knows Lowenbräu, but Augustiner is favored locally.

but have recently enjoyed a minor revival. They are easiest to find in Franconia, where some are very dark and full of character. The Franconian town of Kulmbach has a history of making very dark beers.

Spaten produced what it describes as Munich's first pale lager beer in 1894, though its local rival Paulaner claims to have developed and popularized this style in the late 1920s and the 1930s. The Munich brewers usually call their entrant in this category simply Münchner Hell. In English, this would be best rendered as "Munich Pale." Such beers have been seen in the American market bearing the legend "Munich Light." This suggests that they are low in calories, and that is certainly not true.

The Münchner Hell or Munich Pale type is a malt-accented golden lager that is slightly lower in gravity, and less hoppy, than a Pilsener. The Spaten example has a gravity of 11.2 Plato, or 1045, as against 11.8 and 1048 for the same company's Pilsener. The Hell has an alcohol content of 3.7 per cent by weight; 4.69 by volume. The figures for the Pilsener are 4.0 and 5.07. The Hell has 22 units of bitterness; the Pilsener 38. Some breweries, including Spaten, produce not only these two styles but also a pale lager of the Export type. Spaten's entrant, Spatengold, has a gravity of 12.7 (1051), 4.3 per cent (5.45) and 25 units of bitterness.

It is sad that within this type of range the Münchner Hell, the first pale style of the city, is sometimes regarded as a poor relation. It is also a shame that even the breweries' own beer-halls and gardens may serve just one of the three pale styles. Most of the breweries have more than one of these "house" outlets. Among the Big Six, the brewery most favored by the local beer-lovers, especially for its pale brews, is Augustiner, which regards its tasty, appetizing, Export-gravity Edelstoff Hell as its house specialty.

Augustiner has its elegant, 1890s brewery-tap in the shopping street Neuhauser Strasse. It has a small, popular beer garden called the Augustiner Keller, on Arnulf Strasse, in the brewery quarter, and a much larger one at the Hirschgarten, a public park near Nymphenburg Palace. In summer, wives take a picnic basket and the children, and meet their husbands from the office over a glass of Augustiner at the Hirschgarten.

Augustiner's beers are generally thought to be the maltiest from the Big Six, and Paulaner's the driest (perhaps with a tannic note?). Those from the Hofbräuhaus brewery are on the malty side; Löwenbräu's medium; Hacker-Pschorr's somewhere in the middle; Spaten's very complex, with a good hop note. These are very general categorizations of house character, and difficult to apply over such wide ranges of beers. With their various dark and pale, Oktoberfest and Bock types, and Wheat Beers, the biggest Munich breweries each have at least ten principal products in different styles.

Märzenbier

Opposite: Picnic baskets at the ready as the tablecloth is prepared at the Hirschgarten, in Munich. Families bring their own radishes, sausages and bread, but enjoy the beer of the Augustiner brewery. *Below*: Attendance at the Munich Oktoberfest runs into millions. The city's breweries all have their own tents, each of which can accommodate several thousand people. *Overleaf*: Steins in action at the Oktoberfest.

IT IS EASY ENOUGH for an English-speaker to decipher Märzenbier as "March beer," but it is less obvious why this style is usually consumed in late September and early October.

The name dates from the time when March was the last month in which brewing was possible, before the warm weather brought out the wild yeasts. March was the time when a big brew was made to be stored away as a supply for the summer. It would be made to a fairly high gravity, so that it could quietly enjoy some secondary fermentation in storage, thus insuring a degree of carbonation and protecting it against yeast infection. At the end of summer, in September or October, any beer left in storage would be ceremonially consumed.

In Germany this custom has left a clear imprint: it is Märzenbier that must be consumed in September-October. In some other countries, most notably the Netherlands, Bock beer is served at this time. In Germany, Bock has other seasons, though it, too, is regarded as a beer to be consumed when the weather is uncertain. These traditions of strongish beers for uncertain or cool weather have merged and mixed over the centuries.

The German notion of draining the last stocks of Märzenbier has been transposed and embroidered in some countries to an oft-retailed story about Bock beer. There is a widespread view that brewers spring-clean their kettles (or have an annual scrub in the autumn), and that the residue of a year's boiling is sold as Bock. This misunderstanding amuses brewers and beer-buffs, but does not seem to dissuade anyone from drinking Bock.

Germany has a clear idea as to what style should be served as a traditional Märzenbier. The traditional German Märzen is a medium-strong, malty, amber-red, translucent, bottom-fermenting beer derived from the Viennese method of brewing. A true Märzenbier has an especially long period of lagering, in line with its tradition. Its maltiness is concentrated in its aroma rather than in its palate. The body is malty, but not immense. This is a delicious style of beer, full of the bouquet and sweet spiciness of its amber-red Vienna-type malt, but it is one that has suffered some erosion of both character and popularity in recent years.

Once again, the original example of a Märzenbier in this tradition comes from Sedlmayr's Spaten brewery. It was obviously his technical collaboration with the Viennese brewer Dreher in the mid-1800s that led the innovative Sedlmayr to give his Märzenbier something of an Austrian character.

This style was then adopted by other brewers all over Bavaria and the south of Germany. The Spaten product in this category today has a gravity of 13-13.5 (1052-5), more than 4.0 per cent alcohol (5.0-plus), a good, reddish color of 33, and a mere 21 units of bitterness. The brewery says that it is lagered for more than three months. Like a man wearing both a belt and braces, this product calls itself Spaten Munich Ur-Märzen Oktoberfest. This is intended to leave consumers doubly sure what is inside the bottle.

Although many brewers continue to produce a truly distinctive Märzenbier in the tradition established by Sedlmayr, there has also been much bowing to supposed public demand for paler beers. For many brewers, the term Märzen merely indicates a bottom-fermenting beer with a gravity of 13-plus, a malty accent, and an alcohol content of 4.0-4.5 by weight. Many of these entrants have a more equivocal, pale bronze color of around 18 E.B.C.

Although the traditional Märzenbier is still emphatically available at the Munich Oktoberfest, there has been an increasing consumption of less interesting pale beers in this style.

The connection between Märzenbier and the Oktoberfest is one of timing. Given the moment when it appears, Märzenbier is the natural drink to be consumed at the Oktoberfest. This event was conceived in 1810 not as a beer festival but to celebrate the betrothal of the Crown Prince of

A fresh Sunday morning in late September, in rural Bavaria... and a satisfying Märzenbier from Reutberg.

Bavaria. The "village green" on which it is held, now a huge fairground, is known at the Theresienwiese, after the royal bride. *Wiese* means meadow. *Wiesenmärzen* is a colloquialism for an Oktoberfest beer. This can be confusing for foreigners, especially if they have already encountered the unrelated Weizen and Weisse styles of Wheat Beer.

The festival begins on a Saturday in mid to late September, lasts 16 days, and ends on the first Sunday in October. On the first Sunday, there is a huge parade to the fairground. All the big Munich brewers take part. Five or six million people attend the festival over the duration. Although the average consumption is less than a liter per head, this is not an event for the beer-lover who wants to make a calm appreciation of the products. Every devotee should probably visit the Oktoberfest once in a lifetime, for one day or two. Afterward, the head can be cleared on a side-trip to an Alpine village, where beer might be more thoughtfully enjoyed.

There are several similar festivals elsewhere. The origins of the Oktoberfest as a country fair are slightly better maintained by the other big southern festival, in Stuttgart. This is called the Cannstatter Volksfest. The neighborhood where it takes place is Cannstatt, and in the local dialect the meadow becomes a *Wasen*. The festival takes place at much the same time, beginning around the end of September and running for two weeks into October. Beers of a Märzen type are produced for the event by Stuttgart's three breweries, at the slightly lower gravity of 12.5-plus which is accorded to the style in the state of Baden-Württemberg. The breweries in this instance are Dinkelacker, Stuttgarter Hofbräu and Schwaben Bräu.

The Stuttgart breweries produce beers in a similar style for Christmas and New Year. In this case, they are identified as Weihnachtsbier. Other breweries offer different styles for the holiday seasons, or for various festivals. If a brew is identified simply as a Festbier, it may well be in the Märzen style.

At festivals and country fairs in Germany the favorite foods are chickens, or cockerels, roasted on the spit. This makes for a happy combination. With its sweet spiciness, Märzenbier is an excellent accompaniment to chicken, and even better with pork. It also goes well with spicy dishes. Not only geographically but also in character and role, the Märzenbier of Baden-Württemberg is a neighbor to the Gewürztraminer of Alsace.

In Austria, the term Märzenbier has come to mean nothing more than a brewery's basic lager, albeit at a gravity of 1048-plus and with a sweetish palate. There have been sightings of German-style Märzenbier in other countries, even including Spain, but these are rare. One or two American micro-breweries have made good examples, and Anheuser-Busch has test-marketed a credible interpretation. Stroh's Erlanger is marketed as a Märzenbier but has no obvious claim to the style.

The Bavarian Brewmaster

Munich's master brewer was Gabriel Sedlmayr (*left*) of the Spatenbräu brewery. His pioneering work helped make the city, and the State of Bavaria, synonymous with bottom-fermented beers as the style's popularity spread throughout Europe. The group photograph (*below*), taken during the late 1800s, shows Sedlmayr's three sons (in the front row) with senior members of the Spatenbräu staff. Sedlmayr is credited with having introduced and popularized today's Vienna-style interpretation of Märzenbier.

Bock and Double Bock

IN GERMANY A BOCK is first and foremost a strong beer. It must have a gravity of more than 16 Plato (1064), and probably has an alcohol content of not less than 5.3 per cent by weight (6.7 by volume). Some are much stronger than this. It may be the most potent beer produced by the brewery unless, as is often the case, there is also an extra-strong one, called a Double Bock. That must have a gravity of more than 18, and is likely to have an alcohol content of not less than 5.4 (6.8). Again, it may be stronger. The alcohol content of the famous E.K.U. Kulminator 28-degree version has reached a height of 10.92 (13.5).

Traditionally a Bock beer was dark, but today there are also many pale examples. A brewery may produce both. Bock beers are seasonal, but in Germany different versions are served at several points during the year. Unless the term is qualified by some further description, a Bock is a bottom-fermenting beer, usually with a longish lagering period. A Bock is not made from residue accumulated in the brew-kettles.

The name most probably originates from that of the town of Einbeck, in the state of Lower Saxony. It seems likely that the identity of brews from this town was in time popularly abbreviated to "beck beer" (nothing to do with the brewery of that name in Bremen). Later, that contraction was corrupted into "bock" in the Bavarian accent.

Einbeck was once widely renowned for strong beers, and it still produces some good examples. Its early fame derived from its wide distribution of beer at a time when most brewing was local. As always, beers brewed to be sent on long journeys would have been made to high gravities for their own protection.

At a time when most brewing was carried out by monks or in the courts of kings and dukes, Einbeck had already turned the occupation into a business. The city fathers licensed their citizens to trade as brewers, then taxed them to raise revenue. Einbeck seems to have been the world's first great center of commercial brewing. It fulfilled this role in the early days of the Hanseatic League, the alliance of trading cities and ports that in the 13th, 14th and 15th centuries long preceded modern Germany as a business nation. The reforming theologian who challenged the role of the Church in the 16th century, Martin Luther, was twice fortified by gifts of Einbeck beer. One gift was for his wedding; the second occasion was when he confronted the Emperor at the Diet of Worms. Einbeck could hardly have conceived a more effective advertising endorsement.

The first great beers of Einbeck were made by what would today be called contract brewers. Individual citizens bought malt and hops, and were visited by a town brewmaster, who brought equipment with him. They then worked together to brew the beer, which was fermented in the cellar of the house. The citizens then marketed the beer.

It seems likely that the original Bock would have

The Beer of Martin Luther

At the Diet of Worms, Martin Luther was fortified with Einbeck beer . . . and his portrait was used on the label in the earliest days of exports to the United States.

Although Einbeck beer has been brewed since 1351, it was not bottled until the mid 1800s. This original bottle, still corked, was found in Einbeck in 1965.

Earlier exports went by the cask on drays which were given an armed guard. This dray from the Einbeck museum is perhaps more robust than it looks. It may have traveled thousands of miles on journeys running as far as Stockholm and Amsterdam.

been a strong, dark, top-fermenting Wheat Beer. Wheat was widely used at the time, and it is unlikely that the people of Einbeck knew in the 1200s how to bottom-ferment. Some enthusiasts argue that the need to store beer to fulfill trading orders gave birth to an early form of lagering, but that is open to question.

Today, Einbeck has only one brewery, and it makes bottom-fermenting beers. The company is called the Einbecker Bräuhaus, and is owned by D.U.B.-Schultheiss. It has no fewer than three Bock beers. All are labeled Einbecker Ur-Bock, but one is dark (Dunkel), one pale (Hell) and one amber. The latter is a springtime May Bock. Beers of this type are intended as a warming drink at a time when winter is yielding to spring. After the dark days, it is a pleasure to get out into a beer-garden, even if some inner warmth is needed. This example is marketed from the beginning of March until the end of May.

All three of the Einbecker Bock beers have a gravity of 16.7 (1066.8) and an alcohol content of around 5.5 (6.9). In color, the Hell has 15 E.B.C., the Maibock 23, and the Dunkel 45. All three have a profound, smooth maltiness and a gentle Hallertau hop character.

The spread of Bockbier brewing is attributed to the marriage between a duke from the city of Brunswick, also in Lower Saxony, and the daughter of an aristocrat from the south of Germany. The wedding took place in the south, in Munich. The marriage was in the 1600s, and by the late 1700s a dictionary was referring to "Oanbock" as a very strong beer brewed in the Hofbräuhaus in the city of Munich.

Hofbräuhaus means "royal court brewery." The Hofbräuhaus of Munich is now a public enterprise, owned by the state of Bavaria. Other cities have breweries with similar names, but they are now privately owned. The Hofbräuhaus of Munich continues to brew several types of Bock beer and considers itself to be the home of the style. One argument has it that Duke Wilhelm V of Bavaria already had it in mind to rival Einbeck's success when he ordered the building of the Hofbräuhaus in 1589.

In the spirit of north-south rivalry, the Einbeck connection is dismissed in Munich. There are many other colorful explanations for the name, most of them relating to the fact that Bock means billy-goat in German. It has even airily been suggested that this is the beer for the season of Capricorn. This sign of the zodiac applies from late December to late January, and it is true that some brewers produce a Bock variation as their Christmas beer.

At the Hofbräuhaus the most important Bock season is, once again, May. The prime minister of Bavaria and the mayor of Munich are quite likely to take part in the tapping of the first huge barrel of Maibock each year. This ceremony takes place on May Day. The Hofbräuhaus Maibock has a gravity of 18 (1072), a dense head, an aroma so powerful that it can almost be eaten, a rich start, and a long, chewily-dry malty finish. It has a very deep amber-red color but is regarded as a Helles Bock. Most Maibocks are

Left: The billy-goat symbol rides many a Bock beer in rural Bavaria. The Rosenbräuerei, of Kaufbeuren, has two. *Right*: Fancy packaging does not always guarantee an interesting beer, but this stoneware bottle contains a delightfully liqueurish brew of more than 12 per cent alcohol by volume, broadly in the style of a Double Bock. The beer is Abt's Trunk and comes from a secularized monastery brewery at Irsee, south of Ulm, Bavaria. *Far right*: The strongest Bock beer in Germany is the "28" version of E.K.U. Kulminator. It is lagered at very low temperatures. The true Eisbock, though, is made by the neighboring Reichelbräu brewery.

pale, and usually far more of a bronze-yellow color. Earlier in the year, the Hofbräuhaus produces a darker, winter Bock, of the same gravity, under the name Delicator.

In gravity and style, both of these are Double Bocks. A "single" Bock usually balances its maltiness with a good attenuation and a smooth but definite hoppy dryness in the finish. The Double Bock type ranges from the round to the profound to the enveloping.

The term "single" Bock is never used. Just Bock. Nor is a Double Bock twice as strong. "Double" Bock is a very unGerman piece of hyperbole. "Super Bock" might have been more accurate. Clearly, the idea was to exceed what had previously been the

strongest type of beer. This was achieved by the monks of St Francis of Paula, who probably first made the beer as "liquid bread," to be consumed at the time of Lent. They began to brew in 1634, and to sell their beer commercially in 1780. Their brewery, secularized under Napoleon's rule, is today the biggest in Munich. It is called Paulaner Salvator; the name is used for both the brewing company and its Double Bock, which honors the Savior. About a week before Easter, the first barrel of Paulaner Salvator is tapped, also amid much civic ceremony, at the beer hall and garden of the Paulaner brewery, on the hill called Nockherberg. This is a time of great celebration, set around the saint's day of the brewery, on March 19. Paulaner still has a sense of its history. It was among the first breweries to use refrigeration, and was a pioneer of steam power in the industry.

Paulaner Salvator, the original Double Bock, has a gravity of 18.0-18.5 (1072-1074), and an alcohol content of 5.97 per cent by weight (7.51 by volume). It is a dark beer, with amber highlights. It has a very rich start, a rounded body and a long finish, with some dryness. It is made with three malts and with Hallertau bittering and aroma hops. Its color is 52, and it has 29 units of bitterness. The brewery says that it is lagered for two and a half months, and sometimes longer.

Two of the other Munich breweries have monastic origins. This is obvious in the case of the Augustiner brewery (which was founded in 1328). In the case of Spaten, the founding Sedlmayr family at one stage acquired a former Franciscan brewery (Spaten traces its origins to at least 1397). However, these saintly breweries join most of their contemporaries in paying tribute to Salvator by giving their Double Bock beers names ending in -ator. Augustiner has Maximator. Spaten has Optimator. The Hofbräuhaus has its Delicator. Löwenbräu has Triumphator. Hacker-Pschorr has Animator. It is a shame that Hacker-

Pschorr does not offer a more musical name. A daughter of the Pschorr family was the mother of Richard Strauss. The Pschorrs were patrons of Strauss from his earliest days as a conductor, and he dedicated several of his works to them. The country *Schloss* brewery at Odelzhausen dedicates its well-liked Double Bock to the Munich Opera. It is whimsically called Operator.

"Munich's favorite country brewery," as it presents itself, with some justification, is in the village of Aying. This brewery, called simply Ayinger, has a full range, including an excellent dark lager and an outstanding Double Bock. Despite Ayinger's being a country brewery, its products are available in export markets. Its Double Bock is called Fortunator in Germany and Celebrator in some export markets. It is an outstanding example of the style, mellow and beautifully balanced. Ayinger's beers are served at the Platzl Restaurant, which is noted for its burlesque show. The restaurant stands on the Platzl Square, facing the Hofbräuhaus.

Among the several country breweries that returned to monastic hands after the Napoleonic period, Andechs is especially noted for its luscious, clean, ruby-colored Double Bock. Andechs, a Benedictine monastery by Ammer See, is such a popular day out from Munich that its beer-garden, hall, and restaurant can accommodate 2,000 people.

On the outskirts of Munich, in the market-gardening suburb of Perlach, the Forschungs house-brewery produces the city's highest-gravity beer, St Jacobus Blonder Bock, at 19 dPlato (1076). This pale Bock has a soft, sweet, clean palate, with a big, malty finish. The brewery, at Unterhachinger Strasse 26, Perlach, was originally built as a pilot plant on which the local companies could try out new varieties of barley or hops, or experiment with new beers. It is open to the public only in the summer months (and even then, like many drinking places in Germany, it closes on Mondays).

The strongest Bock beers in Germany are made in the city of Kulmbach, in Franconia. In recent decades, Kulmbach has become as well known for its Bock beers as for its regular dark brews. Among the variations on the Bock theme, the area is especially noted for a version that is frozen at the brewery to concentrate its alcoholic strength. This method rests upon the fact that water freezes at a higher temperature than alcohol. (A factor in the emergence of pure, strong, vodkas in cold countries.) If the beer is frozen and the ice removed, the remaining liquid contains a higher proportion of alcohol. Although the intent is different, the method is reminiscent of that used to remove yeast from Champagne. Germany thus has not only *Eiswein* but also ice-beer.

The best-known Eisbock is made by the Kulmbacher Reichelbräu brewery. It is called Eisbock Bayrisch G'frorns ("Bavarian Frozen"), has a gravity of 24 Plato and an alcohol content of around 8.0 by weight, 10 by volume. It is an extremely dense-

The Father of Them All

The original: Salvator was the first of the doppelbocks. There are more than 120 beers with the -ator suffix. The Munich brewers are well placed to provide the springtime beer-cure for the drinkers of the Nockherberg.

tasting beer, with a lot of alcoholic warmth in the finish. Kulmbacher Reichelbräu has a full range of styles, and enjoys the biggest local sale. It also has a subsidiary brewing company in Kulmbach called Sandlerbräu. Kulmbach also has the Monchshof brewery, noted for its very strong, 28-degree Double Bock.

True lovers of beer know that very strong brews are limited in their application, but a specialty such as this inevitably becomes a legend. In beer-bars far and wide, the initials E.K.U. are spoken with awe. The "E" stands for "Erste" ("First"), the "K" for "Kulmbach", and the "U" derives from the union of two earlier breweries that created the company in 1872. E.K.U. has a full range of products, and its most famous beer is specifically identified by the figure "28" (indicating degrees Plato). It is further described as Kulminator Urtyp Hell, which sounds suitably awesome. Despite the "Hell," it is not especially pale ~ the great density of malt imparts an amber cast ~ but it is not dark, either. It has an intensely malty nose and palate, with a strongly alcoholic character.

E.K.U. "28" guarantees that figure as its minimum gravity, and aims for an alcohol content of 9.8-10.92 by weight; 12.4-13.5 by volume. All three figures have varied. All brewers aim for a particular gravity and alcohol content but work within a band. At these high levels, where conversion of fermentable sugars is difficult, total accuracy is impossible. The "28" is regarded as being reliably and consistently the highest-gravity beer in the world (around 1120 in the British system), though not quite the strongest in alcohol. From a marginally lower gravity of 27.6, the Swiss beer Samichlaus emerges with 11.1 to 11.2 alcohol by weight; 13.7-14 by volume. Again, these figures differ slightly in every analysis that has been made, and there have been many.

Very low temperatures are used in the production of E.K.U. "28," but the brewery says that these are part of the lagering technique, and does not regard its product as an Eisbock. The beer is lagered for nine

Above: **If Munich's mighty Spaten brewery looks rather like an international airport, the city's tiny Forschungsbräuerei resembles the control tower at a dubious holiday destination. No ambivalence about the Bock, though.**

months. The brewery also has a dark Double Bock of 18.5 degrees (6.0; 7.6), called simply Kulminator; and a pale single of 16.8 (5.8; 7.3), E.K.U. Edelbock. Strong beers anywhere else in the world, but in Kulmbach a mere bagatelle.

The Speciality Beers of Franconia

Below: It seems appropriate that when the first railway train in Germany ran, from Nürnberg to Furth in 1835, it was ceremonially loaded with two casks of local beer. The Franconians have a colorful line in locomotion, and an apparent preoccupation with steam and smoke. The realistically steamy model brewery was towed through the streets at a carnival near Bamberg. In Bayreuth, the Maisel brewery, which has a wonderful museum, makes a fruity, top-fermenting product that it calls Dampf ("Steam") Beer. In Coburg, Rauchenfels has the world's steamiest brewing process . . . and a very smoky beer. Smokiest of all are Bamberg's Rauchbiers.

THE MOST COLORFUL assortment of beers in Germany is to be found in the north of Bavaria, in the region known as Franconia. This is the most densely-breweried part of Germany — indeed, of the world. There are more than 250 breweries in the swath of countryside stretching from the Danube north to the frontier with East Germany. To the west are the hop-growing areas of Spalt and Hersbruck (and farther west the Sylvaner grapes around Würzburg). To the east lies the Bohemian Forest.

A beer-lover's pilgrimage through this heaven would step north from Regensburg through Amberg (with nine breweries) to Nürnberg, Bamberg (with ten, and known for its smoked beer), Kulmbach (famous for dark lagers and Double Bock), Bayreuth (where the Maisel brewery makes its fruity, top-fermenting Dampfbier) and Coburg (where Rauchenfels produces its rock-boiled Steinbiere). Some towns have communal breweries where members of the public can brew their own beer. Falkenburg, Neuhaus-on-Pegnitz and Sesslach are examples. Once many towns in the German-speaking world had such municipal breweries.

Nowhere are dark lagers more readily found than in Franconia, especially from the smaller breweries. They range from the tawny and translucent to the almost black. Some of the more rustic examples are also very yeasty. Dark or pale, many of the local beers are offered unfiltered, in a variety of forms.

Krausenbier is found in other parts of Germany, but is at its most common in Franconia. The term implies that the beer has been kräusened before being sold in a yeastily unfiltered form.

A variation is the type of beer that has not been kräusened, and has been allowed to settle in the maturation tank before being sold unfiltered. This

Left: The inferno which heats the rocks that brew Rauchenfels (*lower left*). The beechwood (*inset*) blazes (*big picture*) to kiln the malt for Rauchbier. Both of these Franconian special ties are smoky in their own ways, but Rauchenfels is a brand and Rauchbier a style.

NEW WORLD GUIDE TO BEER

The brewer's star (*left*) hangs outside "Zum Spezial," in Bamberg. *Right*: Not far away, in Bayreuth, the "Steam Beer" brewery of Maisel has an amazing museum.

10 produces nothing else. It even has its own maltings. Spezial's Rauchbier has a gently insistent smokiness and a treacle-toffee finish. It is produced at a gravity of around 12 Plato, as the house lager, and in Märzen and Bock versions, the latter in November.

The best-known example of the style is the Heller brewery's Aecht Schlenkerla Rauchbier, which is produced as a Märzen all year round and as a Bock in November and December. This beer, which has a lovely smoky aroma and long finish, is served at the brewery tap in Sandstrasse. This brewery, too, has its own maltings, so lingeringly smoky that the same character is lightly imparted to its pale beer.

Also in Bamberg, the Greifenklau brew-pub at Laurenziplatz 20 has a very faintly smoky beer. Kaiserdom Rauchbier is produced not far away in Eltmann, as is Maisel's Rauchbier. (This is one of four quite separate breweries called Maisel in Bavaria; it is not connected with the one in Bayreuth.)

Although the style belongs to Bamberg, there are several smoked beers elsewhere. By far the most distinct in Germany is Eichbaum's Rauch-Weizen, a smoked Wheat Beer made in Mannheim, Baden-Württemberg. A lightly smoked malt from the north of Bavaria has been used by the Vernon Valley micro-brewery in New Jersey.

RAUCHENFELS STEINBIERE

A smoky beer of a different style is produced by the Rauchenfels brewery, at Neustadt, near Coburg, on the border with East Germany. This remarkable style is produced by only the one brewery, whose registered trademark is Rauchenfels Steinbiere.

The beer gains its character from an astonishing method of production, revived in the 1980s by an especially entrepreneurial brewery-owner. Stones heated to 1,200°C (2,200°F) ~ again, over beechwood fires ~ are immersed in the kettle to heat the wort. This system is said to have been used in the days when brew-kettles were made of wood, and could not be heated from the outside. It was reputedly practiced in Alpine areas that had plenty of suitable stone, and the Rauchenfels brewery has acquired its own quarry for the purpose. Not only do the hot stones boil the wort, amid much roaring, seething and hissing, they also gain their own coating of caramelized brewing sugars. The stones are later placed in the lagering tanks, where the caramel coating dissolves, creating an almost explosive secondary fermentation.

The end product, which is top-fermenting, has a smooth, rich, smoky palate and a long, rounded finish. It has a gravity of 11.3 (1045), and a tawny color. There is also a companion "stone-brewed" Wheat Beer, Rauchenfels Steinweizen, of a similar gravity.

has only a slight haze and a low carbonation, and is heavily hopped as a protection against infection. It is known as Kellerbier.

In a third variation, the beer may have been matured in tanks that are at least partly open, in which case natural carbonation will be very low. This type of beer will be described as *ungespunderd*, meaning "unbunged." A less specific term, used for any type of unfiltered beer, is Zwickelbier.

The most cursory visit to Franconia is likely to include Nürnberg, where the old town has a good example of a hearty, unfiltered dark lager at Hausbräuerei Altstadhof. This tiny brewery opened in 1984, but uses antique equipment. The brewery, a bakery, and one or two wholefood shops share a courtyard off Berg Strasse.

Elsewhere, this style of beer is best found in tiny, country breweries: this one looking like a timbered inn, seeming merely to be a café; this one resembling a sports pavilion; that one a workshop or garage; this one a hole in the wall; that one more like a cave in a hillside.

BAMBERGER RAUCHBIER

The most promising area for exploration is the area around Bamberg, a lovely baroque town overlooked by a 17th-century Romanesque church. The church was originally part of an abbey, and the monastic brewery has now been converted into a museum of Franconian beer (Tel 0951-53016).

Besides being a tourist town, Bamberg is a center of malting and brewing in Franconia. Its ten small breweries produce dryly malty beers, served in some delightfully cozy taverns, but the town is best known for its specialty, Bamberger Rauchbier.

This is the beer world's answer to a single malt Scotch whisky, especially of the Islay type. Scotch whisky gains its smoky character from the kilning of barley malt over a fire of the local peat. Bamberger Rauchbier takes its smokiness from the kilning of the same material over beechwood logs. Just as Scotland, and notably Islay, are rich in peat, so is Franconia, and especially the area around Bamberg, in beech forests. In each instance, a traditional method has been retained to produce a distinctive local specialty. It is also in Franconia that beechwood chips were commonly employed in a traditional method of fining. (The Hofmark brewery, at Cham, near Regensburg, is a keen present-day exponent of this method.)

Bamberger Rauchbier is a dark brown, bottom-fermenting beer, with an intensely smoky aroma and palate. Locals say that at least three liters of Rauchbier, perhaps four or five, must be consumed before the taste for it can be acquired. They are either being needlessly pessimistic or artfully boosting sales. It is a reflection not on the beer but on timorous palates that some drinkers never learn to like Rauchbier.

The tiny Spezial brew-pub at Ober König Strasse

Weizenbier

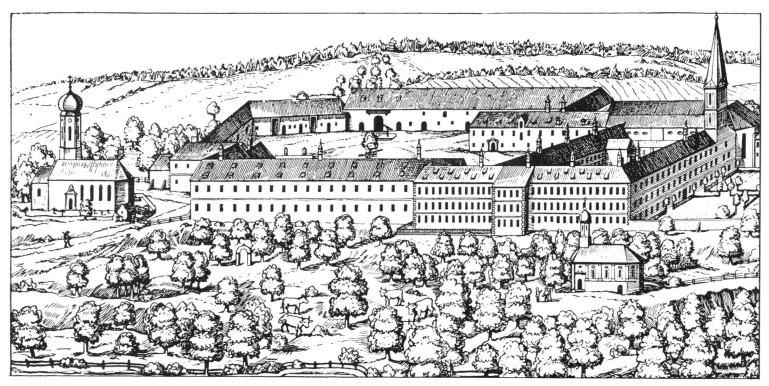

THE FASHIONABILITY OF WEIZENBIER, in places as far apart as Munich and Milwaukee, has been a phenomenon of the beer renaissance. A drinker ordering a Weizenbier usually has in mind a Wheat Beer of conventional strength, in the style that has a clove-like aroma, served in a tall, vase-shaped glass, sometimes garnished with a slice of lemon.

This style is not unique to southern Germany, but is most commonly made there, in the states of Baden-Württemberg and, especially, Bavaria. Within the state of Bavaria, it is made by scores of breweries.

The style is particularly associated with the Hofbräuhaus, in Munich, though the Weizenbiers served there in recent years have been produced to the north of the city, by Bavaria's other state brewery, at Weihenstephan. That renowned establishment regards itself as the world's oldest brewery. Beer is believed to have been made on the site in 1040, though the oldest parts of the present buildings date from a monastery built in the 1600s. It was after secularization that the brewery came into the hands of the state. It is operated on a substantial commercial basis, though it enjoys a close relationship with the University Faculty of Brewing at Weihenstephan.

The most famous place devoted especially to the consumption of Weizenbier is the Schneider beer-restaurant, on Tal Strasse, in Munich. The outstandingly tasty Weizenbiers served there are produced some distance away, at Kelheim, near Regensburg.

The greatest concentration of Weizenbiers is in the stretch of country to the east of Munich. This supports the notion that the style originated from Bohemia, though it is no longer produced there ~ at

Weizen Variations

Below: The number of variations in which Weizenbier may be produced was most clearly shown in the labeling style of this selection from the Sanwald brewery, Stuttgart. Sad to say, the range has diminished since Sanwald was merged into a bigger local brewing company, Dinkelacker.

Left: By contrast with the bowl-shaped glass used for Berliner Weisse, a very tall, vase-like vessel is preferred for South German Wheat Beer, with its distinctive full flavor.

least for the moment. Some breweries in the region produce only Weizenbier. A good number of these are very tiny but one, Erdinger Weissbräu, is a sizable concern. Whereas many of the smaller breweries produce Weizenbiers of intense character and individuality, Erdinger's product is notably clean and subtle. There is much more variation between Weizenbiers than can be found among most other German specialties. This may in part be due to the number produced by small country breweries. Many of their products have a distinct house character, often deriving from their yeast strains.

There is no intentional lactic fermentation in Weizenbier. Only a brewers' yeast, always top-fermenting and usually single-cell, is employed in the primary fermentation. The state bank at Weihenstephan sets aside yeasts suited to this purpose, but they have no taxonomic designation. They are known simply as Weizenbier yeasts. They must, obviously, perform well in the fermentation of wheat. Characteristically, they also act to release from the wort a naturally-produced phenolic compound that creates the clove-like aroma.

This style of Wheat Bear may have four to five days' secondary fermentation at warm temperatures, followed by a week or two of cold lagering. It may then have a dosage of yeast and four or five days' further warm conditioning in the bottle before being released. The dosage in the bottle might be a mix of top- and bottom-fermenting strains. Elsewhere in the world, bottom-fermenting strains are often used for this purpose to insure that the yeast settles in the bottle. This is not necessarily the case in Germany. Many German enthusiasts like to see yeast in suspension in a bottle-conditioned beer. Heavily-sedimented, naturally-conditioned Weizenbier, once thought to be a rustic drink, has in recent times become the most chic type. Its fashionability among young drinkers in the 1980s recalls the similar popularity of cask-conditioned ale in Britain in the late 1970s.

The choice of yeast is central to the expressive palate of a Weizenbier. Apart from clove ~ and sometimes vanilla ~ notes, there are also fruity characteristics, often reminiscent of green apples or of plums, occasionally of fresh blackcurrant or lemon. The latter is accentuated by the habit of adding a slice of lemon, though this custom is not as common as it once was. The fruity character of the beer derives not only from the yeast but also from the use of wheat. In southern Germany, a Weizenbier is made from a mash of at least 50 per cent malted wheat. The rest is barley malt. Sixty per cent wheat is very common.

If a beer from southern Germany is identified simply as a Weizenbier (or, sometimes, a Weissbier or simply Weisse), its gravity may be anywhere from just under 12 to 13.5 Plato (1048-1054). Alcohol content ranges from 4.0 per cent by weight (5.0 by volume) to 4.5 (5.6). Like all Wheat Beers, Weizenbier has only a light hop character, typically in the range 12-20.

A filtered Weizenbier can vary in color from a pale gold to a deep bronze. Brand-names sometimes have allusions to Champagne or crystal. Darker, copper-red or brown versions are also made. They are sometimes identified as Dunkelweizen. A good example is made by the Ayinger brewery under the name Ur-Weizen. Unfiltered versions from the cask, or bottle-conditioned examples, may have the word Hefe ("yeast") somewhere in their name or labeling.

Many breweries also produce a strong Weizenbier, either as a seasonal special, perhaps for Christmas, or year-round. The outstanding example of this variation is Schneider's dark Aventinus, with a gravity of 18.5 (1074) and an alcohol content of 6.1 per cent by weight, 7.7 by volume. This has a lovely complex of Wheat Beer sharpness and luscious, malty sweetness. This strong style is sometimes identified as a Weizenbock.

In all of its variations, and all of its confusing designations, the southern German style of Wheat Beer makes a delicious brew. Its clove-tinged fruitiness renders it a perfect complement to the elderberry-flower fritters with which it is sometimes served.

The sense of a monastery endures at Weihenstephan (*above*), but it is a well equipped modern brewery, from the stainless steel of its kettles (in the traditional shape) to the lagering cellars (*below*).

Berliner Weisse

With a touch of poetic license, one brewer symbolized the three versions of Berliner Weisse as traffic lights. Bowl-shaped glasses are customarily used. The one on the left is the most basic shape. Woodruff (*right*) is the most popular flavor. Woodruff is 4-12in (10-30cm) in height and grows in deciduous or mixed woodland.

Although Berliner Weisse is the best-known beer of the type, Bremen has a similar product. These are sedimented beers, and throw a yeasty haze unless they are handled gently. Some enthusiasts like to drink the vitamin-rich yeast. The engraving (*below*) shows a brewery in Brandenburg in the 16th century.

THE "CHAMPAGNE OF THE NORTH" is said to have been the verdict of Napoleon's occupying troops. It is the most apt of such comparisons ("The Athens of the North" ~ Edinburgh?; "The Venice of the North" ~ Amsterdam?). If there is a Champagne of beers, it is definitely Berliner Weisse, with its unusually pale color, sustained small head, intense sparkle and, especially, its fruity acidity.

No one minds being compared with Champagne but, like those great northern cities, Berliner Weisse has its own identity, too. It is one of the world's classic beer styles, and one that is often misunderstood when encountered for the first time.

It is the most quenching and refreshing of all beers, and one of the lightest. It is feminine, teasing and complex, with no pretensions to great gravity. Typically, its gravity is around 7.5-8.0 Plato, with an alcohol content of just under 2.5 per cent by weight; around 3.0 by volume. It has only four or five units of bitterness.

Berliner Weisse is a Wheat Beer, and it is the principal northern German example in this family of styles. The wheat is malted, and traditionally constituted only 25-30 per cent of the mash. In recent years, percentages have tended to be higher, and it is not unknown for 60 per cent wheat to be used. Traditionally, hops were added in the mash tun, as a natural preservative and an agent of clarification, and not in the kettle. No bitterness is required.

The characteristically fruity acidity derives not only from the use of wheat but, more significantly, from a distinctive method of fermentation and maturation. Throughout, the yeast used is a symbiosis of a top-fermenting strain and a lactobacillus. The presence of such a bacillus would normally give a brewer nightmares, but that is because conventional beers are not meant to contain lactic acid. This acidic characteristic is central to the style of Berliner Weisse. Nor is it a random bacillus. It is a particular strain isolated at the turn of the century by Professor Max Delbruck, one of the founding fathers of the Institute for Brewing and Fermentation Studies (V.L.B.), in Berlin.

Although the isolation of this bacillus was a discovery of great importance to beer-lovers, it was not the only achievement of the Delbrück family. One of the professor's nephews, also named Max, later won a Nobel Prize for his work in California on molecular biology.

The two brewing giants of West Berlin, both principals in large northern groups, each make a Weisse. The Schultheiss company is a member of the larger group, with several breweries in Berlin, but is the smaller producer of Weisse. Its Schultheiss Berliner Weisse is, though, produced in the more traditional — and very painstaking — way. This is not especially evident in mashing and brewing, but very significant during fermentation and maturation. The mash contains 50 per cent wheat. Only hop extract is added — and exclusively in the kettle, which is not taken to a full boil.

In the primary fermentation stage, each new brew is pitched with *Lactobacillus delbrückii*, but also blended with a small proportion of three- to six-month-old wort. After three days' primary fermentation, the wort is then moved to the cellar, where it spends from three to, ideally, 12 months at warm temperatures, between 15°C (59°F) and 25°C (77°F). After this period of "ripening", it is then blended again. This blending immediately before bottling is effectively a priming, or *kräusening*, with wort that has fermented for only one day. There is then a further addition of *L. delbrückii* as a dosage before the beer is bottled. It has four weeks' bottle-conditioning at the brewery, at not less than 18°C (64°F), and ideally at 25°C, before being released. The final product is extremely thoroughly fermented and very low in carbohydrates. It has natural carbonation of around seven grams per litre (about 3.5 volumes). Although it is ready to drink when it leaves the brewery, devotees of the style will keep it

for a further one or two years at 6-7°C (42-45°F), so that its estery fruitiness, acidity and fine fragrance can fully emerge. These lengthy periods of secondary fermentation, ripening, conditioning and maturation comprise a further defining characteristic of the style.

In order to insure a temperature that is neither chilly nor too warm, and to protect the bottle from the light, it used to be customary to bury the beer in the garden. This is a problem for apartment-dwellers. Without their traditional larders, the British have forgotten the taste of real cheese; it would be a shame if the same fate befell Berliner Weisse. Refrigerators are a mixed blessing.

The Berliner Kindl brewery, a member of the smaller of the two groups, is a bigger producer of Weisse. Its Berliner Kindl Weisse is tank-conditioned. It may therefore not qualify as *méthode Champenoise* but is nonetheless a characterful product, with a good acidity.

Kindl neatly divides the name of its Weisse. Strictly, the unbroken phrase Berliner Weisse implies bottle-conditioning. "Berliner" certainly means the beer must be made in Berlin. There are several breweries in East Berlin, still identified by the names of their former owners, Schultheiss and Kindl, but producing beers under the brand of the state monopoly V.E.B. Two of these appear in recent years to have made the specialty of their city, and the product of the Berlin-Weissensee brewery is still bottle-conditioned.

The word *Weisse* means "white." Weissensee means "White Lake"; the name does not indicate that it is full of Berlin Wheat Beer. The term "white" as applied to beer always refers to a wheat style, and derives from the pallor and cloudiness evinced by some of these brews.

Berlin Wheat Beer is always of the same style. Like all Wheat Beers, it is regarded as a specialty and is primarily served in summer. It is customarily presented in bowl-shaped glasses, like giant Champagne saucers, and is usually laced with essence of woodruff or, more commonly today, raspberry syrup. The second version resembles a pink Champagne, or perhaps a Kir Royale.

A product in much the same style is made as a local specialty in Bremen by the Haake-Beck company (the German sister company to the internationally-marketing Beck's Bier concern). This is called Bremer Weisse and has a similar gravity, 7.5, and an alcohol content of 2.4 by weight, 3.0 by volume. It is a little drier, with 11 units of bitterness, and has a fuller, bronze color. The brewery uses its own pure-culture lactobacillus, and centrifuges the beer, but does not filter it. The beer is matured in tanks for four weeks, then has another three months' warm conditioning. It has a heavy sediment and a very fruity, greengage character.

Wheat Beers are a very old style, probably having their origins in the days when farmers harvested fields of mixed grains. Wheat is less manageable for the brewer than barley, and it seems eventually to have been appreciated that the latter made for clearer, cleaner-tasting beers. The husk of the barley forms a natural filter bed in the mash tun.

Once Wheat Beers were made in almost all the brewing regions of Europe. Today they survive as specialties. Berliner Weisse and Bremer Weisse are distinct styles specific to those cities. They are similar to each other, but set apart from other styles of Wheat Beer. Similar traditions are remembered in other areas of northern and eastern Germany.

The city of Hanover was once famous for Wheat Beer, but has not made its local style for many years. Perhaps that will be revived. The type of beer known as Mum, or Mumme, was originally a wheat brew aromatized with herbs. This style was well known in Britain during the Hanoverian period. It is especially associated with the city of Brunswick (in German, Braunschweig). A version is still made there, but as a non-fermented malt extract. Braunschweiger Mumme is today a minor specialty on the lines of other non-fermented products like the Schwarzbier of Bad Kostritz, in East Germany, or Mather's Black Beer, from Yorkshire, England. These products are often made into a shandy with a pale beer.

Although it does not give its name to a style, the northern city of Münster does have a distinctive Wheat Beer, one of a range of interesting products from the old-established and much-loved Pinkus Müller house-brewery. This light, refreshing beer has the brand-name Pinkus Weizen. As already mentioned, in German *Weisse* means "white" and *Weizen* is "wheat." These two similar words are both used to describe Wheat Beers. Berlin and Bremen always identify their products as Weisse. Elsewhere, the two epithets are often interchangeable, though the southern style is more generally known as Weizenbier.

Pinkus Weizen is southern in its name and its gravity (11.1; 1044.4) and alcohol content (just over 4.0 per cent by weight; 5.0 per cent by volume). It is made with 60 per cent wheat malt and has an "old gold" color and some lightly hoppy dryness (25 units units of bitterness).

The Berliner and Bremer Weisse, with their low alcohol content, are among the few products rated in Germany as Schankbier. This is a designation not of style but of gravity, and indicates a beer of 7.0-8.0 degrees Plato (usually 2.0-3.0 per cent alcohol by weight). A beer of a conventional gravity and alcohol content is rated as a Vollbier (11.0-14.0 Plato; 3.5-4.5 by weight). Bock beers and other strong specialties are identified as Starkbier (16-plus; 5.0 per cent or, usually, more).

The term Schankbier derives from the word for a retail outlet. "Table beer" perhaps captures the sense, though it seems less than fair to the Champagne-like products of Berlin and Bremen. Vollbier means "full-strength" beer. Stark translates simply as "strong."

A selection of beers from East Germany. East Germany is among the world's major brewing nations, yet its output is dwarfed by that of its neighbor to the west.

The Brewing Towns of Northern Germany

Cologne and its Kölschbier

The gilded florishes of Alt Köln announce the city-center "brewers' tap" (*right*) for Küppers, biggest brewery in Cologne, and a Kölsch specialist. Bönnsch (*below*) is an unfiltered variation from a brew-pub in West Germany's federal capital.

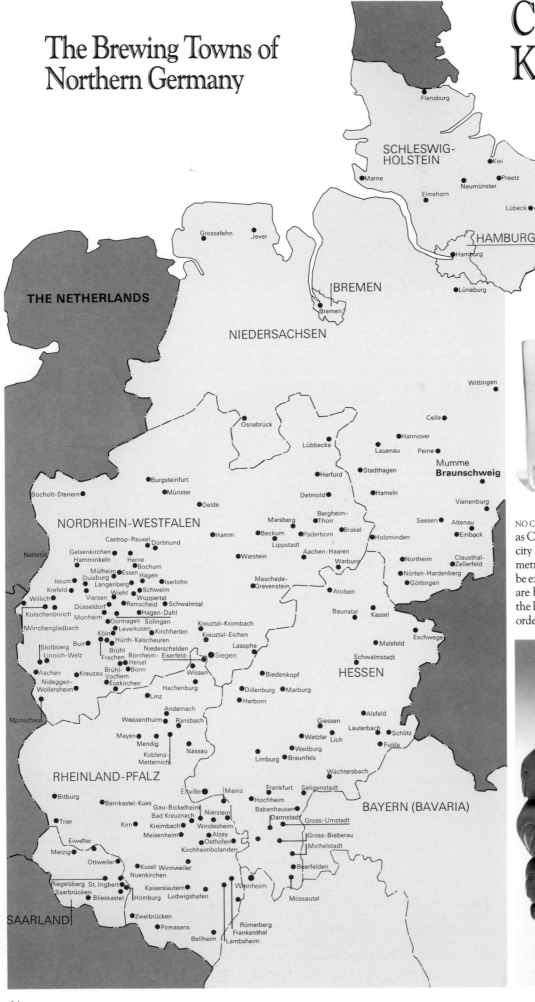

SCHLESWIG-HOLSTEIN
Flensburg
Kiel
Marne
Neumünster
Preetz
Elmshorn
Lübeck
HAMBURG
Grossefehn
Jever
Hamburg
THE NETHERLANDS
BREMEN
Bremen
Lüneburg
NIEDERSACHSEN
Wittingen
Celle
Osnabrück
Hannover
Lübbecke
Lauenau
Peine
Herford
Stadthagen
Mumme **Braunschweig**
Burgsteinfurt
Hameln
Bocholt-Stenern
Münster
Detmold
Vienenburg
Oelde
Bergheim-Thorr
Seesen
Altenau
NORDRHEIN-WESTFALEN
Marsberg
Brakel
Einbock
Castrop-Rauxel
Dortmund
Hamm
Beckum
Paderborn
Holzminden
Nettetal
Gelsenkirchen
Lippstadt
Aachen-Haaren
Clausthal-Zellerfeld
Hamminkeln
Herne
Bochum
Warstein
Warburg
Northeim
Mülheim
Essen
Hagen
Meschede-Grevenstein
Nörten-Hardenberg
Issum
Duisburg
Iserlohn
Göttingen
Krefeld
Langenberg
Wiehl
Viersen
Schwelm
Wuppertal
Arolsen
Willich
Remscheid
Schwalmtal
Düsseldorf
Hagen-Dahl
Baunatal
Korschenbroich
Monheim
Solingen
Kassel
Mönchengladbach
Dormagen
Leverkusen
Kirchherten
Köln
Kreuztal-Krombach
Eschwege
Stolboerg. Buir
Hürth-Kalscheuren
Kreuztal-Eichen
Malsfeld
Linnich-Welz
Brühl
Niederschelden
Laasphe
Frechen
Bornheim- Eiserfeld-
Schwalmstadt
Aachen
Hersel
Siegen
HESSEN
Brühl-
Bonn
Nideggen-
Kreuzau
Vochem
Wissen
Biedenkopf
Wollersheim
Euskirchen
Hachenburg
Dillenburg
Marburg
Monschau
Linz
Herborn
Andernach
Alsfeld
Weissenthurm
Ransbach
Giessen
Lauterbach
Mayen
Wetzlar
Lich
Schlitz
RHEINLAND-PFALZ
Mendig
Nassau
Weilburg
Fulda
Koblenz-
Limburg
Braunfels
Metternich
Wächtersbach
Bitburg
Frankfurt
Seligenstadt
Eltville
Mainz
Bernkastel-Kues
Hochheim
BAYERN (BAVARIA)
Gau-Bickelheim
Nierstein
Babenhausen
Trier
Bad Kreuznach
Darmstadt
Gross-Umstadt
Kirn
Kreimbach
Windesheim
Alzey
Gross-Bieberau
Eiweller
Meisenheim
Osthofen
Michelstadt
Merzig
Kirchheimbolanden
Ottweiler
Kusel
Winnweiler
Beerfelden
Nuenkirchen
Riegelsberg St. Ingbert
Saarbrücken
Kaiserslautern
Weinheim
Blieskastel
Homburg
Ludwigshafen
Mossautal
SAARLAND
Zweibrücken
Pirmasens
Römerberg
Frankenthal
Bellheim
Lambsheim

NO CITY IN THE WORLD has as many brewing companies as Cologne. There are more than a dozen within the city limits, and the same number again in the metropolitan area, which embraces Bonn. As might be expected, some of these are very small, and several are brew-pubs. Most of these breweries specialize in the local style, Kölschbier. This style of beer is usually ordered simply as Kölsch.

Below: The restaurants and taverns of old Cologne proclaim their civic loyalties loud and clear. The Cölner Hofbräu tavern (*bottom* and *below left*) offers a taste of the city in the glass and on the plate.

Kölsch is a wonderful apéritif, and is often served in the local brew-pubs with snacks of "Cologne caviare" (blood sausage), mettwurst (steak tartare), or "half a hen" (an impenetrably whimsical name for a piece of cheese with a bread-roll). If these are ordered "with music," generous helpings of chopped onions are provided.

Kölsch is an extremely pale, golden-colored, aromatic, top-fermenting brew, light in body but not in palate, and very delicate in character. In the English-speaking world, it would be regarded as an ale, though one of unusual pallor and cleanness. Some examples contain a small proportion of malted wheat (10-20 per cent), which heightens their fruitiness and assists head-retention. The producers seek to impart to their beer a definite, but only slight, fruity-winy bouquet. This is regarded as a very important aspect of the style. They also aim for a gentle hop dryness in the finish, flowery but less effusive than in a Pilsener. Kölsch has a conventional gravity, at around 11.5 (1046), and is very well attenuated, emerging with around 4.0 per cent alcohol by weight; 5.0 by volume. The water in Cologne is very soft, and the beer is cold-conditioned, but at temperatures of up to 5°C (41°F). The finished product typically has a bitterness at the upper end of a 20-30 range, and a color of around 8.0 E.B.C.

It is a very subtle style, not at all dramatic, but its appellation has been vigorously protected by the Brewers' Association of Cologne, in both German and international courts. There are 24 Kölschbier brewers within the designated region, and no one else may use this name to describe a beer.

The Cologne brewers' pride and unity in protecting their style has no doubt helped to insure their survival in such numbers. Cologne is also a good city in which to run a tavern. Since Roman days, when the city gained its name (as a Colonial capital), it has been a center of trade and transportation on the Rhine. With its river and its cathedral, it is also a tourist center.

Near the cathedral is the best-known tavern, the Cölner (with the old "C" spelling) Hofbräu, the brewery tap of P.J.Fruh. The brewery is no longer behind the tavern, at Am Hof, but the character of the place is little changed. The Kölsch there is very soft and clean. The Päffgen brew-pub, in Friesen Strasse, produces a hoppier Kölsch, and has a second outlet on the Heumarkt ("Haymarket"). At the other end of the Heumarkt, the Malzmühle brew-pub produces an appropriately malty Kölsch, with a hint of marshmallow in the palate.

The bigger producer, Kuppers, makes a sweetish Kölsch. Kuppers has a restaurant and beer museum at its brewery, at Alteburger Strasse 145-155, a short tram ride from the city-center. The company also has an unfiltered Kölsch, called Wiess. This is another dialect version of the word for a meadow (as in Munich's Wies'n). It does not indicate a Wheat Beer. Not far away, in the Federal capital, a new brew-pub

produces a similar beer which it calls Bönnsch. In Mulheim, on the Ruhr, the Berg-Bräuerei Mann has a product called Mölmsch. With the spread of specialties and the birth of new brew-pubs, no doubt there will be more such brand-names.

Dortmunder

IT MAKES MORE BEER than any other city in Germany (or, indeed, Europe); so, when people think of Germany and its beer culture, why does the proud name of Dortmund not leap into their minds? As a modern, industrial city, Dortmund has certainly suffered for its lack of romance, but it is now beginning to offer more for the visiting beer-lover.

The word Dortmund, or Dortmunder, appears on the labels of about 30 beers in different styles, all brewed in the city, under nine marques. Although some of the companies share plants, or are linked through their ownership, there are no fewer than five major breweries in the city. Two of these have in recent years additionally established separate brew-pubs. One of the city-center landmarks is the huge

letter "U," illuminated at night, on top of the Dortmunder Union Bräuerei. D.U.B. produces well-balanced, mild-tasting beers that are marketed all over Germany. It has traditionally enjoyed its greater success in the south of Germany. Its parent, D.U.B.-Schultheiss, also owns Dortmunder Ritter, which has its own brewery. Ritter's beers, perhaps a little drier and more textured, are especially popular in the nearby industrial towns of the Ruhr valley.

The great rival to D.U.B. is D.A.B. (Dortmunder Actien Bräuerei), which also owns Hansa. These two companies, part of the Oetker group, share a modern plant on the north side of the city. The D.A.B. beers tend toward the light side, with some malty dryness. They are also marketed nationally, and have

Dortmunder Union still occupies its classically 1920s brewery close to the center of the city. The brewery has the look of a rather handsome power station. Its surmounting "U" is a symbol for Dortmund.

A retired brew-kettle serves as a canopy at the new Hövels Hausbräuerei (*below*), in Dortmund. Inside, diners can see the brew-house through a window. Such arrangements have long been popular in Germany, and are being introduced elsewhere in the world. *Right*: Elegant gilded signs announce many German taverns.

traditionally had their greater success in the north. Hansa concentrates on the supermarket trade.

Dortmund also has two sizable privately-owned breweries, Thier and Kronen, both close to the center of the city.

Dortmunder Thier makes hearty, tasty, malty beers. Its products sell well in the neighboring parts of the state of Westphalia, especially to the north and east of the city. In 1984 Thier opened, on its own doorstep in Hoher Wall, a brew-pub under the name Hövels. One of Thier's founders was called Hövels. The traditional kettle and open fermenter of this small new brewery are visible through a lattice window from the restaurant area. In the restaurant entrance, a decorative brew-kettle faces onto a terrace, where beer and food are served in summer. The brewery has made a wide range of excellent seasonal specialties. Its year-round house beer is a bronze, malty bottom-fermenting brew of 13.5 (1054) with the somewhat inappropriate name of Bitterbier. It has also produced a top-fermented, dark revivalist brew called Adam-Bier.

Dortmunder Kronen makes soft, clean, malty beers of some complexity. Its products are the local favourites in Dortmund. The Kronen building, on Märkische Strasse, also houses a museum devoted to the brewing industry of Dortmund. Since 1987, Kronen has owned Dortmunder Stifts, a local brewing company in the south of the city. Kronen has taken over the principal production of the Stifts range, and it is not clear whether there will be any further brewing on the old site in the south. Kronen has also opened a brew-pub, on a separate site, in the market square of Dortmund. At Markt 10, within the Zum Kronen restaurant complex, the Wenker's Bräuhaus, also named after an early brewer, has its copper-faced state-of-the-art brew-house in the middle of the bar area. Its house beer is a lightly fruity, top-fermenting, pale brew, containing 15 per cent wheat, served unfiltered with a heavy yeast sediment. This is called Wenker's Urtrüb. More specialties are planned.

Whereas a wide range of styles are produced in Dortmund, none of the city's brewers has in recent years made a point of the local specialty. Indeed, most of them have stressed their Pilseners, though without great success.

Dortmund, which has been a brewing center since the 1200s, made top-fermenting, dark Wheat Beers for much of its history. In 1843, the city's oldest brewery, Dortmunder Kronen, began to make bottom-fermenting beers. In the 1870s, Dortmunder Union developed a bottom-fermenting beer which won wide renown in Germany. It was so widely marketed that the Dortmund brewers began to refer to it as the Export style.

Beers in this style are now produced elsewhere in Germany, but Dortmund is its home. Dortmunder Export is a recognized style, albeit these days one with a low public profile. Across the border in the Netherlands and Belgium, where it has enjoyed some

appreciation, the style is sometimes abbreviated simply to "Dort." A beer in the true Dortmunder Export style is bottom-fermenting, made from barley malt, with an "old gold" color, drier than a Munich pale type, but fuller-bodied than a Pilsener, and a little higher in gravity than either, at around 13 Plato (1052), with about 4.4 per cent alcohol by weight and 5.5 by volume. It typically has around 25 units of bitterness, and a color of 10.5 E.B.C.

Between the elegance of the fine German Pilseners and the heartiness of the Munich pale beers, the Dortmunder Export style has been overshadowed. Each of Dortmund's principal brewers still has a beer in this style, but its popular reputation is as an unglamorous product favored by coal-miners and steelworkers. Perhaps this macho image should be turned to its advantage. In the meantime, despite its considerable weight, it is trapped in the same kind of shrinking market as inhibits Mild in England.

Düsseldorf and its Altbier

THE WORD *ALT*, MEANING "OLD," is used in labeling to describe a variety of specialty beers in Germany. Whichever the specialty, the implication is that the beer is of a type that pre dates the pale, bottom-fermenting styles most commonly found today. If *Alt* is employed on its own, as a noun, it usually implies the copper-colored style of top-fermenting brew made in the north of Germany and especially associated with the area around the city of Düsseldorf.

An Altbier of this type is the German brew closest to a Belgian or British-style ale. The typical Altbier has a full copper color, a light-to-medium body and lots of hop character. The combination of an all-malt mash and a period of cold conditioning (at up to 8°C; 46°F) makes for a smoother, cleaner, less fruity character than is found in most Belgian or British-style ales. The German way of hopping and the varieties used produce a fragrance, and frequently a considerable bitterness, but not the acidity often present in a British ale.

A good Altbier in this style has a gravity of 12 Plato (1048) or just over and an alcohol content of 3.6-3.8 by weight; 4.5-4.7 by volume. Its color may be around 35 E.B.C., and its bitterness anything from the lower 30s to the upper 50s.

The most widely available example is Hannen Alt (soft and well-balanced), made in Willich and Mönchengladbach. Others are the popular, firm-bodied Diebels, from Issum; the slightly thick-tasting Rhenania, from Krefeld; and several from Düsseldorf: Frankenheim (hoppy and light-bodied), Schlösser (malty but dry) and Düssel (fruity).

For devotees of the style, the classics are the Altbiers produced by the brew-pubs of Düsseldorf. There are four of these. One, Ferdinand Schumacher, at Ost Strasse 123, is in the modern part of town. Despite its location, Schumacher has an old-world atmosphere, and is a pleasant place to rest the legs after a day in the city. Of the four "home-brewed" Altbiers, that at Schumacher is the lightest in body and the maltiest. The other brew-pubs are in the Old Town ~ the term Altstadt seems especially appropriate.

Zum Schlüssel, at Bolker Strasse 43, has something of a coffee-shop style, though its brew-kettle is clearly visible. It has a lightly malty Altbier, with some acidity. The success of this product led the owners also to start the free-standing Gatzweiler brewery, making a similar Altbier.

In Füchschen, at Ratinger Strasse 28, is a large restaurant where patrons share scrubbed tables and eat hearty plates of pork knuckles. Behind it is a tiny tower brewery. The beer is beautifully balanced and complex, with a hop accent.

Zum Uerige, at Berger Strasse 1, is the most famous of the four. It is a warren of inter connected rooms, two of which offer views of the beautiful copper brew-house. There might be old ladies with elaborate hats in one room, students in another, rock musicians or fashion models in a third. Zum Uerige

serves only snacks, but makes its own sausages and marinates malodorous Mainzer cheese in beer. Its Altbier is the hoppiest and tastiest of them all.

All four brew-pubs observe a tradition of occasionally making a single brew to a slightly higher gravity, and perhaps dry-hopping, to produce what Schumacher calles a Latzenbier and the others call a Sticke.

These "secret" beers are offered at the normal price, as a "thank you" to regulars for their year-round custom. On each occasion, the beer is available for as long as a single brew lasts (one day, or two at the most). Each establishment has its own calendar, offering its secret beer either twice or four times a year. The days vary slightly from one year to another, but are usually in the months when business is quiet.

An Altbier resembling those of Düsseldorf but slightly higher in gravity, darker in color and lighter in hop character, is made by the Lindener Gilde brewery, of Hanover. This is named after the great Hanover brewer Cord Broyhan. A quite different interpretation of Altbier, golden in color, with 40 per cent wheat and a slightly lactic character, is made by the Pinkus Müller brewery, in Münster.

A house specialty is the lacing of Altbier with diced fruits that have been steeped overnight in sugar syrup. In summer, strawberries or peaches are used; in winter, perhaps oranges. This combination is served in the stubby, cylindrical glass used in most places for Altbier. Despite the shape of the glass, the fruity version is known as an "Altbier Bowl." Similar fruit-laced drinks are served in several parts of Europe, and are especially associated with Maytime or the harvest months.

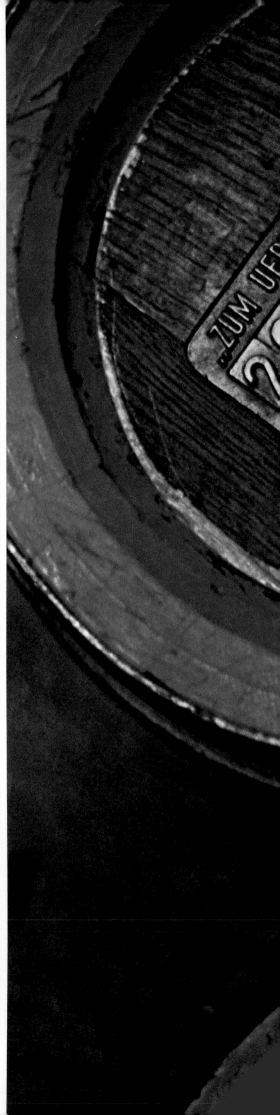

The brew-pubs of Düsseldorf are institutions, none more so than Zum Uerige. Behind its modest façade, it has various rooms that each have their own theme. From the drinking area, the brew-house is visible — and there is copper everywhere. Casks of Altbier are raised from the cellar by a dumb waiter and rolled between the drinkers to the bar. As in many such establishments, the waiters automatically replace empty glasses with full ones, noting each drinker's tally on his or her beermat.

Along with a range of other styles, a pale, golden style of top-fermenting Altbier is produced at Pinkus Müller's, in Münster. Drinkers who have enjoyed a glass are inclined to leave a mark of their appreciation.

German Pilseners

OTHER COUNTRIES may use the term lightly, but in Germany the term "Pilsener" *means* something. It indicates more than just a pale lager. Nor does it merely offer an assurance of some imprecise "premium" quality. It does not stop, either, at implying a gravity somewhere between 11-plus and 12-plus (1044-1048 or more) and an alcohol content of around 4.0 per cent by weight; 5.0 by volume. In Germany, a Pilsener has a definite hop accent, in both its flowery bouquet and its dry finish. That is its most distinctive feature.

The mildest of German Pilseners have around 25 units of bitterness, but 35 is much more typical and figures closer to 45 are not unknown. When the best of German Pilseners have been exported to the United States, they have been rejected as being "too bitter." A more accurate comment would have been "too good for us."

The original beer of Pilsen achieved its renown when Bohemia was officially German-speaking, won its first important award in Hamburg, and remains the biggest-selling imported brand in the Federal Republic. The award in Hamburg was in 1863, but it is interesting to note that this city is still markedly keen on Pilsener-style beers.

Hamburg, a brewing center since at least the 1300s, has a long-established taste for hoppy beers. It was one of the first cities to use hops in brewing, and its market imported the precious flowers down the river Elbe from Bohemia. As a port, it also shipped a great deal of beer, and no doubt its export brews were well hopped for their own protection. The Dehn's brew-pub, at Ost-West Strasse 47, Hamburg, opened in the mid-1980s with a "dark Pilsener." This is nonsense ~ Pilsener cannot be dark ~ but it does suggest a certain infatuation with the style.

Among the old-established breweries in the city, Elbschloss produces the driest Pilsener. This product, called Ratsherrn Pils, has 40-42 units of bitterness, and a lovely, long finish. Elbschloss is a handsome old brewery in the D.U.B.-Schultheiss group.

The much larger Holsten brewery is a major exporter, best known in some markets for its Diät Pils. In Germany, Holsten's "super-premium" Pilsener is Moravia, made by a sister brewery in the old, gabled town of Lüneburg. The name Moravia presumably came down the Elbe in the distant past. Moravia Pils has a big, soft, hop aroma, and 37-38 units of bitterness. It has a finish that is emphatically dry without being in any way abrasive. Moravia is now produced in a modern brewery in Lüneburg, but its original premises nearby house a beer museum and restaurant. Holsten also produces beers under the Dressler name. Dressler formerly brewed in Bremen, and was noted for its Porter.

The other large Hamburg brewery, with the somewhat confusing title of Bavaria St Pauli, and the brand-name Astra, also has a super-premium Pilsener in another town. Its sister company is Jever, based in the spa town of the same name, in the region of Friesland. Jever Pilsener has a Tettnang hop aroma; a clean, dry start; and a very long, bitter finish. It has 40-42 units of bitterness, with its house yeast further contributing to a distinctive dryness.

Left: "Diät" Pils? It all depends how much of the stuff you drink. Jever, from Friesland, is a true Pilsener-style beer and one of the hoppiest in the world. Peter Peters knows this — he brews it. Herr Peters, who likes a five-liter glass, weighs in at 150 kg. *Below*: The haziness is intended . . . indeed, encouraged. That is the whole point of a Kräusenbier. The Beck family of brewing companies presents its Haake Kräusenpils in a crackware glass to heighten the effect.

Although Jever seems to have lost a little bitterness in recent years, it is one of Germany's driest beers.

Bavaria St Pauli takes the second half of its title from its home neighborhood in Bremen. St Pauli Girl claims to take the first half of its name from a one-time monastery brewery in Bremen. St Pauli Girl and Beck's Bier, both broadly in the Pilsener style, but with a rounder, softer character, are produced in adjoining brew-houses in Hamburg. The same complex also produces the hoppier Haake-Beck Pils (33 units of bitterness) for the local market. The Haake-Beck company also has a yeasty Kräusenpils which, not surprisingly, has a little more bitterness. To insure that the yeast is kept in suspension, kegs of Haake Kräusenpils are fitted with a mechanical agitator that kicks briefly into action every eight hours.

Although Pilsener is not regarded as a regional style, and is produced throughout Germany, the far north and the northwest have some of the best

known examples. There are many in the northwest. For beers in the Pilsener style, the clean, soft Herforder and the tasty König are both quite full-bodied. Stauder is firm-bodied and faintly fruity. Krombacher is slightly malt-accented. The fashionable Veltins has a hint of new-mown hay in the nose. Warsteiner is light, dryish, and slightly fruity. Bitburger is very light-bodied with a very good, but soft, hop character.

Veltins and Warsteiner are in an area of lakes, woods and hills called Sauerland, to the east of the industrial Rhine-Ruhr area. They and other brewers in this area have become especially associated with the Pilsener style.

A number of brewers who have made a specialty of the Pilsener style like to identify their products as being "premium" beers. In Germany, this has the connotation that would be identified as "super-premium" in the United States. (Everything is bigger in America.) The designation "premium" was first

used by a journalist in the influential newspaper *Die Welt*. He was merely employing the term to identify a number of especially fast-growing and successful breweries that all specialized in one style, and was not implying that their products were the best. However, the term has stuck.

All of the so-called premium Pilsener breweries are in the northwest except Furstenberg, which is in the Black Forest. Furstenberg, owned by the aristocratic family of the same name, produces a Pilsener that is full-bodied and soft, with a good hop character.

There are, of course, other good Pilseners in the south, but this is an area in which many styles enjoy widespread recognition.

Where Germans Drink

THE BEER-GARDEN and the beer-hall are the most definitively German of drinking places, but they are found widely only in the south, primarily in Bavaria.

Beer-gardens, especially the smaller ones, are usually peaceful places, shaded by trees (invariably chestnuts) and faithful to the scene depicted by painters like Liebermann and Menzel. Munich is said to have 100 beer-gardens. Near the Nymphenburg Palace, the very large Hirschgarten, with Augustiner beer, can accommodate 7,000 people, but still has a family atmosphere.

There is more of a studenty atmosphere at Löwenbräu's huge beer-garden. This encircles the famous pagoda, The Chinese Tower, in a park called The English Garden.

Confusingly, a beer-garden may be called a *Keller*. This usage means simply that the beer is kept in a cellar in the tavern that serves the garden: it does not mean the drinking has to be done in a basement. Imitation Bierkellers in other countries are in fact modeled on a quite different institution, the beer-hall.

As at the Hofbräuhaus, the two can operate side by side; the Paulaner beer-hall and garden at Nockherberg is a very good example of this arrangement. While the beer-garden is notable for its quietude, the hall can be conspicuous for its noise. Once again, drinkers can be accommodated by the thousand, but there is also room for brass bands, singing and swaying.

Each of the Munich brewers has a Bierhalle. The biggest is the Mathaser Bierstadt, owned by Löwenbräu. This hall is in Bayern Strasse, not far from the railway station. The Mathaser has the look of a railway station itself, but its 15 or so inner halls are worth exploring.

Drinking men have always had a weakness for barmaids, and in Bavaria these ladies seem to have inspired countless artists in stained glass. The demure young woman carrying the Hacker-Pschorr is by no means stylized. Those liters of beer are heavy, but there are Bavarian barmaids who can heft eight or more without spilling a drop of femininity.

Right: Even at ground-floor level, drinking places in Bavaria are often vaulted like a cellar. The same style is found also in Austria and Bohemia. This lithograph was produced by Peter Ellmer in 1840.

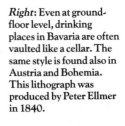

"Hopfen und Malz, Gott erhalt's!" ("Hops and malt — God preserve them!") is an exhortation found all over Germany, and especially in Bavaria. It seems especially appropriate on drinking vessels. The three-liter giant comes out occasionally, but the single and half are more commonly used.

German barmaid, complete with her fistfuls of brimming *Steins*.

Der Bock-Keller in München.

Beer has been drunk from
some extremely elaborate
and decorative vessels.
The examples on these
pages are from the
collection made by Rastel,
the German company
which decorates many of
today's glasses with
brewers' insignia.

1 Glasses, 16th century
2 *Steins* from Altenburg, *c.* 1750
3 "Apostles" *Stein*, Creussen, 17th century
4 Ivory, 18th century
5 Hand-painted lids, *c.* 1850
6 Hand-painted "fox and chicken", 18th century
7 Glass tankard, *c.* 1840
8 *Steins*, Raeren, 1685
9 Battle scene on Dresden porcelain, 19th century
10 View of Nürnberg, ivory, *c.* 1900
11 Skull *Stein*, late 19th century

12 Hand-painted glass and *Stein*, mid-19th century
13 19th-century decorated and translucent glass *Steins*
14 "Fireman" *Stein*, 19th century
15 Decorated glass *Stein*, 19th century
16 "Fox" *Stein*, 19th century
17 "Riding boots" — some modern examples
18 Art Nouveau *Steins* and jug, *c.* 1900

4

5

6

10

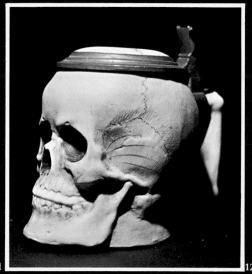

11

12

16

17

18

The Schützenfest

IN GERMANY THERE IS ALWAYS a plausible reason for having a beer. As well as the pre-Lenten Fasching, the springtime Bock celebrations, the village festivals in summer and the October excesses in Munich and elsewhere, there is also the Schützenfest. There are Schützenfests throughout Germany and in émigré communities all over the world. The one shown here took place in the Rhineland. Even in the New World, the annual Schützenfest often provided good cause for a special brew — perhaps a different one each year.

Originally a Schützenfest was a gathering of the town's "sharpshooters," an historic civic vigilante body, which grew into a ceremonial order. Today, such celebrations are beer-festivals. The biggest is in Hanover and lasts throughout the first week in July. A traditional drink is a Lüttje Lage ("little one"), an especially small beer drunk together with a corn schnapps. The northwest of Germany is Korn country. In a Lüttje Lage, the two drinks are not taken as a beer-and-chaser but simultaneously.

The beer in the glass might well be the Broyhan Alt of the local Lindener Gilde brewery. This beer is named after a famous Hanover brewer of the 16th century. He produced wheat brews, but today's Broyhan Alt is in a similar style to those from Düsseldorf. It is slightly darker, quite light-bodied, malt-accented and with a delicate hop character.

Lindener Gilde was originally a civically supported cooperative of home-brewers. In the 17th century, a third of the population of Hanover was in the brewing trade, even though the city fathers

restricted rights to the owners of fireproof houses. The malt might be over-roasted, the kettle might boil away, but Hanover would not burn. Lindener Gilde is now a private company, but the city's Wülfel brewery remains a cooperative, under the ownership of publicans. Such is the brewing tradition of Hanover that Lindener Gilde holds a civic reception on an historic theme each year. There are further celebrations to tap the new winter Bock beer at the beginning of November.

The traditionalist beer of a proud brewing city, and the much-loved local spirit, give a dash of style to the Lüttje Lage. First, the proper grip must be applied, then comes the careful raising of the glass to the lips, and finally the sublime swallow. This is a rare ritual. More elegant than a boilermaker, more profound than a submarino.

GERMANY

The Parthenon of Beer-Drinking

This elevated description flowed from the pen of H. L. Mencken. He was talking about the Hofbräuhaus, which stands on the thoroughfare known as the Platzl, in Munich. The Hofbräuhaus is only 400 years old — some of its vaulted chambers, galleries and baronial turrets are a trifle younger — but it still properly inspires awe. There is no more famous brewery-tap, beer-hall or garden in the world, and the Hofbräuhaus is all three. It can accommodate 4,500 people on its three floors. Inevitably, like the Parthenon, the Hofbräuhaus suffers the rigors of tourism, but which visitor to Athens or Munich would miss either?

The Hofbräuhaus has had its moments of notoriety, and on summer evenings can be a noisy place, yet its garden is a restful place in which to drink a refreshing Weissbier or a sustaining Bock. The Hofbräuhaus still has its own brewery, though not on the same premises. It produces its own bottom-fermenting "H.B." beers, characteristically malt-accented and with a spritzy finish.

The proper time to drink at the Hofbräuhaus is before noon, with a pair of coddled Weisswurst sausages as the stomach's sole defence. (If that seems inadequate, Leberkas may be applied. This local dish is neither liver nor cheese, but a meat-loaf made from beef and pork.) For the rest of the day, Munich will seem even more beautiful than it truly is.

Across the street from the Hofbräuhaus is the Platzl restaurant and cabaret, where Munich presents its own sampling of Bavarian country entertainments. To a feast of yodelling, alpenhorns and knuckles of pork, diners drink Ayinger beer, served from a small barrel placed on each table. The Ayinger brewery has also a tiny still in which it makes a fruit brandy from local apples and pears. This Obstler is served at the Platzl in china tobacco-pipes.

85

SCANDINAVIA

THERE IS A GRAIN of truth in the image of Europe's icy northern lands as the ancestral home of the Vikings, brandishing drinking horns and thirsting for mead or some other spicy brew. Even today, between the forests and fjords (and sometimes in the stately, elegant capitals) there is a deeply-rooted and enthusiastic ritual of home-brewing in the northernmost of these countries. It is no doubt kept healthy by complicated laws and tax structures designed to restrain the commercial sales, and therefore use, of alcohol.

This is the case in Finland, isolated by the Baltic sea; in Sweden and Norway, on the Scandinavian peninsula; and on the island of Iceland. Things are much more civilized in Denmark. It may be a collection of islands and a peninsula, but it is less detachable from the rest of Europe. Only Denmark has a major international brewer, Carlsberg, and that remarkable company played a historic role in perfecting the production of lager beer in the late 1800s.

From the time of the Norse sagas of Viking life to the mannered era of Ibsen and Strindberg, social behavior in these parts has been well documented. Finland's national epic managed to accommodate the creation of the world in 200 verses, but required 400 in which to explain the invention of beer. There would seem to have been beer of some description in Finland for more than 1,000 years. Iceland was not settled until the 9th century, when the Vikings arrived. Its sagas, written in the 12th and 13th centuries, record that the Vikings brewed a strong drink from barley.

They called this beverage *aul*, which evolved into the Finnish word *olut*, the Swedish *öl*, the Norwegian and Danish *øl* and, among other derivations, the English "ale." (Only later did the English import the word "beer," or *bier*, from Flanders.) After drinking *aul*, the Vikings used to go *berseark*, which might explain why they were held in fear and awe by the rest of Europe.

In the 1700s, the art of distillation, which seems to have been brought from the East and introduced by the Moors to Spain, was spreading northward. In several northern countries, the popularity of spirits in this period overshadowed the development of beer.

The oldest of today's breweries in the region was founded by a Russian in Helsinki in 1819, during the Tsarist rule of Finland. The most culturally isolated is probably the one in Lapland, a region defined by the nomadic Mongol people who live in the far north of the Soviet Union, Finland, Sweden, and Norway. The Lapp brewery is in Finland, on the border with Sweden. The northernmost brewery is inside the Arctic Circle, at Tromsø, in Norway. In Tromsø, beer is served with a snack of seagulls' eggs.

In the 1980s, Finland for the first time licensed commercial production of its traditionally home-brewed juniper beer, Sahti. Sweden has a commercially produced mead and a juniper beer.

Denmark has an old style of "white ale," loosely based on a Wheat Beer tradition. Finland, Sweden, and Denmark all have good examples of the Baltic style of Porter. Sweden, Norway, and Denmark have dark Munich-style and amber Vienna-style lagers as well as the more conventional pale type. Norway has Bock beers.

All of these are specialty products, and are not thrust upon the visitor, but the inquisitive beer-lover will wish to find them and try them.

This "Long Ship" drinking vessel dates from 1699. Similar artefacts are to be found in many Scandinavian collections. We know the Vikings brewed a strong drink from barley, but the region's beer history may be even older than that.

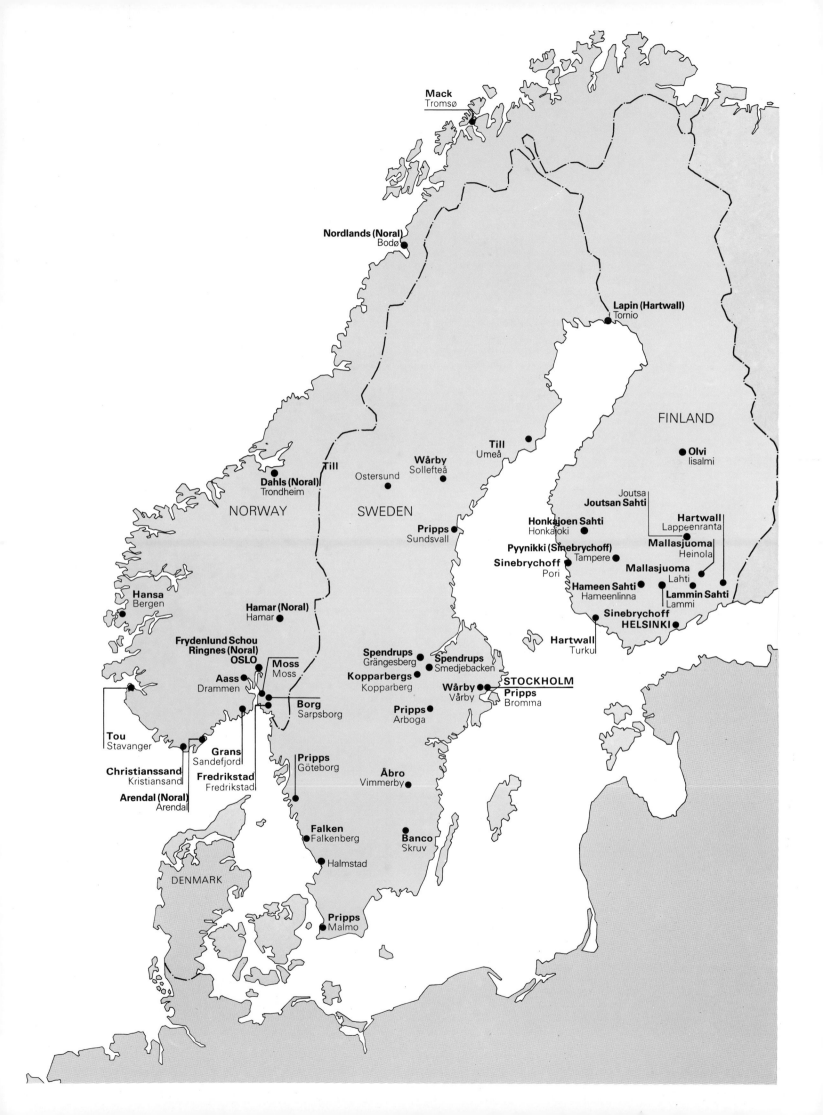

Mack
Tromsø

Nordlands (Noral)
Bodø

Lapin (Hartwall)
Tornio

FINLAND

Till
Umeå

Olvi
Iisalmi

Wårby
Sollefteå

Joutsa

Joutsan Sahti

Dahls (Noral)
Trondheim

Till

Honkajoen Sahti
Honkajoki

Hartwall
Lappeenranta

NORWAY

SWEDEN

Ostersund

Pyynikki (Sinebrychoff)
Tampere

Mallasjuoma
Heinola

Pripps
Sundsvall

Sinebrychoff
Pori

Mallasjuoma
Lahti

Hansa
Bergen

Hameen Sahti
Hameenlinna

Lammin Sahti
Lammi

Hamar (Noral)
Hamar

Sinebrychoff
HELSINKI

Frydenlund Schou
Ringnes (Noral)
OSLO

Moss
Moss

Hartwall
Turku

Aass
Drammen

Spendrups
Grängesberg

Spendrups
Smedjebacken

Borg
Sarpsborg

Kopparbergs
Kopparberg

Wårby
Vårby

STOCKHOLM

Pripps
Bromma

Tou
Stavanger

Pripps
Arboga

Grans
Sandefjord

Pripps
Göteborg

Christianssand
Kristiansand

Fredrikstad
Fredrikstad

Åbro
Vimmerby

Arendal (Noral)
Arendal

Falken
Falkenberg

Banco
Skruv

Halmstad

DENMARK

Pripps
Malmö

Denmark

THE DYNASTIC STORY of Carlsberg is a blockbuster. It features adventure, entrepreneurial daring, family feuding, scientific breakthroughs of world importance, expansive architectural projects, the acquisition of art and antiques on a grand scale, and finally an act of charity the reverberations of which are still being felt around the world.

The background is more colorful than the beers — at least, the mild, pale Pilsener-types (and, indeed, the stronger lagers) for which Carlsberg, and therefore Denmark, are best known internationally. Carlsberg has done more than any other brewery in the world to spread the popularity of lager beers, but its most interesting products are often hard to find outside its home market.

When your homeland is tiny, and you want to sell to the world, you have to make products that appeal to a broad market. It helps if you can use your corporate pedigree to support a slogan promising "Probably the best lager in the world." Even better if you can hire Orson Welles to speak the voice-over, although he might have enjoyed more creative satisfaction making a film of the Carlsberg story.

There never was a Mr Carlsberg. There was the Jacobsen family, farmers in Jutland, the peninsular part of Denmark. In the 1700s, Christian Jacobsen left home to seek his fortune in the big city, Copenhagen. Perhaps the Jacobsens had made beer on their farm; Christian established himself as a brewer in Copenhagen. In his own small way, this first member of the brewing dynasty was an innovator. He was one of the first Danish brewers to introduce the use of the thermometer. His son, Jacob Christian Jacobsen, played a much more dramatic role.

This greater innovator came into the business at a time when Europe was putting itself back together after the Napoleonic wars. Denmark's brewers were at the time making top-fermenting Wheat Beers, but the more cosmopolitan consumers were already talking about the new style of lager beer coming out

Among the elaborate decorations which bring such color to the "New" Carlsberg brewery, none is more imposing than the Elephant Gate. The theme was celebrated in advertising, and still features on the label of a popular beer-brand.

of Bavaria. The enterprising young Jacob Christian went to Bavaria, to Munich, and studied under the great Gabriel Sedlmayr at the Spaten brewery. On his return, he succeeded in producing a lager-type beer in his mother's wash-copper. At the time, understanding of yeast was still sketchy, but Jacobsen realized that that was the secret. If he were to make a lager beer on any scale, he needed a supply of a reliable yeast suited to the purpose.

With this realization dawned one of the most colorful episodes in the history of brewing. It took place in 1845, at a time of great advances in science, when Pasteur was about to unfold the mysteries of fermentation, and Balling was explaining the chemistry of yeast.

By stagecoach, Jacob Christian Jacobsen set out for Munich, a journey that is 600 miles as the crow flies. According to *The Book of Carlsberg*, "he managed to secure two pots of yeast from Brewer Sedlmayr." According to an account published by Spaten, "Gabriel Sedlmayr succeeded in cultivating an especially pure strain of yeast. Under adventurous circumstances, this yeast later arrived at the Carlsberg brewery in Copenhagen."

It is said, believably enough, that Jacobsen kept the pots of yeast cool under his stove-pipe hat as the stagecoach rumbled its way back to Denmark. At every stop, he took the pots to a water supply and doused them to chill them down. The journey must have taken several weeks, but he got the yeast home in adequate condition.

He used the yeast to produce Denmark's first commercially-marketed bottom-fermented beer, which he lagered in storage cellars under the city ramparts of Copenhagen. He had been given royal license to use these cellars. The beer (a dark brown, Munich-style lager) was a success. With money inherited upon the death of his mother, Jacobsen bought land and built a bigger brewery. The land had good water, and was close to Denmark's first railway line, which was being laid at the time. The new brewery was on a hill, for which the word in Danish (as in other Teutonic languages) is *berg*. Jacobsen named the brewery after his son Carl, who was aged five at the time.

The first beer under the name Carlsberg was brewed on November 10, 1847. A few decades later, this brewery became known as Old Carlsberg. On an adjoining site, the son had a brewery of his own, called New Carlsberg.

The missionary zeal with which Jacobsen pursued the scientific aspects of brewing knew no bounds. His friends and working acquaintances included Pasteur, Sedlmayr, the Austrian brewer Dreher, and the great French brewer of the period, Eugene Velten, of Marseilles. All four brewers were on the executive committee of the International Brewing Congress in Vienna in 1873, where Professor Carl von Linde presented a celebrated paper on refrigeration. Two years later, Jacobsen set up the famous Carlsberg Laboratories, not only to conduct

Left: It could be the nave of a cathedral, but in fact it is the brew-house at "New" Carlsberg, Copenhagen. This temple to brewing and other arts remains much as it was when built in 1901, and is still in full use. Carl Jacobsen produced his own drawings for the architect. The building is largely in Florentine style, although there are many other references. On the roof of the brew-house is a bronze sculpture depicting "Thor's Fight Against the Giants" (nothing to do with the Danish beer called Thor). The chimney is shaped like an Egyptian lotus-blossom. At its foot are "chimeras" copied from those at Notre Dame. The elephants that guard the gate are modeled on those at the obelisk in Minerva Square, Rome.

"New" Carlsberg lives as a visible, tactile expression of grace, beauty and boldness: art as an expression of imagination and of dreams. It never seems to be just a memorial to Jacobsen, though today's brewers might argue that the ways in which they spend their petty cash bring pleasure to people at large rather than simply to those fortunate enough to visit the brewery: hot-air balloons, yacht races, baseball — you name it.

research in brewing but also to serve as an endowed institute for the pursuit of scientific activities in the interests of the country. A year after that, the Carlsberg Foundation was established "to benefit science and honor the country."

Perhaps it takes one revolutionary to recognize another. Towards the end of his life, Jacobsen employed a young scientist called Emil Hansen, who had previously done some work at New Carlsberg. It was an historic appointment. In his new job at the Carlsberg Laboratories, Hansen furthered the work of Pasteur, and soon made one particularly important advance. He isolated the first single-cell yeast culture. His next step was to establish which species produced good beer and which did not. Another famous Danish brewery, Tuborg, was having trouble with its brews. This was the period when Tuborg was introducing Denmark's first pale, golden Pilsener-style lager. After being bottled for a few days, the beer fermented to a point where it was turbid and unpleasant. Hansen was able to show that Tuborg was using two "bad" yeast species along with one "good" species. At the Old Carlsberg brewery they were having problems, too. Sometimes the beer smelled bad and was excessively bitter. This was not a good hoppy bitterness but an astringency deriving from some other source. The problem turned out to be with the yeast. Hansen discovered that there were three "bad" species of yeast at work, and one "good" species. Doubts were expressed about his finding, but he pressed ahead with an experiment using the "good" species in 1883. The experiment was a success.

Carlsberg the Charity

Left: The Little Mermaid statue is regarded the world over as a symbol of Copenhagen. It was originally donated to the city as a work of art by Carl Jacobsen, and was one of many such gifts he made. The sculpture has been sited in the entrance to the harbour since 1913. It is the work of Edvard Eriksen. *Right*: An example of the works in the collection of the Ny Carlsberg Glyptothek: Gauguin's famous *Vahine no te Tiare*.

TODAY, CARLSBERG is a charity. A controlling interest in the brewing company is held by the Carlsberg Foundation, to provide funds not only for the pursuit of scientific knowledge but also for the performing arts. To drink the beer is to be a patron of the arts or sciences.

The first grand gesture of philanthropy turned out to have been a mere foretaste. After the Carlsberg Laboratories, and then the Foundation, came the National History Museum. Then, on the death of Jacob Christian Jacobsen, in 1887, the most remarkable gesture of all. His will revealed that he had left his entire brewing business to the Foundation.

The year before he died, Jacobsen and his son Carl had ended a lengthy quarrel. The son, whose great interest was in art and architecture, went on to continue the expansive tradition of philanthropy.

Given the size of Carlsberg today, it is ironic that the dispute had principally been over the scale of production. Jacobsen the father felt that expansion was jeopardizing quality ~ also that his son should pay more attention to brewing and less to the acquisition of works of art.

There was also the question of the style of beer to be made. At first, the father had provided the son with a brewery in which he made top-fermenting, "British-style" beers. It was subsequently decided that the market for the future was in bottom-fermenting lagers. After a period in which the two men had cooperated, their disagreement grew to a point where Carl set up a new brewery next door, in competition with his father. It seems that, following the lead of Tuborg, the younger Jacobsen's brewery switched to Pilsener-style lagers. As to the details of

these events, accounts differ. Clearly both men had very strong personalities, being stubborn and determined.

There followed half a dozen years of lawsuits. Finally, Carl's wife and daughter brought father and son together. Not long afterwards, father and son set off together for a holiday in southern Europe. In Italy, the father died.

Carl Jacobsen was a temperamental and dandyish extrovert. His own brewery was alive with architectural delights, not least the famous decorative gate carved in the shape of two elephants. He set up a fund in 1879 to pay for public squares and gardens in the city, and added to the towers of Copenhagen's skyline by providing a spire for St Nicholas Church and building the Jesus Church. A world-famous donation to his native city was the Little Mermaid statue on Copenhagen's harbor promenade.

Carl Jacobsen assembled a considerable private collection of paintings, sculptures, and antiques, which he housed in an annex to his private mansion.

Today, this annex is used as the Carlsberg Museum, and is open to the 150,000 people who visit the breweries each year. It contains paintings depicting scenes from Carl's time, rarities and curios received as gifts by the family, and early posters.

A large part of the family's personal art collection was given to the nation by Carl Jacobsen and his wife in 1884. This gift was made after the royal collection of sculpture had been devastated in a fire at Christiansborg Castle. The collection, much expanded, is now housed in a magnificent museum on Copenhagen's Western Avenue which was built by the city and the State of Denmark with the family's help. The museum, called the Ny Glyptothek, houses major works by Rodin, including *The Thinker*, no fewer than 73 sculptures by Degas, and works by artists such as Gauguin, Monet, Corot, Bonnard, and Millet. Some of these works were bought for the museum by the New Carlsberg Foundation, which was set up by Carl Jacobsen in 1902. Just as the original Carlsberg Foundation, set up by his father, was endowed to

More pieces from the collection of the Ny Carlsberg Glyptothek. *Far left*: The Impressionist Alfred Sisley's *Waterworks at Bougival*, painted in 1873. *Left*: A Greek head from the 6th century BC and a bust of an Egyptian Pharaoh. *Above:* Kai Nielsen's sculpture *The Water Mother*, a symbol of fertility.

benefit the sciences, so the New Carlsberg Foundation was created to support the arts. Apart from its donations to the Ny Glyptothek, the Foundation has also helped to finance the purchase of works by Titian, Tintoretto, Hals, Tiepolo and Goya for Denmark's State Museum of Art. Gifts to the oddly named Louisiana Museum of Modern Art, at Humlebaek, not far from Elsinore, have included works by Karel Appel, Jean Arp, Corneille, Alberto Giacometti, Barbara Hepworth and Henry Moore, among many others.

The Old and New Carlsberg Breweries were amalgamated in 1906, the profits from both enterprises to be used to fund the Foundations for art and science. In 1914, Carl Jacobsen died. He had said, "I care not for flowers on my coffin when so many people lack fuel for their hearths." Fifty years after the original bequest of the old brewery to the Carlsberg Foundation, a further gesture was made in 1938. "The Carlsberg Bequest to the Memory of Brewer J. C. Jacobsen" was devised to provide short-term assistance for various causes, especially in the performing arts. In 1961, the Carlsberg Foundation offered to pay for the erection and equipping of a Planetarium, which was built during the early 1970s.

The winner of the Nobel Prize for Chemistry in 1972, Dr Christian Anfinsen, was an "old boy" of the Carlsberg Laboratories. Over the years, the Carlsberg Foundation has supported innumerable quests for knowledge: exploration in Greenland, a study of the mysterious migrations of the eel, geological surveys of the sea-bed (hence the naming of the Carlsberg Ridge, in the Indian Ocean), archaeological excavations all over Asia (which have benefited the Danish National Museum, and museums in the countries concerned), ethnographic studies of peoples like the Tuareg, the building of a reflecting telescope in Chile, and countless other works.

Carlsberg and Tuborg had cooperated since the turn of the century, and at the beginning of the 1970s they merged, to form a unified presence as Denmark joined the European Economic Community. Initially, the company was called United Breweries, but in 1987 the name became simply Carlsberg. It was a condition of the merger that the Carlsberg Foundation would have at least 51 per cent of the joint company, which is quoted on the stock exchange. It receives a commensurate proportion of profits to dispose on its charitable works. Initially, and historically through Tuborg and Carling, of Canada, there were links with the Rupert Group, of South Africa. With Carling's acquisition by Elders, of Australia, the last of these links have been severed.

The Beer-Styles of Denmark

AT FIRST SIGHT, the rest of Denmark's beers are mild, lightly malty lagers in the Pilsener style, like the principal products of Carlsberg and Tuborg. As in most brewing nations, first sight is deceptive. Denmark does have several other styles. Since the Carlsberg company is the biggest, its range of products is most extensive, and most thoroughly exemplifies the styles of beer to be found in Denmark.

In addition to its site in Copenhagen, Carlsberg has another, very large, brewery in Denmark, at Fredericia, Jutland. Tuborg has a separate brewery in Copenhagen, making beers to its own specifications within the Carlsberg group. Tuborg has also since 1891 owned the brand-name Kongens Bryg ("King's Brewery"). Before then, Denmark had a Royal Court brewery, mentioned as early as 1443 and apparently founded when the King of Denmark was Christopher of Bavaria. Under the Carlsberg, Tuborg and Kongens Bryg names, the group has about 20 products in its home market. The Carlsberg group also owns Wiibroe (in Elsinore, and with a beer called Hamlet) and Neptun. It additionally has a stake in Ceres and Thor.

The oldest and most unusual style in Denmark recalls the Wheat Beers of earlier days. This is known as Hvidtøl ("white beer"). It is no longer made with wheat, though the brewers still use top-fermenting yeasts. Hvidtøl is made in two variations.

One, confusingly, is dark (in Danish, mørkt). Its exact color varies, but is usually a dark reddish-brown and sometimes almost opaque. This version is made to gravities in the region of 11.0-14.0 Plato (1044-1056), and sometimes higher still, but is barely fermented, so that its alcohol content is slight: 1.2-1.3 per cent by weight (1.5-1.7 by volume). It may also be primed with sucrose before being pasteurized. Mørkt Hvidtøl is very sweet, and may be quite creamy in texture. It can have the aroma and palate of sweet, milky Indian tea or even drinking chocolate. Variations made for Christmas (Jule) and Easter (Påske) are the sweetest. They are not to be confused with the strong lagers identified with the same seasons.

It is a rural tradition to drink Mørkt Hvidtøl with the savory rice pudding that is served as a first course to Christmas dinner, and traditionally followed by goose. Children are permitted to drink this style of beer, and they customarily leave a glass or two, with the rice pudding, outside the house for the Christmas elves.

Lys Hvidtøl means "pale white beer." This brassy-colored version is less sugary, though still on the sweet side. It has a lower gravity (7.5-8.0; 1030-32) and a slightly higher alcohol content (in the region of 2-0; 2.5, or the odd percentage point more). Because low-alcohol beers are not taxed, they are inexpensive. The pale Hvidtøl has the appeal of a pleasant low-alcohol beer at a modest price. It is often also regarded as a table beer for family use. In style, only a light fruitiness and "roughness"

distinguish this pale Hvidtøl from a low-gravity Pilsener-type.

Yet a third top-fermenting variation is known as Skibsøl ("ship's beer"). This was obviously first brewed to ferment out on board ship during a voyage. Skibsøl might have a gravity of 8.0 Plato (1032), and an alcohol content of 1.7; 2.1. It is very dark, and is notable for its smoked-malt character. Only two or three examples of this style survive. It would be a shame if Skibsøl (or, indeed, any of these old styles) were to vanish. In the case of Skibsøl, the difficulty is in finding a modern-day application for the product. Perhaps with a well-spiced apple pastry, as a Danish version of afternoon tea?

Some brewers also have a top-fermenting beer called Maltøl, at a higher gravity (perhaps 17 Plato; 1068) but an even lower alcohol content (0.9; 1.1). This is a very heavy product, similar in style to the malt-extract beers produced in Germany, Latin America, and other places. It is regarded as a tonic, and in some export markets as an aphrodisiac.

These top-fermenting styles are frequently high in brewing sugars other than barley malt. Caramel is often used, and corn may be employed to the tune of anything from 12 to more than 30 per cent, depending upon the variation. A more conventional Danish beer might have 12-25 per cent corn. Some are all-malt.

A style that is on occasion all-malt, and might be expected to be top-fermented, is the Baltic type of Stout, also sometimes labeled as Porter. In Denmark, these products are usually bottom-fermenting, but are nonetheless very interesting beers, with a great deal of taste. Gravities in this style are generally in the range of 18-20 Plato (1072-1080), and these beers have an alcohol content of more than 6.0; 7.5. Carlsberg's example, which variously appears under the descriptions Imperial Stout and Gammel ("Old") Porter, has a lovely, chewy "burnt toffee" palate. Wiibroe has a similar product, described as Imperial Stout.

The second largest brewing company, Ceres, has a version with a very fruity aroma and a rich, sweetish, licorice-like palate, drying in a long finish. It is variously labeled as Stout (sic) or Gammel Jysk Porter (jysk means "from Jutland"). Ceres is headquartered in the important university town of Århus, in Jutland. Ceres and its brother company Thor have five plants between them, under the group name Jutland Breweries. Another sizable independent, Albani, has a powerful, firm, malty Porter. Albani is headquartered in Odense, the town of Hans Christian Andersen. It has three breweries.

In addition to the Stouts (or Porters), there is the occasional blended beer made from this type of product and a regular lager, with a view to approximating the British ale type. Danish drinkers sometimes ask a barman to make this mix for them, by ordering a "half and half."

Carlsberg still makes a product in its original style, a dark-brown, Munich-type lager. This is called

A green beer for Whitsun is one of Denmark's more questionable contributions to brewing science. How odd that the serious-minded Danes, rather than the whimsical Irish, should have been the first to engage in regular commercial production of such a brew. The Irish can console themselves: there is a greater depth of character discernible in the black stuff.

Gamle Carlsberg Special Dark Lager (10.7 Plato; 1042-3; 3.3; 4.2). Gamle and Gammel are different forms of the same word. Gamle Carlsberg is a tasty beer, malty but with some dryness in the finish. Tuborg has a similar product, called Rød ("Red Label"). Another example is Ceres Lager Øl, with a dark amber color, a malty but dry palate, and very good head retention. Albani's entrant in this style is an all-malt beer called simply Odense Lager. In the early days, all lager was dark, and there are in Denmark (and in some other European countries) still vestiges of that usage.

Ceres has a dark lager of a higher gravity (15 Plato; 1060; 5.1; 6.3) called Bering Bryg. This is named after the Danish explorer Vitus Bering (1681-1741). He discovered the seaway now known as the Bering Strait, and is credited with having discovered Alaska.

Carlsberg has a further group of darkish lagers that straddle the Munich and Vienna styles. The strongest of these is its Easter beer. Påskebryg (18.0 Plato; 1072; 6.3; 7.8), with a fairly full color. Then comes C47, a name that could be more evocative, since it celebrates 1847, when the brewery was founded. This beer has more of an amber color, and a gravity of 16 Plato (1064; 5.6; 7.0). Finally, Christmas arrives: the Julebryg returns to the fuller color, but has a gravity of 12.8 (1051; 4.4; 5.5). These are delicious beers, beautifully balanced, with a restrained sweetness in the nose and a malty dryness in the finish.

Below: One of the world's classic examples of advertising illustration, entitled simply *Thirst*, was produced for Tuborg in a poster competition in 1900. The poster has been in use ever since. The artist was Eric Henningsen.

The strongest of the company's pale, golden lagers in the Danish market is the Påskebryg from Tuborg, at 17.3; 1069; 6.2; 7.7. Close behind in this category comes the famous Elephant Beer (16; 1064; 5.8; 7.3). The combination of yeast character, malt specification, gravity and fermentation procedures give this beer a distinctively estery, sweet-fruity character for a lager. Albani has a similar product, fractionally less strong, called Giraf. This type of beer has become almost a minor style in itself, although it has no name. Several other Danish brewers produce similar beers under the description Bock. Although there are obvious similarities, these Danish strong lagers do not have the malty richness, the complexity or the hoppy finesse of a German Bock.

There is nonetheless some poise and balance to Elephant that seems lacking in Carlsberg Special Brew, at 19.2 Plato (1077; 7.1; 8.9). This extra-strong pale lager, the most potent of Carlsberg beers, has plenty of alcohol but not much character. It seems to be all brawn and no brains. Carlsberg Special Brew is made in Denmark but not marketed there. In Britain, where Carlsberg has its own brewery and produces Special locally, the product has been such a success that it has inspired many imitators, some even stronger.

The group's Danish breweries make about a dozen products specially for export. One of the more interesting export products is a dark lager called 19B (in degrees Plato, 18.1; 1072-3; 6.4; 8.0). The ranges produced for the home and export markets are broadly similar, but tuned to meet what the company perceives as local requirements. Beers for Germany are brewed according to the Reinheistgebot.

Carlsberg and Tuborg products are made by about half a dozen associate companies in other countries, and under license by more than 20 other breweries. Other international brewers have similar arrangements, but Carlsberg is notably forthcoming, clear, and precise in explaining its activities.

Denmark has Pilsener-style beers under the Carlsberg label at three gravities. There is Let ("Light") Pilsener at 7.7 Plato (1032-4; 2.2; 2.8). Then Pilsner Hof at 10.7 (1043; 3.8; 4.7). Finally, Sort Guld ("Black Gold"), at 12.9 (1052; 4.6; 5.8). Tuborg also has products in each of these brackets, though the gravities and alcohol contents are not identical.

The Carlsberg products' house character is to be a little on the sweet, malty, slightly buttery side. The Tuborg beers are drier and hoppier. Carlsberg is a bigger name internationally, but Tuborg sells more in Denmark.

Carlsberg's two subsidiaries, Wiibroe and Neptun, each produce their own ranges but also specialize. Wiibroe is preoccupied with a non-alcoholic lager. Neptun does not actually brew; it is supplied with wort, which it ferments. Its specialty is an oddity ~ a green beer. This product was originally made to celebrate the dawn of spring. In Denmark, it is called Pinsebryg ("Whitsun brew"). Other

The collection of Danish costumes below was just one theme from an attractive series of illustrated labels produced by the small Lolland-Falsters brewery, now owned by Faxe. A sample selection of current labels from minor Danish brewers is at the foot of the page.

breweries have products with similar names for this season, but not colored green. Neptun's product is intended to make the same allusion as some of the German infusions of fruit or herbs in beer at Maytime. Its green derives, though, from food coloring. The beer is exported to the United States as Green Rooster and to Japan as Bacchus. If the consumer's eyes remain shut, this product manifests itself as a pleasantly soft, dryish, strong lager of around 6.0 per cent alcohol by weight; 7.5 by volume.

A pinkish beer was for a time marketed under the name Red Eric by Ceres. After Denmark joined the European Economic Community, it emerged that the food coloring used in this product contravened an E.E.C. ruling. The beer, a firm, dry, lager of 13 Plato (1052; 4.5; 5.6) paled to a wholly conventional color. Eric himself would have had no such difficulties, since he traveled away from Europe. When he discovered Greenland in 982, he and his fellow mariners brewed some beer to celebrate Yule, but its color is not recorded.

Ceres and Thor, in the joint guise of Jysk, emphasize their specialty products, notably their Xmas Beer, a round, rich, sweetish, pale lager of 13 Plato (1052; 4.6; 5.8). Ceres has also a strong lager of 16.3 (1066; 6.0; 7.7) that is marketed under two names, neither of which is appropriate to its style: Dansk Dortmunder and Strong Danish Export Ale. This product has a fruity, winy aroma and a big soft body. Thor also has a similar beer, slightly fuller-bodied, at 16.3; 1066; 5.9; 7.6, called Buur. This name was first used to decribe a Danish beer in the 1400s. This powerful beer is popular with women drinkers. Among their everyday Pilsener-style lagers, the Ceres products tend to a clean, malty dryness; the Thor beers have a little more hop character. Both are in the typically mild vein of Danish beer.

Everyday lagers in Denmark tend to have a bitterness in the region of 17-26. At a standard Pilsener gravity, 22-26 is typical. The differences between the products of one brewery and another are not great. The trade-names and label designs

used by Carlsberg are often mimicked by the smaller brewers. References on labels to Skatteklasse give a guide to gravity. Class I has a maximum gravity of 11 Plato (1044). Class A ranges from 11.0 to 13.3 (1053-4). Class B is anything higher. Most beer is bottled, and draft is sometimes hard to find. Draft beer may be flash-pasteurized.

In the late 1970s, the aggressive independent brewery Faxe became fashionable by promoting its unpasteurized beer, but has not done anything especially interesting since. As in some other countries, the term "draft" (in Danish, *fad*) is used to indicate an unpasteurized beer even when it is bottled or canned. Faxe now owns Lolland-Falsters, which produces fresh-tasting, malt-accented lagers. Faxe also acquired Odin, but closed the brewery.

The small independents are Fuglsang (with a pleasant, unpasteurized draft), Hancock, Harboes, Maribo, Marrebæk, Thisted, and Vestfyen (which concentrates on discount products).

Norway

PURITY OF ENVIRONMENT is a feature of all the northernmost countries, but it is more than sparkling mountain water that imparts a cleanness to Norwegian beer. For reasons that no one seems to be able to remember, Norway maintains a Pure Beer Law based on the Bavarian model.

Whatever the private enterprises of its many home-brewers, Norway insists that commercially-produced beers be made from an all-malt mash. This leaves Norway's beers with a distinctively clean palate. As the principal products are not intended to be heavy beers, their all-malt character also manifests itself in a firmness and crispness of what is otherwise a light body. Some Norwegian beers also have very respectable lagering periods. Everyday beers may have two to three months, and specialties may go to six. All are bottom-fermenting, except perhaps for malt-extract types.

In addition to its principal, Pilsener-type, beer, a Norwegian brewery may have a Sommerøl ("Summer Beer"); a Munich-style dark lager, identified as Bayer ("Bavarian"); perhaps a house special (sometimes having been originally brewed to celebrate an anniversary); a Dortmunder Export type, referred to as "Gold Beer"; a Jule Øl ("Christmas Beer"); and a Bokkøl (Bock).

The Pilsener type might typically have a gravity of around 10.8 Plato (1043) and an alcohol content of 3.6 by weight; 4.5 by volume. Being clean and well-attenuated, these beers have little sweetness to balance, so bittering units can be low — in the region of 20-22.

The style known as Summer Beer is a pale lager of around 10.6 (1042) and, again, an alcohol content of 3.6; 4.5. The marginally greater degree of attenuation provides for an even crisper, drier palate. The hopping, fermentation, and lagering are arranged to create a flowery, lightly fruity, character. This style of beer is meant to be quenching.

House specialties vary, but an anniversary beer might have a gravity of 11.4 (1046) with, again, an alcohol content of 3.6; 4.5. In this case, the lower attenuation will make for a more satisfying, textured beer. This might be a pale lager, but with a fuller, "old gold" color.

The Dortmunder Export, or "Gold Beer," type might have the appropriate gravity of 13 (1052) and an alcohol content of 4.5; 5.6. Beers in this style are well balanced and tasty, though on the mild side, with perhaps 24 units of bitterness.

The Munich Dark Bayerøl type usually has a gravity around 11.8 (1047) and an alcohol content of 3.6; 4.5. These tend to be dryish, malty beers, with some coffee and fruity notes. Although there is nothing dramatic about these beers, they do offer a change of pace. In recent years, a consumer organization called "The Friends of Bayerøl" has established itself, in a light-hearted way, to "protect" the style.

The most interesting beers in Norway are the Christmas brews and the Bocks. A Jule Øl may be in the amber Vienna style, at perhaps 15 Plato (1060), with an alcohol content of 4.8; 6.0. These products can have a very good, clean, dry, firm malt accent, and be very tasty. A Bokkøl will have a gravity of around 17.0 Plato (1068) and, again, an alcohol content of around 4.8; 6.0, or slightly more. These are customarily dark, and can be quite rich.

Although the quality of the products is good, consumer choice was for 50 years limited by an agreement among brewers not to compete in each other's territories. This agreement was modified in the late 1980s to permit some limited degree of competition. Whether this was a good thing remains to be seen. Its early impact seems to have been to make the strong brewing companies even more powerful, at the expense of the handful of independents.

The capital, Oslo, has two breweries. One, Ringnes, is well known in export markets, in which it promotes its beer as having a three-month lagering period. Ringnes' beers are very dry. Those from the other Oslo brewery, Frydenlund, are hoppier, with some herbal notes. Frydenlund also has a secondary brand, Schou. Ringnes and Frydenlund are owned by a company called Noral that has in recent years acquired four provincial breweries: Arendals, Hamar, Dahl, and Nordlands.

Norway has nine brewing companies, with a total of 15 plants. Not far from Oslo, in the town of Drammen, is the middle-sized brewery Aass (pronounced "Orse," to the relief of English-speakers and, especially, Americans). This is Norway's oldest surviving brewery, having existed in its present form since 1867. It also produces some of Norway's most interesting beers. Its nutty Juleøl and its creamy Bokkøl are outstanding. The Bock is delicious with the marzipan cake that is a Norwegian delicacy.

Sweden

Farther west, the important towns of Kristiansand and Stavanger each have a brewery, the two owned by a single company. Bergen also has a brewery, which remains independent. Among the smaller towns, Moss, Sarpsborg, Frederikstad, and Sandefjord have breweries. In Tromsø is the Mack brewery, famous for serving its beer with seagulls' eggs.

The styles that may be produced are regulated, and there are joint labels among some brewers for low-alcohol beer, known in Norwegian as *lettøl*. The English-language term "Light Beer" is also used. A non-alcoholic beer under the name Zero is also a shared label.

Although none of the Nordic countries has much of a pub culture, the city of Oslo does have a noteworthy institution called The Original Pilsen Bar. This picturesque establishment dates from 1895, when the Pilsener style was beginning to be known in Norway. It is in Tollbugata, at the corner of Skippergata.

The greatest frustration faced by Norwegian brewers and drinkers alike is the high level of taxation on beer. Even by Scandinavian standards, the government's demands are steep. One result of this is to foster the Norwegian tradition of home-brewing, especially in the very rural areas of the west and north.

As recently as the 1960s, the anthropologist and sociologist Dr Odd Nordland wrote of home-brewing as being an integral part of social life in many rural districts. "Brewing occupies an important place in the economy and household traditions of Norwegian peasant society," he explained.

The custom was deeply rooted in family life, as Nordland recorded, looking back over the years: "It was associated with a multitude of events connected with work on the farm, and with different religious and secular high days and holidays . . . Christmas, Easter and Whitsun . . . funerals, weddings and Christenings . . . the hay-making season and other important events. Everyone brewed at Christmas, no matter how poor they were. The amount of ale brewed, and its quality, added to or detracted from the local prestige of a wedding." Sometimes a dozen or more barrels would be brewed. Old people prepared malt for their funeral beer, and renewed it if they failed to die at the expected time. When a man gathered together his friends for the last time, Nordland explained, he wanted to be sure they had good beer. He quoted an old man as saying: "They will not be putting me into the ground with shame." For hay-making, on the other hand, a less strong brew was prepared. It was thirsty work, but not to be pursued when drunk.

In a throwback to pre-hop habits, other plants have continued to be used by Norwegian brewers during the 20th century. One example is the alder, which was added to the brew in the form of finely-chopped young twigs, with plenty of sap. Even more

widely used was the essence of juniper, the same plant which gave its name, in abbreviated form, to gin. Home-distilling continues to be a national pastime, despite its being illegal, and the links between the production of spirits and of beer are thus consolidated. (Whiskey is distilled in its native countries from a wort which is much the same as unhopped beer.) "There are still many people familiar with the brewing of juniper ale, especially in the coastal areas near Bergen," wrote Odd Nordland. He also noted its popularity in the smaller industrial towns by the shores of the Oslo Fjord. Historically, Norway provided much of the juniper for the great gin-distilling industry of the Netherlands, trading the berries for supplies of the finished product.

A "VIKING-STYLE" mead is produced in the north of Sweden by a medium-sized independent brewing company, Till. There is also a juniper beer in this company's range of brews. Neither of these is a major product, but they are two of the most unusual brews to emerge from Scandinavia. They are also a reminder of the ancient brewing traditions that the Nordic countries have half-forgotten.

The mead, called Röde Orm ("red snake"), has a rich, golden color, with faint hints of honey in the aroma and perhaps the finish. It is really a honey-flavored beer, rather than a true mead. Röde Orm is based on a conventional beer, whereas a mead is actually fermented from honey.

The juniper beer, named Spetsat (the name indicates a sharp, refreshing drink), has a dark, reddish-brown "black cherry" color. Again, the juniper character is faint, though it perhaps comes through in the nose, and there is a resinous herbiness in the finish. Both products are spiced with bog myrtle and angelica, herbs that were widely used to aromatize beer in northern Europe long before the hop was adopted. Each has a lightly sweet fruitiness. Both are low-gravity beers of 8.5 Plato (1034), with 2.8 per cent alcohol by weight; 3.5 by volume.

No doubt bog myrtle and angelica were still commonly employed in the 12th century, when the Hanseatic League began, initially as a federation of Baltic ports. In the League, King Magnus of Sweden laid down laws concerning beer. By the 1600s, the brewers of Sweden already had their own trade guild. When Swedes today sigh that they have no brewing tradition, they are being at worst insular and at best modest.

The beginnings of brewing on an early industrial scale are recalled by a number of Swedish products in the style of ales or Porters. The classic example, the only one that is authentically top-fermenting, is Carnegie Porter, an outstanding brew of great complexity.

Carnegie was one of the many Scots who emigrated east to the port cities of the Baltic region in the late 1700s and early 1800s. He established a brewery specializing in Porter, in Gothenburg (Göteborg). This eventually merged with the local Pripps and Lyckholm family brewery.

Pripps is today the giant of the Swedish beer industry. It is state-owned, through a national enterprise board. Pripps has modern breweries in Gothenburg and Bromma (a surburb of Stockholm, the capital), and one of more traditional design farther north, at Sundsvall. It is the Sundsvall brewery, with copper vessels and open fermenters, that produces the Carnegie Porter.

Carnegie Porter is produced at two strengths. The lower-gravity version has 10.2 Plato (1041) and 2.8 per cent alcohol by weight; 3.5 by volume. This is labeled as Class II. The stronger version has 15.3 (1061-2); 4.5; 5.6, and much better expresses the character of the beer. After a long period out of production, this was restored to the market in 1985.

nose and a long, spritzy finish. Bügel, in a swing-top bottle, is a maltier-tasting Pilsener-type.

The company's principal product is Pripps' Bla. (It does not mean blaaagh; it is Swedish for "Blue.") This is a sweetish pale lager, drying in the finish. On draft, it is called Pripps Fatöl, which in English seems no more flattering, but means simply "keg beer." Nördik Wölf is a clean, dry, brew in the American "light beer" style. It is aimed primarily at the American market, and the umlauts are purely decorative. The company additionally has a beer caled Chess, in what it considers to be the everyday American style (low in character). This is for Swedish kids who want to act American. There is also a beer in the Italian style (light, slightly fruity, spritzy). Birra Italiana, as it is plainly known, was originally aimed at pasta restaurants.

With its regional beers, which have their own character, Pripps has about 20 products, most of them pale lagers. Some are available in two or three gravities, others in only one, so that the total number of specifications is closer to 30. The reason for the variations in gravity is the system in which beers are classified into three brackets according to alcohol by weight.

Class I has a ceiling of 1.8 per cent by weight (2.25 by volume). These brews usually have a gravity of 6-7 Plato (1024-1028), and are really regarded as table beers. Class II permits alcohol up to 2.8 (3.5). These brews usually have a gravity of 8-9 Plato (1032-6), and are regarded as everyday beers. In 1977, a class designated IIB was abolished. This class, with a ceiling of 3.6 (4.5), provided Sweden with beers at what might be regarded as an international gravity (around 11; 1044) and strength. It remained possible to brew at this strength, but the beer was taxed and priced at the Class III level. Class III has a maximum of 4.5 by weight (5.6 by volume). These beers usually have a gravity of 12-13 Plato (1048-53). Some, like the Class III version of Carnegie Porter, have a higher gravity ~ but they must stay within the alcohol ceiling.

Class III beers may be bought only in a restaurant or a State Monopoly liquor store. Such rules of tax class and permitted alcohol levels trouble all of the Nordic countries, but the Swedes seem to agonize over them most. They feel it an infringement of their liberties that, while they can drink a weak beer or ~ admittedly ~ a strong one, they cannot have what everyone else seems to enjoy.

This has become something of an obsession. Beer-lovers argue that it is no coincidence that so many of the world's Pilsener-style brews have alcohol contents of around 3.6 (4.5). That is the perfect level for a Pilsener, they assert. Perhaps 4.0 (5.0) would be even better.

It is possible that Class IIB will be resurrected. Swedes like to ask the question in English: IIB or not IIB? A Danish prince once put the same poser. Class IIB was also known as Mellanöl (medium beer), but that does not have the same rhetorical flourish.

The effective ban on Mellanöl was instituted because it was by far the biggest-selling class of beer. The legislators' attention seems to have been aroused by some eye-catchingly beautiful ads for Pripps' Three Towns (a light-tasting, dryish lager that poses no great threat, or promise). The ads showed young people in idyllic situations.

Were the wicked brewers trying to corrupt the young? The rest of the world does not imagine Sweden to be coy about even the inference of sex, but the rest of the world perhaps forgets the Calvinist elements in Scandinavian mores. All the same, it would have been fairer to attack the advertising, not the beer.

Brewers argued that, without IIB, they would have no proper beer. In putting that argument, they encouraged the anti-beer lobby to pursue a ban. The brewers thus scored an own goal. The ban on IIB encouraged some drinkers to move up to Class III. The legislators had thus also scored an own goal.

The ban caused a round of brewery closures, but also made the survivors more competitive. To the west of Stockholm, an old-established medium-sized brewery in Grängesberg decided it faced closure if it did not compete more aggressively. The Grängesbergs brewery, as it was somewhat anonymously known, restored the old family name of Spendrup's and began to launch new products.

One of these is Spendrup's Premium Beer, bottled and labeled to look like Mumm Champagne. This is a notably smooth beer with a delicate hop character that is well sustained through its aroma, palate, and finish. A Pilsener-style beer with Dortmunder leanings, perhaps. Another, in a bottle that could contain anything from a gourmet salad oil to a men's cologne, is the super-premium Old Gold. It has a dense head; a lovely, flowery aroma; a crisp texture; and lots of hop flavor in the finish. An excellent Pilsener-style beer.

These are both all-malt beers, as are several of the super-premium products from other breweries. In Sweden beer must contain at least 70 per cent barley malt. Common adjuncts are corn or cane sugar. Some of the lower-alcohol beers are primed with malt-extract, then pasteurized. This residual sugar gives them a little texture and "warmth."

There are eight brewing companies, operating 14 plants. A second state-owned brewery, run autonomously, is Falken. It uses that spelling for its corporate name, but renders its brand as Falcon. Its beers tend toward sweetness, sometimes with hints of butteriness. It has a tasty, sweet Julöl, and a very

Although it is not a widely known product, it has some well-known devotees, and its return had been urged by a number of "beer societies" that had been established round about that time.

A year later, the brewery went one better by releasing a vintage-dated edition. The label bears the brewing date, but the beer has six months' maturation in tanks at the brewery, and at least the same period of bottle maturation. It is a filtered and pasteurized beer, but the brewery feels that it develops in the bottle, becoming smoother and gaining some port-like notes. Carnegie Porter has a very dense head; a rich, roasty, "burnt" start; a deep, rounded coffee-ish palate; and a very dry finish.

Pripps has several other specialty products. A copper-colored brew called Dart has some of the bitterness of an English ale, though it is bottom-fermenting. One called Black & Brown, with Scottish-accented packaging, turns out to be a chocolaty, malty lager in broadly the Munich Dark style. A Christmas beer, called simply Julöl, is darker and sweet. Royal, in a bottle designed by Prince Sigvard Bernadotte of Sweden, is an all-malt Pilsener-style beer with lots of Hallertau hop in the popular Munich Dark type named Falken Bayerskt. The latter has inspired several emulators.

There is also a brewing company owned by the cooperative retail stores, although there has been some speculation about the future of this arrangement. The company is called Wårby, and its breweries are at Vårby (near Stockholm) and Sollefteå, (in the north). Its beers tend to be full-bodied and sweetly aromatic. Among the independents, Åbro is a company of considerable brewing skills, and has experimented with specialty products. Its beers are tasty and well-balanced. Banco makes markedly sweet, fruity beers. Those of Appeltofftska tend to be fruity, scenty and dry. The Till company, which operates two breweries, has some admirers for a dry, fruity, pale beer called Sailor. The company cannot live on juniper beer alone.

The Swedish author Harry Martinson once wrote evocatively about his family's home-made juniper beers. One problem in their production, he said, was the uneven ripening of the berries on the bush. "When all the berries ripen at the same time," he wrote, "the Day of Judgment is drawing nigh."

Right: The sun is caught by the brew-kettles at Wårby. This traditionally fitted brewery also uses open fermenters (*below*). An innovation is a top-fermenting Altbier called Kellermeister.

Finland

Sinebrychoff still keeps two dray-horses, which have learned to be sure-footed in the snow. While their dray awaits, Styrkka ("Power") and Fyrkka ("Money") are out of sight, having breakfast.

THE SAHTI OF FINLAND is one of the world's most unusual and distinctive brews. Until 1987, it was made only as a traditional home-brew, but there are now very small producers licensed to offer this product commercially.

Every rustic home-brewer in Finland has his (or more often her) recipe for Sahti. A classic method, especially in the Sahti stronghold of the northwest, around the area of Lammi, is to use equal parts of rye and barley, seasoned with juniper berries. The brew is fermented with bakers' yeast, for about a week, in wooden pails or milk churns, and filtered through juniper twigs and straw. It is often brewed in the sauna, and may be consumed there later.

Sahti made with rye usually has a russet color. A yellow version made with oats is popular in the northeast, around Lahti and Heinola. Both styles are usually hazy. Sahti can have a buttery aroma, drying to a Manzanilla tang at the back of the nose. The palate can be almond-like and bittersweet. The alcohol content varies, but Sahti has the reputation of leaving drinkers legless, like the rough cider in the West of England.

The purchase of Sahti is in itself an endeavor. A Sahti voucher has to be bought from a liquor store of the State Monopoly, and this must then be taken to a producer and exchanged for a supply of the brew. The first brewer to go into production, Pekka Käärinen, is about 200 miles northwest of Helsinki at Lammi, a famous area for the making of Sahti.

All over the world, people who fancy a drink are liable to find themselves thwarted by procedures that render such pleasures difficult. The Sahti arrangement must number among the best of them.

Such routines are usually created to discourage drinking, but this one may simply result from a lack of preparedness on the part of the bureaucrats. Käärinen is an economist who wrote his college thesis on Sahti. When he decided to go into commercial production, there was no legal system ready to facilitate the marketing of his Sahti.

Sahti is more than a curiosity. It is a part of Finnish culture. The Finns are an isolated people whose language is comprehensible elsewhere only to the Estonians (and, very distantly, has the same roots as Hungarian). They seem to have come from Asia and Central Europe and crossed the Gulf of Finland sometime around AD 100-200, bringing with them the custom of brewing. They even had a god of beer and barley, called Pekko.

Even more than their Scandinavian neighbors, the Finns have traditionally gathered and utilized the various berries of the cold north. In addition to juniper beer, in the form of Sahti, they also commercially produce vodkas, liqueurs and sparkling wines from their native fruits. These include Arctic Bramble, Cloudberry, Cranberry and Hawthorn Berry. The pale brown Cloudberry, with its tart, orangey, earthy taste and seedy texture, is served as a delicacy for dessert.

The Finns also grew hops as early as the 1400s, though they no longer do so. In the 1500s, Finnish beer was supplied to the royal court of Sweden, and praised in letters by the kings of that country. Both the Swedes and the Russians have at times ruled Finland, and its emergence as an economically-independent nation-state has occurred only this century. Where possible, it likes to be self-sufficient,

and in the matter of beer its law insists upon the use of fermentable material grown in Finland. The country grows barley, in its own varieties, both two-row and six. Some of the six-row is exported to Scotland and Japan as a raw material for grain whiskey. Finnish beers must contain at least 80 per cent malt. The most common adjunct is unmalted barley. Wheat starches and sugar are also used.

In the late 1800s, when Finland was under Russian rule, it had some of the most advanced breweries in the Tsarist empire. The oldest of today's breweries in Finland was founded in Helsinki by a Russian, Nikolai Sinebrychoff, in 1819. It initially produced mead, Porter and top-fermenting beer. In 1853, an early date for such a change, bottom-fermentation was introduced. At the turn of the century and until 1932, there was Prohibition, and the brewery produced near-beers and malt drinks.

Buildings from the mid-1800s survive in the largely modern brewery, which is close to the center of Helsinki. On one side is a small park, where children sledge when there is snow. Facing the park is the Sinebrychoff family house, built in 1840 and now an art museum. On the other side, a shipyard builds ice-breakers. Even after a century and a half, the Russian name Sinebrychoff is awkward for Finns, so the company's products are usually identified simply as Koff.

After the two world wars, the brewery reintroduced its Koff Porter. Except perhaps for some Sahti, this is the strongest beer made in Finland. It has a gravity of 17 Plato (1068), with an alcohol content of 5.5-5.8 by weight; 6.8-7.2 by volume.

It is an intense, Baltic-style Porter, big and very dry, oil-smooth, full in flavor, with a complex of chocolate, roastiness, fruit, and hop. With an ancestry to match, it was for a time marketed in the United States as an Imperial Stout. It is made with four malts, Northern Brewer and Hersbruck hops, and a fresh yeast every time. The brewery claims that the yeast was originally propagated from a bottle of naturally-conditioned Guinness after World War II. There is a cheeky delight in this claim, but it seems unlikely, and no one can furnish the details. An alternative version has it that the yeast was brought from Dublin in a modern-day version of the Jacobsen-Sedlmayr story. Koff Porter is warm-conditioned in tanks for six weeks. It is not filtered, but is flash-pasteurized.

This product is made in only the highest of the four classes that govern the alcohol content of beer in Finland. These were originally set out according to alcohol by weight, but the measure now used is volume. Class I provides for a maximum of 2.25 by weight (2.8 by volume). Its gravities are typically in the range of 6-7.5 Plato (1024-30). Class II accommodated 2.25-3.0 (2.8-3.7), but is no longer used. Class III offers 3.0-3.7 (3.7-4.7). Its gravities are in the range of 10-11 (1040-44). Class IVA is 3.7-4.5 (4.7-5.6). Its gravities are generally 12-13.5 (1048-53). Class IVB covers beers of 4.5-6.0 (5.6-7.5). Its gravities are 15 (1060) and upwards.

All the Nordic countries limit the advertising of beer, and in Finland it is permitted only for Class I. For this reason, most products are represented in that class as a means of promoting their trade-names. Beyond that, the Class I brews are regarded as table beers. Class III are sold in supermarkets and the very basic type of bar. Class IV are sold in state liquor stores and in restaurants.

Koff also produces a beer in an English-ale style, called Cheers. This hybrid product is really a copper-colored lager, its initial malty fruity-sweetness gradually drying until it is balanced by a substantial hop flavor in the finish. Beer is often served very cold in Finland, despite the climate, and in this form Cheers is completely tasteless. At warmer temperatures, it is a pleasant beer. Cheers is available in Classes III and IVA.

In 1987, the company introduced a Vienna-style lager as a Christmas beer, in Class IVA, with a gravity of 13.5 (1053). This Jouloulot has an amber-red color, a firm, medium body, and a clean palate with a nice complex of maltiness and gentle hop character.

The brewery also has Koff Extra Strong Export Beer, at 15.5 Plato (1062) and 5.5; 6.8. This aromatic, estery, pale lager is not available in Finland, but can be bought on ferries to Sweden, and in export markets. It is in the style of Carlsberg Elephant, and makes an oblique allusion by having a bear on the label. The everyday beers of Finland are clean, sweetish lagers, sometimes with a little fruitiness. Generally, Koff's products have an estery house character. Sinebrychoff also owns a brewery under its own name in Pori. This brewery has its own label, Karhu, and seems to produce slightly sweeter beers. The company additionally owns the Pyynikki brewery, in Tampere, and the beers there are all-malt, with a balancing, slightly "grassy" hop character. This brewery has its own yeast. It produces the Amiraali beers.

There are two other major brewers, Hartwall and Mallasjuoma, and one small company, Olvi.

Hartwall bottles in Helsinki, but its three breweries are elsewhere. One is near the important city of Turku (in the west), and the others are in the provinces of Karelia (east) and Lapland (north). The brewery near Turku, at Kaarina, has as its home brand Aura beer, which is light, with a hoppy dryness. Karelia gives its name to the brand Karjala, which is light, clean and dry. The Lapp beer, Lapin Kulta, has a dash of new-mown hay in the nose. Hartwall's specialty product is a light, clean Wheat Beer, Weizen Fest, made to its specification by the Sigl brewery, of Austria. This well-made, pleasant brew is the only Wheat Beer in Finland.

Mallasjuoma brews at Lahti and Heinola, two cities that are geographically fairly central although they are regarded in Finland as being in the north-east. Its principal brand-name is Lahden, and its products include an extra-strong export beer. The regular Lahden Erikois has a sweetish aroma, a drier palate, and a very quick finish. The company also has a lighter, spritzy product called Sininen, loosely based on the character of Heineken, as an "international" beer.

The small independent Olvi brews at Iisalmi, right in the middle of Finland, in heavily forested countryside. Olvi, owned by a foundation, has a small museum of beer. Its regular beer, which is light and hoppy, is hard to find in the cities. The brewery also has an interesting specialty called Vaakuna. This is a malty, slightly toffee-tasting beer of 13.4 Plato (1054), with an alcohol content of 4.4; 5.5. It has a very full golden color, and is regarded by the brewery as being of the Märzen type.

There will, no doubt, be more specialties. The friendly, everyday bars of Finland may be very basic indeed, and serve their beer frozen flat, but a new gastronomic culture is growing in the cities. Helsinki even has a specialty beer bar, serving just about every brew in the country's limited portfolio. It is called Olutpörssi, and is near the Finnish Bank. It is a chic place, and wags joke that a bank-loan might be necessary to fund a thorough tasting.

The only "primitive" beer to survive in Western Europe is the Sahti of Finland. Traditionally, it is infused in a wooden tub and the mash is filtered through berry-covered juniper branches and straw (*right*). The drink is consumed from a two-handled mini-barrel (*bottom*). The first commercial producer (*below*) has a four-hectoliter system made from stainless steel.

BELGIUM

THE REVERENCE RESERVED for wine in most countries is in Belgium accorded to beer. To the nation's many specialty beers, anyway. The Belgians sometimes use the phrase *méthode Champenoise* to describe bottle-conditioning, and many of their specialties enjoy this form of secondary fermentation. In a café, or at a family dinner, a rare bottle, perhaps vintage-dated, is borne from the cellar slowly, cradled horizontally, so that the yeast will not be aroused from its dreams. There may be a wrap of tissue paper to remove. The seal is opened, or the cage unhooked, as though this were a seduction, and the cork gently drawn. So foamy are some of these specialties that the glass may have been moistened first to calm the brew. The beer is served in its own special glass. Every beer in Belgium has its own glass, belonging not to the style but to the individual label. It may be a flute or a goblet or, often, a variation on a Burgundy sampler.

There are profoundly aesthetic and gastronomic sensibilities toward beer in Belgium. Its highly-developed beer-culture is quite different from those of the leisurely British or the elemental Bavarians.

The world's most wine-like beers are to be found in Belgium. The spontaneously-fermenting Lambic family of the Senne valley are the winiest of all, both in method of production and in palate. Depending as they do upon the wild yeasts in the atmosphere and in their casks, they are also products of the oldest extant method of brewing in the developed world. These are the products most often cited by brewers elsewhere who wish to demonstrate the eccentricity of Belgian beer, but the Lambics are just one example.

The use in fermentation of resident microflora occurs in several Belgian styles. The employment of herbs, spices, and fruits in some Belgian beers pre-dates the universal acceptance of the hop as the agent of seasoning and aroma. There are several distinct styles of Wheat Beer. While monks brew elsewhere, too, only in Belgium and the Netherlands are there defined styles of "abbey" beer (all of a strong ale type).

No other nation has a more colorful, individualistic, or idiosyncratic assortment of beers. There are to some extent regional styles, but the narrower term *streek*, meaning "district," is preferred. Many towns and breweries like to think of their style of beer as being exclusively their own.

Having at times been governed by the Romans, the Spanish, the Burgundians, the Austrians and the Dutch, the people of Belgium are extremely anti-authoritarian, and are not given to accepting rules as to how anything should be done. Each town has its own way of brewing. Why not?

Belgium is a meeting place of Romantic and Teutonic cultures in Europe. As far north as the city of Brussels, French is spoken alongside Flemish. The Romans went just about that far with their linguistic influence, and called the people the Belgians. Later, the Burgundians left at least some of their cultural memories in the region of Flanders. "The Burgundy of Belgium" is a phrase used on both sides of the French-Flemish language line. Only a tiny amount of wine is made in Belgium (although there are dessert grapes); the phrase refers to beer. It is not meant altogether lightly. Lambic-brewers sometimes even macerate·grapes in their beer.

Their reverence towards beer is one of the cultural elements that unite the French-speaking and Flemish communities that principally make up this small country (there is also a small German-speaking region). French-language terms such as Grand Cru are used on beer-labels even in Flanders. The French-speakers might just return the compliment by agreeing that Flanders has more breweries.

These cellars (*above*) are at the Liefmans brewery in Oudenaarde, Flanders. *Left:* the fine Brown Ales, Kriek and Framboise produced by Liefmans are cosseted in tissue paper.

Hop shoots (*below*) are classically served with poached eggs, but they may also be treated as a vegetable.

CUISINE A LA BIERE

Even the most basic café will stock Belgian beers in five or six styles, and there are some specialty bars with selections running into hundreds. While most cafés offer no food, and others simply cheeses, sausages or hotpots, there are also restaurants devoted to *Cuisine à la Bière*.

Meals are presented in which each dish has been prepared with a different beer. Yet another beer will be suggested to accompany each course. This is not the beer cuisine of Alsace or Bavaria, however delicious that can be. This cuisine is at least *bourgeoise,* and sometimes *haute.*

In March or early April, the hop shoots themselves are poached in lemon juice and served as though they were asparagus. They are topped with poached eggs, and served in a mousseline or béchamel sauce, decorated with croutons. This is a peasant dish that has become fashionable. It is one of the least elaborate examples of Belgian beer cuisine. Cherry soup with Lambic beer? Mousseline of pike poached in ale? Pigeon breasts in a sauce made from the Red Beer of Flanders? Feuilleté of pineapple, with a sabayon of Wheat Beer? There is more to this than Carbonnade Flamande.

Among several cookbooks on the subject, one classic manfully restricts itself to "the 300 best recipes for dishes aromatized with beer." There are seminars and published studies on such esoteric topics as the

Below: In front of the monastery of Affligem, hop poles await the climbing of the vine. The abbey gives its name to several beers.

The Belgian attitude toward beer has encouraged the survival of individualistic craftsmen brewers, often working at tiny kettles in buildings that reflect the agricultural origins of their trade. Even in such a land of artisan breweries, there are newcomers. About ten new micro-breweries or brew-pubs have opened in recent years. There have also been six or seven closures of breweries. The total in operation, some sporadically, is more than 100. Beers come and go, but at any one time there are four or five hundred in production, and as many as 700 in the cellars of cafés. In beer styles, there are eight or nine principal families and three times as many variations. This is in a country not much more than 150 miles across at its widest point, and with only ten million people. Belgium has fewer cafés than it once did, but they still number tens of thousands. The number of cafés in Belgium rivals the tally of pubs in England, a country with five times the population. Chez Michel vies for attention with Chez Theo, Café Sport with Café Stadhuis. In some, the table-football spins noisily; in others, especially in Brussels, the Art Nouveau elegance sets a different mood.

With its characteristically pitched ceiling, this traditional wort-cooler at Maes Pils is known in the brewery as "The Chapel".

suitability of certain beers as an accompaniment to particular cheeses.

A light, fruity or hoppy beer might be served before dinner, a strong brew afterward. The standard Pilsener strength is regarded in Belgium as being appropriate for a basic beer. Stella Artois, for example, has 4.0 per cent alcohol by weight, 5.0 by volume. Many of the specialty beers are much stronger.

BELGIAN PILSENERS

The standard Pilseners are regarded as everyday beers, and enjoy a good 70 per cent of the market. They are less distinctive than those of Germany, but more characterful than at least their mass-market cousins in the Netherlands, Denmark and (most certainly) Britain. It is the misfortune of Belgium's Pilseners to be overshadowed in character by their more specialized and stronger brother brews.

Some Belgian producers of Pilseners also make a companion beer of slightly lower strength (around 3.75; 4.6) under the description Export. This is a somewhat confusing designation, especially as some

also make a slightly maltier, more lightly-hopped companion brew under the description Dort. There is also the odd Bock in Belgium, but none of these bottom-fermenting variations is a major style.

Stella Artois is internationally the best-known example of a Pilsener-style beer made in Belgium. It has in recent years lost some of its distinctive "new-mown hay" character, but gained a little cleanness and dryness. The Artois group, headquartered in Louvain, has four subsidiary brewing companies, and about 20 products. These include the slightly stronger and sweeter "Danish-style" Loburg; the sweetish Vieux Temps and drier Ginder, both ales; and the Leffe range of abbey-style brews. Artois also financially backs the De Kluis, in Hoegaarden. Many Belgian breweries have financial links, either directly or through their backers or bankers.

Artois and Jupiler, of Liège, are now affiliated companies. Jupiler is the best-selling Pilsener-type beer within Belgium. It was once on the dry side but is today softer, slightly fruity, and rather lacking in character. Jupiler also produces Lamot, again somewhat neutral. Its subsidiary Kruger, once very

A night out in the town of Hasselt, Limburg, offers Dikkenek juniper beer, plus the excellent Sezoens strong ale — not to mention Fryns' jenever gin.

dry, is now also on the neutral side.

Kronenbourg, of France, owns the brewery in Belgian Limburg that produces Cristal Alken, the hoppiest of the country's principal Pilseners (32 units of bitterness). This is a clean-tasting, unpasteurized beer, with a dash of Saaz hop character. The company also owns a brewery in East Flanders producing Zulte, a good example of the sourish, Burgundy-colored style of the region.

After a period of ownership by Watney, of Britain, the Maes brewery is now back in Belgian hands. It produces a flowery Pilsener-style beer. Bohemian malt, Saaz hops and the Darauflassen "double fermentation" method are used. Maes, which is between Antwerp and Mechelen (Malines), also owns the Union brewery, near Charleroi. There, it brews for the Norbertine fathers of Grimbergen, and makes Cuvée de l'Ermitage.

GIN AND STRONG BEER

There is no other country where strong beers are as commonly served as in Belgium. One reason for this is a law passed in 1919 that forbade the serving of spirits in cafés. This law was part of the same international wave that gave Britain its odd pub hours and other countries Prohibition. It greatly benefited sales of strong beer, even though the traditional jenever of the Low Countries continued to be served under the counter.

Jenever takes its name from its flavour of juniper

Like their German neighbors, the Belgians favor a stemmed glass, often an extended tulip, to heighten the elegance of a good Pilsener-style beer.

This chunky goblet could have come straight from the refectory of a medieval abbey, but it is typical of the style used for today's monastery beers in Belgium.

In color at least, Rodenbach Grand Cru bids to be the "Burgundy of Belgium"... and its house glass is in the style of a Burgundy sampler. The beer is sharp and refreshing.

(in French, *genièvre*). The name was, in turn, abbreviated to "gin" by the English, whose London Dry and Plymouth versions are derivatives. When the drink was first made, present-day Belgium was a part of the Netherlands. Thus Belgian and Dutch gin are very similar. The Belgian law was finally repealed in the mid-1980s, but beer hardly feels threatened by jenever.

Some specialty beer cafés have sister jenever bars in adjoining premises. In the city of Bruges, this is true of 't Brugs Beertje (Kemel Straat 5). In the distilling city of Ghent, Het Waterhuis aan de Bierkant (Groente Markt 9) has a jenever bar nearby. So, in the jenever-producing town whose name it bears, does the Hasselt Café (Maastrichter Straat 38).

The Hasselt Café consolidates its relationship with civic tradition by having a juniper beer called Dikkenek ("Thick Neck," a self-deprecating name for the local Limburg people). Dikkenek is produced for the café by the De Smedt brewery, near Brussels. Juniper was once widely used in brewing. A similar,

The most extravagant among Belgium's beer glasses is shown in this advertisement for the strong dark Kwak. The glass is, of necessity, brought to the table in a wooden bracket. This "stirrup cup" popularized the beer from Ghent to Aix.

The "pink Champagne of the beer world", a Frambozen from the Senne Valley, presents itself in a flute that could equally accommodate the products of Rheims or Epernay.

With its dense yellow color, the intentionally cloudy Hoegaarden "White" Beer bears a passing resemblance to a pastis — especially in the bevelled tumbler that is its house glass.

The thistle glass is the symbol of Scotch Ale — but only in Belgium, where this is a traditional style. The Scots themselves offer no such flourish.

but less assertive, juniper beer is made by the Till brewery in Sweden. An even less assertive one was made by a now-defunct brewery in Philadelphia under the incongruous name Ivy League. The compliment is returned by the occasional hop gin. An example of this rare beverage is the Hopjenever made by a company called Verhofstede, in Nieuwkerken-Waas, near Sint Niklaas, East Flanders.

Interesting drinks and good food (not least oysters and mussels) are a part of the social culture of Belgium. To the immediate south, France is the foreign country that most appreciates the special qualities of its neighbour's beers. To the north, Belgian beer is also well understood in the Netherlands. (Flemish and Dutch are, in written form, the same language.) To the west and east, the British and Germans have a hazier idea of Belgium's contribution.

Despite that, it is a Belgian, the 13th-century Duke Jean I ("Jan Primus," corrupted to "Gambrinus") of Brabant, Louvain and Antwerp, who is honoured as the King of Beer by the Germans and even the Czechs. His name was no doubt spread throughout Europe in the 14th and 15th centuries, when the Flemish port of Bruges was one of Europe's most powerful trading cities.

In Belgium, legend has him as founder of the Knights of the Mashing Fork, whose headquarters are still the gilded and gabled Maison des Brasseurs (with a small museum open to visitors), on the Grand' Place in Brussels. That he was a Belgian has been long forgotten elsewhere in Europe. Since he is said to have invented the toast as a social custom, it could be argued that every land honors Jan Primus, even when the glass being raised contains a liquid other than beer.

The Grand' Place of Brussels is swathed in small streets named after the historic industries and trades of the city — such as the "Brewers' Street" (*below left*). A moment's walk away is the palatial guildhouse and museum that is the headquarters of the Knights of the Mashing Fork. Among the guildhouses set around this most elegant of squares, only the brewers' is still used for its original purpose. Nowhere in the world does an organization of brewers have quite such a splendid address. The elegance surrounding Belgian beer does not diminish the *joie de vivre*.

Hell's Pils is, alas, a thing of the past (*above*), but almost every café in Belgium offers a choice of temptations — rounded off, in this case, with a Trappists' prayer? The map (*right*) outlines the possibilities in full.

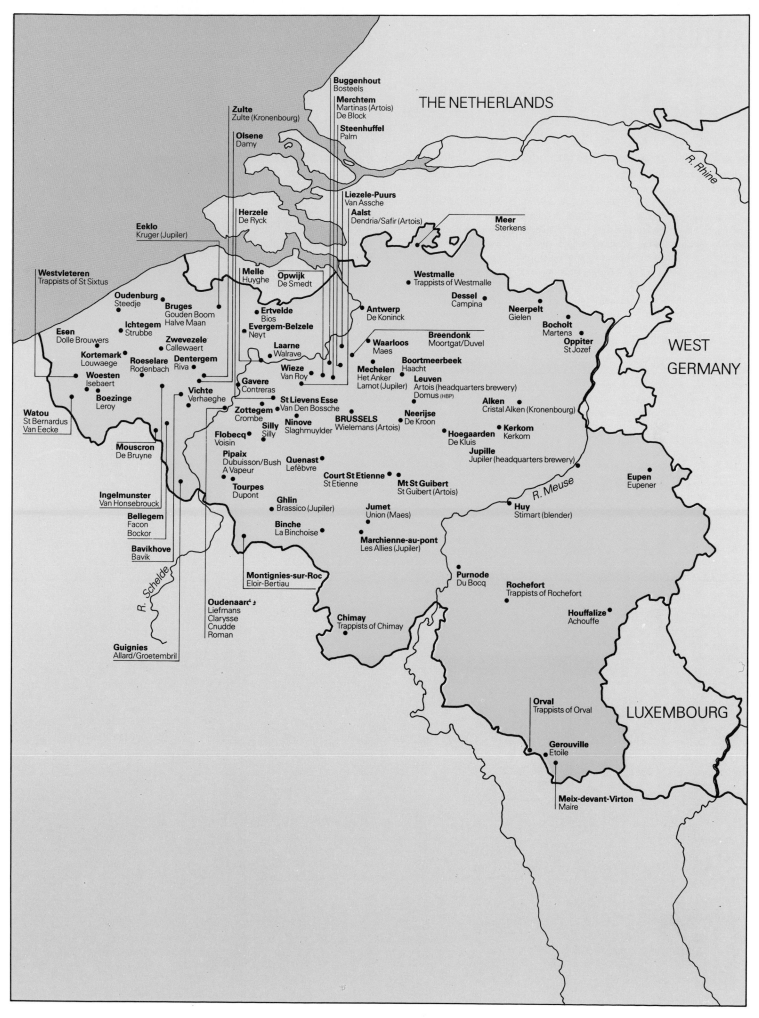

Buggenhout
Bosteels

Merchtem
Martinas (Artois)
De Block

Steenhuffel
Palm

THE NETHERLANDS

R. Rhine

Zulte
Zulte (Kronenbourg)

Olsene
Damy

Liezele-Puurs
Van Assche

Aalst
Dendria/Safir (Artois)

Meer
Sterkens

Herzele
De Ryck

Eeklo
Kruger (Jupiler)

Westvleteren
Trappists of St Sixtus

Melle
Huyghe

Opwijk
De Smedt

Westmalle
Trappists of Westmalle

Dessel
Campina

Neerpelt
Gielen

Bocholt
Martens

Oudenburg
Steedje

Bruges
Gouden Boom
Halve Maan

Ertvelde
Bios

Evergem-Belzele
Neyt

Antwerp
De Koninck

Breendonk
Moortgat/Duvel

Oppiter
St Jozef

Esen
Dolle Brouwers

Ichtegem
Strubbe

Zwevezele
Callewaert

Laarne
Walrave

Waarloos
Maes

Boortmeerbeek
Haacht

Kortemark
Louwaege

Roeselare
Rodenbach

Dentergem
Riva

Wieze
Van Roy

Mechelen
Het Anker
Lamot (Jupiler)

Leuven
Artois (headquarters brewery)
Domus (HBP)

Alken
Cristal Alken (Kronenbourg)

Woesten
Isebaert

Gavere
Contreras

St Lievens Esse
Van Den Bossche

Neerijse
De Kroon

Kerkom
Kerkom

Vichte
Verhaeghe

Zottegem
Crombe

Silly
Silly

Ninove
Slaghmuylder

BRUSSELS
Wielemans (Artois)

Hoegaarden
De Kluis

Boezinge
Leroy

Watou
St Bernardus
Van Eecke

Flobecq
Voisin

Pipaix
Dubuisson/Bush
A Vapeur

Quenast
Lefèbvre

Court St Etienne
St Etienne

Mt St Guibert
St Guibert (Artois)

Jupille
Jupiler (headquarters brewery)

Eupen
Eupener

Mouscron
De Bruyne

Tourpes
Dupont

Ghlin
Brassico (Jupiler)

Jumet
Union (Maes)

R. Meuse

Huy
Stimart (blender)

Ingelmunster
Van Honsebrouck

Binche
La Binchoise

Marchienne-au-pont
Les Allies (Jupiler)

Bellegem
Facon
Bockor

Bavikhove
Bavik

Purnode
Du Bocq

Rochefort
Trappists of Rochefort

R. Schelde

Montignies-sur-Roc
Eloir-Bertiau

Oudenaarde
Liefmans
Clarysse
Cnudde
Roman

Chimay
Trappists of Chimay

Houffalize
Achouffe

Guignies
Allard/Groetembril

WEST
GERMANY

Orval
Trappists of Orval

LUXEMBOURG

Gerouville
Etoile

Meix-devant-Virton
Maire

111

Lambic

A STUDY PUBLISHED on Pieter Bruegel the Elder shows his painting *The Wedding Feast* and suggests that the innkeeper pouring a beverage of a strawy-russet color into a crock is about to serve guests wine or some unidentified liquor. It does not seem to have occurred to the art historian that an old master, especially when painting peasants, might dip his brush in beer. Even at a glance, it is quite clear that that is what the guests in *The Wedding Feast* are to be served. The same type of crock is sometimes used today to dispense a beer of the same color, in the very old Lambic style of Bruegel country. The Lambic family of beers, which includes subsidiary styles like Gueuze, Kriek, Framboise and Faro, presents that same puzzling marriage of simplicity and sophistication that is found in Bruegel's paintings.

Bruegel is a national hero in Belgium and especially to the Flemings. His earthy depictions of rustic life are seen as enduring evidence of the roots and life-force of the Flemish people. (His more frightening images are generally forgotten.) There is a similar affection for Brouwer, a painter with an apposite name, who worked in the same tradition a century later, in the early 1600s, depicting drinking, brawling peasants.

Bruegel lived in Brussels, in its Flemish Old Town. From his home, he could soon have been in the countryside on the western stretch of the Senne valley. The Senne is a small river that flows through, and sometimes under, Brussels. The stretches of the river on both sides of the city were once associated with the brewing of beer in the style known as Lambic, but today the craft is carried out only to the west.

On both sides, the province is Brabant, which is bilingual, but the Lambic breweries are generally Flemish. The style probably takes its name from the very small country town of Lembeek, which in Flemish means "Lime Creek." The reference is to the character of the soil, not to lime trees. Not just the town of Lembeek but also a cluster of perhaps a dozen nearby villages produce Lambic beers. Together, these villages are given the district name Payottenland. They are set in flattish, open country, with small farms and the homes of people who work in Brussels.

Lambic is the most unusual style of beer made in the developed world. First, it is a Wheat Beer — and they are in themselves an unusual, and old, clan of beers. Second, the wheat, which comprises 30-40

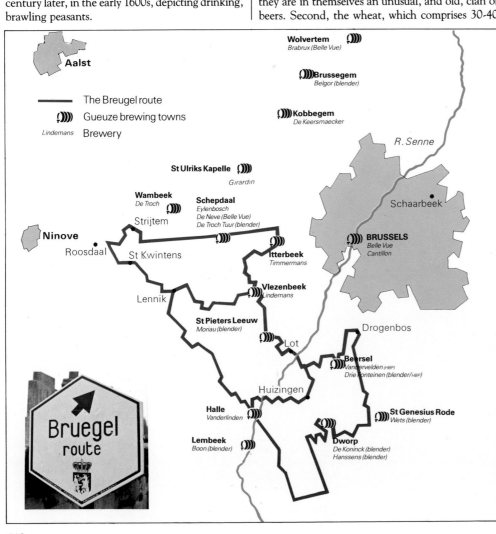

Wolvertem
Brabrux (Belle Vue)

Brussegem
Belgor (blender)

Kobbegem
De Keersmaecker

Aalst

— The Breugel route

⊕))) Gueuze brewing towns

Lindemans Brewery

R. Senne

St Ulriks Kapelle
Girardin

Schaarbeek

Wambeek
De Troch

Schepdaal
Eylenbosch
De Neve (Belle Vue)
De Troch Tuur (blender)

Strijtem

Ninove

Roosdaal

St Kwintens

Itterbeek
Timmermans

BRUSSELS
Belle Vue
Cantillon

Lennik

Vlezenbeek
Lindemans

St Pieters Leeuw
Moriau (blender)

Lot

Drogenbos

Beersel
Vandervelden (HBP)
Drie Fonteinen (blender/HBP)

Huizingen

Halle
Vanderlinden

St Genesius Rode
Wets (blender)

Lembeek
Boon (blender)

Dworp
De Koninck (blender)
Hanssens (blender)

Bruegel route

Gallery of the Brewer's Art

Turbid mash (*top*) at Cantillon, Brussels. The art of the producer lies in the ability to judge the maturity of the basic Lambic brews, to blend them with sensitivity, and to ferment the *mélange* for just the right length of time. *Second from top*: A gallery of tuns at Timmermans' brewery. The froth on the barrels at Cantillon (*above left*) shows that secondary fermentation is taking place. Even after it has been bottled, it still has to be conditioned (*above right*). When the bottles are moved, they are held in the same orientation throughout, so that the yeast will not be disturbed. The whitewash mark provides a guide to help effect this.

per cent of the mash, is unmalted. This is most unusual, and results in a milky-white wort, which may have to be boiled for between three and six hours. Then there is the hopping procedure: the hops are aged for up to three years to diminish their aroma and bitterness. Those characteristics, usually so highly desired, are not wanted. Instead, the hops (which are added in very high quantities) serve their earlier purpose of protecting the beer against unwanted infections. It is in this area that Lambic beers are most unusual: some wild microflora are actually welcomed. That is the defining characteristic of a true Lambic: it is spontaneously fermented.

Spontaneous fermentation is traditional in the production of wine. The yeast that resides on the skin of the grapes did the job of fermentation until recent years, though today specially-isolated strains are widely used. (Indeed, there are campaigners for a return to wild yeasts.) All beer was once also made by spontaneous fermentation, but those days are lost in the mists of history. First, brewers discovered that, if some of the foam were scooped off the fermenting vessels, it could be added to hasten the process next time. Then, between the late 1700s and early 1900s, the workings of yeast began to be understood.

In brewing in the developed world, spontaneous fermentation (at least, as an intentional method) has survived only in Belgium, in this one area on the west side of Brussels. The Lambic breweries are very small. Some are tiny gems of industrial archaeology (in which Belgium is especially rich). One or two had their origins as farms, others as village cafés. Only about 10 are today functioning, although a number of others are still in existence, some of them overgrown by time. There are closures and occasional re-openings.

Each has the traditional slats in the roof, where the magic microorganisms of the valley can enter to have their way with the wort, which lies waiting in an open cooling vessel. It takes just one night for consummation to take place. The finest beers seem to be conceived on autumn evenings, and the brewhouses avoid working in summer, when the yeasts of the atmosphere are just too wild.

Afterwards, the wort (original gravity 12-13 Plato; 1048-52) has both primary and secondary fermentation in wooden casks, often previously used for claret, port, or even sherry. The primary fermentation, which is identifiably vigorous, lasts for six days. The secondary fermentation is not a single event but a chain of reactions that can spread from weeks into months as different yeasts gain the upper hand and the levels of sugars and acids change.

Brewers have been known to sell Lambic that has been in the cask for only a few weeks, but usually even a "young" or "foxy" example (*jong* or *vos*) on sale in a café is three to six months old. It remains young in the eye of the brewer until it is a year old. Only after at least "two summers" is Lambic regarded as being completely mature.

The wild yeasts in the valley include two that have been named *Brettanomyces lambicus* and *B. bruxelliensis* (the latter after the Latin name for Brussels). There are also fruit yeasts and bacteria. There are additionally yeasts and bacilli resident in the brewery and the casks. The casks are arranged in dusty galleries, and the brewers are always concerned about the building being cleaned, in case the microorganisms are disturbed. At work in the casks are *Saccharomyces bayanus* and sometimes *S. cerevisiae*, as well as lactobacilli.

This is an empirical method of producing beer, and no two brews emerge with exactly the same character. Nor are the microbiological conditions the same in any two breweries or for any two summers. For this reason, there is much debate about the exact workings of Lambic fermentation.

This practice is very unusual, but not wholly unknown elsewhere in the world. In Belgium, it is especially associated with cafés, and is a more fundamental version of the British idea of cask-conditioning in the cellar of the pub. Before bottling became common, bars and restaurants in many countries bought wines and spirits young in the cask and matured them in their own cellars. Today, some still earmark their own casks for maturation in the supplier's cellar. The blenders are fermenting the beer, as well as maturing it. Only then do they blend it. The existence of independent blenders of beer is, again, unique to the Lambic tradition.

The faces of Flanders have changed little since Bruegel's time. The Flemings still enjoy a contemplative Lambic beer. The preferred glass is a matter-of-fact tumbler, with just a little fluting as a gesture to style. First, it must be studied (*far left*), then savoured (*above*), and finally enjoyed (*left*).

STRAIGHT LAMBIC

The Belgians have a cavalier attitude toward designation of style, but a beer described as Lambic, with no further qualification, should be unblended. The fermentation method leaves a straight Lambic with no carbonation, or very little.

Good examples have a fruity complexity that is variously reminiscent of a fine dry cider, a Chardonnay or a *fino* sherry. The "toasty" notes sometimes found in a Chardonnay are prized. A "cigar-like" character means a poor Lambic. The overall character should be soft but very dry. Belgian devotees of the style sometimes talk of a "wonderfully sour" Lambic in much the way that a

British ale-lover might rejoice over the intense bitterness of his favorite brew. Sad to say, producers of both these styles have been inclined over the years to blandify their beers to appeal to a wider taste.

Lambic is usually served on draft, although there are some bottled examples. There is one mass-market producer of beers in this family, Belle Vue, and this company also owns two small breweries in Payottenland. One, with the unromantic name Brabrux, produces sweetish versions of Lambic beers. The other, De Neve, has more characterful Lambics, sometimes with an almondy dryness.

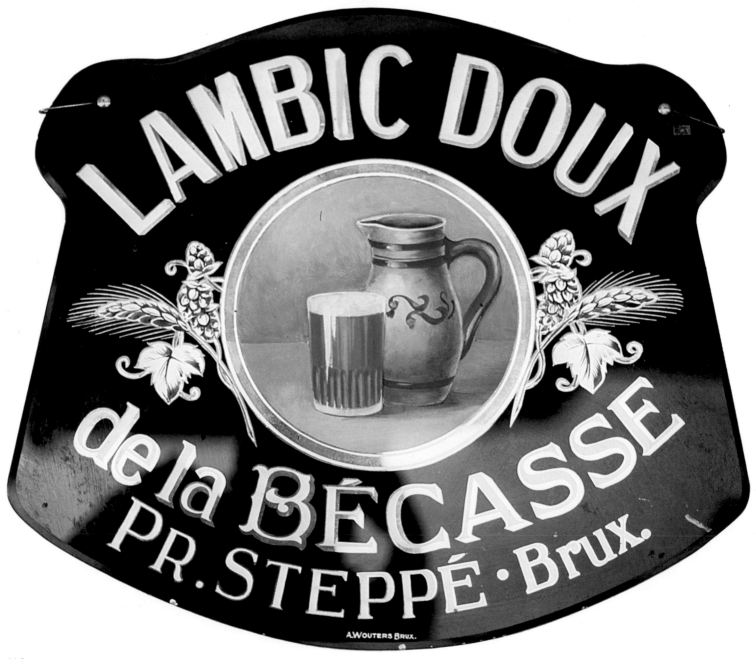

116

Opposite: Open pitchers are still used to decant the beer at the Café Bécasse ("The Woodcock") in Brussels. Much the same arrangement was shown in Bruegel's paintings. A more intense, traditional, Lambic called Bruocsella ("Brussels", in Latin) is offered by Cantillon (*right*). The hearty poster (*below*) for the Lambic family featured in a joint campaign by the Senne Valley brewers in the 1920s. Each brewer overprinted its own name in this remarkably early example of generic advertising. Faro was obviously popular at the time.

One of the larger producers in Payottenland is Timmermans, with fruity, lightly acidic beers. An exporting brewery, albeit on a farmhouse scale, is Lindemans, producing sweetish, clean-tasting beers. Eylenbosch makes young, old and bottled Lambics, a little less dry than they once were. Girardin is a very traditional Lambic brewer with its own fields of the small-grained, reddish-colored Brabant wheat. Its Lambic is clean and soft, with a pleasantly bitter-fruit character.

Experimental attempts have been made to produce Lambic beer elsewhere in Belgium, but the result has never tasted the same. Nor will it, since the combination of microbiological circumstances can never be quite as it is among the 10 old breweries of the Senne Valley. A couple of breweries west of the valley also produce Lambic-based styles but these are not very convincing. The technique involved is to buy surplus casks from Lambic brewers and hope that the wood will have the important resident microflora. An alternative is to buy Lambic beer and blend it with more conventional brews.

There are also five or six Lambic blenders. Because the character of Lambic beer is so greatly shaped by its spontaneous fermentation, and that so influenced by its surroundings, this aspect of production is more important than the brew-house process. The blenders buy wort from brewers, then do their own fermentation. They like to make a comparison with the grower who brings his grapes to someone else's wine press, and comes back with juice to ferment. This is stretching a point: the blenders bring only money, and come back with wort.

De Troch is a small producer, making a full-bodied Lambic, darkish for the style. Vandervelden is another small producer, making good Lambic with some "sour apple" tartness and a hint of pine kernels. Vanderlinden, making a grapefruity Lambic, is a one-man brewery adjoining a typical Payottenland café in Beersel. This village has a moated castle where plays are sometimes performed in summer.

Beersel is a popular spot for an afternoon out, and has several cafés serving Lambic. One, called Drie Fonteinen, matures its own beer. Other examples are the Drie Bronnen and the Oude Pruim. On a fine weekend, the people of Brussels like to take a short drive (or even bus ride) into the Senne Valley, have a walk, and sit down over a Lambic or two, served in simple, fluted tumblers. It is a restful beer, like a pint of English Bitter.

In the capital itself, in the Anderlecht district, which blends into Payottenland, the Cantillon Brewery sometimes bottles straight Lambic from a particularly good cask. These "vintages" are labeled Bruocsella Grand Cru, and can be bought at the brewery. Although Cantillon is a commercial brewery, it is very much a working museum of Lambic (Rue Gheude 56; Tel 5214928). It is also a guardian of the classic Lambic tradition.

GUEUZE

Much Lambic beer is sold not "straight" but in a variety of blended forms. There is a distant analogy with malt whiskey. The most basic blend is between a young Lambic and an old one. The process of blending creates a further fermentation and a degree of natural carbonation. The young Lambic, which still contains some residual sugars, also imparts a degree of balancing sweetness. This blended version is known as Gueuze-Lambic, especially if it is served from a cask.

If the blend has enjoyed its further fermentation in the bottle, it is sometimes identified simply as Gueuze. Flemish is a language of dialects, and the pronunciation of the word Gueuze varies. To describe such a traditional product with a word from the world of computers seems incongruous, but "cursor" is probably as near as any English-speaker can get.

Gueuze might have the same root as the English word "geyser," and may relate to the turbulence of secondary fermentation, but no one is sure. Another theory links the name to that of a Flemish mayor who led resistance to Spanish rule (an echo of Dijon's Mayor Kir, a Communist and anti-Nazi, who inspired an apéritif).

A Gueuze blended from young and two-year-old Lambics might have a further three to nine months of conditioning in the bottle before being released. It will then continue to develop with age for one to two years and a maximum of five. A Gueuze intended for laying down will be corked, and should be stored on its side at 10-15°C (50-60°F). At one to two years, it will have a considerable sparkle, and be medium dry and fruity, perhaps with apple or even rhubarb notes. This latter characteristic can also be found in vermouths. With age, the Gueuze will become drier and more complex. A truly fine Gueuze is especially appreciated with Sunday lunch in a traditional home in the Brussels area.

Some of the most characterful blends come from Moriau, Hanssens and Wets. Perhaps the most sophisticated are produced by a young blender turned brewer, Frank Boon, in Lembeek, the "capital" of the style. Boon uses his best casks in blends that he labels "Mariage Parfait." He learned his trade from the retired Lembeek brewer René De Vits, and bought many of his casks from the former blenders Van Malder, of Brussels.

Most of Brussels's specialty beer cafés take a keen interest in Lambic blends of one kind and another. One is even called Moeder Lambic (Savoie Straat 68, St Gillis). It has a branch specializing in draft beers, also called Moeder Lambic (Boendaalse Steenweg 441, Ixelles).

An easy-to-drink, sweetish blend (identified simply as a Panache) can be tasted at a famous old Gueuze café, the Bécasse, in an alley off Rue Tabora, near the Grand' Place. The beer is traditionally enjoyed with the lactic, creamy Brussels cheese served on bread with radishes. Another famous café, Mort Subite, serves Gueuze of the same name at Rue de Montagne-aux-Herbes, also in the city center. For their style and ambience, these cafés should not be missed. Each is an institution in Brussels.

Mort subite (*above*) means "sudden death" in French, but there is nothing life-threatening about a Gueuze of 5.0 per cent alcohol by volume. The name derives from the Mort Subite Café near the National Bank, Brussels. Staff out for a lunchtime drink and game of dice would switch to a "sudden death" rule if they were needed at the office. A similar story explains the origin of the Italian apéritif Punt e Mes. The Belgians like to joke that Mort Subite is a killer, by punning with the French word for "coffin": "*De bière à bière.*"

Some Lambic breweries, like the Vandervelden "cellar", Beersel (*below*), promote themselves also as working museums. The Old Beersel café (*left*) is next to the brewery. In Itterbeek, Café Sportwereld proudly announces the local product, too (*below left*). *Right*: The cherries head for their second fermentation at the Liefmans brewery.

KRIEK

A Lambic blend may alternatively be given a further fermentation by the addition of whole cherries. The Flemish word for cherry is *kriek.* This style of beer is known as Krieken-Lambic. Sometimes only the word Kriek is used, but this is really insufficient, since some cherry beers are not blended from a Lambic base. A particularly good example is made on a base of Liefmans' Brown Ale. Lambic and other styles are used also as a base for further fermentation with raspberries. This type of beer is known as Frambozen in Flemish, or Framboise in French.

Cherry and to a lesser extent raspberry are traditional, and can produce the world's most elegant beers, often served in Champagne flutes. A good Kriek has an almondy dryness, imparted by the stone of the cherry. A fine Frambozen has an immense bouquet of raspberry, and a delicate sharpness of palate. These are apéritif beers fit for a garden party or a stylish meal.

In recent years, there have been further but sickly variations — made with blackcurrant, peach, banana, and other fruits. These are products not of brewing tradition but of marketing men's daydreams, inspired by the success of sweet liqueurs.

Although the traditional fruits are used as a fermentable material, they also aromatize the beer, and were probably employed for that purpose before hops were universally accepted. These products are not wines, but beers, because the fruit is used on a base of fermented barley and wheat.

The traditional method is to use whole fruit, preferably cherries from the Schaarbeek growing region, near Brussels. Although few cherries are grown there these days, there are still sufficient to find their way into the better Kriek beers. Some brewers even have arrangements to pick cherries from trees in the gardens of private houses. Schaarbeek has its own variety of small, dark, dry-tasting cherry. This is allowed to ripen, and perhaps later to dry, until it is almost prune-like, its fermentable sugars concentrated.

The fruits are picked in late July and early August. Some brewers add them to straight Lambic, others to Gueuze. The beer stays on the cherries until September or October at the latest. If it is kept there longer, the cherry-stone bitterness will be too great. Elderberries are sometimes also used, for their color. When the fruit has fermented, there may be a further blending with additional beer. The beer may then be bottle-conditioned for a further five or six months before it is released. Sometimes fruits are stored so that a second batch can be made. This is known as "late-bottled" beer. Some producers print on the cork the years when the beer was brewed and the cherries picked.

Every brewer has his or her own methods, and there are many variations. Some first make their fruits into a syrup, which they call a coulis. Others use essences, and produce beers with a bonbon sweetness. If real fruit is used, the additional fermentable sugars will slightly increase the strength of the beer. This also varies, but is typically in a range of between 4.25 and 5.25 by weight (5.3-6.5 by volume).

The best producers of Gueuze generally make a good Kriek or Frambozen. Lindemans is one of the best-known producers of Kriek, and Boon makes some outstanding examples. Cantillon is noted for its Frambozen, especially a still version called Rosé de Gambrinus. This also contains a proportion of cherries.

Rosé de Gambrinus is a doubly vintage-dated Frambozen (Framboise). The earlier date indicates the time of the brewing, the later the year of the raspberry harvest. There are approximately 350g of raspberries in each 75cl bottle. The farmhouse brewery of Lindemans depicts the raspberries on its Frambozen and the cherries on its Kriek, but others are more flamboyant.

Opposite: Faro was seen as the Father of Beers in the early 1800s, when this illustration was produced by the caricaturist De Loose. Several of the styles listed in its caption still exist and some, like Pauwel Kwak, have even been revived. *Below right*: Pertotale is the Faro of the Frank Boon brewery.

FARO

The oldest extant style of blended Lambic, called Faro, is made with the addition of sugar or caramel. Often, sugar is used in the brown crystal form provided with coffee in fancy restaurants and hotels. "Candy sugar" in this form, either brown or white, is a material that has traditionally been employed by brewers in Belgium. In Faro, its role is to create a "sweet and sour" beer.

Some cafés serving a very sour straight Lambic will offer with it sugar and a muddler, providing a do-it-yourself Faro. Several of the Lambic brewers also produce a ready-made Faro, though it is today a minor style. If the brewer does the blending, the sugar will eventually ferment out. This is not a problem in a quick-turnover draft Faro, but it means that the bottled version is usually pasteurized to prevent further fermentation. Some Lambic producers do make this bottled, pasteurized type, including Lindemans and Boon. Also, some conventional brewers use the term "Faro" simply to indicate a sweet, dark beer with no real claims to the style.

The antiquity of the style can be judged from the name, which is thought to derive from the time of Spanish rule. Some brewers of the product see its name as coming from the Latin *farina,* implying a grain-based drink, a "Barley Wine." In modern Spanish, *faro* is a familiar word meaning "idea."

Although it does not resemble a British Barley Wine, Faro probably was once stronger. A variation that is no longer served was diluted with unfermented wort, or simply water. This was called Mars, though no one is sure why.

In the days of Spanish rule, Flanders was a far-flung territory, its towns fragmented and isolated. The Lambic variations did not reach Brussels until the mid-1700s. As the city grew, they were on its doorstep, and at the beginning of this century Faro was the everyday beer of Brussels, as Mild Ale was in London or Dark Lager in Munich. Between achieving its modern nationhood and being dragged hither and thither in two world wars, Belgium was late in adopting "modern" brewing methods.

That, and the Flemish sense of independence, are no doubt the reasons for the persistence of Mother Lambic and her family amid the flood of mass-marketed Pilsener-style beers. It is a remarkable survival.

DEDIÊ AUX BRASSEURS, NÈ

FARO REGALE SES AMIS À L'OCCASION
Notez Bien, Ces bières jusqu'a la premiere Separation sont de Bruxelles   Gand et les de
A. Père Faro. B. Susse Lambic. C. Jef Half en half D. Lieven
Liere   Hoegaerde   Termonde
I. Janneken Kavesse. K. Pié Hoegaerds. Pauwel Kwak. L. Med

CIANTS DE BIÈRE, CABARETIERS ET À TOUT LE MONDE.

FARO HOUDT FEEST TER GELEGENHEYD VAN DEN VREDE.

LA PAIX

t. E. Karel — Pays de

ines

n-Bruynen. — Depose

Waes.
Drydraed. F. Tonne Leuvens G. Lamme Peeterman. H. Luppe Diest Diesters.

Anvers
M. Signor Geersten-bier N. Colas brune. O. Bruynen Bacchus. & &
Louvain Pays Wallon Ypres.

White Beer

THE ORANGE MUSCAT of the beer world? There is both an orangey character and a remarkably Muscat-like, honeyish aroma to the style of "White" Wheat Beers historically associated with the eastern part of the province of Brabant. These are undoubtedly Belgium's dessert beers, and they fulfill that role better than any in the world.

Fruity, pale Wheat Beers in a variety of local versions were once widespread in the east of Brabant. There were more than 30 White Beer brewers in the valley around the small town of Hoegaarden during the 1700s, but the last closed in 1954. A dozen years later, an enthusiast, Pieter Celis, salvaged an old brew-house and set about restoring the style. His brewery De Kluis ("The Cloister" or "The Hermitage") and his Hoegaarden White Beer captured the imagination of young drinkers. The beer became very fashionable. Before long, the old equipment was in a museum, and today De Kluis has a modern, but very handsome, brew-house. Expansion has been so demanding that De Kluis is now financially backed by Artois.

The old Hoegaarden beers had a pronounced lactic character, like that of Berliner Weisse. Today's product is not so obviously lactic, but it is distinctive enough, and has inspired one or two keen emulators. It is also exported. In English-speaking markets, it is identified as Hoegaarden White. (The name of the town is pronounced "who garden.") In Flemish, it is known simply as Oud Hoegaards, and identified as a Witbier. In French, it is described as a Bière Blanche.

Oud Hoegaards is brewed from 45 per cent wheat. It contains also oats, to a proportion of five per cent. The wheat and oats are raw, and the remainder of the mash is barley malt. The gravity is a conventional 12 Plato (1048), and the beer has an alcohol content of 3.8 by weight, 4.8 by volume. The use of oats is old-fashioned and unusual, and perhaps adds a hint of oily smoothness, but Hoegaards's distinctive features do not end there. More significant is the spicing of the beer with Curaçao orange peels, coriander and a third "secret" ingredient. Cumin seeds, perhaps? A top-fermenting yeast is used. After the primary fermentation, the beer is bottle-conditioned with a different culture. When it is very young, the beer has a little lactic sourness, but it gains a "demi-sec" honey character within a couple of months. It is intended to retain some of its "white" cloudiness, though this clears with time to a shimmering quality that the brewers call a "double shine."

A similar beer, aromatic and pale but made solely from barley malt and to a higher gravity (18.4; 1076; 6.0 per cent alcohol by weight; 7.0 by volume), is called Hoegaarden Grand Cru. This noble, complex beer will evolve in character for three to four years. These beers should be stored and served at 12°C (53-54°F).

Hoegaarden also makes a slightly darker Wheat Beer, of conventional gravity, called Echte Peeterman — as well as several other colorful, spicy strong specialties. *Echte* means "genuine," and the

The rescued brew-house at Hoegaarden in 1966 (*above left*) and the scene there 20 years later (*left*). The community named a street after the famous "White" Beer. *Above*: The same brewery's pale Grand Cru is a classic in its own right, and its Forbidden Fruit is a deliciously spicy, strong dark ale seasoned with coriander.

name Peeterman is a reference to the parish saint of the city of Leuven (in French, Louvain). Peeterman was the name given to an old style of Wheat Beer once widely made in Leuven.

The last Peeterman to be produced in Leuven faded from the scene in the late 1970s. Another was made nearby in Lubbeek until well into the mid-1980s. In the same part of the country, a sweet, cidery, very cloudy beer called Dubbel Wit is made by the De Kroon brewery, at Neerijse. Leuven for the moment does not have an entrant, though the Domus brew-pub, opened in the mid-1980s, will surely revive the style. Perhaps some brewer will try to produce it with figs as a fermentable material. Within

living memory, a Leuven White Beer was brewed in that way.

In the Hoegaarden style, there are two further examples, both made on the opposite side of the country, in West Flanders. The Riva brewery, at Dentergem, makes a Witbier with a lot of sweet, apple-honey character. A version of this has been exported under the name Wittekop. The yeasty, cloudy Brugs Tarwebier (Bruges Wheat Beer) is made in that city by the Gouden Boom brewery. In East Flanders, the less spicy Oudenaarde's Witbier is made in that town by Clarysse.

Red Beer

IF COLOR WERE the only criterion, the popular soubriquet "The Burgundy of Belgium" would best be applied to the highly-distinctive Rodenbach beers, made in the province of West Flanders. As Burgundy suggests not only a color but also a particular aroma, palate, and texture, the comparison is incomplete. In aroma and palate, the Rodenbach products have a hint of Madeira, and perhaps even of passionfruit, and in texture they are light-to-medium, with an intention to refresh, but their defining characteristic is their sourness, with not only lactic but also acetic notes.

Rodenbach is the name both of a family that founded a brewery in the town of Roeselare and of that company's products. It is a registered brand-name, and cannot be used by any other brewer to identify a beer of similar style. No one else can therefore say "Type Rodenbach" on a label, though brewers can whisper it to define the style of their products. There is no recognized designation, though the Rodenbach brews and several others in the region could be described as sour Red Beers of a style that belongs to West Flanders. Rodenbach might also be regarded as a variety of Old Ale.

Among the Red Beers, Rodenbach is the undisputed classic, made by the most traditional method. The red color comes in part from the use of Vienna malts, but a greater contribution is from the tannins and caramels of the massive, vertical tuns of uncoated oak in which Rodenbach beer is matured, and in which it gains its distinctive sourness. These vessels make a remarkable sight, reaching from floor to ceiling. The smallest contains 15,000 liters of maturing beer, the largest 60,000. There are almost 300 of them, filling ten or a dozen halls, as though this were a winery or a brandy distillery.

Only a handful of breweries anywhere in the world use the unusual procedure of aging their beer in uncoated wood, and none has such a forest of tuns as Rodenbach. It is a unique brewery, a living phenomenon of beer's history. The brewery has had its ups and downs; it is to be hoped that its tuns are not permitted to become "too costly" to maintain, like Bass's Burton Union System in England.

The basic Rodenbach is made by the classic old method of blending young and matured beers. Seventy-five per cent of the blend is young beer, though even this has five to six weeks of maturation, during which period it undergoes a secondary fermentation. This takes place in metal tanks.

The young beer is brewed to a gravity of 11.4-11.5 Plato (1045-6). The beer intended for aging has 13.0 (1052). Four varieties of malt are used, and 20 per cent corn grits. A double decoction mash is employed. Hopping is with Brewers' Gold and Kent Goldings, though much of their character is lost in the aging process. This is not intended to be a hoppy beer. An important contribution to palate is made by the Rodenbach yeast, which is an amalgam of at least five strains.

After secondary fermentation, the beer intended

The ceiling-high oak tuns (*left*) are the essential ingredient in Rodenbach as well as in Grand Cru and Alexander. The maintenance and rebuilding of the tuns, using numbered staves, is a major task for the brewery.

for further maturation goes on to spend not less than 18 months, and sometimes well over two years, in wood. During this time, there is a third sequence of microbiological activity, caused by lactobacilli and acetobacters. The lactic acid develops in the beer, and the acetobacters are resident in the wood.

Although much of the matured beer is used in the blending of the regular Rodenbach, some is held back to be bottled "straight" as Grand Cru. This beer is so tart that it is sweetened slightly with sugar before being flash-pasteurized. It is not intended for laying down. Some of its admirers would welcome an unsweetened, unpasteurized version, perhaps to a slightly higher gravity.

The regular Rodenbach is a tasty, sour-and-sweet, refreshing beer but the Grand Cru has a bigger character all round. Like many "old" beers, it has its own distinctive freshness — a paradox of brewing. That freshness is sustained throughout, especially in the powerful bouquet, but also in the "passionfruit" palate and the long finish. There is a teasing complex

of fruity freshness and older, Madeira-like notes. Although the whole point of these beers is their tartness, some drinkers sweeten them with a dash of Grenadine syrup. For its 150th anniversary, the brewery made a sweeter version named Alexander, after its founder. This blends some of the freshness of the Grand Cru with a cherry flavor. The Regular Rodenbach has an alcohol content of 3.7 per cent by weight, 4.6 by volume. The Grand Cru and the Alexander have 4.1, 5.2.

Several breweries in West Flanders produce beers that are broadly similar in style, though none has the same extent of wood aging, or the depth of character. These products include Paulus, Bacchus, Vichtenaar and the sweet Bourgogne de Flandres. A drier, more lactic example with a confusingly similar name and a longer pedigree is Vlaamse Bourgogne, from Bios, in East Flanders.

Brown Beer

THE WORLD'S MOST complex Brown Beer, in a style that might loosely be regarded as an Old Ale, is made by Madame Rose Blancquaert-Merckx and her son in the lovely, old Liefmans brewery (which traces its origins to 1679), in the historic town of Oudenaarde, in the province of East Flanders.

Like West Flanders, the eastern province has a tradition of sourish beers. On both sides of the provincial border, these beers have tended to become less sour over the years, to meet the alleged public taste for sweeter products. The boundary between the styles is a fuzzy one. In general, those from East Flanders are the least sour. Their color tends to be less reddish, more of a brown hue. Madame Rose's classic example is bottle-conditioned. The center for their production is the area around Oudenaarde, which once had 20 breweries. There are still two or three in the Oudenaarde area, another three or four in striking distance, and about 10 beers being made in broadly this style in Belgium as a whole.

Madame Rose, as she is always known, makes by far the finest of these sour-and-sweet Brown Ales, and the defining classic of the style. Madame Rose, after studying theater and ballet, joined the company as a secretary and eventually found herself running it, seeing it through turbulent times and winning a great following for its beer.

The brewery has a remarkable amount of copper, not just in its kettles but also in its fermenting and blending vessels. The Liefmans beers are of the type made from a blend of young and old. They are brewed from four types of malt and a similar number of hop varieties, and undergo a most unusual procedure in the kettle: they are simmered for a whole night. Lengthy boiling, though not this long, is a feature of Lambic production, with its turbid mash. Why it should be done in the case of a Brown Ale, no one knows, but it always has been. The beer is pitched with a yeast that has some lactic character. After fermentation, it is matured at ambient temperatures in metal tanks.

The basic Liefmans has six weeks' maturation in tanks, and is blended with a smaller proportion of beer that has been aged for eight to ten months. It has an original gravity of around 12 Plato (1048) and an alcohol content of 3.7 by weight, 4.6 by volume. The older beer is bottled "straight" as Liefmans Goudenband (Gold Riband). It has a gravity of about 13 Plato and an alcohol content of 4.4; 5.5. Goudenband is bottle-conditioned (without a dosage) in the brewery's own *caves*. It is intended to be laid down, and reaches its peak at about two years.

For a dark Old Ale, Goudenband has an elegant, spritzy character. It has a great depth of flavor, with Montilla notes and sometimes a hint of dry cherry. Perhaps the latter is suggested by the brewery's Kriek. Liefmans also has a Frambozen. These are wonderful apéritif beers.

The town of Oudenaarde also has Brown Ales from Cnudde and Clarysse, the latter under the Felix label, and in a less sour style from the nearby Roman brewery. Similar beers are made in the area by the artisanal breweries of Crombé, in Zottegem, and Van Den Bossche, in St Lievens-Esse.

Madame Rose's Mighty Brew

Clarity, aroma, palate…? Madame Rose Blanquaert-Merckx (*left*) likes to check the maturity of each batch herself before agreeing that it can be released. Her classic brews have their final maturation in the bottle in the cellars at Oudenaarde. The beers are available in a variety of oversized bottles, including (*right*) Nebuchadnezzars for very good customers. A Nebuchadnezzar contains enough beer to fill 20 normal bottles. Liefmans' classic is its Goudenband Brown Ale, but the brewery produces also a Kriek and a Frambozen. *Below*: A tax document, dated 1679, testifies to the antiquity of the brewery.

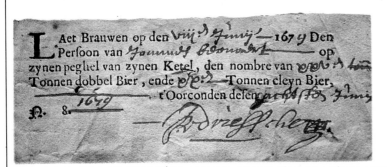

Saison

SEASONAL BEERS for summer, or harvest time, are usually low, or at least modest, in alcohol and light-to-medium in body. Modesty can be measured only against what is deemed to be conventional behavior. Lovers of specialty beers in Belgium are accustomed to drinking strong, heavy brews even in warm weather.

Saisons are the summer and harvest specialties for French-speaking Belgium, the area sometimes known as Wallonia. In particular, they are made in Hainaut, and especially in the western part of that province and the bordering areas. There are about a half-dozen breweries in this stretch of countryside, and perhaps twice as many Saisons to be found in Belgium as a whole.

In tradition, and to some extent in style, these are top-fermenting counterparts to the Märzenbiers of Germany. Saisons vary greatly in gravity, from 13 to 20 Plato (1052-80). At the lower end, they might have an alcohol content of 4.5 by weight, 5.6 by volume; at the upper end, 6.0 (7.5). The characteristics of the style are a powerful car-bonation; a creamy soft texture; a full orange color; a very fruity, citric sourness; sometimes a hint of iron; and often spicy notes.

Saisons tend to have a crystal malt character, but this is very well attenuated. Some interesting yeasts would seem to be used in these beers, and they usually have some weeks of maturation. All are warm-conditioned, often in both tank and bottle, and some also have a period of cold conditioning. In some, spices such as licorice root are added. They represent a minor style, but within it are some well-respected beers.

The most widely marketed example is Saison Regal, from the very commercially oriented Du Bocq brewery, which has a huge portfolio of brands. Despite having its attention thus diverted, Du Bocq produces a pleasant Saison. The best example of the style is the bottle-conditioned Saison Dupont Vielle Reserve, which is on the dry side and very complex. Other good bottle-conditioned Saisons are Voisin, Pipaix, La Châtelaine, Lefèbvre 1900, Silly (the name of a place, which does not seem funny in French) and its stronger companion Double Enghien. Most are bottled with a drawn cork.

Flanders has no similar style but, in its name and its label design, a beer called Sezoens makes its own allusion. Sezoens is a brand-name, not a style. The beer is made by Martens, in Limburg. It is a lovely beer, a golden, very hoppy, top-fermenting brew of 13.5 Plato (1054). Another Flemish beer of a similar character is Straffe Hendrik, from Bruges.

Two of the most antiquated artisan breweries in Belgium, both making delightful products. Crombé (*left*), at Zottegem, specializes in brown beers. *Right*: The malt mill of Brasserie à Vapeur, a brewery known for its Saison Pipaix, which contains a considerable selection of spices. When the last owner retired the brewery was acquired by two schoolteachers, both Greens. Their first label was less elaborate than its predecessor. *Below*: The Crombé brewery tap.

Specialties

THE INDIVIDUALITY OF Belgian beers is, in all senses, staggering. Apart from those specialties that fit into clear families (the Lambics, the White Beers, the Flemish sour variations, the Saisons, the abbey beers), there are many others that do not. Being top-fermenting (whether spontaneous or not), all of these categories could loosely be described as ales. Sometimes the English-language word "ale" is even used on labels in Belgium. Beers described in this way are usually copper-colored, with a gravity of 12-13.5 Plato (1048-54), top-fermenting, fruity, perhaps sweetish, sometimes spicy. That style of brew is often identified simply as Spéciale in a café.

Beyond those, there are a number of brews that are broadly ales but not labeled as such, in a wide variety of gravities, colors, and moods. Some of these are so distinctive as to constitute a style in themselves. The Flemish beer-writer Peter Crombecq, in his book *Biersmaken*, divides Belgian brews into 19 styles, 16 of them top-fermenting, and still fails to position some of the classics. Small wonder, the Belgian brewers would say: every beer is its own specialty.

BELGIAN ALES

The presence of British troops in Belgium during two world wars probably gave the country its taste for Stouts and Scottish and English Ales. Several of these are still produced under license, often to a significantly higher gravity than they would offer in their home country. There are also ales with British names that are the creations of Belgian brewers. These British-style products probably introduced the English word "ale," but Belgium already had its own, similar, top-fermenting brews.

There is a particular concentration of brewers in this style not far from Brussels, beyond Payottenland, in the northwest corner of the province of Brabant, between the main roads to Ghent and Antwerp. The Artois subsidiary Martinas produces Ginder Ale at Merchtem. De Smedt makes the soft, lightly fruity, rather "English-tasting" Op Ale at Opwijk. Palm produces several ales at Steenhuffel. Its basic ale, well rounded, with a clean, citric character, is Spéciale Palm. A less characterful sister product is called Spéciale Aerts. This has a big brother called Aerts 1900, with a higher gravity (17.5; 1070; 5.9; 7.4), that is also dry-hopped.

One of Belgium's classic ales, though its name makes no reference to any style, is De Koninck, produced in the province and city of Antwerp. De Koninck is Antwerp's local brew, and discerning drinkers in the city are rightly proud of it. De Koninck is an all-malt, top-fermenting beer of 12 Plato (1048), brewed by direct flame in a cast-iron kettle. It is cold-conditioned and emerges with an alcohol content of just over 4.0; 5.0. De Koninck is best sampled in its draught form. Opposite the brewery, at the Pilgrim Café (Boomgardstraat 8), drinkers sometimes add a sprinkle of yeast to the beer. This is hardly necessary; it already has a yeasty,

fruity aroma, with some very distinctive malt notes and a Saaz hop character. In the heart of Antwerp, the beer is available at the city's oldest café, Quinten Matsijs (Moriaan Straat 17). It is a perilously drinkable brew.

STRONG GOLDEN ALES

The Devil features in the names of several Belgian beers, and in a variety of spellings. Duvel is one. This is another example of a beer that has no designation of style on its label, at least in the Belgian market. It is also a good example of a Belgian beer that is a style in itself, and widely imitated. Its emulators usually have brand-names implying devilment. Examples are Lucifer, Teutenbier and Deugniet.

The devilish name is appropriate. This remarkable, beguiling beer looks, and at first sip may

Belgian ales (*left* and *top right*) and British-style favourites past and present (*above*). Belgian brewers like Lamot were once proud to feature British-style ales and Stouts, made to a higher gravity than was common in London, Burton or Edinburgh. In contrast, when continental lagers are produced under licence in Britain they are often reduced in specification.

maltings, and can maintain a very precise control over specification.

There is also the question of the brewery's yeast, and the very rigorous process of fermentation and conditioning. A pure-culture, single-cell yeast is used. The strain was one of 20 isolated in the 1930s from a McEwans yeast by the great Belgian brewing scientist Jean De Clerck. The beer is top-fermented, then cold-conditioned at 0°C (32°F) for two to three weeks. It is then bottled, with some further yeasting, and warm-conditioned for a week or two so that the yeast can create a secondary fermentation in the bottle. It is then cold-conditioned in the bottle at 3°C (38°F) for a further month or more.

The classic, bottle-conditioned version of Duvel has a red label. A green-label version is filtered. The classic Duvel should be stored at 14°C (57°F), or a little less, and will express its character most fully if it is served at that temperature. After three months, and no more than six, it will have reached its peak. Its aroma should offer Saaz hops (the beer has 31 units of bitterness), a clean, soft maltiness, and a fruity hint of Poire William. Top-fermenting ales will not normally stand up to being served well chilled, but Duvel does, and is often presented in this form. Neither are brandies usually chilled, but an *alcool blanc*, like Poire William, is, of course.

STRONG DARK ALES

Belgium has as many strong dark ales as Burgundy has appellations. Two of the classics are produced in Mechelen by the brewery Het Anker. This company's local specialty, Mechelsen Bruynen (16 Plato; 1064; 5.2; 6.5), is worthy of a wider exposure, but tends to be overshadowed by its big brother Gouden Carolus (19 Plato; 1076; 5.6; 7.0).

Both of these beers have a deep, Burgundy color. They are rich and sweet, creamy in texture, complex in palate, with a big, malty aroma and only a light hop character. They are bottle-conditioned, and the Gouden Carolus will benefit from six months' storage. The brewery recommends it be kept at 15°C (59°F). The company also issues "vintage" batches that have already been bottle-matured for a year at the brewery. The city of Ghent, in East Flanders, has an amber strong ale, spiced with anis, called Stropken (17.5 Plato; 1070; 5.5; 6.75). This is produced for the specialty beer café Hopduvel (Rokerel Straat 10) by the Slaghmuylder brewery. East Flanders has also the licorice-tasting dark brown Pauwel Kwak (18.5 Plato; 1074; 6.8; 8.5).

even taste, wholly innocent. It has an extremely pale, golden color (6.5 E.B.C.) and a soft, light palate. It also has a gravity of 17.5 (1070) and an alcohol content of 6.8 per cent by weight, 8.2 by volume. Its deceptive lightness derives in part from the very pale malt used. As might be expected, two-row barley is used. The brewery (near the old city of Mechelen, in the province of Antwerp) has its own

Three student brothers who began making beer at home as a hobby acquired this 1840s brewery (*left*) when the owner fell ill. The three are now in the professions but, led by architect Kris (*below*), the family still runs the brewery on a part-time basis.

The Materfamilias (*above*) is a keen participant in the venture. The products are all strong ales, including the award-winning Oerbier, honeyish Boskeun, hoppy Arabier and high-gravity Stille Nacht (8 per cent alcohol by volume). The family call their company The Mad Brewers.

West Flanders has a whole selection of strong ales from De Dolle Brouwerij ("The Mad Brewers"), at Esen, near Diksmuide. This family of enthusiasts rescued an old brewery, restored it, and work at weekends to produce specialties like the deeply Burgundy-colored, luscious, smooth smoky Oerbier, with 6.0 per cent alcohol by weight, 7.5 by volume. De Dolle Brouwerij welcomes visitors (Tel 051-502781), and provides a lively insight into the artisan style of Belgian brewing.

The strongest brew in Belgium is called simply Bush Beer. This is nothing to do with the German and American Busch breweries. With the Belgian penchant for English ale-names, the brewery's owners, who are called Dubuisson, decided to translate theirs. *Buisson* in French is "bush" in English. Bush Beer is very similar in style to an English Barley Wine. It is even hopped with Kent Goldings. It has a gravity of 24 Plato (1096), enjoys ten to twelve weeks of lagering, and emerges with an alcohol content that has provided analyses in the band of 9.28-9.76 by weight 11.6-12.2 by volume. It is not pasteurized, but nor is it bottle-conditioned. It is a clear, copper-red beer, with a chewy, nutty palate and a hoppy finish. The brewery is on the Brussels-Lille road at Pipaix, in the province of Hainaut, and this mighty beer is its sole product.

All of these strong dark ales should be served at a natural cellar temperature. Most are presented in a *copita* or goblet.

Abbey Beers

IN THE ABBEYS OF FRANCE, the monks may prefer to earn their daily bread by making Montélimar nougat or Chartreuse liqueur, but in the beer lands of Belgium and the Netherlands, Germany and Austria, there can be no doubt as to which path they should follow. In Belgium, some also make cheese and bread. In Germany, some not only brew beer but also make fruit brandies; that is perhaps being too liberal. The Germans and the Austrians have not been sufficiently zealous to develop their own monastic style of beer.

Only in the five abbey breweries of Belgium and the one (in the adjoining province of North Brabant) in the Netherlands have monks developed their own classic style. As these six are all Trappist abbeys, that is the stylistic designation given to their beers. Only they may use the terms *Trappistenbier* and *Bière des Pères Trappistes*.

As a means of raising funds for their own support or for pastoral work, other monasteries in Belgium commission commercial brewers to make beers for them, or licence their names, and they generally offer the same style of product, but theirs should properly be identified as *Abdijbier* or *Bière d'Abbaye*. These terms are also used loosely to describe beers in the same style made by commercial brewers and dedicated to former abbeys or hermitages in their localities. Every café in Belgium wants to have an "Abbey Beer," and every brewer wants to make one. Although those made in the Trappist monasteries are the classics, there are some excellent abbey beers of less holy origin.

In all countries where there are abbey breweries, the monks tend to have at least one strong specialty. This may simply derive from the idea that a monastery is a special place in which to brew, and should offer a beer which reflects that. It is more likely, though, to derive from the tradition of brewing a full-bodied beer that could serve as "liquid bread" during Lent.

In the days when most water was not safe to drink, monks brewed to meet their own needs. The tradition grew in times when the only travelers were pilgrims and the only inns run by monks. They brewed beer for their guests, to accompany their meals. Monks made beer in all of the traditional brewing nations until the Reformation, and continued to do so in Catholic countries until Napoleon enforced secularization. Afterwards, the keenest re-started.

The abbey of Orval, one of today's brewing monasteries in Belgium, traces its history to 1070, and enjoyed an important position in European monastic life in the 1600s. Napoleon brought that to an end, and monastic brewing in Belgium began again in 1836, at Westmalle.

When the church was the principal clearing-house for knowledge and education, monks were the first brewing scientists. Belgium's greatest brewing scientist, Jean De Clerck, was buried at the abbey of

Scourmont, in Chimay. One of his notable followers has been Father Théodore, who made Chimay into a great brewery and is now in semi-retirement.

Within the tradition of making full-bodied brews, the Belgian abbeys have stayed on the path of top-fermentation, the specialty of their country. They have also pursued the Belgian tradition of bottle-conditioning. Some, though by no means all, abbey beers also gain a part of their character from the Belgian practice of using candy sugar, in this instance as a fermentable material rather than purely a sweetener.

The popularity of candy sugar derives from the agricultural background of Belgian brewing. In a small fragmented country, farms have traditionally been little and have worked from a modest capital without elaborate equipment. Beet is widely grown, and farmers traditionally extracted their own sugar by making a syrup and allowing it to crystallize on stretched threads of cotton or linen. If the syrup is allowed to caramelize, it produces brown crystals. If not, the crystals are white. This very basic technique of refining continues today on an industrial scale. It is a method that leaves a lot of flavor in the sugar, in the form of proteins and salts.

Candy sugar was originally used, especially by farmhouse brewers, because of its availability. Its use has continued not only for that reason but because of the characteristics it imparts to beer. All candy sugar seems to contribute to head retention, aroma, texture and flavor. The dark type imparts a rum-butter note. The pale type is used in the dosage for Champagne and other sparkling wines, as well as the typically bottle-conditioned specialty beers of Belgium. Although the sugar is highly fermentable, its still leaves some flavor. In some of the strong beers made in Belgium, so much alcohol is formed that it inhibits fermentation, leaving behind plenty of residual sugar.

The style meant in Belgium by "Abbey Beer" is a strong, full-bodied, top-fermenting ale, always bottle-conditioned, usually with plenty of residual sugar. Within that overall style, there are a number of sub-categories, and each of the Trappist abbeys has its own interpretations.

Each also has its own attitude to the outside world. The abbey of Orval is something of a tourist attraction, with ruins to see and a gift shop selling beer, cheese and fresh-baked bread, but the present-day cloister may not be visited except by prior arrangement. Nor is that possible for casual visitors to any of the monasteries, though some, notably Chimay, admit guests who pre-arrange to spend a few days there at a "retreat." All supply a café, restaurant or auberge nearby, in some cases owned by the abbey, but these are well separated from the monasteries. All will accept pre-arranged visits to their brew-house (at least by males) but with varying degrees of reluctance. In the breweries, a brother in his habit will often work alongside secular employees, of whom there are a growing number.

WESTMALLE

The Trappist abbey of Westmalle, in the province of Antwerp, was the first of today's generation to brew, but initially produced beer only for the consumption of its own brothers. It started to sell its beer in its own village in 1872, but did not operate on a commercial scale until about 1920. Although its beer has been sold to the public for more than 100 years, and is very well known, Westmalle goes about its business quietly. Behind high, red-brick walls, the present turn-of-the-century monastery edifice appears sternly through the elm trees. The brew-house is in a striking 1930s building.

Like most of the abbeys, it has a beer of modest gravity brewed primarily for the brothers to drink with their meals. This beer, of 11 Plato (1044), has an alcohol content of about 3.4 per cent by weight, 4.25 by volume. It is a pale, golden top-fermenting beer, very aromatic and dry and quite delicious. In addition to this basic beer, the abbey produces for commercial sale a stronger (16 Plato; 1064; 5.2; 6.5) beer called Westmalle Dübbel. This "double" version has a dark, amber-brown color and a rich maltiness that gives way to a hoppy dryness in the finish. The abbey is best known for a third, yet stronger, beer called Westmalle Tripel.

This "triple" has a gravity of 20 Plato (1080) and an alcohol content of 6.4; 8.0. It reverts to the pale style. It is a very distinctive beer, combining its high gravity and top-fermentation with the exclusive use of Pilsener malts, but chaptalised with pale candy sugar. The beer is hopped with English Fuggles, a number of German varieties, and Saaz. It has between one and three months' warm maturation (10°C; 50°F) in tanks, is re-yeasted, primed with invert sugar, then bottle-conditioned for three to four weeks at 20°C (68°F). It is a beer of great complexity, with its faintly citric fruitiness, its roundness and its strength. It seems to peak in condition in six months to a year, though 1927-vintage bottles are still in good condition. It should be stored at 16°C (60°F), and not served at less than 12°C (54°F). A wonderful restorative. With this classic brew, Westmalle inspired a sub-category among abbey-style beer, usually identified as Tripel. Several secular breweries now produce a Tripel. Good examples include Witkap Tripel and Tripel Isebaert.

WESTVLETEREN

The smallest of the abbey breweries is St Sixtus, at Westvleteren, in West Flanders. This abbey has a tiny old brew-house of classical Flemish design, overlooking the hop-growing area of Poperinge. Despite its location, Westvleteren does not produce hoppy beers. Indeed, they are sweet, spicy and fruity. All of its beers are dark, and there are four of them, in ascending order of potency: Double (green crown-cork); Special (red); Extra (blue) and Abbot (yellow).

The Abbot (in Flemish, *Abt*) is one of Belgium's

strongest beers. It has a gravity of 21-22 Plato (1084-88) and an alcohol content in the range of 8.0-9.25 by weight; 9.5-10.5 by volume. It is also one of the most tasty beers, spicy, raisiny and creamy. An after-dinner liqueur among beers, served in the goblet that is always used for the abbey style.

Westvleteren's production is very small. Its beers are available by the case at a sales window at the monastery, and next door at the Café De Vrede. They are hard to find elsewhere, though the abbey does licence commercial production to a nearby brewery. The beers made in the abbey are identified as Westmalle; those from the licensee as St Sixtus. Its St Sixtus Abt 12 (the number refers to the Belgian method of indicating gravity) has an alcohol content of 8.0; 9.5, and a very lively, yeasty, sweet fruitiness, with notes of honeydew melon. A very interesting and satisfying beer in its own right.

CHIMAY

The first monastery to brew on a commercial scale, by far the biggest today and still expanding, is the monastery of Notre Dame, on the hill of Scourmont, at the hamlet of Forges, in the township of Chimay, in the province of Hainaut. The monastery is often known as Scourmont, but the brewery is always called simply Chimay. It is pronounced "she may," which seems singularly inappropriate for a monastery, but no one minds. The monastery is set in woodland in the Ardennes, close to the French frontier.

It was the first of the abbeys to brew commercially, in the 1860s, and it is credited with having introduced the term "Trappist Beer." Both commercially and in its religious works, it is an ambitious abbey. While other monasteries may brew only to support themselves, or to pursue pastoral work in their own community or nation, the brothers of Chimay have carried on their abbey's work in several countries. Chimay produces a classic range of three principal beers, each identified by the color of its crown cork (in French, *capsule*). Its Chimay Red (15.75 Plato; 1063; 5.5; 7.0) sets the house

Phoenix Beer

The chocolaty Grimbergen Dubbel and the drier, more vinous Tripel are produced by the brewery at Jumet for the brothers of a Norbertine abbey to the north of Brussels. St Norbert (1080-1134) was born in the Rhineland and founded his first community at Prémontré, France. He established the abbey at Grimbergen, which is believed to date from 1128. The abbey was destroyed in religious wars, and "rose" again on several occasions. It adopted the Phoenix as its symbol in 1570. These pictures show the church's choir stalls, the cloister, two of the windows and, of course, a vat. Although the story of Christ's own times of solitude and contemplation inspired the hermitages of early monasticism, modern orders derive from the rule of St Benedict (480-547), who founded the abbey of Monte

Witkap Pater peeks through the spokes of the old compressor at the Slaghmuylder brewery. The name alludes to the "White Friars" — ie the Cistercians. The Witkap range are good examples of abbey-style beers from a secular brewery.

Cassino, Italy. The Benedictines eventually became more involved in society; the Norbertines took this further, becoming a pastoral order. The Cistercians (taking their name from the abbey at Cîteaux, Burgundy), sought to restore a sense of austerity, and were followed by the even stricter settlement at La Trappe, also in France.

character, with a reddish-brown color, a notably soft palate, and a hint of blackcurrant. Its Chimay White (17.75 Plato; 1071; 6.3; 8.0) is a quite different beer, with a tawny color, firm, dry and hoppy, and with a quenching acidity. It is a beer of immense finesse. The brewery is very proud of this product, sales of which have grown rapidly, and its production has been extended to the Netherlands, to the Trappist monastery of Schaapskooi. The strongest of the regular range is Chimay Blue (19.62 Plato; 1078; 7.1; 9.0). This reverts to the soft, fruity character that is typical of Chimay. It is vintage-dated and can be laid down. It should be stored at 18°C (64°F), and served at that temperature.

Some admirers find a Zinfandel spiciness in Chimay Blue. Others say that, with age, it gains a port-like character. Analysis has revealed that, after five years, aldehydes occur that are similar to those in port. For those wishing to lay it down, Chimay Blue is also available in a bottle with a drawn cork, under the name Grande Réserve. Other "special editions" have been produced.

ROCHEFORT

Even by the standards of Trappist monks, those at the abbey of St Rémy, at Rochefort, are quiet. Little is heard in public from this monastery brewery, which is known for its strict observance. For some years, its beers were rather variable, but recently its Rochefort 10 (representing Belgian degrees; about 7.2 per cent alcohol by weight; 9.0 by volume) has developed into a splendid beer, with a rich, deep, chocolaty palate. The brewery is in the province of Namur.

ORVAL

Each of the monasteries has its attractive visual features but none is more striking architecturally than Orval, the present buildings of which were designed and constructed in the 1920s and 1930s. It incorporates Romanesque-Burgundian influences, and has a dream-like purity of line.

There is a single-mindedness to the brewery, too. Alone among the abbeys, it produces only one beer. The brewmaster says that Orval likes to do just one thing, and do it to perfection. While it is still recognizably an abbey beer, it is quite different from any of the others, especially in its dryness. It is immensely complex, with a distinctive, orangey color and an intense bitterness, almost sour. It is so distinctive that admirers talk simply of "Le goût d'Orval."

The beer has a gravity of 13.5-14 Plato (1054-6) and an alcohol content in the range of 4.2-4.5 by weight; 5.2-5.7 by volume. It has an all-malt mash, but white candy sugar is used in the kettle. Hallertau hops are used for bitterness, but so are Kent Goldings. There is a further addition of Kent Goldings for aroma. The emphasis on this variety is obviously an important influence on palate, but so is the procedure of fermentation and maturation.

After the primary fermentation, the beer has a secondary for six to seven weeks, at 15°C (59°F). During this period, it is dry-hopped. It is then bottled with a second, multi-strain yeast, and primed with sugar. It is bottle-conditioned at the brewery for two months at 17°C (63°F). It should be stored at a good cellar temperature, around 11°C (52°F), in a dark place (like all beer, but this one is very delicate) and will reach its peak between one and three years. It is heavily sedimented, and should be poured gently. It is an apéritif as powerful as an Italian *amaro*. It would surely win the approval of Orval's first monks, who came from Calabria.

The name means "Valley of Gold." Legend has it that a princess lost a golden ring in a lake in the valley, and said that if God ever returned it to her, she would thank him by building a monastery. When a trout rose from the lake with the ring in its mouth, the princess was as good as her promise.

Orval is near Florenville, in the Belgian province of Luxembourg. There are two Luxembourgs: one is a Belgian province, the other an independent country. The latter, the Grand Duchy of Luxembourg, is just over the border.

THE NETHERLANDS

The idealized Dutch girl in the poster looks as though she might indeed be "always welcome," but the text refers to the beer. It seems to maintain that De Sleutel beer has been consumed for five centuries — an exaggerated claim. The brewery no longer exists; the brand-name is now owned by Heineken.

EVEN THE MOST CASUAL beer-drinker has heard of Heineken, though not everyone can place its country of origin. Heineken is Dutch. It comes from the country popularly called Holland and properly known as the Netherlands, but it is the most internationally marketed of all beers.

Everyone knows about Heineken, perhaps its stablemate Amstel, probably their cheeky rival Grolsch, conceivably also some of the several brands that emerge from Oranjeboom in Rotterdam and the old Three Horseshoes brewery in Breda. It is less well known that the Netherlands has a cluster of smaller old-established breweries, and now a growing number of new micros making beers in quite different styles.

Regular Heineken is an everyday Dutch beer. These are usually lightly fruity, mild interpretations of the Pilsener style of lager, at or around the classic gravity. Traditionally, some Dutch brewers have also produced their own interpretation of the Dortmunder style; most have offered a sweet dark brown lager of low gravity; and several have at the beginning of October released a seasonal Bock (sometimes spelled without the "c" in the Netherlands).

The country has always had some Stouts, but made by bottom-fermentation. For many years, only the Netherlands' lone monastery brewery made top-fermenting beers. Now, there are also Dutch brewers producing Wheat Beers in the German and Belgian styles, the occasional Altbier, a "sweet and sour" ale similar to those from Flanders, and several other top-fermenting specialties.

An everyday beer in the Netherlands is ordered as a Pils. It will have a gravity of around, or very fractionally less than, 12 Plato (1048); 4.0 per cent alcohol by weight, and 5.0 by volume. The bigger brands have a bitterness in the 20-25 range. Some of the smaller brewers go for a more characterful 25-30. Dutch interpretations of the Dortmunder style vary, but are sometimes quite high in gravity. The dark lager — a vestigial memory of the earlier, Munich, style — will usually be identified as Oud Bruin ("Old Brown"). It typically has a gravity of around 9 Plato (1036), with an alcohol content of around 2.8; 3.5, sometimes less. (In some export markets, Heineken has its stronger Special Dark, at 12.3; 1050; 3.9; 4.9.) A Dutch Bock will usually be dark, and often sweet, with a gravity of more than 16 (1064) and an alcohol content of 4.8-5.6; 6.0-7.0.

That was a standard range until the beer revival spread to the Netherlands in the mid-1980s and introduced many new specialties, especially from the new micros.

They are, of course, small beer to Heineken, founded in 1864, in the city of Amsterdam, in the

Below and *bottom*: Amsterdam's "Beer King" shop in Paleisstraat, just behind the Royal Palace, stocks more than 700 brews. There are several such specialists in the Netherlands: another (not shown) is D'Oude Gekroonde Bier en Wijn Winkel, at Huidenstraat, Amsterdam.

The original Mr Heineken went into business in 1864, in Amsterdam, and opened a second brewery in Rotterdam ten years later. The Heineken "beer-brewery company" started to produce a bottom-fermented beer in the "Bavarian" style which was sweeping Europe and North America. In its local Dutch market, Heineken has separate ranges of products under both its own name and the Amstel trademark. It has also minor brands like De Sleutel, Hooijberg and Van Vollenhoven. The De Ridder brewery is operated as a separate entity.

Above: It is on the Meuse, in historic southern cities like Maastricht, that the pre-Lenten Carnival reaches its beeriest proportions.

province of North Holland, by a family that is still a substantial shareholder. Within a decade of its foundation, it was exporting to the Dutch colonies, and it today does more international trade than any brewer in the world. It produces more than 40 million hectoliters of beer each year, in its three Dutch breweries and through about 20 companies elsewhere in the world in which it has a majority stake and 70 or 80 in which it has a minority share, a technical consultancy or merely a licensing agreement.

The regular Heineken is made to a similar specification in most markets. The original is called Heineken Special Export in Britain, where a much lower-gravity version is sold as an everyday lager. Specification is slightly reduced in the United States, where many states insist that a produce of 4.0 per cent alcohol by weight be termed a Malt Liquor.

The Netherlands has a population of only about 14 million, representing a tiny local market for any product, including beer. The provinces of the north are Protestant, cautious, and not given to roistering. Amsterdam, a city apart, has been cosmopolitan and

outward-looking since its golden era as a center of world trade in the 1600s. Other very small countries on the rim of the Continent (notably Denmark) must export (beer, among other things) to thrive, but only the Dutch are actually up to their knees in water. The Dutch trade to survive, and Heineken is one of their most successful exporters.

Heineken remains headquartered in Amsterdam. It finally stopped volume production there in 1988, though the option was kept open to operate a micro-brewery on the site.

A couple of decades earlier, it had bought its neighbor Amstel (named after the river of Amsterdam), and subsequently closed that brewery. Amstel still has its own range of beers, produced with a different yeast. In the Netherlands, Amstel has a "super-premium," all-malt, Pilsener-type beer called 1870. This is a dryish beer, especially in the finish, but is not especially distinctive. In North America, the Amstel brand is especially associated with a hoppy, dry Light Beer. Elsewhere in the world, Amstel is usually a sweetish, spritzy, quenching beer with a light body and not much aroma. When grandfather

Heineken went into the business, he bought a brewery called Hooijberg ("Haystack") which had already been operating for three centuries, though he stayed there for only four or five years. The Hooijberg name is still used for one of the company's several Bock beers. The old Hooijberg site is now occupied by a well known tourist restaurant and hotel, the Port van Cleve. Heineken has been at its present site, not far from the Museum Square, since 1868. In the 1950s, Heineken bought the De Sleutel brewery, which has long ceased to operate, and its brand vestigially survives. Another old brand, represented by an interesting product, is Van Vollenhoven. This is a bottom-fermenting, but tasty, Stout of 16.2 Plato (1065; 4.8; 6.0). It has a rich start and a nice dash of roasty and hoppy dryness in the finish.

In the Netherlands, production is now centered at a large plant in Zoeterwoude, near The Hague, in the province of South Holland, and at s'Hertogenbosch (often abbreviated to Den Bosch), in the Dutch part of Brabant. This province is in the south of the Netherlands, but is north of Belgian Brabant. It is therefore known in full as North Brabant. The Dutch

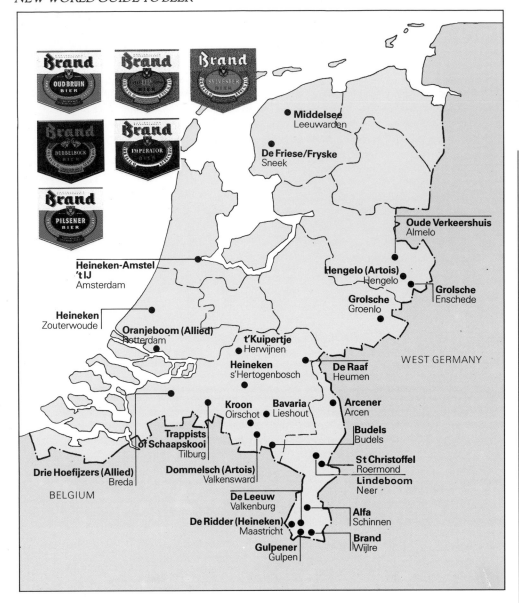

also have a province of Limburg, which borders the Belgian one of the same name. Some distance to the east is the German city of Limburg. All three Limburgs are historically linked.

The south of the Netherlands, especially Dutch Brabant and Limburg, is predominantly Catholic. Those provinces have considerable affinities with the neighboring parts of Belgium and, to a lesser extent, Germany. They are beer-drinking regions, and they have the biggest share of the country's breweries, especially the smaller ones.

South Holland has the Oranjeboom ("Orange Tree") brewery in Rotterdam, and Brabant has the old Drie Hoefijzers ("Three Horseshoes"), in Breda, both owned by Allied, of Britain.

The Oranjeboom beers tend to be the firmer in body of the two, and the Drie Hoefijzers beers more fresh-tasting, but the orientation of these breweries is due less to production than to marketing. At any one time, they may have between them 20-odd brands in the domestic market and more (with Anglo-Dutch names like Royal Post Horn) in export territories. In the specialty market, Drie Hoefijzers has heavily promoted its Klassiek, a reddish-gold top-fermenting brew of conventional gravity, with a slightly syrupy palate and finish. Neither brewery has recovered from a lengthy period of corporate daftness when their names and products were subordinated to Skol,

Allied's forgettable attempt at an international brand.

Allied's portfolio includes also Trappist-style beers under the Koningshoeven name. These are produced under contract by the De Schaapskooi monastery, near Tilburg, also in Brabant. The Koningshoeven beers are perhaps maltier and cleaner in accent than De Schaapskooi's own brews, which are labeled La Trappe. A dark Dubbel (5.2; 6.5) has a sherryish nose, drying out in the palate. A Tripel, full in color for the style, has a yeasty, dryly fruity palate, with some hints of coriander. It has an alcohol content of 6.4; 8.0. Schaapskooi has varied its range over the years, but is a proud brewery, making some characterful products.

Also in Brabant, between Tilburg and Eindhoven, at Oirschot, the very small brewery De Kroon ("The Crown") has among its products a Vienna-style beer called Egelantier. This has a conventional gravity but a full, bronze color, a medium body, and some toffeeish notes. Another very small brewery in Brabant, taking its name from its home village of Budel, has three specialties. Budels Alt is in the Düsseldorf style, but very fruity, and brewed from a highish gravity (13.5; 1054; 4.4; 5.5). Parel is a top-fermenting pale beer of 14 Plato (1056; 4.8; 6.0), but with less character. A beer broadly within the abbey style, called Capucijn (16; 1064; 5.2; 6.5), is most

unusual, with notes of applewood smoke and a sharp texture. This beer is top-fermented, then bottle-conditioned with a lager yeast. Budels also offers a pleasantly hoppy Bock.

There are two larger enterprises in Dutch Brabant. The Swinkels family's Bavaria brewery, in Lieshout, is Dutch despite its name. It has a wide range of labels, and specializes in the supermarket trade. The Belgian giant Artois has the Dommels brewery, in Valkenswaard. This brewery's specialties include a fruity, strong, pale lager called Dominator (4.8; 6.0). Dommels produces the bottom-fermenting beers in the range of the distributor Hertog Jan ("Duke John"). The top-fermenting Hertog Jan beers are produced by Arcen, in Limburg.

Set around the old Hanseatic city of Maastricht, in Limburg, is the tightest cluster of breweries in the Netherlands. Heineken now owns the small De Ridder brewery, in Maastricht. This brewery has as its specialty a creamy, fruity, pale lager called Maltezer (5.2; 6.5).

The nearby village of Gulpen gives its name to one of the most interesting among the old-established independents in the Netherlands. Gulpener has long been known for its super-premium Pilsener, called X-pert, which has a conventional gravity but a lot of Tettnang hop in both aroma and flavor (35 units of bitterness), and six weeks' lagering. While a typical Dutch Pilsener might have 10-25 per cent adjuncts, X-pert is all-malt. This is often true of specialty beers in the Netherlands. Gulpener also has a Dortmunder-type. This has a gravity of 15.5 (1062), an alcohol content of 5.2; 6.5, and an aromatically malty character. The most interesting of Gulpener's products is a revival of an old Maastricht style that seems to have vanished between the wars. The style was known as Mestreechs Aajt, and this is being used as a brand-name by Gulpener.

The brew is a low-gravity counterpart to the reddish Old Ales that are produced across the Belgian border. Gulpener started the process of creating the new beer by exposing to the atmosphere wort that had undergone a primary, but not a secondary, fermentation. This process was carried

When Mestreechs Aajt was first revived, the matured blending beer was aged in wine casks. The result was too vinous, and the brewery commissioned its own, new, oak tuns. The trouble merits the fancy wrap for a distinctive low-gravity beer.

The porcelain-style bottle for Royal Brand Beer makes a very attractive presentation. It is a pleasant beer, too, though Brand has several more interesting products. Within the Pilsener style, Brand UP is a fine brew.

In common with many other countries, the Netherlands underwent a period of considerable temperance activity during the early part of this century. This poster came later, in 1935.

Bottom: Leon Brand is a member of a well known brewing family, but he wanted to fire his own kettle. He found the 80-year-old copper dome in a farmer's barn. Brand makes batches of 15 hectoliters, and lives at the front of the brewery. His Christoffel beer is outstanding.

out not at the brewery but "in a special place." The wort became inoculated with lactobacilli and *Brettanomyces*.

The brewery then spent three years experimenting with secondary fermentations before it found the character it needed. Each of these fermentations took 14-16 months, in wooden barrels. The object was to persuade the lactobacilli and *Brettanomyces* to take up residence in the wood. Once this had been achieved, the required fermentation could be achieved in a year. Beer fermented in this way is then thoroughly filtered, and blended with a proportion of the company's dark lager. The winy, fruity, sourish, wild-fermented beer represents about 25 per cent of the blend. The sweet, brown lager accounts for the rest. The two flavors blend beautifully, without any further fermentation in the bottle. The final alcohol content is 2.8; 3.5, and the beer is presented as a light, but tasty, summer quencher.

There is an irony to Gulpener's intentional production of an acidic beer. In the days before refrigeration, when beer frequently went sour in the barrel during summer, breweries would sell this as vinegar. Gulpener's vinegar was so popular that the company has continued to produce it, albeit by more conventional means. Most brewers would have nightmares about making beer in a plant that also created acetic acid, but at Gulpener the two production facilities are separated by the busiest highway in Europe. Any acetobacters that try to cross the road are likely to end their journey in either Lisbon or Copenhagen. The beer and the vinegar remain safely separated, and the latter is also used to produce a mustard. That a brewery should produce mustard is unusual but not unique. In England, Greene King has such a product. Its East Anglian neighbor Ridley's even has a mustard seasoned with Fuggles hops.

In the Netherlands, the Maastricht area also has the renowned Brand brewery, at Wijlre. There was a brewery in the village of Wijlre in 1340, and one on the present site in 1743. The present business traces its history from 1871. A hundred years later, it was accorded the honor of being able to style itself the

Royal Brand Brewery. This style, bestowed by the Queen of the Netherlands, is greatly prized.

In the summer of 1945, Brand's brewery was put at the disposal of the United States Army, and provided beer for American troops as they advanced toward the Liberation of the Netherlands. Today, the company's regular Pilsener-style beer is marketed in the United States as "Royal Brand Beer," in an opaque white bottle that gives the appearance of being ceramic. Advertisements announce "the royal beer from Holland," and show a line of windmills. Within the Netherlands, Limburg is a province in its own right, as are South and North Holland. It is in the Netherlands, but not in Holland. Nor is it noted for its windmills.

In general, the Pilsener beers from this part of the Netherlands have slightly more character than those from elsewhere. Brand's Pilsener is outstandingly clean, with a hoppy elegance speaking of Hallertau and Hersbruck. It has 28 units of bitterness. Anyone who enjoys this beer, and many do, will find a more assertive character in the company's long-established super-premium Pilsener, Brand UP. The name suggests a soft drink, but the UP stands for Urtyp Pilsener. This is all-malt, with a minimum of six weeks' lagering. It is hopped with Hallertau, Tettnang, Spalt, and Saaz, and has 36 to 37 units of bitterness. It has a soft, aromatic and tasty hop character, with a long dry finish.

Brand also produces a distinctive (in both its amber color and its clean, aromatically malty character) strong beer called Imperator (17.5 Plato; 1075). This has between 5.2 and 5.6 per cent alcohol by weight; 6.5-7.0 by volume. Despite its "-ator," it is a single Bock, and produced year-round. The company also has a newer Double Bock, at 18.5 (1074; 6.0; 7.5). This has a lovely Beaujolais color and a rich palate. Brand's particular specialty is its aromatic, cleanly fruity, very complex, bottle-conditioned Sylvester (18.5; 1074; 6.4; 8.0). This was originally made by a highly unusual procedure: it was bottom-fermented, then given a secondary fermentation with a top yeast. It is now entirely top-fermented, and this is very evident in its character. It is brewed in late August or early September, and released in November. The brewery would like stocks to be exhausted by the end of January.

Just to the north of Maastricht is the brewery De Leeuw ("The Lion"). Its specialties are a soft, notably malty, pale beer of conventional gravity under the name Jubileeuw (originally produced for the brewery's centenary); a well-liked Dortmunder-type called Super Leeuw (13.5; 1054; 4.7; 5.9); and a smooth, dryish, Düsseldorf-style Venloosch Alt. It also offers a distinctively dry, roasty Bock.

The strongest of the Dutch "Dortmunder" types is produced a little farther north in Limburg, where the province slims to a strategic isthmus between Belgium and Germany. At Schinnen, the Alfa brewery makes the sweetish Super-Dort, at 16-16.5 Plato (1064-66), with an alcohol content of 5.6; 7.0.

This brewery's beers are all-malt, balanced with a good Hallertau and Saaz hop character.

One of the driest Pilseners in the world is produced by a new micro-brewery, St Christoffel, named after the patron saint of its home town, Roermond. This former coal-mining town is at the point where the river Roer (Ruhr) flows into the Maas (Meuse). St Christoffel is owned by a member of the Brand brewing family. Its first beer, called simply Christoffel Bier, is an all-malt Pilsener with 43-44 units of bitterness. It is very hoppy indeed in aroma, palate, and finish, with a good Hersbruck character. The beer is marketed in swing-top bottles and two-liter flagons.

A Vienna-style lager called Gouverneur, amber-red, malty, soft, and very easily drinkable, was

launched as a specialty in the mid-1980s by the Lindeboom ("Linden Tree") brewery, at the village of Neer, in the north of Limburg. This small, family-owned, old-established brewery was already well respected for its clean, delicately hoppy Pilsener.

The pioneers of the micro movement in the Netherlands were a group of employees made redundant when Allied closed its small De Vriendenkring ("Circle of Friends") brewery, amid farmers' fields at the village of Arcen, north of Venlo. This town is in the Dutch Limburg but on the end edge of the Rhine-Ruhr conurbation of Germany. The redundant workers, one of whom was a brewer, managed to buy De Vriendenkring and turn it to the production of a wide range of top-fermenting specialty beers. These are marketed under the Arcener brand and the label of the distributor Hertog Jan. The range is constantly evolving, but has included a light, delicate, Bavarian-style "white" Wheat Beer, Arcener Tarwe; a dry, thinnish, Düsseldorf-style Altforster Altbier; a strong (20 Plato; 1080; 7.2; 9.0), pale Winterbier; a smoky, strong (5.6; 6.5) Stout; and a rich, fruity, strong (8.0; 10.0), bottle-conditioned Barley Wine named Grand Prestige.

The brewery has its own tap-room, with a children's play area which offers swings and a climbing frame (an unusual service perhaps, but some of the Firkin brew-pubs in London have similar facilities). Courses in beer appreciation are offered at the brewery; Arcen's pre-Lenten carnival opens with the tapping of beer at the brewery; there is a weekend beer festival at the beginning of July; and the brewery has a tent at Arcen's Wednesday market in summer. (Arcense Bierbrouwerij, Kruisweg 44, 5944 EN Arcen, the Netherlands. Tel 04703-2427.)

A farmhouse maltings and brewery dating at least from the 1700s, and defunct for 60 years, was re-opened, with its own café and small museum, in the mid-1980s near the city of Nijmegen, in the province of Gelderland, in the east of the Netherlands. The revived brewery, called De Raaf ("The Raven"), is at Rijksweg 232, Heumen (Tel 080-581177). Its principals previously ran a health-food store, and their beers are made from organically-grown barley and hops. The Raaf brews include a Belgian-style "white" Wheat Beer called Gelderse Witte; a very complex and tasty bronze-colored ale, No. 12; abbey-style beers; and a varying selection of other specialties. In general, these are assertive brews, with an excellent balance of fruitiness and hop character.

A village schoolhouse at Herwijnen, Gelderland, is the unlikely location of a tiny micro-brewery called t'Kuipertje (appropriately, "The Little Copper"). Its early brews have been very fruity and spicy, with notes of ginger, cinnamon, and aniseed. There are also plans for a micro-brewery at Oss, to be called Maasland.

The Grolsche brewing company takes its name from the little town of Groenlo, in Gelderland. The company has a second brewery at the larger town of

Enschede, in the adjoining province of Overijssel. Grolsche spells its corporate name with a final "e" and its brand without. This very old-established company, which traces its history to the 1600s, was for years seen simply as a country brewery, catering for what is by Dutch standards a far-flung provincial area. In the 1950s, Grolsche decided to phase out as "old-fashioned" the ceramic swing-top on its bottles. This decision was quickly reversed. Local consumers let it be known that they were very keen on the Grolsch bottle. "They could re-seal it, you see," joked one of the owning family at the time. "That meant that they didn't have to drink a whole bottle at once. Very careful people, these Dutch Calvinists." In the 1960s, the Grolsch bottle was set among other craft artefacts by the Dutch fashion photographer Paul Huf, in a low-key advertising campaign of some memorability.

Grolsch became a nationally-marketed product in the Netherlands, and is now widely sold in other countries, too. Although other breweries had continued sleepily to use swing-top bottles, the conscious pursuit of this style has become especially associated with Grolsch. In the early days of its national popularity, Grolsch perhaps also benefited from a freshness of taste, due to its being unpasteurized. It still is, even for export, and it travels well. Several of the small breweries in the south omit pasteurization, but the larger companies, with wider distribution, are not customarily so bold. At its freshest, Grolsch has a hint of new-mown hay in the nose. It is arguably the best of the mass-market beers from the Netherlands, but these days the smaller brewers have many more individualistic products.

The giant Artois has a second Dutch brewery in the town of Hengelo, Overijssel. This brewery has a standard range, but it does also offer a Hengelo Speciaal which is similar to its southern counterpart Dominator.

The first brew-pub in the Netherlands opened in 1987 in the nearby town of Almelo, offering a top-fermenting ale of 4.4; 5.5. The pub is known as De Almelose Bistro 't Oude Verkeershuis.

No doubt there will be more. In Staphorst, where the fundamentalist community have been known to stone cars and ritually throw cow-dung at people

Left: Grolsch was never the only beer to come in a pot-stoppered "swing-top" bottle, but it is by far the best known example. The bottle gains attention for the product, though it could also be considered a distraction. Grolsch's real claim to fame should be that it is unpasteurized.
Top: The 'tIJ brewery in Amsterdam.

who offend their sexual mores, a brewery is planned to produce a strong, top-fermented ale called Marquis De Bosch. This has initially been contract-brewed elsewhere, which might be a safer arrangement. There are plans for a brew-pub at a chic restaurant, the Stadskasteel, in the old city of Utrecht, in the middle of the Netherlands. Another is planned in the far southwest, at Goes, in Zeeland.

As a little country, the Netherlands has an affection for smallness. For a time, the smallest brewery in the country was undoubtedly De Friese Bierbrouwerij, in the village of Uitwellingerga, in Dutch Friesland. This province has a recognized language of its own, in which the brewery is De Fryske and the village Twellingea. The village once sank into the marshy soil, and its name means "coming out of the well." The brewery, which is in a cowshed, has produced a number of strong ales, beautifully balanced, and with a dry, slightly sour fruitiness. In Leeuwarden, the provincial capital of Friesland, a home-brewer has commercially marketed cherry and elderberry beers under the name Middlezee.

The most Dutch of all locations for a micro-brewery is beneath a windmill. That the brewing building should formerly have been a public bath-house is a refinement worthy of colorful old Amsterdam, where this arrangement is to be found. The windmill is occasionally set to work, and has been used to grind the malt for the brewery.

The brewery is named 't IJ, after the nearby stretch of water on which Amsterdam harbour stands. Its products also have odd names, like Natte (meaning "Wet"), Zatte ("Drunk"), and Struis ("Ostrich"). In colloquial Dutch, an "ostrich" can mean a large ungainly woman.

These are all abbey-style beers, very profound in palate and fruity (tasters have found notes of melon and mango) with a notably dry house character. Natte is a "Double," at 4.8; 6.0. Zatte is a "Triple," at 6.4; 8.0. Struis is intended to be a "Super Double," with a claimed alcohol content of 8.0; 10.0, which would make it the strongest beer in the Netherlands. The brewery also has a "Super Triple," slightly less strong, but dry-hopped. This is called Columbus, which is meant to imply the discovery of new territory.

The principal of 't IJ, Kaspar Peterson, is a former songwriter and singer with the Dutch band Drukwerk. They have their own café in Amsterdam, at the corner of the Singel and the Brouwersgracht (appropriately, Brewers' Canal).

Amsterdam has also a number of renowned specialty beer cafés. The pioneer was the Gollem, in Raamsteeg, off Spuistraat. The bartenders who made that famous now have their own establishments. The most central, and atmospheric, is In De Wildeman, at Kolksteg 3, off the Nieuwendijk shopping street. The bigger selection of beers is at Het Laatste Oordeel, behind the Royal Palace, at Raadhuisstraat 17. These two cafés, which

Above: Trappist fathers make and market very characterful beers in the style of their order at the Schaapskooi ("Sheepfold") monastery, near the city of Tilburg, in North Brabant. This is the only abbey brewery in the Netherlands.

Right: Café Gollem, in a typical Amsterdam alley, was the first specialty beer bar in the city. Today In De Wildeman and Het Laatste Oordeel enjoy a particular patronage.

open in the afternoon and evening, are among the founders of the Alliance of Beer-tappers (Alliantie van Bier Tapperijen), which publishes a list of such specialty outlets all over the country.

The Netherlands also has a campaigning organization for beer-lovers called PINT (Promotie Informatie Traditioneel Bier). This body can be reached at Post Box 3757, 1001 AN Amsterdam, Netherlands. It organizes the Netherlands' principal beer festival, devoted to the Bock style, in late October each year.

There is a national beer museum in the old De Boom brewery premises in the cheese town of Alkmaar. The museum is open from the beginning of April to the end of September (Tel 072-113801). Its bar attempts to stock every Dutch beer. This would once have been easy. Happily, it is becoming much more difficult.

LUXEMBOURG

SANDWICHED BETWEEN the Belgian province with which it shares a name, Germany, and the Lorraine region of France, the tiny Grand Duchy of Luxembourg could be perceived as a beer country, but this is debatable. To supply a population of 350,000, scarcely enough to fill a decent-sized city, this tiny country has no fewer than five breweries, but the variety of their products is less impressive.

The bordering parts of Belgium, Germany, and France are not the most colorful in brewing terms, and Luxembourg's beers are not very assertive in character.

The brewers are beginning to extend their ranges slightly, but all the beers are for the moment bottom-fermenting. Although it is one of the Benelux countries, and has a currency tied to that of Belgium, the Grand Duchy has both economic and gastronomic links with Saarland and Lorraine. In general, its beers are German-accented. Perhaps mild lagers go best with pike, pork, and fruit pastries.

Typically a brewer might have a Pilsener-type of 11.5 Plato (1046) or a little more, perhaps a super-premium version at 12.5 (1050), sometimes a Dortmunder-style of 13.5 (1054), perhaps identified as a "de luxe," and in some instances a dark-brown Bock of 16.5 (1066). Some beers are all-malt, but others use up to 25 per cent adjunct, usually corn. Lagering times vary from three to five weeks or longer. The basic Pilseners usually have around 24 units of bitterness.

The biggest brewery is Diekirch, in the town of the same name, across the border from Trier and Bitburg. It produces a clean-tasting, firm-bodied Pilsener. The second largest is Mousel et Clausen, in Luxembourg city. This company has also taken over the range of the former Henri Funck brewery. Its everyday beer is called Henri Funck, and its slightly hoppier Pilsener is identified as Mousel et Clausen. Brasserie Nationale, a merger of the former Funck-Bricher and Bofferding breweries, produces a light, aromatic, Pilsener type. The small Simon brewery, at Wiltz, across the border from Bastogne, makes a Christmas beer in broadly the style of a dark Bock. The very small Battin brewery, in Esch-sur-Alzette, across the border from Metz, produces a full range of styles, including a sweetish Bock.

Luxembourg also has local wines, crisp, dry and white, and fruit brandies. It has high consumption figures per head for beer, wine and liquor. The Luxembourgers themselves are keen diners, and they are helped in their endeavors by highly-paid bureaucrats from the various European and international institutions headquartered in their country.

The labels of Luxembourg . . . Brasserie Nationale's Meisterbock and Christmas beer are both pale lagers. Mousel has a premium brew called Royal Altmunster and a dark Luxator, both at about 13 degrees.

Steam-brewing, European style

Brewer Albert Mousel proudly presents his products (above). At the time, brewers took great pride in their use of steam power. "Steam brewery" did not have the same meaning in Europe as it did across the Atlantic. It was a big moment when a new boiler was delivered to the brewery. M. Mousel was succeeded by his son (far right).

Brasserie Simon Wiltz Luxembourg bière blonde du type pilsen

THE BRITISH ISLES

Left: The famously "flat"
pint of English ale still
leaves plenty of lacework
in the glass of this thirsty
drinker, a professional
rabbit-catcher caught off
duty at his favorite pub
in the West of England.

THE REST OF THE WORLD is often puzzled by the brews of the British Isles. Are they really served warm? Flat, too? Aren't they all frighteningly dark? How can people enjoy something called "Bitter"?

The traditional brew of Britain is ale. It was a spontaneous consumer campaign to defend traditional ale in Britain that gave birth to the micro-brewery movement throughout the developed world.

Even to the most eclectic drinkers from other parts of the world, it seems remarkable that the British have remained so loyal to ales that these brews continue, albeit only just, to outsell lagers. Britain has brewed lager since 1882, but that style has still not quite achieved its long-predicted clean sweep. To true British ale-lovers, it seems extraordinary and unpatriotic that any English, Welsh or Scottish drinker would, on his or her home ground, drink even the best of lagers. Nevertheless, in Britain, many lagers are produced under licence from foreign brewers, often to a lower specification than the original. Would a French drinker in Bordeaux choose a fake Liebfraumilch (or even, for that matter, a real one)? In more matters than drink, the unconcernedness of the British is both their strength and their weakness.

That insouciance can also make social attitudes hard to decipher but, as in some other countries, fashions in beer change. Ale, once regarded as the workaday drink, is now generally regarded in Britain as the more sophisticated tipple. Lager, once for maiden aunts, is now supped by the English hooligan soccer supporters who are infamous throughout Europe. Even in Britain, lager beers are almost always served chilled.

Most British ales should be served at a natural cellar temperature, ideally around 13°C (55°F). No product that is fermented at warm temperatures will express its flavor fully if it is more than lightly chilled. The ideal serving temperature is even more sensitive to the manner in which the brew has been conditioned. If it has also been matured at an ambient or cellar temperature, as have many of the classic British ales, that is how it should be served. This has nothing to do with national taste, or a supposed lack of refrigerators in Britain.

A well-run pub in Britain will keep its cellar, and serve its ales, in the optimum temperature range. In winter, the cellar may have to be heated. In summer, or year-round in these days of central heating, bottled ales in a warm bar might be lightly chilled on a cold shelf. Lagers served on draft from a warm cellar will be flash-chilled.

Any publican in Britain who excessively chills his ales, and some do, should be punished by transportation to Australia. In some other countries, British ales are frequently served under refrigeration; the customer who orders, or accepts, them in this form is easily parted from his or her money. The distinction has to do with palate, not color, but the majority of British ales should be treated like most red wines.

Most British brewers make several styles of ale, among which the type known as Bitter is by far the

What look like witches'
cauldrons (*right*) are in
fact open brew-kettles.
This touch of tradition is
found at the Caledonian
Brewery, in eastern
Scotland.

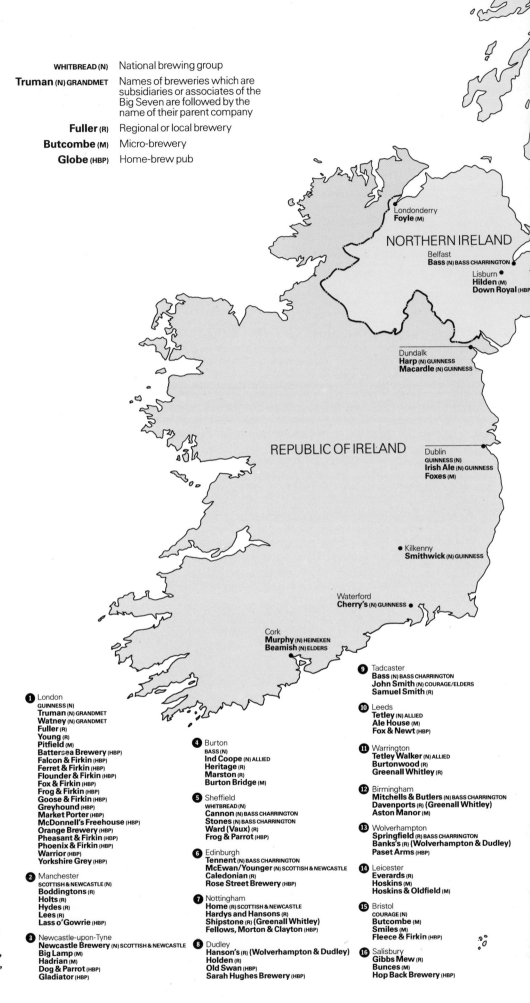

WHITBREAD (N) National brewing group

Truman (N) GRANDMET Names of breweries which are subsidiaries or associates of the Big Seven are followed by the name of their parent company

Fuller (R) Regional or local brewery

Butcombe (M) Micro-brewery

Globe (HBP) Home-brew pub

Londonderry
Foyle (M)

NORTHERN IRELAND

Belfast
Bass (N) BASS CHARRINGTON

Lisburn
Hilden (M)
Down Royal (HBP)

Dundalk
Harp (N) GUINNESS
Macardle (N) GUINNESS

REPUBLIC OF IRELAND

Dublin
GUINNESS (N)
Irish Ale (N) GUINNESS
Foxes (M)

Kilkenny
Smithwick (N) GUINNESS

Waterford
Cherry's (N) GUINNESS

Cork
Murphy (N) HEINEKEN
Beamish (N) ELDERS

❶ London
GUINNESS (N)
Truman (N) GRANDMET
Watney (N) GRANDMET
Fuller (R)
Young (R)
Pitfield (M)
Battersea Brewery (HBP)
Falcon & Firkin (HBP)
Ferret & Firkin (HBP)
Flounder & Firkin (HBP)
Fox & Firkin (HBP)
Frog & Firkin (HBP)
Goose & Firkin (HBP)
Greyhound (HBP)
Market Porter (HBP)
McDonnell's Freehouse (HBP)
Orange Brewery (HBP)
Pheasant & Firkin (HBP)
Phoenix & Firkin (HBP)
Warrior (HBP)
Yorkshire Grey (HBP)

❷ Manchester
SCOTTISH & NEWCASTLE (N)
Boddingtons (R)
Holts (R)
Hydes (R)
Lees (R)
Lass o'Gowrie (HBP)

❸ Newcastle-upon-Tyne
Newcastle Brewery (N) SCOTTISH & NEWCASTLE
Big Lamp (M)
Hadrian (M)
Dog & Parrot (HBP)
Gladiator (HBP)

❹ Burton
BASS (N)
Ind Coope (N) ALLIED
Heritage (R)
Marston (R)
Burton Bridge (M)

❺ Sheffield
WHITBREAD (N)
Cannon (N) BASS CHARRINGTON
Stones (N) BASS CHARRINGTON
Ward (Vaux) (R)
Frog & Parrot (HBP)

❻ Edinburgh
Tennent (N) BASS CHARRINGTON
McEwan/Younger (N) SCOTTISH & NEWCASTLE
Caledonian (R)
Rose Street Brewery (HBP)

❼ Nottingham
Home (R) SCOTTISH & NEWCASTLE
Hardys and Hansons (R)
Shipstone (R) (Greenall Whitley)
Fellows, Morton & Clayton (HBP)

❽ Dudley
Hanson's (R) (Wolverhampton & Dudley)
Holden (R)
Old Swan (R)
Sarah Hughes Brewery (HBP)

❾ Tadcaster
Bass (N) BASS CHARRINGTON
John Smith (N) COURAGE/ELDERS
Samuel Smith (R)

❿ Leeds
Tetley (N) ALLIED
Ale House (M)
Fox & Newt (HBP)

⓫ Warrington
Tetley Walker (N) ALLIED
Burtonwood (R)
Greenall Whitley (R)

⓬ Birmingham
Mitchells & Butlers (N) BASS CHARRINGTON
Davenports (R) (Greenall Whitley)
Aston Manor (M)

⓭ Wolverhampton
Springfield (R) BASS CHARRINGTON
Banks's (R) (Wolverhampton & Dudley)
Paset Arms (HBP)

⓮ Leicester
Everards (R)
Hoskins (R)
Hoskins & Oldfield (M)

⓯ Bristol
COURAGE (N)
Butcombe (M)
Smiles (M)
Fleece & Firkin (HBP)

⓰ Salisbury
Gibbs Mew (R)
Bunces (M)
Hop Back Brewery (HBP)

The United Kingdom and the Republic of Ireland have no shortage of breweries, most of which produce ales. The lagers brewed in the two countries lack distinction, but there are some excellent Stouts. Mild is still brewed, but demand for it seems to be steadily shrinking.

most popular in England and Wales. There are different traditions in Scotland and Ireland. The term Bitter is intended to suggest a brew with more hoppy dryness than its companion style, Mild, which is today less widely available but still well worthy of appreciation. None of this has anything to do with "Bitters," which is a term used to describe a style of Continental European liqueur that often tastes of quinine or gentian and is variously used as an apéritif, digestif, or hangover cure.

The color of a Bitter varies from one brewery, or product, to another but most are in the range from pale bronze to a full copper-red. A low-gravity Bitter is sometimes described as a Light Ale, especially in its bottled form. The term relates to its weight, not its color or calorie count. A premium-gravity Bitter, which may well have the fuller copper color, is nonetheless sometimes identified as a Pale Ale. This distinguishes it from a darker Brown Ale. A stronger brew may be called an Old Ale, and one of special potency a Barley Wine, though these terms can overlap. Most breweries in England and Wales make ales in several of these styles and in a number of sub-categories.

In addition to ales, a handful also make a Porter. More make a Stout, usually sweet in Britain and dry in Ireland. These styles are very dark, almost black. Most make at least one lager, usually in a mild and nondescript "international" derivation of the Pilsener style: not as hoppy as a Czech or German Pilsener; not always as clean as a Dutch or Danish version; not as light as the North American examples. In the British Isles, it tends to be just "lager" — a commodity: there has emerged so far no tradition of style. Nor is lager yet really accepted as being beer in the British Isles. When the British drinker talks of beer, the subject is really ale. In Ireland, it may be Stout.

The color, gravity, and palate of each style of ale will be determined as much by density and breadth of that particular brewery's spectrum as by any national consensus. All of these are recognized as principal stylistic descriptions, but they are not as precisely defined as are the classics in Germany, for example. There is also more idiosyncrasy in the house character of the entire range from one brewery to the next. In part, this is perhaps because the British are not Germans. It is, though, also due to the greater individuality of ale yeasts, some of which represent an amalgam of several strains.

There are also several regional accents, some more clearly defined than others. These are especially evident in the case of Bitter. The individuality of each brewery's interpretation, and the regional differences (albeit not *appellations*) are another reminder of Bordeaux.

There is also some regional loyalty to particular styles. Mild enjoys its greatest popularity in the West Midlands (around the cities of Birmingham, Wolverhampton, and Dudley) and the Northwest (Greater Manchester, in particular). The type of

Brown Ale available as a minor style in most parts of the country (very dark, low in gravity, and extremely sweet) does not prevail in the Northeast (York, Sunderland, and, especially, Newcastle). There, a deep amber, premium-gravity, medium-sweet style of Brown Ale is favored.

CASK-CONDITIONED ALE

In its most traditional form, British ale is cask-conditioned. This is what is meant by "real ale." The term indicates that the ale goes into the barrel with some residual sugar and living yeast, and enjoys a secondary fermentation there. If at the end of primary fermentation there is insufficient residual sugar or yeast, the ale may be given a dosage of either, as in Champagne production. The object is to offer a living ale, with a natural carbonation in the cask. This is a gentle carbonation, but the ale is not actually flat. (The natural carbonation level might be 0.75-1.0 volumes.)

If an ale is conditioned in the cask, it must obviously be served on draft. To the British, this is not a serious limitation. Another remarkable aspect of drinking in Britain and Ireland is that more than 85 per cent of all beer, whether ale or lager, is bought in the pub, club or (less often) restaurant. More than 75 per cent of the total is served on draft. No other country approaches this figure (next is Czechoslovakia, with 45 per cent). More than half of Britain's 75,000 pubs serve at least some of their ale cask-conditioned. Usually, only Mild and Bitter ales, and perhaps a strong, winter brew, are served in this way.

Even pubs that serve cask-conditioned ales may also carry others in a filtered and pasteurized draft form. This is known as "keg" ale. This is like a supermarket offering both a mature Cheddar and a processed cheese. Where both forms are available, true ale-lovers will always opt for the cask-conditioned product. This may be identified by the wording on the hand-pump or tap, but that is not always the case. It is most likely to be drawn from the cellar by a hand-pulled, mechanical pump, or very occasionally tapped by gravity from a cask on the bar. Electric pumps are also sometimes used, and they can be hard to distinguish from the CO_2 pressure systems used to serve keg ale and lager.

Cask-conditioned ales can be difficult for the publican or the cellar manager to keep well. The yeast in the cask has to be given time to settle, and encouraged to do so by the addition of finings (a substance made from the swim-bladder of the sturgeon). During the period of natural carbonation, the excess has to be released by the venting of the barrel. For this purpose, there is a vent in the bung. This can be occupied by a "soft peg" that is porous or a "hard" one that is not. For a time, the two may have to be alternated. The easiest system is for all of this to be done at the brewery and for the ale to be decanted into new casks before leaving for the pub. This "bright" ale is not quite "real."

Truly "real" ale reaches its peak of condition in the cellar of the pub. The brewery may already have added the finings, though more might be required at the pub. The cellar manager will monitor each cask for clarity, natural carbonation, and — most important — palate. An ale that has not reached its peak of condition tastes hard and "green." If it has passed its peak, its fruity acidity will have turned vinegarish. New casks must peak on time to meet changing demand. Cellar-keeping is a craft. The world is not full of such craftspeople, especially at the rates of pay offered in some pubs. In the cellar, a cask normally takes from 24 hours to three days to settle. Some special products may take longer, even a week. Long periods of maturation at the pub are not common, but some ales may take two or three weeks to reach their peak of complexity. There are instances of strong ales being kept at the pub for six weeks before being broached, and lasting a further six, but that is unusual.

Once tapped, a cask of ale is normally consumed within 24 hours, and few will remain enjoyable for more than three or four days. Once the ale has reached its peak, it is no longer producing CO_2. As the ale is drawn from the cask, space is filled by oxygen. To protect the ale from oxidation, some brewers keep it under a blanket of CO_2 pressure. In this system, the CO_2 is not used to dispense the ale, and should not have sufficient pressure to be absorbed in it. Many brewmasters feel this is the best of all worlds, but other ale-lovers are unconvinced. The more that a brewery tries to anticipate problems and protect its ale, the less robust the end product sometimes tastes.

An over-protected "real ale" may be hard to distinguish from the more gently processed of keg brews; a cask-conditioned ale handled by a craftsperson in the cellar is a revelation. During its short life, a cask of pub-conditioned ale (perhaps a better term?) will evolve in character. Nor will any two casks be identical. Brewers worry about consistency, which they mistake for quality. Ale-lovers enjoy comparing today's pint with that served yesterday. Or Friday's cask with Monday's. The same wine is not meant to taste identical from one vintage to the next. It should, of course, be recognizably itself — but to identify the subtle differences is a part of the pleasure.

Any publican worthy of the name should care about his ale and know how to look after it. By no means all do. A landlord with a real understanding of the art and a flair for it is sufficiently noteworthy for his pub to win a widespread reputation.

Cask-conditioned ale is ale at its very freshest: still "alive" in the cask. The freshness can be a shock — a delicious one — a frisson of pleasure. In any good beer, freshness leaves the flavors unmasked, but the living yeast imparts a special character to a cask-conditioned ale. The yeasty fruitiness, the suggestion of sweetness in the Pale Ale malt and the hoppy acidity attain a height of complexity. An English

Below: The unique coopers' shop at the Samuel Smith brewery, in Yorkshire. "Sam's" is the only brewery to make its own barrels, though some others employ coopers for repair work. Virtually all of Samuel Smith's cask-conditioned ale is served from wood.

Over page: A celebrated photograph used to promote the ales produced by the Eldridge Pope brewery, Dorset. Beer advertisers have always been keen on the youth market. This company goes further, with implied claims of eternal youth.

Bitter in this form is, indeed, the beer world's answer to a red wine from Bordeaux. The soft-fruit character, that touch of sweetness, and the hoppy dryness do for the ale what the oak does for a Pauillac.

In some instances, the cask in which the ale is conditioned is made from wood. One or two breweries retain a policy of using only wood. A few more have a mix of wood and metal casks. Most use metal. Despite the loyalty of the few (Samuel Smith's brewery even has its own coopers), an organization called The Society for the Preservation of Beer From the Wood has been reduced to the status of being, so

to speak, a splinter group. This is sad, in that this small group of conservationists pre-dates the much more successful, and far larger, Campaign for Real Ale. Both organizations foster traditionalism.

"Real ale" does exist in the bottle, but there are only a few specialties produced in this form. Britain is first and foremost a draft country. If ale does have a secondary fermentation in the bottle, as in the *méthode Champenoise*, this provides a lively sparkle and a quite different character. The few ales that are marketed in this form by British brewers are prized, and in character they represent something of a bridge across the North Sea to Belgium.

THE CAMPAIGN FOR REAL ALE

The cask-conditioning of draft beer has survived as a widespread tradition only in Britain. There are some vestigial parallels in Belgium and Germany, but not quite the same thing. The scale of the British tradition made it worth saving when it seemed to be dying out, with the great growth of the national brewing groups and the "modernization" and "rationalization" of the late 1950s, 1960s, and early 1970s. At the time, the convenience of marketing filtered and pasteurized "keg" ale, and its ease of handling by pub staff, was diminishing British brewers' interest in cask-conditioning. With that,

149

Lads of the Village. 193

DORSET BROWN ALE

Are first in

GEORGE CHAINEY, 87.   **JAMES HIGGINS, 87.**   **SAMUEL**
TOTAL

their commitment to any sort of quality, as opposed to consistency, seemed to be on the wane.

In 1971, a group of drinking friends decided to start a consumer campaign to save "real ale." The idea was born out of enthusiasm, and they did not realize that they were starting a national consumer movement. There were journalists among the founders, and their contacts (not to mention their commitment to beer-drinking) no doubt helped.

More important, they had struck a nerve. Thousands of drinkers had felt concern at the future of British ale, but had believed "progress" to be inevitable. They had not protested, but now they had exemplars and a forum. The Campaign for Real Ale (known by the acronym CAMRA) started, and still publishes, a monthly newspaper called *What's Brewing*. Its paperback *Good Beer Guide* (identifying the pubs that best serve cask-

Bradford Abbas, Dorset.

NG. 90. THOMAS COOMBS. 89. SIDNEY PARSONS. 81.

434 YEARS.

conditioned ales) became a best-seller and remains an annual standard work.

The interest aroused by CAMRA made it possible for columnists and authors to write on beer as a product of some consequence. A weekly column in a respected newspaper —

The Guardian — was a particular help.

CAMRA's Great British Beer Festival, held in a different city each August, is an opportunity for ale-lovers to sample the products of local and regional brewers from all over the British Isles. It also offers the national brewing groups the chance to show that

they still produce cask-conditioned ales as well as their more heavily-advertised mass-market products. The festival lasts for a week, and attendance runs to tens of thousands.

At its height, the campaign had more than 25,000 members. Although the number has diminished a

The Harbour Inn at Southwold, East Anglia, is occasionally cut off by flooding at high tide, leaving drinkers trapped in the bar. It serves Adnams' ales, which are especially complex in character. Students of these brews have sometimes been stranded there for days.

little since then, hundreds of new members sign up every time a brewery faces takeover or closure. People pray only when they fear the Devil. When an intended brewery closure is announced, the campaign coordinates public demonstrations. Perhaps coffins bearing beer barrels will be carried through the streets. There will be local — and sometimes national — media coverage. Breweries have been saved, and for a time closures ceased altogether.

For every card-carrying member, there are another five or six who no longer pay their dues but still subscribe to the idea. For every one of those, there are another ten sympathizers. The British Press may by now regard the campaign as an old story, but it still phones CAMRA whenever beer is an issue: whether over quality, availability, price, legislation, or whatever. The organization has become a valuable clearing-house for information.

At first, brewers dismissed CAMRA as a bunch of know-nothing amateurs, but in fact some brewers were educated by the campaign. Through its informed questioning and its publications, they learned to appreciate their own products and to describe their qualities to others. Some brewers still resent the public airing of controversial issues, but most have seen that CAMRA has done them a service, and many enjoy regular contact with their local branches.

Cask-conditioned ale, so nearly abandoned, is now — in marketing parlance — a product segment. A brewery that wins an award at the Great British Beer Festival makes sure to publicize its success.

Cynics point out that, of British brewers' total output, well under 20 per cent is cask-conditioned ale, and that this was roughly the share when the campaign started. The percentage is often said to be diminishing — yet the figure quoted is almost always the same. The share is hardly the point. Without CAMRA, there would probably be no cask-conditioned ale today. It has been saved, at least for the moment. If the market-share of cask-conditioned ale has been preserved, through generations of new drinkers, the campaign has been an extraordinary success.

When the campaign began, it seemed to face an immovable obstacle: in Britain, the majority of pubs are owned by brewers, a situation that is forbidden in some countries, notably the United States. Since they controlled the principal outlets, the breweries could in theory dictate which beers the consumers would buy. In practice, the campaign showed that the consumer could fight back. It was an astonishing demonstration, especially because the British brewing industry is dominated by its own Big Six (in descending order of size: Bass, Allied Breweries, Whitbread, Watney, Courage, Scottish & Newcastle). At the time, through acquisitions of local breweries, the Big Six had around 70 plants. They now have 30-odd principal plants, though they also own several "captive" micros and brew-pubs. In

1972, a year after the foundation of the campaign, the Selby Brewery, which had been closed since 1954, reopened. At the time, there were about 90 old-established breweries. After a decade and a half, there were still 70-odd, owned by about 60 companies. In 1973, a restaurant in Somerset began to brew beer for its customers. That business metamorphosed into the Miner's Arms micro-brewery, which still operates at Westbury-sub-Mendip. Over the next dozen years, littered with openings and closures, the number of completely new micro-breweries in Britain at one point reached more than 90. The number of old-established brew-pubs had fallen to four, but a new one opened in 1974: the Mason Arms, in Witney, Oxfordshire. That no longer brews, but the number of these establishments did at one point rise to 75. By 1987, closures were outstripping openings, but the micro and the brew-pub had by then become an accepted

Above: A CAMRA funeral march for the Lancaster brewery Yates and Jackson. Later that year, 1985, a wreath garlanded the brewery's empty place at the Great British Beer Festival. *Right*: This march helped delay, but not prevent, the takeover of Matthew Brown, of Lancashire. The company, too, had contested the takeover. Matthew Brown still operates, but is now owned by Scottish and Newcastle.

part of the scenery. David Bruce, a former employee of Courage and Theakston's, moved into brew-pubs in 1980 and built up a chain of ten or more in less than a decade. Peter Austin, formerly an employee of North Country Breweries, has either built or acted as consultant for more micros than anyone. His home base is the Ringwood Brewery, in Hampshire, but his expertise has brought new beers to the United States, China, and Africa.

The Privacy of the Pub

SMOKE ROOM

BAR PARLOUR

LUNCHEON

BAR

The more extravagant style of pub, dating from the Victorian and Edwardian periods, is wrapped in stained, frosted and etched glass to thwart the prying eyes of outsiders. The dark souls inside had their sins illuminated by gaslight (now converted to electricity, at The Vines, Liverpool, *above*) and their ambience softened by a flourish of decorative delights. These examples are all from Northern cities: Liverpool, Greater Manchester and Leeds.

LOUNGE

Porter

LIKE A FADING RECOLLECTION of an interesting encounter, Porter lingers in bars all over the world. Brews called Porter are made in China, in Eastern Europe (especially the Baltic countries) and in North America. It is rightly suspected that they are of British antecedence. They are always dark, and often nearly black. They usually have a roasty palate, but beyond that there is little agreement.

Surely, they should never be bottom-fermented, but many are. There are, though, a couple of top-fermented Porters in the Baltic region, and several excellent examples among the new micro-brews of Britain and the United States. Some are rich, with notes of sweetness, but surely it is dryness that should dominate?

Brew-lovers know that a Porter should, indeed, be top-fermented, but other questions are less clear. Some of the old ghosts that loom through the darkness have a great gravity, perhaps in the 1070s, and are consequently very strong. The newer examples are more likely to be in the 1050s or 1040s and of a more conventional strength.

The difficulty lies in knowing what constitution Porter enjoyed in its prime. It is the most elusive of styles, yet it continues to exercise a particular fascination among beer-buffs. A journalist once tried to recreate the sound of the jazz cornet-player Buddy Bolden. He wanted to establish whether Bolden could, indeed, have been heard across Lake Pontchartrain. The search for the authentic Porter is almost as hopeless.

Porter became internationally known because it was the principal beer style in Britain, and especially London, during the country's greatest period of industrial and economic growth and consequent global influence. The style seems to have emerged in the early 1700s, reached a peak around 1800, and largely vanished between the two world wars. In the 1940s and 1950s, most British pubs still had signs over their doors announcing that they were licensed to sell "ale and porter," but the latter style was not available.

It continued to be brewed in Ireland until 1973, though toward the end it was assembled as a blend in the pub — which is how the style is said to have begun. The valedictory Irish blend was made from that country's Draught Guinness and a second brew produced especially for the purpose by the same company. Although this brew was made in the Guinness brewery in Dublin, its last hold-out of availability was in Belfast. In its final years, it was especially associated with the north east of Ireland. When the last barrel had been drained to the point of expiration, it was draped in "Guinness Black." The Irish know how to hold a wake, and they did.

In 1978-9, at the peak of interest in "real ale" traditionalism, two British breweries decided to revive Porter in its home country. One of them was Penrhos, a micro-brewery set up with the technical assistance of Peter Austin and the financial help of comedian and actor Terry Jones (made famous by the cult British television series *Monty Python*). Sad to say, the Penrhos brewery eventually closed. The other Porter was made by the old-established and highly regarded small brewery of Timothy Taylor, in the little town of Keighley, Yorkshire. Both the brewery and its Porter survive. One or two further revivalist examples have been introduced since. One made by the Burton Bridge micro-brewery is, at its best, a very convincing modern interpretation.

The fascination exercised by Porter derives in part from its having been the first product of industrialized

157

In the British Isles, Porter seemed to have breathed its last gasp in Belfast (*left*), but it was resurrected by breweries like Pitfield (*right*). Pitfield, in London, is a prize-winning micro-brewery attached to The Beer Shop.

brewing anywhere in the world, and in part from its refusal to die. The very old Porters that are still produced have for beer-lovers the same appeal that a surviving steam railroad might have for a steam buff. The micro-brewers who are reviving the style wish to feel that they are being true to tradition. They also want to produce an interpretation of Porter that has its own place within their range of more current styles.

It has been argued that the original Porter did have a gravity of around 1070, but that this somehow diminished over the decades to a point in the 1050s or lower. Eventually, the higher bracket seems to have been filled by the style now known as Imperial Stout, and the lower one by Dark Mild. Hence Porter's becoming lost in London fog. It now seems to have rediscovered itself, and to be settling into an identifiable form.

A modern, English-speaking Porter has a gravity in the 1040-50 range. It is black in color, almost opaque, perhaps with mahogany highlights. It resembles a Dry Stout but is lighter in body and less creamy. Its dryness is coffee-ish and fruity. The lighter body derives from a greater attenuation. The coffee-ish dryness emerges from the use of malts that have been highly roasted, although not to the degree required for a Stout. The fruitiness emerges from the top-fermenting yeast. This quality is not masked by bitterness, though a modern Porter nonetheless has a definite hop character. The bitterness is in balance, and not as intense as in the best of Dry Stouts. This modern manifestation is a credible descendant of the original, and has a place in the portfolio of a brewery that may also produce at least one style of Stout.

The elusiveness of the original results from its great age. A beer known as Porter is said to have been produced in 1722. There was little technical literature on brewing at the time. Nor is Porter mentioned in the 1735 edition of *The London and Country Brewer*, a standard work. Mentions of Porter begin to emerge around 1740-50, but they are not as helpful as they might be. By this point, more general literature was describing Porter as a universal drink in Britain.

The starting point for the technical description of a beer is usually its original gravity, but the means of measuring this — the saccharometer, or hydrometer — did not come into use until the period between the 1750s and 1780s. From early recipes, an extrapolation can be made, but this is not a very accurate method. Varieties of barley and methods of malting in use at the time would have produced a lesser extract of fermentable sugars than can be achieved today. Recipes talk of "brown malt" but it is not clear today exactly what that meant.

The British beer-writer Dr Terence Foster, who now lives in the United States, has taken a particular interest in Porter. His studies have led him to believe that the original version had a gravity of around 1070. Perhaps this was so. Or perhaps the first run from the mash-tun yielded this kind of extract.

A resultant high-gravity Porter may sometimes have been set aside for the export trade with Baltic Europe. With its high gravity, it would have contained plenty of residual sugar to ferment during the journey. This would explain why some Baltic brewers still regard Porter as a high-gravity style. Those that bottom-ferment their Porter do so simply for convenience; they are primarily lager-brewers. In Charles Dickens' London, manual workers undoubtedly eased their lives with strong beers, but by the time average gravities were being computed, in the late 1800s, the figure was in the upper to mid-1050s. At that point, a good deal of the beer being consumed was still Porter.

There is nothing to suggest that all Porter had the same gravity. Since the notion of measuring gravity was new, the idea of an agreed standard is unlikely. It is also possible that most Porter was a blend of two or three runs through the mash-tun. The term "small beer" seems to have meant a brew produced to a low gravity from the second or third water. Porter is said to have originally been brewed to combine the merits of three lesser styles (Pale, Brown, and Old ales) that were commonly blended by the drinker in the pub. Since Pale Ale was not a well-developed style at the time, this probably meant the watery third run. A blend of all the house styles was ordered as "Entire."

The decorative stonework in some London pubs still offers "Entire," though drinkers are not recommended to try and order it. They would undoubtedly be met by blank incomprehension.

The idea of a drinker mixing his or her own blend, albeit under different names, has never altogether died. It may be a means of producing a more enjoyable drink or simply a way of expressing individuality. Spirits-drinkers order cocktails, wine-lovers occasionally have a spritzer or a Kir, and there are a number of mixes made with beers of various types. As fast as the producers seek to offer these blends ready-made, new ones become popular. In 1722, a brewer called Ralph Harwood decided to offer his customers a ready-made Entire, and that is said to have been the birth of Porter.

Although his establishment sounds as though it may have been a brew-pub, Harwood's idea was soon taken up by the larger companies that were emerging. A brew-pub does not have to deliver its beer. A free-standing brewery does. Free-standing breweries were a new idea at the time. Industrial capitalism was in its infancy. It may be that the draymen delivering the new style of beer shouted, "Porter!" to announce their arrival. A more commonly-accepted theory is that the drink was a popular restorative among the porters in London's produce markets.

The history-making Mr Harwood had the Bell Brewhouse in Shoreditch, not far from several important markets. In 1742, a young brewer named Samuel Whitbread started a business nearby, in Old Street. He, too, specialized in Porter. Within three years, Whitbread had made a short move to Chiswell Street. By 1760, Whitbread had built a Porter tun room, "the unsupported roof span of which is exceeded in its majestic size only by that of Westminster Hall." Whitbread is today a national giant, and its Chiswell Street premises, with tun room, are used as offices. The company no longer makes a Porter.

Much was made of the size of Porter breweries, and especially of their storage tuns, and reports from the time say that the beer had to be kept until it was "racy and mellow." As to how long it was matured, less is certain. Figures of between four months and a year or more have been mentioned, though the latter must surely have applied only to a very high-gravity Porter. The longer periods seem to have been necessary to attenuate thoroughly the malts used in the earliest days of Porter-brewing. In those days, there was no means of artificial refrigeration, and storage exposed the beer to the danger of infection. No doubt this was why brewers of the time used what seem today to be very high hopping rates. The hops protected the beer against infection (and did not yield the degree of bitterness that would be expected from a similar dosage of today's varieties).

In brew-pubs, such maturation as was thought

A modern-day revivalist home of Porter is the Orange brewery and pub, Pimlico Road, in a chic quarter of central London. It offers a fruity-chocolaty Porter, a Light Ale and two stronger brews bearing the district names SW1 and SW2. It is not strictly a free house, since it is owned by Grandmet.

necessary would have been carried out in barrels, and there would have been no need to keep a large stock; the publican simply brewed for his own customers. With the emergence of free-standing commercial breweries, serving a city that was experiencing a great period of growth, the size of stocks held would reflect prestige. This was a time of new commercial competition, technological advancement, feats of engineering and architectural swank.

"Absurd braggadocio surrounded the brewing of Porter," says Roger Protz, in his *Great British Beer Book.* The Meux brewery built a Porter tun so big that 200 people were able to sit down to a celebration meal in it. As brewers vied with each other to build ever-bigger tuns, the tide turned in a tragicomic fashion. In 1814, a Porter tun burst at the Horse Shoe brewery, near Tottenham Court Road, in London. The deluge swept away buildings, and eight people were killed by "drowning, injury, Porter fumes or drunkenness." The "fumes" were probably natural CO_2, which still sometimes causes fatal accidents at breweries. Perhaps the great Porter tragedy gave rise

to the many bad-taste jokes about such incidents. ("At least it was mercifully quick, wasn't it?." . . "On the contrary, he climbed out of the tun three times to relieve himself.")

Although Porter was a London style, it quickly spread to other parts of Britain. It took longer to reach Ireland. Guinness, founded in 1759, was producing only Porter by the turn of that century. "Plain Porter" become the beer of the Irish working man, and proved especially durable in his country.

Discussing the exile of Jame Joyce, his admirer Anthony Burgess once said: "You cannot write in Dublin, there's too much talk . . . the book can be spent in a couple of pub conversations." Burgess, himself in part of Irish origin and from a pub-keeping family, knows better. Dubliners cannot stop writing any more than they can desist from drinking. Every Irish author seems to have something to say about Porter. Even Donleavy, who is American, mused: "When I die, I want to decompose in a barrel of Porter and have it served in all the pubs in Dublin. I wonder, would they know me?"

When it lost its ascendancy, Porter was usurped by Extra Stout, also produced by Guinness. This dry style of Stout became the national beer of Ireland, where it is also made by Murphy's and Beamish (*see* page 181). The word "Stout" originally referred to the strength of beer, but its significance gradually seems to have shifted towards body. The expression pre-dates Guinness. Before Guinness started brewing, Swift wrote:

Should but the Muse descending drop
A slice of bread and mutton chop
Or kindly when his credit's out,
Surprise him with a pint of stout.

These two closely-related styles, Porter and Dry Stout, are among the most intense of beers, but make a surprisingly delicious accompaniment to certain dishes. Porter was at its peak in London when oysters were still plentiful around the Thames estuary. Their combination was renowned. It sounds an odd match, but it was made in heaven. Swift was right about mutton chops and Stout. If you can find the mutton chops.

Pale Ale

THE DAYS WHEN ALL BEER was either dark or cloudy are so long gone that it seems odd of the British still to celebrate pale clarity. Even odder, why call an ale that is usually copper-colored, or at least reddish-bronze, "Pale"? Yet they do. A great many British brewers have a product called Pale Ale.

There is, of course, nothing wrong with an opaque black or brown brew, and some styles are meant to be yeastily cloudy; but sparkling clarity was a novelty when brewers first achieved it. This happened earlier in Britain, with reddish Pale Ales, than it did in Bohemia, with Pilsener lager (or Bavaria, which still identifies a golden brew as a Helles).

The term Pale Ale could loosely be applied to almost any Bitter in Britain, and to some examples of other styles, but in general it is not. In practice, it is usually reserved for what the marketing men would call a "premium" Bitter, and most often (though not always) in its bottled form. When Pale Ale was introduced, its novelty made it seem sophisticated, and that association has to some extent remained. (Again, a precedent for Pilsener in Continental Europe.) At the time of its fashionableness, the bottling of beer was becoming more widespread; that association, too, has lingered.

Because of the different levels of carbonation necessary to keep a brew in good condition on draft and in the bottle, the two never emerge with an identical character. In Britain, with its strong tradition of draft ale and its custom of cask-conditioning, the difference is often greater than elsewhere. Companion draft and bottled ales sometimes have different names or stylistic designations. Sometimes, their specifications have diverged just slightly. On other occasions, they have become truly separate products.

A classic Pale Ale has an original gravity of more than 1045 and probably closer to 1055. It has a copper color, in the range of 20-35 E.B.C. Its palate is clean and complex, with an accent on yeasty fruitiness, a dash of Pale Ale malt character, and a dry, hoppy finish (more than 25 E.B.U., and perhaps closer to 45). Some of the finer examples are dry-hopped. Some are also warm-conditioned, at 12-14°C (54-58°F) for a couple of weeks or a month. A few brewers produce a higher-gravity Pale Ale, in the range 1065-70, but still attenuated to a relative lightness of body. A fine example of this type is Courage's Bulldog Pale Ale. A good Pale Ale makes an excellent accompaniment to red meat dishes.

The first famous Pale Ale was produced by a largely forgotten London brewer named Hodgson in the mid-1750s, but the style became especially associated with the town of Burton, in the Midlands. Burton had been the site of a monastery, and had a brewing history dating from at least the 1200s. It has never altogether lost a reputation for darker styles, but in the 1800s its Pale Ales won it yet greater renown.

It remains a small town, somewhat lost in the industrial area between Birmingham, Derby, and Nottingham, but it is still a sizable brewing center. The home of Bass, Britain's biggest brewing company, it has an old and important brewery owned by Allied; a classic independent, Marston's; the former Everard's brewery, which is being turned into a working museum; and a micro-brewery, Burton Bridge. In terms of beer styles, it ranks with Dublin, Dortmund, Munich, and Pilsen.

Burton is on the River Trent, often considered to be the dividing line between the North and South of England. The Trent valley was well known for its brewers at least as early as the 1600s, and its beers are mentioned in the writing of Defoe. London's Porter brewers had to compete with Burton in the export trade. This was because, through the Trent Canal, Burton had access to the Yorkshire port of Hull, serving the North Sea and thus the Baltic market.

That trade was impeded by the Napoleonic blockade of 1807, and never fully recovered.

Burton's own local style of ale had been a dark nut-brown, but in 1822 the Allsopp brewery developed a pale type. The head brewer is said to have produced the first successful batch in a teapot. During the war with France, the Burton brewers had begun to look at other markets, and they found sales for their Pale Ale in the Indian Empire.

The ale sent to India was brewed to a high gravity, so that it could continue to mature at sea, and hopped heavily, to protect it from infection. The term India Pale Ale, or I.P.A., is still used by brewers in Britain and elsewhere to indicate a "super-premium" hoppy example of the style. Although the designation is used carelessly, a good I.P.A. has a bitterness rating at least in the 40s, and sometimes far

The Bass at the Folies-Bergères

The label so carefully observed by Manet in his 1882 painting, *The Bar at the Folies-Bergères* **(right), was still in use when these bottles (below right) were sold, probably in the 1930s. The red triangle was the first trademark to be registered in Britain (and possibly the world), as the certificate (right) shows. The engraving below shows the Bass brewery in 1834.**

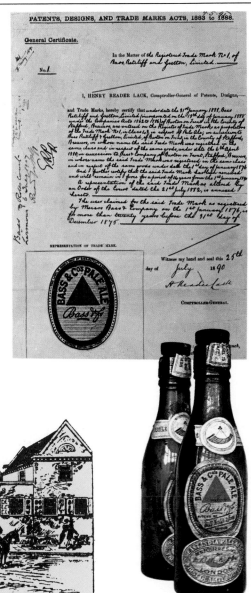

higher even than that.

London faced such competition from Burton that some southern brewers decided to open plants there. The famous old London firm of Truman (now linked with Watney) started a Pale Ale brewery in Burton. The Romford brewery of Ind Coope moved into Burton, and years later took over the great Allsopp company. The owning family had been involved in brewing locally since the Crusades. Hugh de Allsopp had fought in the Holy Land under Richard Cœur de Lion, while his family at home were learning the brewing trade from monks in Burton. A later Allsopp was brewer to Charles II. The merged companies of Ind Coope and Allsopp are today a principal component of Allied Breweries. Its flagship Pale Ale, Double Diamond, has had a variety of incarnations over the years. The company is better known among ale-lovers for its splendid premium draft, Burton Bitter.

The classic Pale Ale from Burton is Worthington White Shield (1052). This is an ale of extraordinary complexity: fresh-tasting, yet mature; clean but with a great depth of palate; round, but also firm and dry. It begins assertively then mellows out to a long finish. White Shield is bottle-conditioned, and its sediment of yeast haunts shaky-handed bar staff who have over-indulged the previous evening. Most drinkers like their White Shield decanted in sparkling condition. "Would you prefer to pour it yourself?" the bartender is inclined to ask, solicitously. Because of the bottle-conditioning, it is not commonly found outside Britain.

White Shield was originally bottled *au naturel,* but for several decades it has been filtered and then given a dosage of yeast. The dosage used in bottle-conditioning and the original yeast in fermentation are different strains.

The Worthington brewery, founded in 1744, was long ago merged with Bass, which dates from 1777. Worthington White Shield has a family relationship with the cask-conditioned ale Draught Bass. Whether that product is a draft Pale Ale or a premium Bitter is a theological question. It is an especially individualistic ale, and one that is much appreciated. Again, being cask-conditioned, it is not exported. Indeed, it is one of the most difficult ales to keep well. At the peak of its condition, it has a soft, almost (but not quite) sour fruitiness that is irresistibly more-ish.

The complexity and character to be found in White Shield and Draught Bass are not necessarily

With an angel's blessing, the horses of Samuel Smith prepare for their round. This is the main street of Tadcaster, a town of three substantial breweries: Samuel Smith's is behind the arched doorway. The Angel and White Horse is the brewery tap.

Heavenly Unions

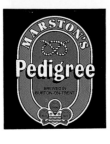

The ranks of linked barrels (*above*) are fermenting vessels at the Burton brewery of Marston's. As the beer ferments, its own turbulence forces it upward through the "swan-neck" tubes into a trough (*right*). As it settles, it flows back into the barrels. This system is now unique to Marston's. The Burton Unions system makes ales of a very distinctive character. It is to be hoped that Marston's continues with this labor-intensive but traditional method.

evident in all the many other products of the company. The widely exported Bass Ale is in some markets a far blander product.

Both White Shield and Draught Bass were originally fermented in a system of linked wooden barrels known as "Burton Unions." The hall of Burton Unions was a magnificent sight, and it made beer to match. At the beginning of the 1980s, and against the advice of at least some of their marketing consultants, Bass decided they could no longer afford to maintain this antiquated system. Had the final decision been in the hands of anyone with the slightest real interest in beer, at least some small part of the system would have been retained to make a specialty product. Its removal from service was an incongruous act from a company that runs in Burton one of the world's finest beer museums.

No one can be altogether sure how the Burton Unions system worked its magic. It was a circulatory system, and its influence would have been to train the yeast to develop in a particular manner. Yeast is a living organism, greatly influenced by its environment and highly individualistic. The yeast that lived and worked in the Burton Unions imparted its own particular fruitiness to the beers it helped make.

When the system was no more, the brewmasters at Bass had to find a way of continuing to maintain a yeast that was of the same character. The life of the yeast could never be exactly the same, but Bass has done as good a job as anyone could have hoped. Oddly, once the White Shield has been brewed and fermented in Burton, it is taken to another Bass brewery, in Sheffield, Yorkshire, for the dosage. Bass has 13 breweries, including one in Walsall which is famous for producing only Mild Ale.

One other brewer continues to use the Burton Unions system, albeit not for all of its products. This brewer is Marston's, a sizable independent. Marston's classic Pale Ale (or premium Bitter?) is its Pedigree. This has some Burton Unions character in its dash of fruitiness, with perhaps a hint of eating apple in the nose; a nutty maltiness; and a flowery, hoppy finish. Pedigree is a recognized delight on draft, but it is also excellent in its bottled form. It is an ale of great elegance, in a remarkable range of fine products, from a "Premier Cru" brewery.

The use of different fermentation systems dates from the time when brewing literature was scarce, research facilities did not exist, and communications were less pervasive than they are today. Each centre of brewing had its own methods. It is possible to travel in some beer countries and notice that each of the older breweries in a stretch of countryside has much the same technical design. They were probably the work of the same engineer, like stations on a branch railroad.

The great brewing centers of Europe have similar histories: perhaps first a monastic tradition; then the evolution of a local style that caught the imagination of the day; no doubt also some brewers who were

willing to invest in expansion and seek distant markets. All of this is usually built on wet foundations. Most brewing centers first assumed that role in the days when clean water was hard to find. The character of their water may also have played a part in creating their style of brewing. The water of Burton has a high gypsum content, which makes it well suited to the production of Pale Ales, with their characteristically robust palates. When brewers elsewhere in the world add gypsum to their water for this reason, they sometimes say they are "Burtonizing" it or "adding Burton salts."

Just as the Burton Unions method of fermentation imparts a fruity character, the Yorkshire Square system provides for a clean, round palate. And just as the water is ideal for Pale Ale in Burton-on-Trent (which is in the county of Staffordshire), so it is in Tadcaster, Yorkshire.

Several breweries, including a couple in the adjoining Midlands county of Nottinghamshire, have Yorkshire Square fermenters. Three notably use these vessels in a traditional way: the Mansfield brewery, in Nottinghamshire; Tetley's, of Leeds, Yorkshire; and Samuel Smith's, of Tadcaster. "Sam's" still has exclusively stone squares. This system, again, offers a circulating method of fermentation, but with quite different surface areas, materials and configuration.

"The Burton of the North," they called Tadcaster in the late 1800s. It is little more than a village, but it still has three breweries. Bass has a large plant; another national giant, Courage, has a brewery under the John Smith name; and there is "Sam's," which is still family-owned.

The Bass brewery makes a cask-conditioned Special Bitter. The two Smiths were branches of the same family, and John's was once a great Stone square brewery. Those days are long gone, though John Smith's has reintroduced cask-conditioned ale. Samuel Smith's, which traces its origins to 1758, is today the classic Yorkshire Square brewery.

"Sam's" has an extensive range of ales and Stouts, all with a definite Yorkshire Square character, especially in their roundness. They are all, also, on the malty side, though each makes an assertive statement of its own style. With Britain's preference for draft ales, the cask-conditioned products are best known in the home market. The well-rounded and profoundly tasty (a hint of sherry wood?), cask-conditioned Museum Ale (1047) might best arouse the palates of beer-lovers elsewhere. Its companion, Old Brewery Pale Ale, is exported to various European countries and to the United States.

Bass made a point of the designation Pale Ale in the days when it found a place in Manet's *Bar at the Folies-Bergères*. Today, Samuel Smith's makes the same stylistic point in some farther-flung places. It travels well; it is a fine Pale Ale; and it is the classic product from one of the world's great brewing regions.

Left: The Yorkshire Squares at Samuel Smith's are the only ones still in use. Each wall of the vessel is cut as a single slab from the quarry. Although the deep lower chambers are not visible, the length of the slate slabs can be judged against the brewery worker. Theakston's has two slate squares, but they are not of the Yorkshire design. Stainless-steel Yorkshire Squares are used by Tetley's, another classic brewery in the county.

Right: Many breweries have more than one Bitter. The local London brewery Young's has an "ordinary" Bitter and a Special. Some drinkers prefer the "ordinary." Classically, Bitter is a style served on draft from hand-pumps like those on the right. Young's has an outstanding bottled Export Bitter, also known as Special London Ale.

Bitter

THE BRITISH ARE NOT PEDANTIC, and they are not keen on extremes. If a particular brewery's house character is to produce sweetish ales, it may still call one of them its Bitter. Perhaps the others are even sweeter than the Bitter. A beer does not have to be very Bitter to be given that sobriquet, although it may be.

The term dates from the time when every brewery produced as its everyday ales a Mild and a Bitter. Some still do. Each brewery's first concern was to distinguish its own principal products from one another. Whether its interpretations of Mild and Bitter were the same as those of another brewery was unimportant, though obviously there were affinities of style. Because everyday drinking is done in the pub, the terms Mild (always) and Bitter (usually) apply to draft ales. Some breweries produce two Milds (a dark and a pale), and most have two examples of Bitter (an "ordinary" and a "best"). Bitter is always, in British terms, pale, meaning translucent: a few have an "old gold" color; some are bronze; the greatest number are copper-red.

As against the house Mild, the companion Bitter should certainly be dry. Some are dry by any standard. The dryness derives from a hop emphasis. Whereas some examples certainly have plenty of aroma and may be dry-hopped, this is secondary.

The foundations of the style should surely be the generous use not of aromatic varieties but of bittering hops. To beer-lovers from countries where delicacy of bouquet is prized, it sometimes seems that British brewers care little for aroma and add all their hops at an early stage of the boil. Even a Bitter that is notably aromatic will have a smack of hops (the classic variety being East Kent Goldings), rather than a delicate bouquet. Aromatic or not, a truly memorable Bitter always has a depth of hop taste and acidity in the palate and finish.

If the British were more logical, they might simply describe as "Pale Mild" some of the sweeter examples of Bitter. Brewers would resist this because, despite its gentle name, Mild is out of fashion. Bitter, notwithstanding its slightly threatening description, remains popular. The greatest gastronomes in Western Europe, the Italians and French, have no difficulty in relishing drinks and other products that are bitter, and described as so. In Britain, it was not until the lower-gravity versions of the principal dark style, Porter, had metamorphosed into what was sometimes known as Sweet Mild Ale that the counter-description Bitter gradually came into use for the draft version of the pale product.

Its acceptance as a formal style was relatively recent. Although it is listed as an "important" style in the pseudonymous 1934 work *A Book on Beer,* it was still being placed in quotation marks in 1949 in *The Brewer's Art,* published by Whitbread. In the period after World War II, Mild gradually lost ground, and "a pint of Bitter" became the most popular call in the pubs of England and Wales.

It would be easy today to imagine that all ale is Bitter; many drinkers believe the two terms to be synonymous. Of the two, it is ale that has a faintly colloquial ring, and Bitter that sounds correct.

Even a generation weaned on Coca-Cola seems to recognize the term Bitter. Perhaps it benefits from its British matter-of-factness. It is hard to imagine an American brewery calling a beer "Bitter," although some of the new micros have been so bold. In Britain, no brewing company goes so far as to describe its product as "Ordinary Bitter," although such a brew is constantly ordered over the bar.

"ORDINARY" AND "BEST"

An "ordinary" Bitter may have a gravity as low as 1035; a premium Bitter may be in the mid- to upper 1040s; a strong Bitter may be in the 1050s. Most breweries have at least two gravities of Bitter, and some have three. The "ordinary" may be simply called Bitter and the premium "Best," but this is not always the case. "Best" can mean almost anything, and many breweries have specific brand-names for each Bitter. In some instances the differences between them concern more than gravity. They may have quite different specifications.

Most drinkers will vary their choice according to their mood or the circumstances, but the low-gravity products are always popular. It is the genius of British brewers to produce ales of very low gravity and alcohol content which are nonetheless bursting with taste. These are enjoyed not only because of their relatively low price, or because the drinker has to drive, but also because they can be consumed without excessive effect. So long as they are not planning to drive, drinkers can enjoy several pints in an evening.

Bitter is the ale over which to talk. It is soothing, restful, relaxing and just slightly appetizing. It is meant for sessions in the pub with friends. After the success of the Campaign for Real Ale, there were attempts to foster similar consumerist movements to fight the case for decent bread and proper cheese. They did not enjoy such support. People care about bread and cheese, but you cannot spend an evening debating . . . conspiring . . . dreaming . . . over even the finest stone-ground granary or farmhouse Cheddar.

There is another reason for the success of Bitter at the lower gravities. As its name says, it is meant to be bitter, to whatever degree. That hop-acid bitterness cannot emerge so well in a bigger ale. It cannot fight its way so well through the malt. When the Campaign for Real Ale became a force in the land, most brewers sought to make their products more widely available in cask-conditioned form. Often the products they chose were their super-premiums.

This choice may have been motivated by pride as well as commercial considerations, but it was resented by many CAMRA members. "Very nice," they responded, "but what about a good ordinary Bitter, at a price to match?" On their side, there was some hair-shirtedness to the argument, but there was also a fair point.

As a result of CAMRA's interest, the local and regional brews of Britain are now often available outside their own areas, but cask-conditioned ale is a notoriously poor traveler. Not every drinker has the opportunity to sample each ale in its natural habitat, but the chance is worth seizing if it arises. A wine tastes best on its own soil, in its own social and gastronomic environment. The same is true of all beers.

Like most wines, and especially those of Bordeaux, the Bitter of England and Wales has its own accent from one area to another. From whichever brewery, an "ordinary" may well be less malty than a premium Bitter, but the house character will be evident in both.

London and the surrounding counties of the Southeast have some dry, hoppy, and sometimes

aromatic, examples, from classic breweries like Shepherd Neame (in the brewing town of Faversham, amid the hop gardens of east Kent), Young's and Fuller's (both in London) and Brakspear (one of several excellent breweries in the Thames Valley).

Young's "ordinary" Bitter (1036) is not quite as flintily dry as it once was, but its Special (1046) has gained in hoppiness and weighs in at an impressive 40 E.B.U. The brewery also has a remarkably hoppy and aromatic bottled product identified as a Bitter in the British market: Young's Special Export Bitter. This magnificent brew is known in some markets as Special London Ale. It has an original gravity of 1062 and not less than 50 units of bitterness (the brewers aim for 55). There could be a whole hop garden in every bottle.

Fuller's dry-hopped Chiswick Bitter (1035.5) illustrates as well as any brew in the world just how much flavor can be packed into a low-gravity beer. The same brewery's delicious E.S.B. (1055+) is the strongest regular Bitter in Britain. The initials stand for Extra Special Bitter. The gravity is by no means

massive, but it is high for a Bitter. Between these two products is the complex, satisfying London Pride (1041.5). For the lover of Bitter, this is a remarkable range.

The east of England has some rather tartly fruity interpretations of Bitter. The small country brewery of Ridley's and the larger independent Greene King afford good examples. Greene King's renowned Abbot Ale (1048) combines this tart, fruity attack with a very powerful palate. Further east, Adnams' ales have a dry complexity. Perhaps Roger Protz is right when he detects a whiff of sea air. In Lincolnshire, Bateman's XXXB (1048) is an immensely tasty Bitter: at first malty, then fruity, and finally hoppy.

In the North, Yorkshire is known for its full, creamy, nutty Bitter, sometimes with the sweetish character of the hop variety Bullion. Old Mill, one of Britain's outstanding micro-breweries, even has a product called Bullion Bitter. There is also a Bullion character in Tetley Bitter (1035.5). Specifically within the category of Bitter, this is the one that typifies the Yorkshire style, albeit from a somewhat

Hop-vines in molded plasterwork climb round the door of Shepherd Neame's brewery (*left*) in rural Faversham, Kent. The brewery is in the heart of hop country. *Above*: Stooks of barley decorate the label of Lees' Harvest Ale. Wisteria said to have been planted at the turn of the century climbs the walls of Fuller's brewery (*right*), in urban London. Fuller's Extra Special Bitter is a classic.

autonomous subsidiary of the national group Allied. Across the Nottinghamshire border, Mansfield Brewery has similar ales. Both of these breweries use Yorkshire Squares, made from stainless steel. Samuel Smith's "stone square" Old Brewery Bitter (1038.9) is full and round. Timothy Taylor's colorful range of products includes the appropriately full-bodied Landlord (1042), again with a Yorkshire sweetness, but with more hop character than some of its neighbors. Across the Cleveland border, Cameron's is noted for its nutty Strongarm (1040).

The Northwest, especially the Greater Manchester area, tends toward a dry Bitter. The dryness of Holt's Bitter (1039) is fruity, hoppy, and austere. This is a much-appreciated Bitter locally, from a brewery with the lowest of public profiles. Its neighbor, Hyde's, is so quiet as often to be overlooked, and that is unforgivable. Hyde's produces a soft, clean, fruity Bitter (1036-7), with a long, hoppy finish. The sizable independent Robinson's has a soft, well-balanced Bitter (1035), with a hint of acidity, among a range of interesting ales. The large independent Boddington's has an unusually pale Bitter (1035) which has lost some of its distinctive dryness. The small old Lees brewery has a Bitter (1038) of malty dryness. Lees is also noteworthy for a massively hoppy, bottled extra-strong brew called Harvest Ale (1100; 10.5 per cent alcohol by volume). This is made each year from the new season's malt (Maris Otter, from Yorkshire) and hops (Goldings, East Kent). Although it is not bottle-conditioned, it is vintage-dated for laying down. A

wonderful beer, and an efficacious nightcap. To drink Harvest Ale is to be bathed in hop oils, with all their soporific effect, and to enjoy the dreams of Fielding's Tom Jones.

In the Midlands, the town of Burton is inclined to make fruity, elegant Bitter (*see* Pale Ale). However, its Burton Ale (1048), from Ind Coope, is uncompromisingly a premium Bitter. It has a mighty depth of flavor, an aromatic fruitiness, and a great deal of hop character. In the West Midlands, Bitter tends to be sweetly malty and fairly light-bodied, though it can nonetheless be subtle and interesting. Holden's produces some very good examples.

Wales tends towards sweetish, malty Bitter which is often quite big in body and full in color. The examples best known outside Wales are from the Felinfoel brewery, in Llanelli. The town is famous for Rugby Union and the manufacture of tinplate, and Felinfoel produced Britain's first canned beer. The Welsh themselves have a great regard for the very malty, but dry and distinctive Brain's S.A. ("Special Ale"), a premium Bitter of 1042. "It's Brains you need" is a famous slogan. The brewery is in the middle of Cardiff, the capital.

The West of England has some examples of Bitter that are notably soft and fruity. In Dorchester, Eldridge Pope has a well-balanced Bitter (1033) and two other excellent draft ales that are broadly in this category: its dry I.P.A. (1041) and the sweeter, complex Royal Oak (1048). The county of Dorset also has Britain's only thatched brewery, Palmer's, producing a lightly dry, hoppy-nutty I.P.A. (1039.5).

Yet another Dorset brewery, Hall and Woodhouse, makes the outstanding tasty, hoppy Tanglefoot (1048). In Bristol, the national giant Courage produces its dry-hopped, malty-fruity Directors' Bitter (1046). In Devizes, the old country brewery of Wadworth's makes its lovely I.P.A. (1034), with lots of acidity, and its 6X (1040), with a hint of Cognac wood. In Swindon, Arkell produces its complex, assertive Kingsdown (1050). Swindon also has an excellent micro-brewery, Archer's, and there are many others in the West.

General de Gaulle once used the example of cheese to explain the individuality of his people. He said that the French could be united only under the threat of danger: "Nobody can simply bring together a country that has 265 kinds of cheese." Britain has about the same number of Bitter ales.

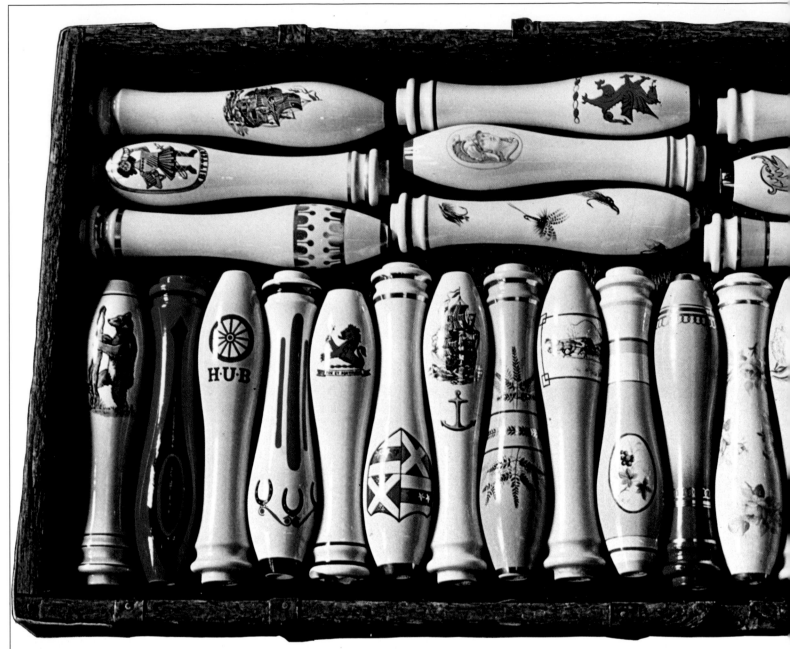

Hand-Pulled Ale

The hand-pump is one of the classic accoutrements of the English pub, but the genuine article serves as much more than a decoration. Some country pubs still tap their ale from a cask behind the bar, but that can be too warm a place for the health of the brew. The introduction of the hand-pump (*near right*) in the 1770s enabled the publican to keep his ale in the cellar. A natural cellar temperature is still the only one at which a cask-conditioned ale will mature properly. The

hand-pump is a simple mechanical device (*far right*). It does not use CO_2 pressure, so there is no gas in contact with the beer. Outside Britain, the genuine mechanical system is rarely seen. *Centre*: These plain-and-simple handles were photographed in a London pub. *Above*: These decorative handles were hand-painted at a pottery in the Midlands of England. Some were designed exclusively for breweries which have since vanished.

Mild

Below: The West Midlands has always favored mildly-hopped ale. In 1987, John Hughes re-opened his grandmother's brew-pub, the Beacon, at Sedgley, near Dudley, where he produces a deliciously creamy dark Mild of a hefty 1058.

THE WELL-REGARDED Fuller's brewery has been known to promote its Mild Ale as a harvest product. The brewery is in a place called Chiswick, which was once known for its market gardens. After a back-breaking day picking lettuce, the local people no doubt enjoyed a few pints of Mild. Today, Chiswick is a residential neighborhood well inside the boundaries of Greater London, and less Mild is sold. The brewery still makes it, but no longer in cask-conditioned form.

As Porter's sweeter, gentler young brother, Mild was originally a London style. Today, the style is very hard to find in the capital, although the Greyhound brew-pubs, in the district of Streatham, has a rich fruity example called XXXP. One of the best interpretations of a pale Mild is still made just outside London in the county town of Hertford, by the McMullen's brewery. It is called A.K. Mild and has a gravity of 1033 and a beautiful balance of malt, fruit and restrained hop.

The idea of a low-gravity brew to refresh manual workers is not exclusive to Britain. Nor is the notion that it should be low in hop bitterness (which is what Mild means). When a thirst has to be quenched, a hoppy brew can be too drying. Mild became a brew for miners and foundry and mill workers, but there is no obvious logic to its continuing to thrive in some industrial areas and not others.

The strongest loyalty to Mild is in the West Midlands, where it is still identified as something of a regional favorite. Pale and dark Milds (and a tawny in-between) can be found in this region, usually at a gravity of around 1036. The most widely-known examples are the dark Milds. The very small Batham's brewery has an appetizing, fruity example in a deep copper color. The Bass subsidiary Mitchells and Butlers has one brewery, Highgate, devoted entirely to the style. Highgate Mild is dark brown, smooth, and tasty, with a nice balance of maltiness and fruitiness. Bass's closest national rival, Allied, has the award-winning Ansell's Mild, made in Burton, among several entrants in this style. It is slightly drier, with fruit and chocolate-coffee notes in both its aroma and its palate. The very large independent Wolverhampton and Dudley Breweries are to some extent Mild specialists. Their Banks's Mild is malty, tasty and medium-dark. Their Hanson's Mild, made in another brewery, is similar, but nuttier. A chocolaty but well balanced dark brew called Merrie Monk, from Marston's, is also sometimes regarded as a Mild, though it is of a higher gravity (1043) than is normal for this category. It is something of an isolated, unclassifiable product that other brewers might nonetheless do well to emulate.

The second hold-out of Mild is the Northwest, especially Greater Manchester. All of the local breweries make Mild, and both the pale and dark styles can be found. Robinson's produces a very good pale Mild, dry and lightly fruity. Thwaite's, in the nearby brewing town of Blackburn, is noted for its very dark Best Mild, which has an intense palate and

some licorice notes.

Although not all breweries produce a Mild, many continue to do so, in most parts of England and Wales. Its problem is that low sales have led to its being withdrawn from many pubs and largely vanishing in some areas. In less consumerist times, it was often heavily dosed with caramel, and could be sickly sweet. Since the climate created by CAMRA, some brewers have taken a greater interest in their Mild.

A good example of a lighter-colored type might be made with Pale Ale malt, and have a color of 24 E.B.C. and a bitterness of 22. The dark type might gain some of its character from chocolate malt, have a color in the range of 60-90, and have a bitterness between 15 and 25.

Although a Mild is not necessarily very attenuated, its low gravity makes for a modest calorie count.

Brown Ale

Many a fisherman has been glad to return to harbor at Southwold and warm himself with a pint of Adnams' Brown Ale. The version shown here, dryish for the style and with a gravity of 1042, is now marketed as a draft winter warmer, called Adnams' Old Ale.

IF BRITAIN HAS A DESSERT BEER, it is Brown Ale. There is no *pourriture noble* in the barley fields of East Anglia, but the technique of producing crystal malt has a similar effect. It is even more reminiscent of the "stoving" used in the production of Madeira. The gentle stewing that is applied to the barley in the making of crystal malt concentrates its natural sugars into a condition known as "luscious" by brewers. These "luscious sugars" have a toffeeish richness.

The "Muscat" aroma evinced by the Hoegaarden type of Wheat Beer made in Belgium does not manifest itself in an English Brown Ale, but a warm sweetness does. It is the beer world's Malmsey.

In his 1956 *Book of Beer*, Andrew Campbell was cautious on the use of beer as an accompaniment to dessert: "The flavor of beer is not really appropriate to very sweet entremets . . . there is at least one exception, for Brown Ale is excellent with apple pie."

A suitably English (as well as American) choice, but surely not the end of the matter. Certainly, an English dish would seem appropriate, but does that leave the way open for treacle tart, or some more toffeeish delight? Campbell was hesitant about "acid fruit," but what about the sweeter eating apples of Kent? Best of all, nuts and a glass of Brown Ale in the soporific afternoon that follows an English Sunday lunch. Such brown brews were bracketed with "brandy and water, turtle soup, roast sirloin, haunch of venison, Madeira and cigar smoke" by that most English of writers, George Orwell, albeit in ascetic mood. He conjured this blend to describe the atmosphere of Thackeray's work.

Such clubby opulence hardly befits brews with names like John Brown, Bob Brown, Danny Brown, Nut Brown, Forest Brown, and Sussex Wealdman, but even their honest Englishness has been forgotten in recent years. Brown Ale was seen in a different mood by the satirist and jazz singer George Melly, in his autobiographical work *Owning Up*. He described Londoners from the south of the river Thames as transpontine people who drank Brown Ale and dealt in used cars. These days, such people drink lager, or vodka and tonic, so perhaps Brown Ale is due for a new image.

Brown Ale was originally a London style. Full-colored brews in general, whether the related styles of Brown Ale and Dark Mild, or Porter and Stout, were traditionally associated with London and the South, because they were the styles best suited to the local waters. Burton switched to Pale Ale when it was realized that this style could be brewed especially well with a water rich in gypsum (calcium sulphate), whereas London's supply has a relatively high proportion of calcium carbonate and some sodium chloride. In *A History of English Ale and Beer*, H.A. Monckton points out that these salts favored the production of "luscious" brews.

The southern type of Brown Ale, very dark in color, almost opaque, definitely sweet in palate, and low in gravity and alcohol content, is brewed all over England. There was a time when every brewery had

an example, but many are now happy simply to carry in their pubs a brand made by one of the national giants.

The best known example is probably Mann's Brown Ale (1034-5), from Watney's. Mann, Crossman and Paulin was originally an east London brewery. Watney's has always brewed in west London, but is now a national group. The two have been merged for many years.

A particularly good brew in this style is King and Barnes Brown Ale. King and Barnes is a country brewery with a modern plant, south of London at Horsham, Sussex. Its entrant, subtitled *Dark* Brown Ale (1031-35), has a dense head, a lovely, clean sweetness in the start, and a gentle dryness in the finish.

A good southern-type Brown Ale might be expected to have a color of around 125 E.B.C. and a bitterness of about 20 E.B.U. Crystal malt provides the signature, even though the percentage used will be well inside single figures. Many brewers also use black invert sugar, and often caramel.

The prefix "dark" is not normally used to identify the southern, and conventional, type of Brown Ale, though it is a useful description. There is another, quite different, type, with a translucent, deep amber color, a medium gravity and alcohol content, and a medium-sweet palate. While the southern type of Brown Ale has experienced declining sales for many years, this second variation has grown in popularity.

In 1987, two new examples were launched by the Cornish Brewery, better known as Devenish, of Redruth. One is called Strong Brown, at 1042-48, the other Extra Strong Brown, at 1052-58. Both are in a range of well-made all-malt brews, made without additives, under the insignia "Real Steam Beer." They are not Steam Beers in the American sense, and the term was clearly conceived as a marketing device. However, they are made in a way that is unusual in Britain. They have a two-stage primary fermentation, and they are cold-conditioned. The whole range is malt-accented and notably clean-tasting. Appropriately, the malt accent is especially evident in the case of the two Brown Ales.

Cornwall is the extreme southwest of England, but this style of Brown Ale is associated with the opposite of the country, the Northeast. The most characterful northern-type Brown Ale is made by Samuel Smith's. In Britain, it is known as Old Brewery Strong Brown Ale. In some markets, it is called Nut Brown. It is, indeed, nutty-tasting — and well rounded, complex and rich. It has a gravity of 1048-52, 34 units of bitterness (the maltiness has to be balanced) and 65 E.B.C. (it is fuller in color than its local rivals).

Just a little farther north, the Vaux Brewery, of Sunderland, has Double Maxim, at 1044, with 22 units of bitterness and 42 of color. This has its origins in a special brew produced to celebrate the return of Captain (later Colonel) Ernest Vaux from the Boer War, where he served with a Maxim Gun

King and Barnes' excellent, Southern-style example spells it out: Dark Brown Ale. Newquay is in the West, but its Brown is Northern-style, like Double Maxim from Sunderland.

detachment. There was at first a "Single" Maxim (subsequently known as Light Brown Ale); the "Double" came much later.

By far the best-known example of the type of Brown Ale made in the Northeast comes from Newcastle Breweries. In the local market, bottled beers of this type were offered in Amber and Brown variations, but the latter became the more popular. When Newcastle breweries linked with the Scottish firms of McEwans and Younger's to form a national grouping, its Brown began to enjoy a wider distribution. Although the city of Newcastle is firmly in England, its brewery's cross-border links sometimes lead to its Brown Ale being wrongly thought to be Scottish. This often happens on beer-lists in the United States.

Across the river Tyne, the Federation Brewery (owned by working men's clubs) has a distinctive and enjoyable entrant called High Level Brown Ale. The name is taken from one of the bridges across the Tyne (though not the one upon which the Sydney Harbour Bridge is modeled). The ale has the light buttery note that is the brewery's signature.

English Stouts

THE OLOROSO OF the beer world? The cream sherry? Or the Bailey's Irish Cream? If the first comparison seems to flatter, the last under-rates. Sweet Stout (though rarely identified as such on the label) is the definitively English type. Within Britain, it may no longer be identified as a Milk Stout, as it once was. That ruling is intended to protect the consumer from confusion, though Sweet Stout is not an especially befuddling drink. Its defining ingredient is, indeed, a milk sugar — lactose. Chocolate malt is also a part of the signature.

The most widely-available and best-known example is Mackeson Stout, which has a stylized milk churn on the label. This product is made by Whitbread, and has been produced at several of the company's breweries. In Britain, it has a gravity of 1038-42. Whitbread aims for the higher end of this bracket. Lactose is used both in the kettle and as a priming. After being primed, the Stout is chilled, to stop fermentation, and fined, but not pasteurized. The priming means that it is sweeter and fuller than its gravity suggests. In other markets, notably the Caribbean, Stouts are associated with higher gravities; so in the Americas, Mackeson is in the mid- to upper 1050s.

The original Mackeson brewery, in Hythe, Kent, is thought to have been founded in 1669. It was acquired by the Mackeson family in 1801, later passing to Jude, Hanbury, which was bought by Whitbread in 1929. Mackeson Milk Stout, as it was originally known, was first brewed in 1907 and has been marketed nationally since 1936. It is said that a farmer sought the right for his cows to pass through the brewery yard at Hythe, and this consolidated the notion that milk was indeed added to the Stout.

Being outside Britain, the Guernsey Brewery, in the Channel Islands, is still able to call its entrant Milk Stout. Cream Label can hardly be debarred, and that is the name used by Watney's for its Sweet Stout. Farm Stout and Meadowsweet are no more. Sweetheart is a well-liked Stout from Tennent's, the Scottish subsidiary of Bass. In all, there are about 20 brands, though the number is declining. A very good example of the style is made by the oddly-named Home Brewery, in Nottingham. This company is a subsidiary of Scottish and Newcastle. Its Home Stout has just enough hoppy dryness to give a bittersweet note to the chocolate-malt character. There are gently roasty notes, too, in the full palate. A well-rounded, smooth brew.

In the once-British island of Malta, the local brewery adds vitamin B to its Lacto Stout, so popular is it with nursing mothers.

Like a sweet sherry or an Irish cream liqueur, these products seem best cast as a relatively innocent mid-afternoon sustainer. In his 1889 classic *The Curiosities of Ale and Beer*, John Bickerdyke recalled: "Macklin, the actor, who lived to be a centenarian, was accustomed to drink considerable quantities of Stout sweetened with sugar, at The Antelope, in White Hart Yard, Covent Garden."

British Stout? Well, the sweet type has been made throughout the British Isles, but the style is really English. McMullen's still makes fine ales but no longer a Stout. Mackeson is the best known. Home Stout is a good example. Eldridge Pope's Huntsman no longer has a Milk or Oat Malt Stout, but Samuel Smith's has a revivalist example. Who will be first to reintroduce Oyster Stout — the British or the Americans?

A sweet drink called "Sheffield Stout," after the city, is still sometimes made in Yorkshire. It is a mix of Mather's Black Beer (a non-alcoholic, malt-extract product made in Leeds) and lemon soda.

Such eccentric behavior should have been rendered unnecessary during the 1800s. Under political pressure to use the products of Britain's Caribbean possessions, brewers began to utilize sugars derived from cane. The influence of these sugars has helped shape modern British brews, and in small quantities should not offend the purist.

Several other ingredients have been used in Stout over the years. Essence of oyster was employed by some breweries, notably Castletown, on the Isle of Man. Oyster Stout is no longer made in Britain, despite the harmony enjoyed by these two items. In 1988 the Red Hook brewery of Seattle, Washington State, carried out development work with a view to producing an example. The state is an oyster-growing area. Even without the oyster, Stout is regarded as an aphrodisiac in many parts of the world.

Oatmeal Stout was a recognized variation on Sweet Stout. It vanished in the late 1950s, but was revived in the 1980s by Samuel Smith's. Oatmeal was used for its nutritive qualities and for fullness of body and flavor. In Samuel Smith's Oatmeal Stout (1048) it imparts a particular silkiness of texture. This is a complex but soothing brew for a restful afternoon, and a magnificent revival of the style.

Samuel Smith also makes an excellent Dry Stout, primarily to offer in its own pubs as an alternative to Guinness. Like the famous Irish brew, this is identified as Extra Stout. Several other English breweries are toying with this idea, after years in which Dry Stout has been regarded as an exclusively Irish style. The tireless Smiths also have an excellent Imperial Stout (*see* "Russian" Stout).

Old Ale

THE CLASSIC OLD ALE OF ENGLAND is a specialty product from the Greene King brewery, of Bury St Edmunds, in the county of Suffolk. The ale is called Strong Suffolk, and is hard to find. It is an endangered product. In the CAMRA newspaper *What's Brewing*, in November 1986, Greene King's head brewer admitted as much, but said he was determined not to let Strong Suffolk disappear.

The ale is produced only occasionally, and is a blend of two brews. The first has a gravity of 1106 and is aged in unlined, covered oak vats for between one and two years, during which time it gains a vinous character. A dosage of ten per cent of this brew is then added to a dark ale of 1052. The end result is an ale of 1058 of claret color and medium body, with a winy, bitter-fruit nose and palate and an iron-like note. Drinkers offended by a hint of iron should stay away from this ale, as from Lafite and Cheval-Blanc. Neither of those, on the other hand, would stand up to pickled herrings. They, too, are an East Anglian specialty, and the two pleasures have been combined at dinners of the Incorporated Brewers' Guild.

Strong Suffolk is the only surviving (so long as it does) British example of the style of brewing that is associated with West Flanders, and especially with the Rodenbach brewery, in Roeselare (Rouliers, in French).

East Anglia and the Low Countries are separated only by the sea, yet through the ages it has joined them. Beer made with hops first entered Britain from Flanders, in the 15th century. The Dutch helped drain the Fens (and there are still windmills in East Anglia). The Flemings brought the textile industry that once enriched East Anglia. It seems, though, that the English introduced — at least in methodical practice — this style of brewing to Flanders. There are, of course, broader comparisons, stretching from English Barley Wine to Belgian Lambics, but there is both a geographical and a technical proximity between Strong Suffolk in Bury St Edmunds and Rodenbach in Roeselare.

It is not always easy to determine the difference between an Old Ale and a Barley Wine. Both are terms used in Britain to describe strong brews. What does seem to be the case is that, if a brewery has both, the Barley Wine will be the stronger.

An Old Ale is usually dark, and often a draft product, though neither of these characteristics is a rule. Strong Suffolk is a bottled product, but is made by a process of aging. That would seem to have been the original meaning of Old Ale, though in general it no longer is.

Was aging originally carried out in order to mature the product, or was a strong Old Ale brewed for another purpose? Before the invention of refrigeration, it was impossible to brew in summer, because of wild yeast problems. Only a very strong ale could be stored during this time without being infected. What happened to ale that was returned because it had gone sour? Only a powerfully strong

and very thoroughly fermented ale could mask the infection.

Today, the term "old" is used in the names of many ales that have not necessarily been aged for long periods, though some may have been. Some have gravities in the upper 1040s; many are much stronger. They may be rich, but not as intensely so as most Barley Wines. They may be strong, but they do not all have the — not so much winy as spirity — warmth of the latter category.

At the lower end of the gravity band, Old Hookey, at 1049, is fruity, malty, and smooth. This is from the lovely old tower brewery of Hook Norton, at Banbury, Oxfordshire. An outstanding example is Dark Star, at 1050, from the Pitfield micro-brewery, in London. This is a fruity brew, with a depth of flavor and a dry finish. Wadworth's Old Timer (1053) is another fruity entrant, with a fresh, peachy character. Although it is not identified as being "old," Young's Winter Warmer (1055) is a superb example. This seasonal ale (November-February) is luscious and fruity, yet surprisingly dry. Ringwood Old Thumper (1060) is fruity, with apple notes, and is smooth and satisfying.

In blind tastings a consistent winner is Old Peculier (1057). This is a soft, rich, remarkably well balanced Old Ale, with a great complexity of yeasty fruitiness (especially blackcurrant, but many other notes, too) complemented by a malty sweetness (notably chocolate) and hoppy dryness in the background (Fuggles and Northern Brewer). Six or seven different malts and brewing sugars are used, and the beer is dry-hopped. Old Peculier is made by Theakston's, which has in succession been acquired first by Matthew Brown, then by Scottish and Newcastle. It is to be hoped that the character of this product can be maintained. Theakston's own brewery is in the village of Masham, near Ripon, North Yorkshire.

At the stronger end of the spectrum, Marston's again has a fine brew, Owd Roger (1080), with its huge, creamy head, vanilla notes, and completeness of palate. Another fine example is Robinson's Old Tom (1080), fruity and sherryish, with lots of warming alcohol in the finish.

The two classic strong ales of England are hard to classify: should they be regarded as Old Ales or Barley Wines? Both are bottle-conditioned.

One is from Gale's, a brewery near Portsmouth. Gale's is known for the character of its ales, all of which are very fruity. Its extra-strong brew is called Prize Old Ale (1092-98) and is available only in the bottle. It comes in a corked bottle, and is naturally conditioned. It is a very intense ale, with a dry fruitiness and alcoholic warmth that would not be out of place across the water in Normandy. A Calvados among beers.

The other is from Eldridge Pope, of Dorchester, and is Britain's strongest ale. It is not identified as an Old Ale, and in style has more in common with the Barley Wines, though it exceeds even the best of them in character. It is definitely an Old Ale in that maturation is a part of its production process. Most of the maturation, though, takes place in the bottle. This profound, stylish brew is called Thomas Hardy's Ale, after the poet and novelist, whose work was largely set in his home county of Dorset, and who wrote with great enthusiasm of the local ale.

Thomas Hardy's Ale has a gravity of 1125.8, 9.9 per cent alcohol by weight, and 12.48 by volume. It is made only with Pale Ale malt (from Maris Otter barley), hopped with Fuggles and Goldings, dry-hopped, and warm-conditioned for three months. The yeast is pitched twice for fermentation, and a third time for conditioning.

Thomas Hardy's Ale was first released in 1968 for a literary festival to mark the 40th anniversary of the poet's death. In 1986, with an eye to the symmetry of the dates, the brewery arranged a tasting of different vintages. The director of the brewery's wine and spirit department, himself a Master of Wine, described the '68 Thomas Hardy as "elegant, but still creamy, Madeira-like." At least one new vintage is released each year, and the brewery recommends that it not be opened for a further five. Enthusiasts who know this beer appreciate that, newly released, it will be overpoweringly syrupy . . . but it is hard to abide by the five-year embargo.

Magnificently bulbous kettles, seasoned with whole hops from the sack, yield tasty ales for the brewmaster at Eldridge Pope. Many breweries make commemorative ales, but Eldridge Pope is particularly well known for such specials. Its vintage-dated Thomas Hardy's Ale has for years been rated Britain's strongest, at 12.48 by volume. In 1988 another West of England brewery, Cornish, sold for more than £1,000 at Christie's, in London, a considerably stronger old ale, at a claimed 15.86 per cent. It was presented as the world's most potent brew, though at the time it was still awaiting entry into the *Guinness Book of Records*.

Barley Wine

WHEN THE BRITISH BEER STYLE known as Barley Wine began to be produced by the new generation of small American brewers, the authorities who govern labeling were perplexed. How could an ale be labeled as a wine? Wouldn't the consumer be confused? Eventually, the American brewers had to settle for a clumsy compromise: "Barley-wine-style Ale."

Of course it is an ale, not a wine. It is an ale that tastes as strong as a wine, and is usually marketed in small bottles, called "nips." It might also be served in a wine glass, though that is true of any beer, especially one to be presented with a meal, and certainly if it has a big bouquet. That is why the Belgians are so fond of Burgundy samplers.

Traditionally, British brewers call their strongest ale a Barley Wine. That is what the term indicates. It seems clearly to derive from the folksy comparison with wine, though another explanation is tempting. In order to achieve high alcohol content, the brew was traditionally left to mature in the cask for many months, and rolled from time to time, so that the yeast would be roused to fight one last battle in the conversion of sugars to alcohol.

During this long time in the wood, the ale would have gained a vinous character from the resident microorganisms. It is hard to find a winy-tasting example today, though one has been successfully produced in the traditional manner by the Commonwealth brew-pub in the United States.

Barley Wines are made in both pale and dark types. Among the best renditions of each are two made in London. A fine example of the pale type is Fuller's Golden Pride (1084-92), remarkably dry for an ale of such strength, with the smoothness and warming finish of a Cognac. A hearty dark type is Young's Old Nick (1084), liqueurish and fruity, with a hint of banana. There are many other examples from independent brewers, among them the less strong (1066) but very dry and intense Bishop's Tipple, from Gibbs Mew, of Salisbury; the toffee-ish, luscious Tally-Ho (1071-5), from Adnams; and the very fruity (reminiscent of a Belgian Triple) Elizabethan (1090), from Harvey's, of Lewes, Sussex.

Among the national giants, Bass has its dark No.1 Barley Wine, and Whitbread the best-known pale example, Gold Label. The latter is the most widely available Barley Wine in Britain. It has a gravity of 1098, spends three hours in the kettle, and is warm-conditioned at 10°C (50°F) for two months. The bottled version is filtered but not pasteurized. This product is also available in the can, in which form it is, of course, pasteurized. For its gravity, it is a mellow and drinkable brew. Watney's dark Barley Wine, Stingo (1076), is notable for a roasty, Stout-like character in the finish.

The Dorset company Hall and Woodhouse also has a Barley Wine called Stingo — an earthy, tasty, brew. It is odd that one brewing company from the South and another from the West are the upholders of the name Stingo, since it was originally a Yorkshire designation, applied specifically to a strong ale. The Watney's product is exported to the United States, but what would the authorities there have made of Stingo if that were offered as the sole description of the item?

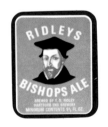

Gold Label

Strong as a double scotch Less than half the price

The ad on the left was a classic for candor and simplicity of message. Nationally marketed Barley Wines like Gold Label have replaced many local brewers' offerings, but with luck the Devil will live for ever.

"Russian" Stout

By Imperial Warrant

The London shipper A. Le Coq (founded by a Belgian) printed its publicity material (*far right*) partly in Russian. *Below*: A gift of Stout much appreciated by the Empress led to a warrant to supply the court. In the early 20th century, increased tariffs encouraged Le Coq to buy a brewery (*right*) within the Russian Empire, at Tartu, in Estonia. The brewery displayed its wares at local fetes (*lower right*).

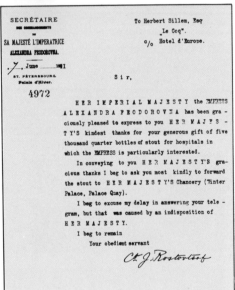

IT WAS AN INDUSTRIAL REVOLUTION, not a political one, that made "Russian" Stout. As the first nation to have its industrial revolution, Britain was able to brew on a large scale before it had good roads, in the days when the easiest export route was by water. The island nation imported wine from the sunny south, and exported strong, warming brews to the north.

Probably first under the name Porter, and later as Stout, brews were shipped from London out of the Thames estuary, and from Burton through the docks at Hull. Export versions would have been brewed to a higher gravity, so that they could enjoy a secondary fermentation at sea. This would protect them against infection. So, no doubt, did a high hopping rate. The notion of a drink reaching its final condition at sea is not unique to this style of Stout, or to India Pale Ale. The same situation helped to shape the lager-brewing traditions of Bremen and Hamburg, the akvavit of Norway and the wines of Madeira.

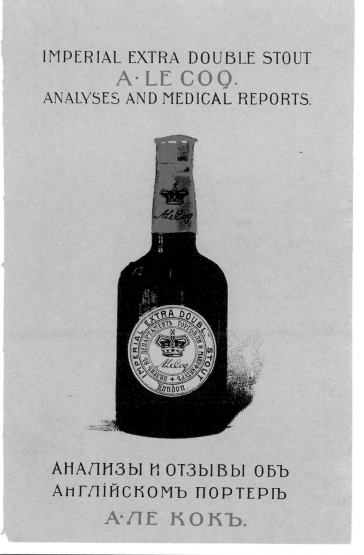

IMPERIAL EXTRA DOUBLE STOUT
A·LE COQ.
ANALYSES AND MEDICAL REPORTS.

АНАЛИЗЫ И ОТЗЫВЫ ОБЪ
АНГЛІЙСКОМЪ ПОРТЕРЏ
А·ЛЕ КОКЪ.

Strong Stouts and Porters were shipped from Britain to the north of Germany, the Scandinavian countries, Finland, Prussia, Poland, and Russia. Eventually, all of these countries began to brew their own, and some still do.

This style of Stout was especially popular in Russia, where a British shipper supplied the Imperial Court. As a result of this, the style came to be known variously as "Russian" or "Imperial" Stout.

In London, the Anchor brewery (one of many in the world to bear this name) shipped Stout to the Baltic from at least the 1780s until World War I. Dr Samuel Johnson, the writer and lexicographer, was briefly involved in the affairs of this brewery and its sale to Barclay and Perkins (later acquired by Courage). He said of the transaction: "We are not here to sell a parcel of boilers and vats, but the possibility of growing rich beyond the dreams of avarice."

Courage announced in 1980 that it would stop brewing in London, but it has continued sporadically to produce its Imperial Russian Stout in its other plants. Some bottlings have been filtered at 1098; others in the classic, naturally-conditioned form at 1104. It still has some weeks' warm conditioning, but not the 18 months of old. Nonetheless, it is still one of the most intense-tasting brews in the world, its "burnt-currant" character verging on being tar-like. It is a brew for lovers of rich fruitcakes, Christmas pudding, or Pedro Ximinez sherry.

Courage has shown some interest in protecting Imperial Russian Stout as a brand, but Samuel Smith has a product in the same category, currently available only in the United States. Although this has a lower gravity (1072), it is immensely rich, with a full "burnt currant" character. So is the honeyish Imperial Stout made by the Grant's micro-brewery, in the United States. Grant's actually uses honey, but

the dominant note in all Imperial Stouts derives from a combination of their esters and their roastiness. The high gravity makes for a particularly distinctive ester character.

In Continental Europe, the terms Porter and Imperial Stout are both used in the Baltic region for brews in this style. Bottom-fermenting versions are produced in Denmark; top-fermenting examples in Sweden, Finland and Karlsruhe, Germany.

The former Le Coq Stout brewery in Tartu, Estonia, was nationalized by the Soviet Union. Compensation of £240,000 was finally paid out in 1971. The brewery still stands. In the Baltic ports of Poland, a Scottish style of Stout, spiced with rose-hips, is still remembered. An extract is sold so that a version can be produced at home.

The inner gates of Traquair House provide access for summer visitors, who can sample its "château-bottled" beer. Bonnie Prince Charlie took refuge in the house during his campaign to seize the crown from the Hanoverian George II. The main gates will remain closed until a Stuart is returned to the throne of Britain. The present brewer/Laird is a member of the Stuart family.

Scotland

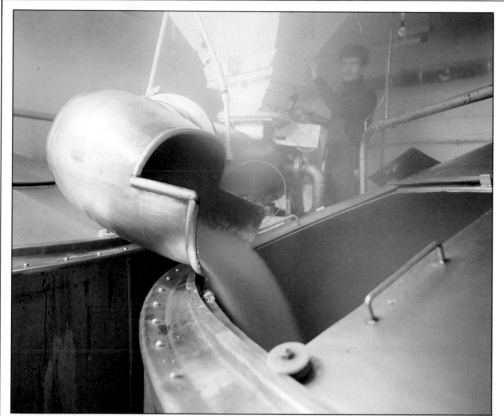

It is an aromatically steamy moment as the mash-tun is charged at the Caledonian brewery. The brewery's antique equipment extends to open brew-kettles, a very rare feature. The buildings, too, are traditional in style, though the maltings were last used in the early 1980s. The brewery is not far from the center of Edinburgh. Its strongest ale is colorfully labeled as MacAndrew's in the United States and St James in Italy. The names are mock-Scottish, but the ale is outstanding.

JUST AS IT WAS ONCE a great literary capital, and remains a center for education and insurance, Edinburgh was also one of Europe's most famous brewing cities. That tradition has been allowed to diminish, but thankfully not to vanish. The capital city still has three free-standing breweries and one tiny brew-pub, and Scotland has its own styles and traditions.

As a cold country, Scotland is well suited by its tradition of full-bodied, malty ales. These are often, but not always, dark. They are made to a full range of gravities, but Scotland is especially known elsewhere for its strong ales. In a separate tradition, Scotland produced lagers at a relatively early stage, and even they have tended to be slightly fuller-bodied than those produced south of the border.

In the classically dark Scottish ales, a defining ingredient is black malt. This provides color and dryness, though it is often underpinned with the sweeter crystal malt. The largest share of the grist is still Pale Ale malt, but that is hidden by the more colorful and flavorful defining ingredients. The ales are not quite as attenuated, nor as heavily hopped, as those south of the border. They are meant to taste malty, and they do.

The counterpart to England's Mild in Scotland is called Light, or Sixty Shilling (rendered as 60/-), and is likely to have a gravity of 1030 or a little more. Light refers only to its relative weight. In color, it is usually dark, which can be confusing for the foreigner. The nostalgic "shilling" system is said to refer to past tax rates, though it may at one time have represented the price of a cask. The counterpart to an "ordinary" Bitter is called Heavy, or 70/-, at around 1035 or a little more. This is usually paler, but tawny. The counterpart to a premium Bitter is called Export, or

The writer John Buchan was born in Broughton, and the local micro-brewery there names its principal ale after his novel *Greenmantle*. The very pale ale Merlin also offers an historical/ literary allusion. The name Old Jock, though, puzzles Americans.

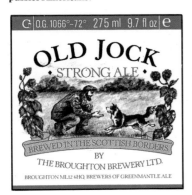

80/-, at 1040 or a little more. This is usually full in color. The counterpart to an Old Ale or Barley Wine, especially if it is presented in a nip bottle, may be identified as a Wee Heavy.

The British giant Bass has two breweries under the Tennent name, in Edinburgh and Glasgow, primarily concerned with lager. It also owns the brand Fowler's Wee Heavy, well remembered as an outstanding Scottish ale associated with Prestonpans, in the border country. Today, Fowler's is brewed for Bass/

Tennent by the respected independent Belhaven. A full range of well-made and typically Scottish ales is produced by Belhaven, and it is to be hoped that their quality is not put under strain by the company's considerable expansion.

Allied Breweries makes Scottish ales, under the Archibald Arrols name, in Alloa. This is an old brewing town, which still has the well-regarded independent Maclays. Its ales, also typically Scottish, are much-loved but hard to find.

The country's own giant is Scottish and Newcastle Breweries. The Scottish brewery of this company is in Edinburgh. Its dark ale, Younger's No. 3 (1043), has a long-established cult following in England. This is in the rich, dark style that might be deemed simply a "Scotch ale." In Belgium and the United States, the 1088 McEwan's Scotch ale packs a more obvious punch.

Edinburgh's Caledonian brewery regained its independence in a management buy-out in the mid-1980s. This magnificent brewery, built in 1869, offers by far the best evidence of the city's brewing traditions. It is a piece of industrial archaeology, with its open, direct-flame coppers as the highlights. Its products have a lovely, clean, yet complex, malt character, and it is especially noted for its Caledonian Strong Ale (1080; 5.7 per cent alcohol by weight; 7.1 by volume). This is marketed in the United States under the name MacAndrew's.

Behind Edinburgh's elegant Princes Street is an alley called Rose Street which was once lined with pubs. It is a shadow of its former sins, but it still has a brew-pub, at 55-57 Rose Street. This produces a very enjoyable, well-balanced but malt-accented 80/- ale called Auld Reekie (an unflattering nickname for Edinburgh, and one it hardly deserves). A 90/- is also sometimes produced.

In Aberdeenshire, at Ruthven, the Borve House brew-pub produces a splendidly rich and smoky Extra Strong (1085). Other micro-breweries have come and gone. One that certainly seems set to survive is Broughton, in the hamlet of the same name in the border country. This produces ales that are relatively dry for Scotland, though its strong brew, Old Jock (1070), has a clean maltiness and lots of taste. The label seems sensible enough in Scotland, where Jock is simply a common nickname, but it causes some puzzlement to American visitors, who tend to think first of the sporting connotations.

The most Scottish of breweries is at the castle called Traquair House, at the village of Innerleithen, near Peebles, also in the border country. The Lord of the Manor (in Scotland, he is known as a Laird) discovered not long after he succeeded to the house that it had once brewed its own ale. He stumbled upon the brewing equipment in a run-down stable block and, with the help of his good neighbors at Belhaven, set it to work again.

It is the only British brewery to ferment all of its production in uncoated, wooden vessels. It produces a cask-conditioned draft brew called Bear Ale (1050-55), but is better known for its Traquair House (1073-1080). This is usually filtered and pasteurized (at Belhaven) but there have been naturally-conditioned bottlings. There are also frequent commemorative specials. Traquair House is a classic, dark Scottish ale, rich and full, but with its sweetness balanced by oaky dryness. A vintage port among beers.

A Haven Still?

"Bavaria cannot produce the like," said the Emperor of Austria. "Belhaven beer is the Burgundy of Scotland..." "The best small beer I ever had," said Boswell. The brewery, in the seaport and resort of Dunbar, has its origins in a 14th-century monastery. It has greatly expanded in recent years, had several changes of ownership, and smartened up the folksy labels shown here.

Ireland

Ireland is the country in which to drink dry Stout, but it has also its own distinctive style of ale, as evidenced by the selection below. Many younger drinkers in Ireland fail to appreciate their Stouts, and ale even less so.

THE TRADITION OF IRELAND is to brew Dry Stout, famously Guinness, but also Murphy and Beamish, both of which have become more widely available in recent years. Ireland also has its own style of ale, noted for its reddish color, full body and sweetish, sometimes slightly buttery, palate. Irish Ale is a minor category, but an interesting one.

Stout has never been threatened by ale, but it is rapidly losing its market-share to lager among the young. Although Guinness moved early into the lager market, through its subsidiary Harp, there is nothing Irish about the character of that product. Nor about any other lager produced in Ireland. They are much the same Pilsener-derivatives as are found in England, and no more interesting.

The Porter and Stout family came late to Ireland, perhaps because it is both a provincial and a conservative country. Stout has been helped to thrive by the same conservatism, in Dublin and Cork as well as the rural areas. If Ireland's Stouts are borne as a badge of national pride, that seems right and proper. They are products of distinction, very enjoyable, undoubtedly among the great beers of the world, and strongly identified with the Irish by everyone else.

Amid the mahogany and marble of a Dublin pub, a pint of Guinness has a reflective quality to ease the passage of wisdom and wit. In Cork, Beamish or Murphy go with the shellfish. In a country pub, Stout soothes the singing. A thin, cold pint of "international" lager can do none of these things. No country in Europe exports a higher percentage of its beer than Ireland. Most of this is Guinness, much sent to Britain, despite the presence of a large branch-brewery near London. Ireland will never make that kind of money selling lager.

Guinness clearly tastes best at a natural temperature, but on draft it is often served lightly cooled. Like a new Beaujolais, it is sufficiently robust to survive this. Warm and cool Draught Guinness are almost like two separate drinks; the same, of course, is true of Beaujolais.

Draught Guinness in Ireland is unpasteurized, because turnover permits that. Ambience aside, this is why it seems to taste better in Ireland than anywhere else. The taste has nothing to do with Liffey water. Neither the Liffey nor Holy Water make Guinness great, though the rain that falls on the Wicklow Mountains may help. Purists object that Draught Guinness is served under CO_2 and nitrogen pressure. It is a shame that the natural carbonation of draft brews is a forgotten art in Ireland, but the method pioneered by Guinness does make for a very creamy pint.

The purist, for that matter, prefers the bottled version, Guinness Extra, as sold in its naturally-conditioned form in the pubs of Ireland and parts of Britain. Quite right, too. In this version, the fresh character unmasks all the complexities of palate, especially the hop notes. All good Stouts are roasty, but the complex of that character with the hoppiness

A Stout Threesome

The Guinness brewery in Dublin was the biggest in the world when the engraving above was made, in about 1890. The size of the mash-tuns and their mechanical operation bear witness to the sophistication of the brewery at that time. Guinness, founded in 1759, became a joint-stock company in 1886. *Right:* The two other Stout-brewers which survive in Ireland were established in the city of Cork in 1792 and 1883.

of Guinness makes for something more. The palate, and the texture, also gain from Guinness's use of a proportion of roasted unmalted barley.

Not only is Guinness purported to be pumped straight out of the Liffey, it is also popularly believed to be stronger in Ireland than elsewhere. This is the exact opposite of the truth. In Ireland (and Britain) Dry Stouts have a gravity in the range of 1038-42 (around 3.5 per cent alcohol by weight; 4.3 by volume). They are thus kept in a tax band, and range of potency, in which they can be regarded as everyday, "session" brews. Elsewhere, 1048 is more common. In the tropics, they reach the 1070s. The

tropical version of Guinness has its richness offset by the blending-in of some intentionally-soured Stout prior to its being stabilized by pasteurization. This unusual technique is another variation on the methods used in the past to produce strong Porters, Old Ales and Barley Wines.

Both of the "other" Dry Stouts are brewed in the city of Cork. Murphy has a gentle but firm body and a lightly roasty accent. Murphy, too, has traditionally used a proportion of roasted, unmalted barley. It once took its water from Our Lady's Well, now a small shrine. It also had its own maltings, now a visitor-reception center. The Stout and whiskey

179

In Ireland, bars often look like shops, and may serve as both. The shop-fronts may offer beer or whiskey, wine, tobacco, tea, groceries and services ranging from car-hire to embalming. Usually, their name is simply that of their owner.

Below: The blessing of the beer. A ceremony to dedicate a new brew-house at Murphy's, in Cork, in 1985. To the right of the priest is Dr Garrett Fitzgerald, who was Prime Minister of the Republic at the time.

The Brewery on Friary Hill

New micro-breweries in Ireland have had a hard time, and the last of the small independents ceased production in 1956. Astonishingly, this tiny brewery at Enniscorthy, County Wexford, has since licensed its Ruby Ale not only to Pelforth, in France, but also to the mighty Coors in the United States. The Irish brewery was powered by a water-wheel until 1952. A doorway in the brewery dates from 1456, when there was an abbey on the site, which is still known as Friary Hill. Relics from the brewery can be seen in the town museum.

Murphys were branches of the same family. The brewery, which traces its history from the 1850s, has been greatly restored and modernized since it was acquired by Heineken in the mid-1980s. Beamish goes back to the 1790s, though its incongruously Tudor façade was built in the 1920s. The company has been controlled by Carling of Canada since the 1960s, and is therefore now owned by Elders of Australia. Its Stout is softer and more chocolaty, especially in its draft form.

It could be that the taste for Stout dictated the fullness of flavor to be found in Irish Ales, though it is also true that they seem to share some notes with their Celtic cousins in Wales and (to a lesser extent) Scotland. Their distinctiveness could have its origins in the strains of malting barley used, or in the yeasts. The slightly buttery note sometimes found would be a defect in a lager, but is part of the character of several excellent tasty ales.

Ale production in Ireland is dominated by a company set up by Guinness with Allied Breweries. The company is called Irish Ale Breweries, and its products are, in ascending order of sweetness: Macardle's and Phoenix, Perry's, Smithwick's, and the newer Twyford's. There is also a Smithwick's Barley Wine.

In the North, near Lisburn, the Hilden micro-brewery has produced some tasty, fruity-malty, naturally conditioned ales. This is a brave attempt, but "real ale" is not well understood in Ireland. An especially Irish-tasting ale called Dempsey's was made by a micro-brewery which foundered. The ale has continued to be produced under license in the United States, but to a much lesser degree of character. An even odder arrangement is the survival of George Killian's Ruby Ale, last produced in Ireland in 1956 but still brewed under license in a modest approximation of the Irish style by Pelforth, in France, and in a lighter-bodied version by Coors of Colorado. "Irish-style" ales with no obvious roots in the "Auld Sod" have also been produced by a number of breweries in North America. Some are laughable, but at least one ~ McNally's, from the Big Rock Brewery, of Calgary, Alberta ~ is very good.

FRANCE

THE WORLD'S MOST DEVOTED gastronomes appreciate beer, as naturally they would. Why else call one of their favorite dining places a brasserie? The French know, though others forget, that *brasseries* means "brewery." The first brassiers were brewery-taps or brew-pubs. The classics, like Brasserie Lipp, in Paris, still serve beer as their staple drink, for those with enough clout to get a table.

Though they are perennially fashionable, brasseries are not intended to serve the most *haute* of *cuisine*, nor do they as a rule provide the most interesting of beers.

The northwest, especially the area around Lille, produces the most colorful beers, and offers them with its own, underrated, cuisine (mussels, excellent lamb and mutton, dishes cooked with jenever gin, leeks, several local cheeses). Good rendezvous of beer and food can be made in the towns of St Omer and, especially, Arras. The northeast, especially the area around Strasbourg, is better known as a brewing center, and to some extent for its gastronomy, but its beers are more conventional, and more likely to be served with the predictable (but still enjoyable) pork and sauerkraut dishes. They do not stand up so well to the local pâtés and goose dishes.

From the northwest, Belgian, and especially Flemish, influence seeps as strongly as ever across the border. The old region of Flanders spreads into France, running from Dunkirk to Lille to Valenciennes to Cambrai. Flanders and Artois are gastronomically good beer regions. So is Picardy, all the way to Champagne.

There are a good dozen small breweries in this part of France, mainly within the "counties" or Départments du Nord and Pas de Calais. In the Channel ports, every supermarket is filled with good beer, though British day-trippers tend to buy the better-known, less interesting, brews.

Some of the northwestern beers are top-fermenting, and most of the rest have an ale-like character, even if they are actually made with a bottom yeast. Just south of the Belgian border at Crespin, near Valenciennes, there was once a monastery that is remembered in a tart, fruity, bottle-conditioned, abbey-style beer called Réserve St Landelin, from the local Rimaux brewery.

Just south of Valenciennes, a brewery with the Flemish name of Duyck produces Jenlain, a classic in the style the French call Bière de Garde. Jenlain has a deep amber color (25-plus E.B.C.), malt and fruit in the nose, and notes of vanilla or licorice in the finish. It is an all-malt, top-fermenting brew of 16 Plato (1064; 5.2 per cent alcohol by weight; 6.5 by volume), with 25 units of bitterness. It is filtered, but not pasteurized.

The original idea of a Bière de Garde was a brew that could be laid down: a top-fermenting beer of medium-to-high gravity that was bottle-conditioned. Some beers identified in this way are still top-fermented, and the occasional one has a secondary fermentation in the bottle. Others are filtered but not pasteurized. A Bière de Garde is typically made with several malts (perhaps three) and to a gravity in the range 15-19 (1060-1076), with one to three months' maturation, a color of 25-40, and around 25 units of bitterness. Alcohol content varies from 4.4 to 7.5 or more. These beers represent a distinct regional style. It may be a minor one, but it is worthy of attention, and it embraces some delicious beers.

An outstanding example of a top-fermenting, bottle-conditioned Bière de Garde is La Choulette, which counterpoints a citric fruitiness with a hoppy dryness. This is produced by the brewery of the same name, in Bouchain, in Département du Nord. The same brewery makes a paler beer in a similar style, whimsically called Sans-Culottes. It has also pioneered raspberry beer in France, with a Framboise based on La Choulette.

Another good top-fermenting example is Trois Monts, Bière de Flandre: dryish, beautifully balanced, complex, it is a delicious apéritif beer. This is from the town and brewery of Saint Sylvestre, also in Département du Nord. This brewery in addition makes a top-fermenting, heavily-sedimented, "March Beer" (Bière de Mars). In the same area, a tiny, one-man, part-time brewery called Caudrelier produces a dry, smooth, fruity, top-fermenting beer of great character, called Iris.

No brewery anywhere has a more interesting *raison d'être* than Brasserie de Dorignies, near Douai. It was founded in 1985, with some public funding, to provide work for handicapped people. It

Above: The great French scientist Louis Pasteur was the father of modern brewing. His work on yeast enabled brewers to work in a far less empirical fashion. The process of pasteurization is, though, a mixed blessing.

In addition to Jenlain, beers like Trois Monts and La Choulette are fine examples from the Northwest. All three can readily be found in the supermarkets of the Channel ports. They make a good accompaniment to the cheeses of the region.

Keeping the Haute Tradition

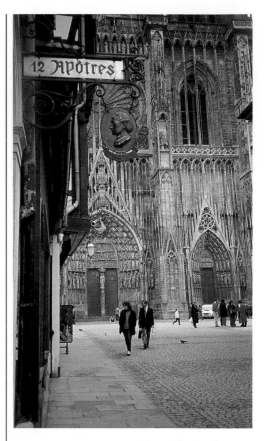

Rimaux is typical of the tiny breweries that eke out a living around the Franco-Belgian border. These very old artisanal breweries produce distinctive and individualistic beers on a very small scale. They are usually operated by a family, with little additional help.

Above: The "Twelve Apostles" have a beer in the shadow of Strasbourg cathedral. Les Apôtres give their name to a small, well run specialty beer café in the heart of France's biggest brewing city. *Right*: A brewery-sponsored festival in Alsace. Many of these small festivals take place in the North each summer. *Left* and *below*: Specialty beers from the Northwest.

has 15 employees, and produces an amber beer called Ste Hildegaarde and a pale brew, Orient Express. Both are sweetish, tasty, lightly fruity, bottom-fermenting brews in broadly the style of Bière de Garde.

A considerable selection of brews in broadly this style is produced in the Département du Nord, under a variety of labels. Among the several tasty examples are the well-balanced Réserve du Brasseur, from the Semeuse brewery, at Hellemmes; the perfumy, strong Septante 5, from Grande Brasserie Moderne, at Roubaix; and the lively, soft, sweetish Franklin's Ale and slightly lighter Pastor Ale, both from the town and brewery of Annoeullin. Grande Brasserie Moderne makes several interesting beers, including a strong, chewy, fruity-malty Spéciale Christmas. In Pas de Calais, at Bénifontaine, near Wingles, the

Castelain brewery salutes the local industry with its profoundly fruity Ch'ti, which has a drawing of a coal-miner on the label. Ch'ti is produced in brown, amber, and blonde versions. The brown has a distinctively port-like aroma and palate. "Ch'ti" is patois for a Northerner. The brewery also has a lighter-tasting, fluffier Bière de Garde called Des Coulonneux, in honour of the local pigeon-racers. Another product is an unusually pale, organically-grown beer called Jade (3.7; 4.6). This is light and dry, but with some fruitiness.

One of the best known examples in this style outside nrance is the clean-tasting, relatively hoppy, St Léonard, from the Facon brewery, in Pas de Calais. In 1985, Facon introduced France's first Wheat Beer. This brew is called L'épi de Facon, and its name refers to an ear of wheat. It is a very pale

beer, bottom-fermented, with an alcohol content of 4.16 per cent by volume; 5.2 per cent by volume. It has a notably clean palate and the slightest hint of grapefruity sharpness arising from the wheat. Facon continues to operate, although it is one of four small breweries acquired in recent years by the St Arnould group, previously known as wine and food distributors.

Douai (which is near Lille) has the world's strongest truly golden lager, La Bière du Démon (21.7; 9.6; 12). For its weight, this beer is surprisingly dry, but with honeyish notes. It is brewed by Enfants de Gayant, which owns the Boxer brewery in Switzerland. Enfants also produce a very sweet Bière du Désert, which promises *plaisir torride,* but turns out to be not especially interesting. In recent years this company has been producing also the malty

The cosmopolitan beer-bars of Paris (*below*) serve brews from Bavaria and Ireland, Burton ales from England, and Dutch lagers . . . but the man in a bar at Champigneulles (*bottom*) probably requires no such distractions.

Below: Today's French selection includes several Bières de Garde, a Wheat Beer, more than one pale allusion to a Double Bock, and a "Malt Whisky" beer to warm the Auld Alliance. None has graphics to match this period piece from Phénix. *Opposite*: Pêcheur is French for Fisher, which is most often rendered as "Fischer" in its native — bilingual — Alsace. Although it usually uses the German name, the Fischer brewery struck a peevish blow against the *Reinheitsgebot* Purity Law.

Lutèce Bière de Paris. This is a bottom-fermenting product in the general style of a Bière de Garde.

Lille has the large Pelforth brewing company, making several pale lagers and a top-fermenting, strong Brune (really a Brown Ale). This product (17.3; 1070; 5.2; 6.6) has a deep claret color, a big body, and a malty palate, drying in the finish. The brewery also produces, as a top-fermenting ale, George Killian's Bière Rousse, at 16.8 (1067); 5.2; 6.6. This is a malty, full-bodied, tasty interpretation of the one-time Irish Ale.

Pelforth and Union de Brasseries (whose brands include Porter 39, "33," and Slavia) are partly controlled by Heineken, whose own French-brewed beers include Mutzig and Ancre. Stella Artois also has interests in France, with Vezelise as one of its brands. The biggest French group is BSN, which includes Kronenbourg and Société Européenne de Brasseries (Kanterbräu, Champigneulles, La Meuse, and others).

Kronenbourg has breweries in Strasbourg and nearby Obernai, both in the Département Bas-Rhin, which is in the region of Alsace. The Strasbourg area, and especially nearby Schiltigheim, is the traditional center of lager-brewing in France. The Pêcheur group (Fischer, Adelshoffen, Gruber) is based there. So are the much smaller Meteor and Schutzenberger.

Historically, Alsace and to a lesser extent the neighboring region of Lorraine have been greatly influenced by Germany. Traditionally, this has been evident in their beer and their cuisine. German was once the predominant language in Alsace, but is now less evident, and its accent has diminished in the local beers.

French lagers are generally light and sweetish, sometimes with a slight fruitiness. Some have very short lagering periods, and a proportion of 20-30 per cent adjuncts is usual.

The regular Kronenbourg as produced in France has a gravity of 12.7 (1050), and 23 units of bitterness. The super-premium version, called 1664, has a little more character.

The Fischer beers are smoother, and the Gold (16; 1064; 5.1; 6.4) has a good hop character. Fischer Export is the much lighter standard beer, sold in the United States as La Belle Strasbourgeoise. It has some hop in the nose but not much in the palate (17 units of bitterness). Fischer has an enjoyable Bière de

Mars: a clean and sweet bronze-colored lager, with a malty aroma and a notably soft texture. The company also produces the very lightly smoky Adelscott (16.2; 1065; 5.2; 6.5), a pale amber lager made with Scottish-style whisky malt.

Surrounded by far bigger groups, Fischer has sought to maintain momentum by innovation. It frequently announces revolutionary new products, one example being a beer concentrate. These ideas do not always take the market by storm. The company's president, Michel Debus, instigated the action that defeated the *Reinheitsgebot* in the European Court. This was a dubious achievement.

Among the more characterful beers from the Strasbourg area are those of Meteor, which is actually in Hochfelden. It has a hoppy Pils and a maltier lager called Ackerland Blonde (14.5; 1058; 4.4; 5.5).

Perversely, the term Bock is used in France to indicate a low-gravity beer (perhaps because it is served in a large mug?), but some French brewers do produce an extra-strong lager. An example is

Schutzenberger's Jubilator (16; 1064; 5.5; 6.9). This is a pale beer, with a fresh, perfumy aroma and a softly fruity finish. Across the border in Lorraine, at Metz, the Amos brewery produces pleasantly malty lagers. Not far from Metz, France has a new museum of beer, at the town of Stenay.

Strasbourg has an excellent speciality beer café, Aux 12 Apôtres, at Rue Mercière 7, within sight of the cathedral. Paris has many, among which the Académie de la Bière, at Boulevard de Port Royal 88, is a good example.

A newer development is the spread of British-style micros or brew-pubs. The pioneers have been Les Brasseurs, in Lille; Deux Rivières, in Morlaix, Brittany; and St Amant, near Clermont-Ferrand.

SWITZERLAND

Left: Feldschlosschen. The name means "Castle in the Field" and would seem an odd description for any other brewery, but Feldschlosschen is built to look like a castle, at least on the outside. On the inside, Schloss might be better translated as "palace" — or is this another case of the style that could be termed "Brewers' Ecclesiastical"? To observe as much is not to mock, but to be awestruck. Even the old compressors and boilers whirred and bubbled in a room decorated with friezes that might have seemed fitting in a banqueting hall. The man in the stained-glass window was one of the firm's founders, Theophil Roniger. Feldschlosschen in its present form was his dream.

THE IRISH MONK who became St Gall may have been the father of brewing in the modern world. St Gall, a Benedictine, was one of the missionaries who brought classical learning and traditions back from the islands and Celtic fringes to the mainland of Europe after the barbarian invasions. In the seventh century, he founded what became an abbey at what is now the textile town of St Gallen, north of the Alps, and not far from the meeting point of Switzerland, Austria, and Germany. The abbey had several brew-houses by the eighth or ninth century, though all that remain of them now are ruins.

St Gallen was an important abbey in the European empire of Charlemagne, and its influence would have been felt widely. Today, the stretch of Europe between the Alps, the Rhine, and the Danube embraces beer cities such as Strasbourg in the west and Munich in the east.

The town of St Gallen still has a brewery, and the canton has more breweries than any other in Switzerland. The nearby canton and city of Zürich also have their claims to significance in the modern world of brewing.

The Zürich brewery Hürlimann has over the years become a specialist in yeast culture. Since brewers first realized that promiscuous yeast was their biggest source of problems, they have always helped each other keep a clean moral climate. If a brewer had fermentation problems or sour beer, he would start afresh with a clean yeast obtained from a neighbor. There is scarcely a brewer anywhere who has never had such a problem. A handful of brewers in various parts of the world eventually became known for their yeasts, and began to make a business of supplying other companies. Hürlimann is one of the best known, and supplies yeast to brewers in about 30 countries.

In working to maintain and develop strains, a yeast bank will naturally concern itself with the ability of each culture to ferment wort at various temperatures and in various cycles of time, to produce alcohol, to settle, and to leave a pleasant background aroma and palate. One difficulty in producing the stronger beers is that, as fast as it ferments the wort, the yeast becomes stunned by the alcohol that it is creating. In the course of working with its house yeast, Hürlimann therefore developed a strain that would ferment to very high levels of alcohol.

A strong beer was made with this strain as a Christmas special. The beer was called Samichlaus ("Santa Claus"). When it emerged from maturation, it appeared to be the strongest beer in the world, and was submitted to the *Guinness Book of Records*. The Guinness book, published by a brewing company but honorably disinterested, ratified Samichlaus as the strongest in its 1982 edition. In 1988, a previous holder, the E.K.U. (Kulminator) brewery of West Germany, sought to win back the title. A new entrant came from Cornish Breweries (Domesday Ale) of Britain.

There is an element of fun, and publicity value, to this contest. A beer as strong as these heavyweights can be so rich as to be almost a trial for the drinker. The alcohol makes itself known quickly, too; a bottle of beer contains a considerably longer drink than the usual glass of wine, yet this brew matches the heftiest of reds for potency.

Samichlaus has an original gravity of 27.6 Plato and an alcohol content of 11.1-11.2 by weight, 13.7-14.0 by volume. Although it has a predictably malty nose and full body, Samichlaus is not as overwhelmingly syrupy as it could be. To some degree, its sweetness is balanced out by the alcohol notes. It has a surprising firmness of body and a brandyish finish. It should be served from a small wooden barrel suspended from the neck of a St Bernard dog on mountain rescue duty.

The Hürlimann brewery traces its history to 1836. The brewery was established on the site of a vineyard, whose auberge still stands, a half-timbered house among the jumble of more modern buildings in their various architectural styles. The brewery's workshops are decorated with medieval-style symbols of their trades: plumbers, carpenters, builders, beer-samplers, and so forth. The building that was originally the brewer's house looks like something out of a Gothic horror movie. Hürlimann makes one of the strongest beers in the world — as well as one of the weakest.

Samichlaus is brewed only once a year, on December 6, the day when the Swiss celebrate St Nicholas (Santa Claus). It is matured throughout the following year and released next December 6. Its high strength is achieved through the length of maturation, as well as the selection of yeast culture. Although Hürlimann does not disclose every detail of its method, it seems likely that the yeast is "roused" occasionally by the transfer of the beer from one tank to another.

The original version of Samichlaus has a deep red-brown color. A Hell ("pale") version is still reddish, but translucent. Even the original can be quite hard to find in Switzerland, and the pale was introduced only for export markets. It is an irony that, with its interest in yeasts, Hürlimann has also been among the pioneers of non-alcoholic beers, in its case Birell. This class of "beer" has also become something of a Swiss specialty.

Very strong beers are somewhat at odds with the careful, tidy Calvinism of the country. The Swiss are also very proper in declining to use the term Pilsener for anything other than the original Czech product. The terminology is further complicated by the country's use of several languages. An everyday beer is identified as *Lager* in German; *Bière de Fermentation Basse* in French; and *Birra Invecchiata* in Italian. Beers in this category may have a gravity between 10.5 and 12.0 Plato (1042-1048) and an alcohol content of 3.36-4.24 by weight; 4.2-5.3 by volume.

Hürlimann's regular pale beer, identified simply as Lager, has a gravity of 11.6 (1046) and an alcohol content of 3.8; 4.7. It has a lightly hoppy nose; a light-to-medium, firm body; and a rather quick finish. It has 22 units of bitterness. Hürlimann also produces a more aromatic, hoppier, lighter-bodied pale lager called Five Star, which is the only major entrant in the De Luxe class (12; 1048; 4.1; 5.12; 26-28 units of bitterness). Hürlimann claims to lager its everyday beer for two months and its specialties for three. Lagering times are generally quite long in Switzerland, and the use of adjuncts limited, though the country's brewers no longer follow the *Reinheitsgebot*. Most beers in the domestic market also benefit for being unpasteurized.

The category called Special, in which most brewers have entrants, has gravities in the range of 11-13.5 (1044-1054) and an alcohol content of 3.8-4.6; 4.8-5.7. This is a growing category, especially among draft beers. An overlapping category variously described as Festbier, Märzen, or Bock has gravities of between 12 and 13.5. Beers in this category are usually marketed for three or four weeks over Christmas and Easter. A beer labeled "strong" (*Stark* in German; *Forte* in French and Italian) must have a gravity of at least 14 (1056) and an alcohol content of not less than 4.32; 5.4. In all categories, both pale and dark beers may be found.

Hürlimann, which has an extensive range, produces a tasty dark special called Hexenbräu ("Witches' Brew"), which is very malty, but less sweet than might be expected, with some "burnt" treacle-toffee notes. It is brewed from a gravity of 13.5, but has only about 4.0; 5.0 per cent alcohol. Hürlimann's Festbier is similar, but with a lower hopping rate and therefore more sweetness. Another hearty dark special is made by Warteck, of Basel. (Warteck also has an enjoyable Altbier in the Düsseldorf style. This is lightly fruity, slightly carbonic for the style, but with a nicely hoppy finish.)

Hürlimann has two tasty entrants in the strong beer category called Dreikönigs ("Three Kings"). Despite their names, these are not Christmas beers. The three kings adorn the coat-of-arms of a district of Zürich. The pale Dreikönigs (16; 1065; 5.4; 6.7) is very malty in both nose and palate. A dark version (19; 1076; 5.9; 7.3) has a Burgundy color and a richer palate, with some sweet fruitiness. A similar beer, with a wonderful aroma, is produced by Haldengut, under the name Albani Bräu. It has a reputation, well deserved, of being a good nightcap. There are also popular beers in this category from Gurten, of Berne, and Müller, of Baden.

Four giants dominate the Swiss brewing industry, and their everyday beers are all very similar. Hürlimann's are in general cleanly malty and fairly light, with a spritzy finish. The company also has an interest in the Zürich Löwenbräu brewery (unconnected with its Munich namesake). Swiss Löwenbräu's beers are characteristically mild and dry. Hürlimann and Löwenbräu also co-operate with another half-dozen independent breweries, mainly in the east.

The large Cardinal group is headquartered in the university town of Fribourg, in the west, on the border of the German- and French-speaking regions. The brewery adopted its present name in 1890, when the archbishop of Fribourg was elected a cardinal. This company produces flowery, light, dry beers. Its range also includes a top-fermenting dark beer called Anker, broadly in the style of a Düsseldorf Altbier. It also produces Moussy, a well-known non-alcoholic beer. Cardinal has subsidiary breweries in Wädenswil and Rheinfelden.

The beautiful Feldschlösschen brewery is also in Rheinfelden, a salt-water spa not far from Basel. (There is a larger town, also called Rheinfelden, on the opposite bank of the Rhine, in Germany.) Feldschlösschen has a castellated, turreted exterior, looking like a baronial fortress This was completed in the 1890s; the interior was further embellished in 1908 and extended, in grand style, in the 1950s.

There are other brew-houses in the world with stained-glass windows, but none as elaborate as the portraiture at Feldschlösschen. The marble pillars that support the plaster ceiling give the brew-house an opulent quality which compensates for the lack of cathedral height to be found at Carlsberg. Other

breweries have decorative tiling, but none as ornate as that at Feldschlösschen, where the mosaics and molded illustrations watch over not only the kettles and fermenters but also the steam boilers.

Feldschlösschen's beers have a slightly fruity house character and a distinctive bitterness. The Feldschlösschen group includes Gurten, of Berne, and Valaisanne, of Sion, in the French-speaking southwest. The group also cooperates with Haldengut, of Winterthur, and Calanda, of Chur.

Calanda is one of three Swiss breweries that produce Wheat Beers, in a light, clean, interpretation of the southern German style. The others are Frauenfeld, in the town of the same name, and the Ueli brewery, at the Fischerstübe beer-restaurant, in Basel.

Thirty of Switzerland's breweries are in the trade's national association, which operates as a cartel. The Ueli-Fischerstübe brewery is among the four that remain outside the association (the other mavericks being Boxer, of Lausanne, and Lupo and Wäfler, both in the canton of Lucerne).

The Fischerstübe is a small, café-style restaurant at Rheingasse 45, in the center of Basel. It is owned by a man whose principal profession is as a radiographer. He is an independent-minded and resourceful man, who objected to his beer supply being controlled by the cartel. At the back of the restaurant, behind a window, he built a small brewery, with the help of Otto Binding. (A member of the family who once owned the large Frankfurt brewery, Binding also built his own establishment at Eltville, in Hesse.) The Ueli ("Jester") brew-house is tiny and very pretty. It has a six-hectoliter copper kettle in the traditional shape, set into mosaic tiles. The brewmaster climbs a domestic stepladder to look inside. He produces an exceptionally clean-tasting pale lager and special, a lightly toffeeish dark beer, and a plummy-tasting Weizenbier which has a sweet start and a tart finish. The restaurant also features mixed drinks made with beer. These are better enjoyed as a joke than as a drink (beer with Nescafé?), but even the stolid Swiss have their whimsical moments.

The Rosengarten brewery, of Einsiedeln, produces a beer that is intended to taste of corn, and does. It is called Maisgold, and contains 30 per cent corn. In some parts of the world, that would not be unusual.

The Restaurant Fischerstübe, in Basel, looks like the sort of place where Swiss ladies with hats meet for coffee, cakes and gossip. Behind this façade, it produces and dispenses three or four different styles of beer, and the gossip takes place over pretzels.

AUSTRIA

Below: The entrance to the Klein Schwechat brewery, built in the early years of this century by Anton Dreher and once the hub of the world's greatest brewing empire. *Second from bottom*: The pavilion in the grounds of the Klein Schwechat brewery. This building dates back to the times of Maria Theresa, when the land was part of an extensive hunting area. *Bottom*: Gleaming copper producing Schwechat's super-premium, Steffl.

ONE OF THE WORLD'S classic beer-styles originated in Austria, specifically in its capital, Vienna. Elsewhere in the world, there are still reddish-amber lager beers that pay tribute to the Vienna style. The distinctively full color originally came from a specification of malt similar to that used to make Pale Ale in Britain. The term "Vienna malt" is still sometimes used by older brewers in other countries. This style of "cured" malt produces not only the reddish tinge but also a sweetish, textured palate which dries in the finish.

Like Vienna's role as an imperial capital, its style of beer seems to have faded as abruptly as the last waltz. Today's Viennese brewers are unsure about the style. Was it really reddish, or just a very full old gold? There were, of course, no E.B.C. figures in those days. In the post-war period, Austrian brewers have regarded a lager beer with a full yellow color, a malty sweetness, and a low hopping, as being in the Vienna style. Only recently has there been an attempt to reintroduce a more distinctive interpretation.

The style was originally introduced, probably in 1841, by the great Anton Dreher, whose brewery at Schwechat, on the outskirts of Vienna, is still in production, and growing. In parts, it resembles a grand country estate rather than a brewery. Its imperial-style buildings, clad with creeping plants, set around a series of courtyards, dotted with poplars and park benches, seem positively rustic. An early baroque pavilion, believed to date from the 1750s, is reputed to have been used as a hunting lodge, or perhaps for illicit trysts, by Maria Theresa, Archduchess of Austria, Queen of Hungary and Bohemia, and ruler of much of Europe. There are barons and counts and aristocratic families at every twist and turn of the Austrian brewing industry. This rambling estate is actually a busy, working brewery. Only when a turn-of-the-century listed building emerges as a power plant does the industrial aspect of the place become apparent. Once hunting country, Schwechat is now an industrial satellite of Vienna.

Dreher was one of the most important innovators in brewing history, like his collaborator Gabriel Sedlmayr of Munich. In size, his Schwechat brewery was second only to Pilsner Urquell. Dreher had a brewery in Bohemia, at Michelob. He had another in Hungary, at Budapest (still operating, under state ownership). There was another, at Trieste, which gave rise to today's Dreher company in Italy. That company is the only one now to have the Dreher name, and it is today based in Milan and owned by Heineken.

Beer is mentioned in the history of what is now Austria in the year 990, in a tax demand. The tax was required to be paid in either beer or wine. At least one of today's breweries can trace its history to the 1200s. One account says the Dreher family were already brewers in the 1600s. The brewery at Schwechat seems to have been founded in 1632 by an aristocrat, and bought by the Drehers in 1796. By the 1870s, their beer was being exported as far afield as Japan. The original Austrian Dreher company

ceased in the 1930s. There are no more male Drehers (at least, not of the brewing family — it is a common name, meaning "turner"), but a female descendant has a farm near the Schwechat brewery.

The brewery at Schwechat is now one among five in an Austrian group with the unmemorable name of Österreichische Bräu-Aktiengesellschaft ("The Austrian Brewing Corporation"). Unwieldy, too. It is usually known simply as Bräu A.G., though there was for a time a German company with the same unimaginative name. The Austrian company now has its headquarters in Linz.

The Schwechat products are identified by the name of the brewery. Like its location, the Schwechater brewery today is a mix of tradition and industry. It still has a handsome, traditional, brew-house; it uses a double decoction mash; its hops are a mix of pellets and extract, with some Saaz; it has dispensed with its open fermenters, but it still *kräusens* its beers.

The basic Schwechater Lager (12 Plato; 1048; 4.1; 5.2) has a soft maltiness. The brewery also has a light, smooth premium beer called Hopfenperle (12.4; 1050; 4.2; 5.3), with a dry finish. The same brand-name is used on a premium beer by Feldschlösschen, in Switzerland. This is coincidental. Neither the companies nor the products have any connection. The beers are not a thousand miles apart geographically, or in taste, though there is perhaps more roundness to the Swiss one.

Schwechat also has a super-premium, called Steffl, at a little over 13 (1052; 4.4; 5.5), with a slightly fuller body and some fruity-hoppy notes. In an international context, Austrian beers are on the sweet-fruity side. Within Austria, those of Vienna

Below: The Nüssdorf brewery and pub opened by Baron Hendrick Bachofen von Echte on the banks of the Danube. The façade is that of a one-time customs house.

Right: Austria has far fewer clearly defined beer-styles than Germany, but its 60 or more operating breweries produce a wide range.

are generally the sweetest. In the Bräu A.G. group, this is true of the Schwechat beers. The group has a fruitier range under the Kaiser name, made in several of its breweries. It also has hoppier beers under the Zipfer brand. These are made in Upper Austria, at Zipf, not far from Salzburg. The hoppiest is the aromatic, very pale, sherbety Zipfer Urtyp (12.5; 1050; 4.3; 5.4).

In the province of Salzburg, the group has the Kaltenhausen brewery, which has since 1986 made Edelweiss. This is one of four or five Weizen or Weisse beers produced in Austria, all in light interpretations of the southern German style.

The second largest grouping is Styrian Breweries (Steirische Bräuindustrie), headquartered in Graz. Its home province has a tradition of hop-growing, although most of the Styrian variety used today comes from across the border in Yugoslavia. The beers in the Austrian province of Styria have the country's characteristically sweet fruitiness, but they do also have some hoppy balance.

Within the Styrian Breweries group, Graz has the Reininghaus and Puntigam beers. The Reininghaus beer has a good balance of malt, fruit, and hop. The Puntigam product seems sweeter and fluffier. The company's brewery in Leoben-Göss gives its name to a more widely marketed range. This selection, under the brand Gösser, includes some quite assertive beers, with a good malt-hop balance. This is best expressed in the Gösser Spezial. The promising-sounding Gösser Stiftsbräu, named after the brewery's founding monastery, turns out to be a very sweet dark beer of 12.2 Plato (1049) but only 2.9; 3.6. The Renaissance Benedictine abbey now houses a brewery museum. Styrian Breweries also

has a share in the substantial Adambräu brewery, of Innsbruck.

Third and fourth places are contested between the local breweries of Salzburg and Vienna.

Salzburg has the Stiegl brewery, founded in the year that Columbus discovered the New World. Hence its malty-sweet, but also well-hopped Columbus (13 Plato; 1052; 4.3; 5.3). There are some links between Bräu A.G. and Stiegl, through common shareholders.

Vienna's local brewery is Ottakringer, which takes its name from the working-class neighborhood where it stands. It is proudly local and concerned for its traditions. In particular, it uses a large quantity of Saaz blossoms, and its beers have a fresh, flowery aroma and malty roundness. Ottakringer likes to call its Gold Fassl Spezial (13; 1052; 4.5; 5.6) a Vienna type, for its soft but substantial maltiness.

In 1987 the company launched a beer closer to the original style. To celebrate the 150th anniversary of the business, Ottakringer produced a reddish-bronze beer (25 E.B.C.) at 13-13.5 Plato, with a malty aroma; a lightly sweet, soft start and a dry, rounded finish. This beer was identified simply as Ottakringer 150 Jahre, without reference to style.

Until the mid-1980s, most Austrian breweries had produced much the same range. The Austrians use the designation Schankbier, or sometimes Abzug, for a low-gravity brew. They admit the term Pils for any hoppy lager between 11 and 13 Plato. They employ the description Lager (or, confusingly, Märzen) for a beer of a full, yellow color and a gravity of between 12 and 12.8 (1048-51) that is generally malty in character. *Spezial* indicates a beer of 13-plus. Bock suggests 16-plus and an alcohol content of more than 5.5; 7.0. Starkbier suggests a brew of 20 Plato (1080) or more.

Lagering periods vary widely, from five to 15 weeks. No artificial colorings or chemical additives are permitted, and some beers are all-malt. Where adjuncts are used (often rice), percentages vary from less than 15 to more than 20. Up to 25 per cent is permitted. Although the big corporations are dominant, there are 54 breweries, owned by 47 companies.

In Vienna, the Fischer Gasthof brew-pub and beer-garden at Billroth Strasse 17, Döbling (Tel 316264), established itself in 1986 with a product in the Munich Pale type, and plans for a Bock. A more unusual range of products has been offered by Vienna's first brewery-restaurant, founded in 1984 by Baron Hendrik Bachofen von Echte in the wine-cellars of his Schloss, at Nüssdorf, a village at the end of the tram line (Tel 372652).

Baron Bachofen, whose family once operated a much larger brewery at Nüssdorf, produces top-fermenting beers. He began with a bronze, dry Doppelhopfen Hell (30 per cent wheat; 11 Plato; 1044); the chewy, malty St Thomas Bräu, broadly in the style of an Altbier (12.25; 1049); a seasonal variation on this, made with smoky whiskey malt;

and the chocolaty, fruity-dry, Sir Henry's Stout (13.75; 1055).

The cellars also accommodate thousands of bottles of sparkling white wine, including some under the Baron's own label. Early attempts to make a black velvet from Sir Henry's Stout produced too sweet a drink, but research will no doubt continue.

In the center of Vienna, the Bierhof (Nagler Gasse 13) offers a number of variations on local beers, including the odd unfiltered example, and one or two interesting imports. It is best visited after 5 o'clock in the evening, and its various floors should be explored. Its interior is beautifully decorated, on beery themes. Specialty beer bars are new to Vienna, but the Old Town has an interesting range of imports at Krah Krah, in Rabensteig.

Northwest of Vienna, the Zwettle brewery has a lightly hazy Zwickelbier with some apple notes. South of Vienna, the Piesting brewery has a sweetish Altbier.

In the province of Salzburg, at Obertrum, the Sigl brewery popularized Wheat Beers with its well-made Weizengold, a clean, soft interpretation with a pearl-like fruitiness. The Cooperative brewery in Ried, Upper Austria, and the Grieskirchen brewery in the same province, both make Wheat Beers. Grieskirchen's is an especially good example, and the same brewery makes a soft, notably tasty Pilsener. A hearty Wheat Beer is produced by the small Huber brewery, which makes some characterful products, at St Johann, in the Tyrol.

Salzburg has a brewery owned by Augustine monks but operated by a secular company. Schlägl, north of Linz, has a brewery run by Premonstratensian brothers. These two breweries both make clean, soft, malty beers. Between Salzburg and Linz, the Eggenberg brewery of Vorchdorf has an interesting range, including a celebrated 23-degree Bock. This is a fresh-tasting, beautifully-balanced beer, with a long, hoppy finish.

Salzburg has always had a few beer-halls. There are plans for brew-pubs in Graz and elsewhere. Austria is rediscovering its traditions.

193

EASTERN EUROPE

EAST GERMANY AND CZECHOSLOVAKIA are special cases, with their own heritage of brewing, but their influence (and that of British Porter-brewers, Bavarians, and Austrians) spread to their neighbors long ago.

One of the most recent missionaries has been Prince Luitpold of Bavaria, who has been helping the Hungarians develop brew-pubs, generally producing Munich-accented pale lagers.

Hungary, or at least its capital city Budapest, rests on a bed of beer. By happy coincidence, the quarrying of stone to build Buda's twin town of Pest left enormous rock caverns where beer could be lagered. They were put to use by the great Austrian brewer Anton Dreher in the mid-1800s, and are still maturing beer. The brewery is today called Kőbánya. Its most interesting products are all-malt: a lightly hoppy Pilsener-type jubilee beer called Kőbányai 125 (11 Plato; 1044; 4.0; 5.0) and a dark, sweetish Bock, identified in Hungarian as Bak, at 18 Plato (1072; 6.0; 7.5). A 12-degree (1048) Pilsener-type called Rocky Cellar has 20 per cent adjuncts and a low bitterness (22 E.B.U.). Another at the same gravity, called simply Budapest, has 24 units of bitterness. At 13 Plato (1052), Mátyás has more adjunct (30 per cent) but also more bitterness (27).

Hungary has five old-established breweries, whose products also include some malty dark lagers, the odd high-gravity specialty (up to 22 Plato; 1088), and the occasional Porter.

All of the Balkan countries have breweries, and Bulgaria has some pleasantly dry beers, labeled with their gravities in the Balling system (typically 12, 12.5, 13; 1048, 1050, 1052).

Most East European countries display the gravity in degrees Balling or Plato on the labels of their beers. Several have a number of low-gravity products, then Pilsener lagers in the 11-13 range, and the occasional stronger Porter. Although they vary greatly, many East European lagers seem to score better on hop character than on malty softness. They are often attenuated to a considerable dryness, with grainy-fruity notes.

There was once a Polish Pope named Clement. As he lay dying, he made an urgent utterance which sounded like the creation of a new saint. Then the people at his bedside realized that he was, in fact, asking for a beer.

Poland has more than 70 breweries and about 40 maltings. It also grows hops, near Lublin. The area of cultivation is around Krasnystaw, where growers have a beer festival every September. The Tatra mountains and the old city of Cracow give their names to light hoppy beers from the brewery at nearby Zywiec. Also in the Cracow hinterland is Okocim, making slightly softer beers. These two breweries export some of their products. Several of the local beers are unfiltered and unpasteurized. In the north, the Gdansk Langfuhr brewery has a good example. Nearby, the brewery at Elblag makes an all-malt Pilsener.

In volume, the Soviet Union is one of the biggest brewing countries in the world, thanks to the size of its population. In consumption per head, it is far lower. For many years, the consumption of beer was encouraged. Beer was seen as a drink of moderation, as opposed to hard liquor. Under Mikhail Gorbachov, even beer seems unsure of its position.

The Soviet Union has about 60 brands of beer, some national and others local, made in 3-400 breweries. The most important in shaping the character of the beer is the national test-brewery in Moscow. This small brewery, built in 1863, is next door to Tolstoy's house (Ylutsa Liva Tolstovo 23). The director in charge is a woman brewer. There are plans to build a beer-hall in the cellar of the brewery.

Moscow's best-known hall is the Zhiguli Cellar, off Kalinin Prospekt. For drinkers in groups, beer is served by the pitcher. Moscow alone has 79 beer-halls, 45 beer-bars and 31 beer-stalls. The quality of their beer, the fact that they become overcrowded, and the leaving of litter (especially the remains of fish snacks) are popular topics for letters of complaint to the newspapers.

The most widely available beer is Zhiguli, an 11-degree (1044) Pilsener type (3.2; 4.0), with a good head formation and retention, a tasty hop bitterness, and a thinnish finish. Slavanskoye is a hoppy, well-attenuated Pilsener type of 12 degrees (1048; 3.7; 4.6). Moskovskoye, at 13 (1052; 3.7; 4.6), is fuller-bodied, with a maltier character and some notes of new-mown hay. Everyday beers contain about 20 per cent adjunct, variously unmalted barley, corn or rice. They usually have three weeks' lagering. Yantar, at 19 (1076) is a fuller-colored, amber strong lager with a complex of hop bitterness and estery, winy notes. It is lagered for two to three months.

The oldest breweries date from the mid-1800s, but there are far more from the 1950s and 1960s, several built with Czech assistance. Although some small breweries have been closed, the Soviet Union has such a large land area that the cost of transport can render economies of scale counter-productive. (The Soviet brewers seem to have realized this sooner than those in the West.) In the early days of the Campaign for Real Ale in Britain, two of its members reported having enjoyed a well-hopped, Bitter beer, dispensed by water-pump from wooden barrels at a café in the Caucasian mountains, at the village of Pasanauri, on the military road connecting Ordzhonikidze with Tbilisi.

No one has ever been able to find the place again.

Column right: All the wine-producing nations of the Eastern Bloc have beer too, but Hungary takes a special pride in its brewing industry. "Rocky Cellar" evokes the ghost of Anton Dreher.

194

Column left: Russian beers. The industry tries to cope with a greatly growing demand . . . and to assuage the trenchant critics in the Moscow beer-halls.

Left: In Poland, cafés like this one serve their beer on draft, but they are by no means universal. In restaurants, bottled beer is more usual, and it thus has a certain snob-appeal. Brewers cannot keep up with demand for bottled beer.

195

SOUTHERN EUROPE

THEY GROW AND DRINK wine in southern Europe, but that is no longer all. Wine may be fine for momma and poppa, and for peasants in Calabria, but the fashionable young in cosmopolitan cities like Rome and Milan prefer to be seen drinking beer. Italy's love-affair with Giovanni Barleycorn has been a minor phenomenon in the beer world in recent years.

Brewers of interesting beers in Britain, Belgium, and Germany have found a growing demand for their products in Italy, and the local companies have responded by making some specialties of their own. There is beer in all the other countries of southern Europe, ranging from the everyday to the modestly interesting, but nowhere else is there a selection of specialties such as can be found in Italy.

Locally-produced specialties come and go. With the popularity of products from the British Isles, there will no doubt be more brews like McFarland (13.5 Plato; 1054; 4.4; 5.5), which is broadly in the style of a Celtic "Red Ale," but actually an Italian product. It is bottom-fermented, and could have more character, but it offers a change from the spritzy, very light lagers made in their several breweries by its Milan-based producers, Dreher (owned by Heineken). The Austrian brewer Dreher introduced beer to this part of the world in the 1860s and 1870s.

Perhaps the most exotic specialty to emerge in Italy in recent times has been Splügen Fumée, made with medium-smoked Franconian malt. This is a bright, copper-colored beer, with a definite, though restrained, smokiness in both aroma and palate. There have been several other Splügen specialties, including a tasty strong lager called simply Red (18; 1072) and a Bock of 15 Plato (1060). Splügen is the name of a mountain pass. These beers are produced by Poretti (in which Carlsberg has a share). Poretti is based in Varese, north of Milan.

La Rossa, with a profound, copper color and a rich maltiness of aroma and palate, drying in the finish, combines the strength of a Double Bock (18; 1072; 6; 7.5) with the spiciness of a Munich Märzen. La Bruna, dark brown and tasty, with just a hint of roasty dryness, is a strong (16; 1064; 5; 6.25) interpretation of the Munich style. Sans Souci, with a flowery hop aroma and a smooth, malty palate and body, is in broadly the German Export style (15; 1060; 4.5; 5.6). All three are produced by the family-owned Moretti brewery, headquartered in Udine, the elegant capital of the province of Friuli, north of Venice.

The regular Moretti beer, a clean, lightly hoppy Pilsener-type, is one of the better everyday brews in Italy. Next to Moretti's offices is a restaurant that in winter sells a more highly-hopped, unfiltered version under the name Integrale ("whole"), an Italian counterpart to a German Kellerbier. Moretti is known for its wonderfully Italian "mustachioed man" logo. In his honor, the brewery also has an all-malt Pilsener-type of 12 (1048), with 25 units of

bitterness and the splendid name Baffo d'Oro ("Golden Mustache"). Everyday Italian beers have 20-22 units of bitterness.

An early attempt at a brew-pub in Sorrento failed but no doubt there will be others. The smallest brewery in Italy is the family-owned Menabrea, at Vercelli, between Turin and Milan. The middle-ranking Forst brewery is also family-controlled. This brewery, at Bolzano, near the Austrian border, produces faintly smoky-tasting beers, including a good dark lager.

The biggest company, with several breweries, is Peroni. Within the light, Italian style, its beers are sweetish, with some balancing fruity dryness, and quite firm-bodied. Peroni's premium product is

Nastro Azzurro. This beer has been slightly reduced in gravity, to 12.5 (1050). It was formerly a Speciale, which implies a gravity of 13-plus (1052). The term Doppio Malto is also used in Italy, implying a gravity of 15-plus.

Peroni also produces the similar Raffo beer. The company owns one-third of Wunster, with the remainder in the hands of the Belgian group Artois. Peroni and Kronenbourg jointly own Wührer. Peroni itself is family-owned, but Kronenbourg has a minority stake. The German Oetker group had a brewery in Italy, but this has now been sold to a private owner. It continues to produce Oetker's brand Prinz Bräu.

The major international groups also have

Left: The classic Southern European figure of the Mustachioed Man is based on a character spotted in a trattoria by brewer Menazzi Moretti in 1942. The brewer snapped the drinker, and the photograph was used as the basis for a painting that became Moretti's trademark. *Below*: Moretti's "Double" Brown is symbolized by a drawing that might today cause the odd punch to be thrown in anger, though it has the same disarming mockery embodied in the Mustachioed Man. The illustration is said to date from early this century.

BIRRA MORETTI
FABBRICA FONDATA NEL 1859
UDINE

Malta – The Ale Island

Farsons' ales are made with hops, malt and yeast imported from Britain. The water is Burtonized, and an infusion mash is used. Cisk Lager is made with yeast from Denmark and hops from Germany, Belgium and Yugoslavia.

Far left: The handsome exterior of the headquarters of Moretti in Udine, Italy. The fountain, alas, sprays water rather than the company's products. *Left*: From top to bottom, labels from the beers of Hellenic Breweries (Greece), Keo (Cyprus), Union (Yugoslavia) and Zlatorog (Yugoslavia).

widespread interests in the brewing industry of Spain. The biggest brewing company in Spain, El Aguila, is part of the Heineken group. Mahou is part-owned by Kronenbourg. The San Miguel group sounds Spanish but, in a reversal of colonial roles, is actually Filipino. La Cruz del Campo is part-owned by Stroh. Damm is part of the Oetker group. Union Cervercera is controlled by Carlsberg. Henninger is also represented.

Spain has produced beer for far longer than might be expected. Brewing goes back to the 1500s, when the king of Spain (and duke of Burgundy) was the emperor Charles V, born in the city of Ghent. Sad to say, Belgian influence has long waned.

The everyday beers are light-bodied lagers, but there are also tastier premium brews in broadly a Dortmunder Export style, at 13 Plato (1052), with an alcohol content of more than 4.0 per cent by weight; 5.0 by volume. There is also the occasional Munich Dark type, and several breweries have strong, malty products in the range of 15-17 Plato (1060-68), with alcohol contents of between 4.8 and 6.0 per cent by weight (6-7.5 by volume). Among the premiums, there is a nice hop aroma and bitterness to Especial Rivera, from Coruña. Among the stronger beers, the same brewery has a good example, Estrella Extra. Others include Keler 18, from San Sebastian; Ambar Export, from Zaragoza; Voll-Dam, from Barcelona; and Tropical Oro from the Canaries.

There has been brewing in Portugal since the 1600s, and in the 1800s there was French, German, and Danish influence. Today, Danish influence is strongest, and most of the beers (from two brewers on the mainland and a couple in the islands) are mild lagers. However, Dortmunder and Munich styles, and even a Sweet Stout, have also made appearances. The most interesting beer at the moment is a rather Belgian-tasting top-fermenting ale with the inappropriate name Bohemia. This is produced by Sagres, which plans also to make it in a new brew-pub in the center of Lisbon.

In the Mediterranean, Malta is an island of top-fermentation. Its Farson's brewery makes a genuine Milk Stout (1045); a darkish Mild called Blue Label (1039); a very pale, dry ale, Hop Leaf (1040); and a fuller-bodied one, Brewer's Choice (1050). The brewery also produces Cisk, a mild lager with some hop aroma.

In the Adriatic region, Yugoslavia is a significant hop-growing country. The hop gardens are principally in Slovenia. This is also the home of the biggest-selling beers, from Union, in the city of Ljubljana. There are more than 30 breweries, and there are a few strong, bottom-fermenting Porters. As might be expected, most of the beers are hop-accented lagers.

Heineken, Henninger, and Löwenbräu have interests in Greece, which still has a German-style Purity Law. There is a tasty local lager named Keo and a Carlsberg brewery on Cyprus.

CANADA

THE FASHION for Canadian beers across the United States border reached a peak in the mid-1980s, and even touched the shores of Britain. While major Canadian brewers were enjoying some success in these markets, far more interesting beers were being produced in their backyard by some of the new micros and brew-pubs. In Canada, these are sometimes known by the quaint term "cottage breweries."

Sensibly enough, Canada likes to present a picture of clear skies and rocky mountain streams when it addresses a foreign audience. What could be cleaner and fresher than a beer made in such a location? Of course, Canada's big cities are pretty clean, too. The country's "Big Three" brewers — Molson, Carling, and Labatt — all have plants in the frontier provinces, but most of their beer is made in the big cities near the border. Those are the places where most Canadians live. Molson is headquartered in Montreal, Labatt in London, Ontario, and Carling in Toronto.

The biggest independent — Moosehead — is, indeed, in a remote part of Canada. Its breweries are in the maritime provinces, at St John, New Brunswick, and Dartmouth, Nova Scotia. Its beers are mainstream Canadian products, with the slightest dash of extra character, notably in their Saaz-accented, delicate hop note.

Besides an image of cleanness and freshness, Canadian beers for years offered a little more hop character than the major products of the American market. As major brands of beer everywhere have become more international, the difference between the Canadian and American products in this respect has diminished. In general, Canadian brewers often use six-row barley, and this can impart a slightly husky taste to the beer. They also use a lot of corn, which can create a creamy sweetness. The balance of these two elements could be taken to represent a "Canadian character."

The popular notion that Canadian beers are much stronger than those of the United States is exaggerated by the different ways in which the two countries express alcohol content. A standard beer in Canada is identified as having 5 per cent alcohol. This is by volume, and would indicate 4 by weight. Alcohol content is not so rigidly standardized in the United States, but in most states a premium beer has 4.5 by volume, 3.6 by weight.

Until recently, western Canada made almost exclusively pale lagers, while the east, and especially the province of Quebec, sustained a fading loyalty toward ale. The western lagers were extremely light, and the eastern ales were very gentle in character and golden in color. For the big brewers, this is still the picture, but the micros present almost a mirror image.

The first micros and brew-pubs, in the early to mid-1980s, were in the west. They made less, but in a much more traditional, characterful style. Today, there are micros or brew-pubs in most parts of Canada, with products that vary from the most intense to the bland and thin. In the late 1980s, openings and closures have been constant. Nor has life been made less confusing for the beer-lover by the number of micros with the word "island" in their name. Canada has a very craggy coastline.

The best example of a new western ale brewery in Canada is on Vancouver Island, at the town of Victoria, provincial capital of British Columbia. This is a brew-pub, called Spinnakers, at 308 Catharine Street. It produces outstanding, top-fermenting ales and Stouts, served by hand-pump from the conditioning tanks or occasionally by gravity from a cask on the bar. Its Extra Special Bitter (1049-50) is beautifully balanced; its Mount Tolmie Dark (1047) is a classic strong Mild, of which Britain should be envious; its dry Empress Stout (1052) is again a

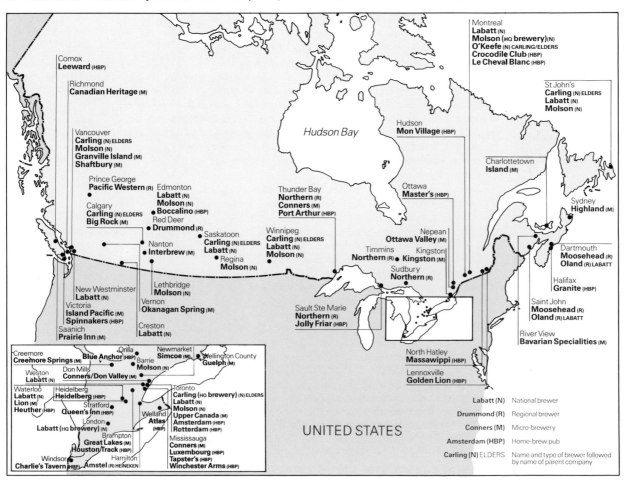

Upper right: New pioneer of cask-conditioned ale John Mitchell pulls a pint of his own brew at Spinnakers, in Victoria, British Columbia. Upstairs, drinkers are offered an Extra Special Bitter, a Dark Ale and a Stout. *Right*: Downstairs, the kettle gets a cleaning.

Comox
Leeward (HBP)

Richmond
Canadian Heritage (M)

Vancouver
Carling (N) ELDERS
Molson (N)
Granville Island (M)
Shaftbury (M)

Prince George
Pacific Western (R)

Edmonton
Labatt (N)
Molson (N)
Boccalino (HBP)

Calgary
Carling (N) ELDERS
Big Rock (M)

Red Deer
Drummond (M)

Nanton
Interbrew (M)

Saskatoon
Carling (N) ELDERS
Labatt (N)

Regina
Molson (N)

Winnipeg
Carling (N) ELDERS
Labatt (N)
Molson (N)

New Westminster
Labatt (N)

Lethbridge
Molson (N)

Victoria
Island Pacific (M)
Spinnakers (HBP)

Vernon
Okanagan Spring (M)

Saanich
Prairie Inn (M)

Creston
Labatt (N)

Hudson Bay

Thunder Bay
Northern (R)
Conners (M)
Port Arthur (HBP)

Montreal
Labatt (N)
Molson (HQ brewery) (N)
O'Keefe (N) CARLING/ELDERS
Crocodile Club (HBP)
Le Cheval Blanc (HBP)

Hudson
Mon Village (HBP)

Ottawa
Master's (HBP)

Nepean
Ottawa Valley (M)

Timmins
Northern (R)

Kingston
Kingston (M)

Sudbury
Northern (R)

St John's
Carling (N) ELDERS
Labatt (N)
Molson (N)

Charlottetown
Island (M)

Sydney
Highland (M)

Dartmouth
Moosehead (R)
Oland (R) LABATT

Halifax
Granite (HBP)

Saint John
Moosehead (R)
Oland (R) LABATT

River View
Bavarian Specialities (M)

Sault Ste Marie
Northern (R)
Jolly Friar (HBP)

North Hatley
Massawippi (HBP)

Lennoxville
Golden Lion (HBP)

Creemore
Creemore Springs (M)

Orilla
Blue Anchor (HBP)

Newmarket
Simcoe (M)

Wellington County
Guelph (M)

Weston
Labatt (N)

Don Mills
Conners/Don Valley (M)

Barrie
Molson (N)

Waterloo
Labatt (N)
Lion (M)
Heuther (HBP)

Heidelberg
Heidelberg (HBP)

Stratford
Queen's Inn (HBP)

Toronto
Carling (HQ brewery) (N) ELDERS
Labatt (N)
Molson (N)
Upper Canada (M)
Amsterdam (HBP)
Rotterdam (HBP)

London
Labatt (HQ brewery) (N)

Welland
Atlas (HBP)

Brampton
Great Lakes (M)
Houston/Track (HBP)

Windsor
Charlie's Tavern (HBP)

Hamilton
Amstel (R) HEINEKEN

Mississauga
Conners (M)
Luxembourg (HBP)
Tapster's (HBP)
Winchester Arms (HBP)

UNITED STATES

Labatt (N)	National brewer
Drummond (R)	Regional brewer
Conners (M)	Micro-brewery
Amsterdam (HBP)	Home-brew pub
Carling (N) ELDERS	Name and type of brewer followed by name of parent company

be found anywhere. Calgary has a second micro-brewery, producing the sweetish, light Appaloosa Lager Beer. Edmonton, Alberta, has an English-accented ale from a micro called Strathcona. The big brewers have plants in Saskatchewan and Manitoba, but these have yet to prove fertile territories for micros. They are thinly-populated provinces, and even their big cities do not have the most metropolitan of tastes. In a country as huge as Canada, transportation costs are enormous, and that is one reason why the big brewers have so many, scattered provincial plants. The other reason is that beer may not, by law, be "exported" from one province to another. This device is intended to protect the economies of the farther-flung provinces.

A beer-lover in one of the cities of Ontario or Quebec can find it difficult to lay hands on the product of a micro-brewery in another province. Sometimes, the quickest way is to pop across the border and see whether it can be found as an import to the United States. In some cases this can be done by local taxi.

Ontario has several micros and a growing number of brew-pubs. In Waterloo, Ontario, the well-appointed and sizable micro Brick's makes a pleasant, all-malt Premium Lager and a Bock. Its Red Baron is less interesting. Waterloo also has a brew-pub, in the Heuther Hotel. This building once housed a well-known brewery, and the tradition has been revived with a clean-tasting lager and Canadian and English-style ales. This city additionally has a Labatt brewery and a Seagram distillery and whisky museum.

The first free-standing micro in Canada to offer cask-conditioned ales was Wellington County, in the nearby town of Guelph, formerly an important brewing center and perhaps to be so once more. In the early days of Wellington County, the outstanding character and integrity of its products bemused the trade and public alike. Historically, the Guelph area has links with the Arkell brewing family in England. This was marked in a nutty Bitter called Arkell (1038), the initial product along with Wellington County (1052), a fruity-hoppy Special Bitter. Iron Duke (1062), a malty, vinous, strong winter ale, came later. Special Pale Ale is a filtered product which in character falls somewhere between the Arkell and the County. Another micro, much larger, is planned in Guelph by a descendant of the local Sleeman brewing family, with assistance from Stroh, of the United States.

The unusual phenomenon of a multiplying micro-brewery began in 1986, at Port Credit, in the municipality of Mississauga, on the western edge of Toronto. The Conners micro, founded there, has since expanded through branch breweries elsewhere in Ontario, at Don Valley and Thunder Bay. Among its early products, its Best Bitter perhaps represents the character that Canadian-style ale once had. Its Conners Ale, with more fruit and dryness, is pitched between the Canadian and English traditions. Its

model of the style. Several other brew-pubs and micros are on Vancouver Island, but their performances have varied. There have also been an especially large number of openings and closings in the province of British Columbia.

The city of Vancouver itself has a new, free-standing micro-brewery, called Shaftbury, pro-ducing a Cream Ale (in style, more reminiscent of an English Mild) and a Bitter. Vancouver also has a longer-established micro in the trendy-touristy shopping neighborhood called Granville Island. Its first product was Island Lager, with a hoppy aroma and finish, and a soft, malty palate. Then came the tawny Island Bock, deliciously malty, with some balancing hop. More recently the brewery has produced an excellent seasonal Märzen, which has a firm malt character and lots of hop in the finish.

Between the coast and the Rockies, near Lake Okanagan, at Vernon, British Columbia, a micro-brewery has produced an immensely tasty, fruity, rounded strong Old English Porter (19.5; 1078; 6.8; 8.5). It has also made a dark, sedimented Wheat Beer (a Dunkel Hefe-Weizen) and a particularly good lager, with a lovely balance of clean maltiness in the aroma and hop character in the finish. The brewery is called Okanagan Spring.

The Big Rock brewery is (despite its name) a micro, in Calgary, Alberta. It produces very characterful, fruity, sweetish ales and a Porter, all unpasteurized but tightly filtered. Its McNally's Extra Ale (1065-70; 5.6; 7) is a most distinctive product: strong, full-bodied, smooth, with a buttery maltness which is balanced by a restrained hop character. Canadian, of course, but as good an Irish Ale as can

The Big Three

John Molson left Lincolnshire, England, for Canada in 1782 and four years later founded the brewery that his descendants still control. It is the oldest brewing company in the Americas.

Of the Big Three in Canada, it has perhaps the most characterful products overall, although the differences are not great. The light-tasting Molson Golden is its basic ale. Its Export, also marketed as Molson Ale, has a little more character, especially in its fruitiness. Molson Stock Ale is tastier again. Brador (5 per cent alcohol by weight; 6.25 by volume) is a top-fermenting Malt Liquor. Among the Big Three, Molson has the tastier Porter, produced at its brewery in Barrie, Ontario.

Both Molson and Labatt are heavily diversified corporations. Labatt is controlled by a splinter of the Bronfman (Seagrams whiskey) family. By far its most distinctive brew is its I.P.A., a golden ale with some hop in the aroma, a firm body, and malty sweetness in the finish. Labatt subsidiary breweries produce two of the best known regional

beers, Kokanee and Schooner. Neither is exceptional.

Carling was once an international brewer, but it gradually withdrew to its home territory, and is now owned by Elders, of Australia. In Britain, Carling Black Label remains a major brand of lager, but in the hands of Bass. In Canada, Black Label is outsold by the company's sweeter Old Vienna. This is an

everyday lager with no serious pretensions to the Vienna style. The full name of the company is Carling O'Keefe. The company has a carbonic, fruity ale called O'Keefe.

Two former Carling plants are now operated by unions, under the name Northern Breweries. Two breweries formerly owned by the entrepreneur Ben Ginter now operate independently under the names Pacific Western and

Drummond. These breweries all produce typical Canadian beers. Moosehead exports its regular Canadian Lager to the United States, but its Pale Ale and Ten Penny Stock Ale have more character. Heineken also has an Amstel brewery in Canada, in Hamilton, Ontario. This produces a Moosehead-inspired brew, Grizzly, and a local product for Hamilton, Steeler.

Imperial Stout has a misleading name. It is not a strong brew, but a Dry Stout of conventional Canadian strength. It is very tasty, though, with a smooth, roasty palate. Mississauga also has some colorful and interesting beers at Tapsters Brew-Pub (100 Britannia Road E).

In the heart of Toronto, the micro Upper Canada Brewing Company has made some characterful products, with frequent specials. It has experimented with dry-hopping and cask-conditioning. Upper Canada's Dark Ale has over the years lost some of its "pears in cream" character, but is still a fruity brew, with plenty of hop in the finish and lots of character all round. Among top-fermenting styles, the brewery has also produced a refreshing appetizing, Wheat Beer. Its basic Upper Canada Lager has a tasty balance of malt and hop; its stronger Rebellion Malt

Liquor (4.8; 6.0) has a spicy character; its True Bock (16; 1046; 5.2; 6.5) is tawny in color, with a malty aroma and start and a long, coffeeish, dry finish.

Toronto's first brew-pub, The Amsterdam (John Street), began with a Vienna-style lager, but has now widened its range. Its Festive Ale, with a dash of Chimay character, is an interesting product.

North of Toronto at Newmarket, a new micro-brewery has started with Brown Ales. Newmarket Brown Ale makes an allusive name. The brewery is called Simcoe, after the nearby lake. Farther north, near Collingwood, the Creemore Springs micro-brewery is putting great care and skill into the production of a beautifully balanced, tasty lager which is hand-packaged in screw-top soft-drink bottles. The Ottawa Valley micro-brewery makes Canadian-style brews from malt extract. The

province of Quebec has a scatter of brew-pubs, but has been slow in developing free-standing micros. The maritime provinces have two micros, both beginning with light-bodied pale lagers: Highland, Sydney, Nova Scotia; and Island, at Charlottetown, Prince Edward Island. There is also a new "Bavarian-style" micro-brewery at Dieppe, New Brunswick.

The most ambitious pioneers of the brew-pub movement seem to like the geographical extremes of the country. The former Ginger's, now called the Granite Brewery and Tavern, is in a landmark building at 1222 Barrington Street, Halifax, Nova Scotia. Its products, served by hand-pump from a conditioning tank under blanket pressure, include one called simply Peculier. Confusingly, this brew (1056-8) is modeled on Marston's Owd Roger. What next — Burton Unions?

THE UNITED STATES

THE UNITED STATES produces a greater volume of beer, by far, than any other country. There are single breweries in the United States that make as much beer as entire European nations. The United States is, in that sense, the world's greatest brewing country.

Does most mean best? The big brewers of the United States lead the world in the production of light-bodied and exceptionally mild-tasting beers in a very distant derivation of the Pilsener (or, to be more general, Bohemian) style of lager. Contrary to popular belief, these beers are not, by international standards, especially low in alcohol content (3.2-3.9 per cent by weight; 4.0-4.9 by volume). Nor are they, by any means, all that the United States has to offer.

These mass-market beers are made to the highest standards of quality control, but they are more notable for their consistency than for their individuality. They are the beer world's answer to a generic Chablis rather than a Chardonnay from Burgundy. Their first intention is to win widespread acceptance. They seek to offend no one, and therefore offer little to excite anyone. Should any drinker nonetheless become excited, there is always the option of an even lighter-bodied version of the same style. This is identified, with breathtaking understatement, as "light beer." (The beer world's precursor of "light wine"; what else?)

These mass-market products are advertised so heavily that many Americans are unaware of any others. Foreigners can be forgiven for a similar ignorance, but the truth is surprising and exciting: the United States does have an increasing number of beers in other, quite different, specialty styles.

Some of these lesser-known specialties not only are very well made but also have great character. They would be regarded as outstanding in any of the great brewing nations. Many of them are produced by new micro-brewers.

The big American brewers can sell a large volume of beer because their country has more people than any other in the Western world. Exports do not account for a very large share of the volume. The light-tasting, mass-market beers are purported to be universally appealing and easily drinkable, but this is open to question. Per head, American men and women do not buy a great deal of beer. In per capita consumption, the United States stands behind perhaps a dozen other nations. However large their sales, neither the brewers nor Madison Avenue can count their efforts an unqualified success.

In all brewing countries, beer is consumed more by men than by women, but in no other developed nation is its advertising as simplistically macho as it can be in the United States. In most countries, drinking is a rite of passage for young men growing up, but nowhere is the ritual as pervasive as in the United States. These are limitations. Without them, American brewers could sell more beer. Paradoxically, the nation's voluble temperance movement might also be disarmed. When the measure of their success is questioned, American brewers are apt to reply that their heritage does not provide for a "beer culture." The Bohemians, Germans, Dutch, British, and Irish who settled so much of the country might argue about that.

Perhaps the Dutch would best understand that the land of conspicuous consumption also has a strong streak of puritanism. As it happened, when the Pilgrim Fathers sought a place to make a permanent landing in America, they did so, according to their diaries, "our victuals being much spent, especially our beer."

The first commercial brewery in the United States seems to have been established some time after 1612, in Lower Manhattan. As the settlement of the country proceeded from east to west, so did the development and growth of the brewing industry. The first famous American breweries were in the East; much more recently, in the late 19th and early 20th centuries, the big names have been in the Midwest; today, California leads in volume, and the West offers the greatest variety and appreciation of beer. In Northern California and the Pacific Northwest, beer and wine are happy bedmates.

Far from lacking in a beer culture, the world's most cosmopolitan country is enriched by the traditions of all its founding nations. It made almost every type of beer before Prohibition — and is now beginning to do so again.

The rediscovery of beer in the developed world is proceeding faster in America than anywhere else. Other nations had elements of Prohibition, but none as rigorous — or destructive to variety — as that in the United States. Hundreds of small breweries went out of business. The survivors have been inclined to present beer as though it were a convenience grocery product. Another factor is that, while in all nations variety has been diminished by mass-marketing, this has nowhere been more overt than in the United States: today people are rejecting uniformity and opting for the particular beers they prefer.

As the most cosmopolitan of nations, the United States has a particular dynamic for conformity. When grandma made her own pasta, she seemed like an immigrant, not an American. Mother did things the American way, and served convenience pasta. Today's generation are confident about being American, and occasionally make their own pasta once more. People in their millions still drink famous, familiar brands of American beer, but a few are sufficiently confident to try something different, perhaps even a return to older traditions.

In a fiercely competitive nation, it is hard to escape the notion of winners and losers. For a time, it seemed that the United States would eventually have only one brand of beer: Winnerbräu or, perhaps, Winnerbräu Light. Even today, many Americans could name only three or four.

The giants are, in descending order of size:

The Anchor Brewery of San Francisco was founded in 1896. Almost a century later, the "discovery" of Anchor was an early sign of the beer revival. It is most widely known for its Anchor Steam, but the brewery also produces a Wheat Beer, an ale, a Barley Wine, and a Porter. In addition to these classic styles, it has its celebrated specials for holidays and other occasions.

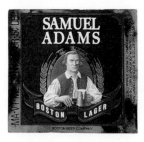

The Maine lobster, the mountain lion of Vermont and a somewhat eccentric 80-year-old picture of a whaler from Massachusetts Bay provide images of New England to rival Samuel Adams.

Anheuser-Busch (producer of Budweiser and Michelob); Miller; Stroh (which owns Schlitz); Bond, of Australia (Heileman and Pittsburgh Brewing); Coors; and Pabst (with Falstaff and General Brewing).

There are fewer than 20 old-established regional and local independents, but at least 40 new microbreweries established themselves in the decade from the late 1970s. In the mid-1980s, more than 20 brew-pubs were set up in a period of three or four years, and many more were planned. On top of this, about 20 "contract brewers" have established a market for their products. These are companies that develop and market their own beers but have them produced under contract by existing breweries.

From a low point of fewer than 40 brewing companies on the eve of the 1980s, the number more than doubled, and promised to triple, in less than a decade. At a conservative estimate, the United States has well over 300 beers, and that figure excludes the ones that are merely labels. Several of the old independents bottle their principal products under a wide variety of labels which recall long-gone breweries with a vestigial local following.

In the worst days, critics of capitalism could have argued that the free market was reducing the consumer's choice. At the eleventh hour, everything changed. Upholders of the economic system could reply that its self-regulating mechanism had tripped into action.

The result is now a far greater choice for the consumer, if he or she can find it. Being by definition very small, most of the micro-breweries serve local markets. This creates a regional variety that should be a delight but that is so unfamiliar as to bewilder some American consumers. They find it hard to conceive of a brewery as being like a winery or a cheese dairy, making a local product — or even like a family-run restaurant, with its own cuisine.

THE NORTH EAST REDISCOVERS ITS BREWING TRADITION

There were once emphatic regional differences in brewing within the United States, and they never totally died. The Northeast, especially New York State, has maintained the Colonial tradition of ale-brewing, and may yet be glad of this. Ale was once regarded as the élite style in the United States and, a century later, is regaining this position. Just as a middle-aged generation dismisses it as being "old-fashioned," a younger crowd is rediscovering ale. This rediscovery has been largely inspired by the micro-brewers. By no means all of them brew ales, but many do. (In an inversion of tradition, many of these new ale brewers are on the opposite coast, in the Northwest.)

Ale has for some time been misunderstood by many Americans, who have regarded it as a craggy outsider, not a member of the family of beer-styles. This is because beer has not been appreciated to embrace a family of styles. To many Americans, "beer" means only one style: the familiar national type of lager. Hence the misconceived, but common, question: "What is the difference between ale and beer?"

Most (though not all) of the old-established American ales have over the years paled to a golden color and light palate, often with a sweet creaminess. Some are primed with sugar before being pasteurized. Only a slight fruitiness, sometimes with a hint of tartness, identifies them as being ales. Some breweries have a product described as "Cream Ale." This American variation was initially, and still sometimes is, a blend made from both ale and lager. Most of the new, micro-brewed, ales have much more character, and are closer to the original colonial version.

Not all of the old-established ales are made with top-fermenting yeasts, though some are, and this is usually true of the new, micro-brewed examples. The "establishment" brewing industry organization in the United States, the Beer Institute, does (commendably) define an ale as being top-fermented. It also notes that this is a rapid method of fermentation and defines the temperature cycle as being 14-21°C (58-70°F). Even an American ale that is not made with a top yeast is likely to be fermented at high temperatures. This at least provides for the fruitiness that should characterize an ale.

Traditionally, the Northeast tended to have the hoppiest brews, and this was especially true of its ales, though that is no longer markedly the case. Although the term "ale" has everything to do with fermentation method and nothing to do with strength, some states' laws insist that a brew bearing this description must contain more than 4.0 per cent alcohol by weight. In some states, any beer that has more than 4.0 per cent must be labeled an ale even if it is not. These laws, framed after Prohibition by anti-drink bureaucrats with no understanding of beer, oblige brewers to mislead and misinform the public in a variety of ways.

One of the principal ale-brewers in the United States is also the nation's biggest independent, Genesee, in the sizable industrial city of Rochester (perhaps better known as the home of Kodak), in New York State. With a capacity for four million barrels, Genesee is very large indeed for an independent, and is inevitably the frequent subject of takeover speculation. Despite its size, it is well known to consumers only in pockets of the East; such is the scale and sprawl of the United States. However, devotees of its products have an affectionate regard for "Genny" (pronounced with a soft "G" as though it were a girl's name). It produces a sweetish Jubilee Porter (inherited from the now-defunct Fred Koch brewery); the golden-colored, top-fermenting, 12-Horse Ale, light-tasting, but with a dash of fruity tartness in the finish; a thinner Cream Ale; and a range of lagers.

Genesee's products are noteworthy not because they are exceptional, but for the opposite reason: because they typify the style of ale usually produced by the old-established American breweries.

Also in upstate New York, the much smaller (800,000-barrel) F.X.Matt brewery, in the town of Utica, makes an ale in this style. Utica Club Cream Ale is pale and fruity, with some of the sweetness and fullness that is the house character of this brewery's products. Matt, old established and family-owned, is a proud and friendly brewery. Its other products include a good Pilsener-style beer, Saranac 1888, and perhaps the best example of a Malt Liquor, Maximus Super (4.8-5.2 by weight; 6.0-6.5 by volume).

"Malt Liquor" is an American term for a pale, golden-colored lager with a light-to-medium body but relatively high alcohol content. Some are agreeable enough, but few are high in malt, and none is a liquor. Several contain a high proportion of sugar, and some are fermented with the help of artificial enzymes. They are popular as a cheap "high" among the urban poor. The style originated in the Midwest, at the now-defunct Glueck's brewery of Minneapolis.

The style of ale that is most associated with the old-established brewers of the Northeast is also made by several small companies in Pennsylvania, and by some larger ones in the Midwest. After Genesee Cream Ale, the best-known example of that variation is made in Cincinnati, Ohio. There, the combined Hudepohl and Schoenling breweries produce the soft, golden Little Kings Cream Ale (as well as sweetish malty lagers under the Christian Moerlein label).

Probably the best-known among all the old-established ales in America is Ballantine's — such an icon that two cans were once the subject of a Jasper Johns painting. Ballantine's has over the years moved from Albany, New York, to Newark, New Jersey, to Providence, Rhode Island, and is currently produced in the handsome Falstaff (former Berghoff) brewery at Fort Wayne, Indiana. The regular Ballantine Ale has both sweetness and hoppiness. Among the old-established, golden-colored ales of America, it is the hoppiest. However, the Ballantine name is at least as celebrated for its copper-colored India Pale Ale. The I.P.A. is markedly hoppier in the finish, and stronger. The Ballantine ales are fermented in open wooden vessels, and begin their maturation there. They are dry-hopped. Among the old-established ales of America, the other notably copper-colored example is made in the far West, in Seattle. That product, Rainier Ale, was in its more robust days known as "The Green Death."

The new micro-breweries have changed the topography and geography of American beer and as a result the East is no longer pre-eminent even in its specialty, ale. It has, though, gained some excellent new ale breweries. So much so that, even in the golden style, its old-established ales are outshone by a

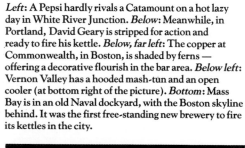

new, micro-brewed product. This stylish newcomer is produced in the unlikely setting of White River Junction, a one-street town in Vermont. It is called Catamount Gold, and its restrained fruitiness is balanced with a splendid, American varietal, hop aroma and palate. The brewery also has a slightly more assertive and fuller-colored ale called Catamount Amber. Both are top-fermenting, all-malt brews, very smooth and clean.

Among the new generation of ale-breweries in the East, Mass Bay, in Boston harbor, is another good example. Its Harpoon Ale has a bronze color and medium palate, with a citrus-apricot accent, but nicely balancing hop and malt notes. Geary's Pale Ale, from Portland, Maine, has a full, copper color, plenty of fruit, and lots of crisp, hoppy dryness. It is a whole-hearted, English-style ale, fermented with Ringwood yeast. The British Ringwood brewery was also the inspiration of the East's first micro, Newman's, which turned out to be somewhat ahead of its time in trying to revive ale-brewing in Albany, New York.

Full ranges of English-style ales, including excellent "winter warmer" Barley Wines and Stouts, kept under blanket pressure but served by hand-pump, are available at two brew-pubs in the East: Commonwealth, at 85 Merrimac and Portland, near Faneuil Hall, in Boston; and Manhattan Brewing, on Thompson at Broome, in SoHo, New York. Despite its origins as a contract brew from F.X. Matt, New Amsterdam Amber has its showpiece Tap Room at 235 11th Avenue and 26th Street, in Chelsea, New

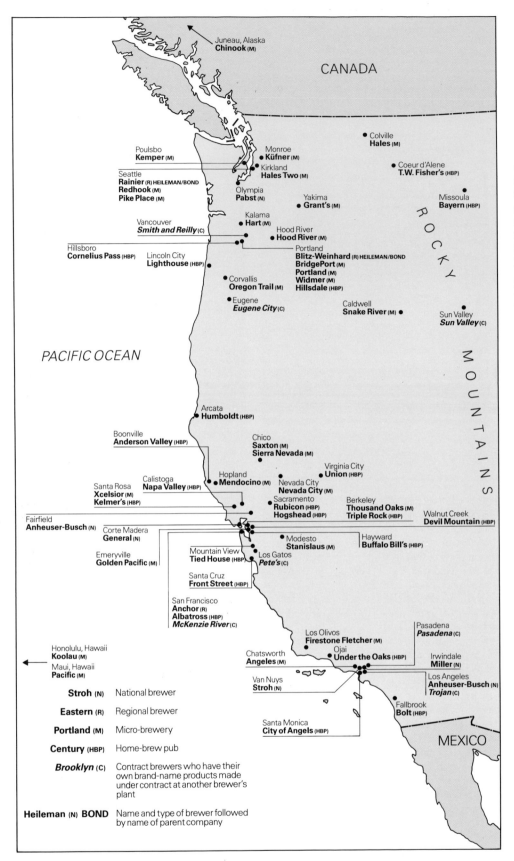

Samuel Adams Boston Lager is not specifically described as a Pilsener, but it is the best example of the style made in the United States. It has a slightly fuller color than a classic Pilsener, but it is nonetheless golden rather than bronze. Its defining characteristics are its elegance and its hoppiness, its flowery aroma and dry finish. It has a softly malty background reminiscent of that to be found in some Pilseners from the South of Germany. Samuel Adams has a sister beer called Boston Lightship. Despite its allusive name, this is not specifically marketed as a light beer. It is, though, relatively low in calories (98 per bottle), and very light indeed in alcohol (2.3 by weight). It has an aromatic hoppiness and plenty of dry maltiness. If it were identified as a light beer, it might be considered the best example of the style. These two beers are from the Boston Beer Company. Despite their strong Boston identity, they were initially produced in Pittsburgh, pending the restoration of the former Haffenreffer brewery.

The most uncompromisingly traditional lagers in today's America emerged from an unlikely place — a ski resort in Vernon, New Jersey — in the mid- and late 1980s. A businessman involved in the resort took his enthusiasm for beer to extraordinary lengths: he built a revivalist brewery largely inspired by that at Eltville, near Wiesbaden, Germany. The question was whether such a venture could survive on an unschooled, family audience at a seasonal resort, or whether it would have to move closer to a big city.

The Vernon Valley Brewery set out by importing all of its malt, some lightly smoked, from Germany; by using an open cooler; and by fermenting and lagering its beer in wooden casks. The huge lagering casks were re-pitched each year like those at Pilsen. The brewery's early range included an unfiltered Pilsener, served like a Zwickelbier, with a yeast sediment; a beautifully-balanced Dark Lager, with a coffee-toffee richness; and a lightly syrupy, liqueurish Bock, with an alcohol content in the region of 5.5 per cent by weight.

It is to be hoped that these outstanding beers stay in production. The Dark Lager is surely the finest produced in the United States in living memory. The Bock is scarcely less interesting, though it has a hearty rival under the name Skipjack Doppel, from the Chesbay micro-brewery at Virginia Beach.

The first lager beer brewed in the United States is said to have been produced in Philadelphia in 1844 or soon afterward. This seems early, since the Bavarians and Bohemians had perfected their lager styles only at the beginning of that decade. However, there are several references to lager brewing in the United States in the 1850s, sometimes with yeast shipped from Europe.

The British colonial ale tradition and the newer, Germanic lager method prospered side by side for many decades, but a long-term shift was inevitable. Besides brewers of British and Dutch origin, there had always been Germans, but there was a wave of

York. This very enjoyable beer is something of a hybrid between a Vienna lager and an ale. A wonderfully aromatic dry-hopped version, described as New Amsterdam Ale, is available in some outlets.

All is not ale in the Northeast. Lagers are far more common but less often interesting. None of the once-famous local lagers any longer belongs to the Northeast. Schaefer and Piels are brands owned by Stroh; Rheingold and Schmidts by Heileman. New

York City could do more to support its new local brews, but it is not a city with widespread appreciation of good beers.

In Boston, local pride has perhaps been better engaged by a beer named after Samuel Adams. It is a bonus that the Bostonian revolutionary politician was at one point a professional brewer. (George Washington also brewed, but his commercial interest was in whiskey-distilling.)

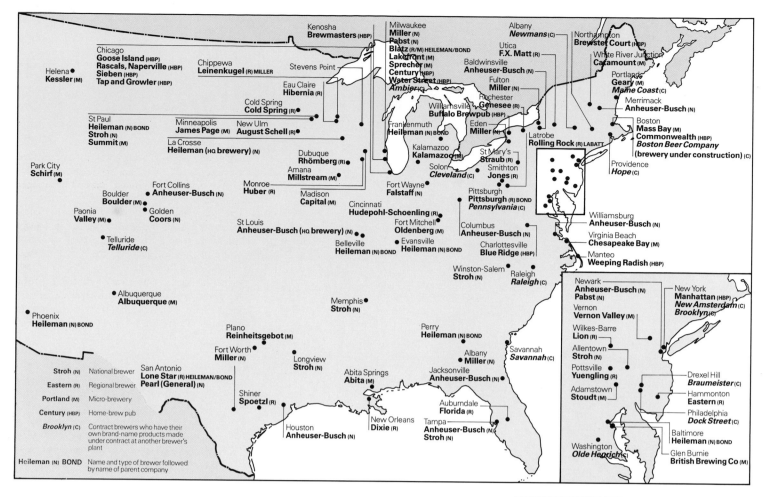

Helena
Kessler (M)

Chicago
Goose Island (HBP)
Rascals, Naperville (HBP)
Sieben (HBP)
Tap and Growler (HBP)

Chippewa
Leinenkugel (R) MILLER

Stevens Point

Eau Claire
Hibernia (R)

Cold Spring
Cold Spring (R)

St Paul
Heileman (N) BOND
Stroh (N)
Summit (M)

Minneapolis
James Page (M)

New Ulm
August Schell (R)

La Crosse
Heileman (HQ brewery) (M)

Kenosha
Brewmasters (HBP)

Milwaukee
Miller (N)
Pabst (N)
Blatz (R/M) HEILEMAN/BOND
Lakefront (M)
Sprecher (M)
Century (HBP)
Water Street (M)
Amber (C)

Albany
Newmans (C)

Northampton
Brewster Court (HBP)

Utica
F.X. Matt (R)

White River Junction
Catamount (M)

Baldwinsville
Anheuser-Busch (N)

Fulton
Miller (N)

Rochester
Genesee (R)

Portland
Geary (M)
Maine Coast (C)

Merrimack
Anheuser-Busch (N)

Boston
Mass Bay (M)
Commonwealth (HBP)
*Boston Beer Company
(brewery under construction)* (C)

Providence
Hope (C)

Williamsville
Buffalo Brewpub (HBP)

Frankenmuth
Heileman (N) BOND

Eden
Miller (N)

Latrobe
Rolling Rock (R) LABATT

Park City
Schirf (M)

Fort Collins
Anheuser-Busch (N)

Boulder
Boulder (M)

Golden
Coors (N)

Paonia
Valley (M)

Telluride
Telluride (C)

Monroe
Huber (R)

Madison
Capital (M)

Dubuque
Rhömberg (R)

Amana
Millstream (M)

Kalamazoo
Kalamazoo (M)

St Mary's
Straub (R)

Solon
Cleveland (C)

Smithton
Jones (R)

Fort Wayne
Falstaff (N)

Pittsburgh
Pittsburgh (R) BOND
Pennsylvania (M)

Williamsburg
Anheuser-Busch (N)

St Louis
Anheuser-Busch (HQ brewery) (N)

Cincinnati
Hudepohl-Schoenling (R)

Fort Mitchell
Oldenberg (M)

Columbus
Anheuser-Busch (N)

Virginia Beach
Chesapeake Bay (M)

Manteo
Weeping Radish (HBP)

Belleville
Heileman (N) BOND

Evansville
Heileman (N) BOND

Charlottesville
Blue Ridge (HBP)

Albuquerque
Albuquerque (M)

Winston-Salem
Stroh (N)

Raleigh
Raleigh (C)

Memphis
Stroh (N)

Newark
Anheuser-Busch (N)
Pabst (N)

New York
Manhattan (HBP)
New Amsterdam (C)
Brooklyn (C)

Vernon
Vernon Valley (M)

Phoenix
Heileman (N) BOND

Plano
Reinheitsgebot (M)

Perry
Heileman (N) BOND

Wilkes-Barre
Lion (R)

Allentown
Stroh (N)

Fort Worth
Miller (N)

Longview
Stroh (N)

Albany
Miller (N)

Savannah
Savannah (C)

Pottsville
Yuengling (R)

Drexel Hill
Braumeister (C)

San Antonio
Lone Star (R) HEILEMAN/BOND
Pearl (General) (N)

Shiner
Spoetzl (R)

Abita Springs
Abita (M)

Jacksonville
Anheuser-Busch (N)

Adamstown
Stoudt (M)

Hammonton
Eastern (R)

Philadelphia
Dock Street (C)

Houston
Anheuser-Busch (N)

New Orleans
Dixie (R)

Tampa
Anheuser-Busch (N)
Stroh (N)

Auburndale
Florida (M)

Washington
Olde Heurich (C)

Baltimore
Heileman (N) BOND

Glen Burnie
British Brewing Co (M)

Stroh (N)   National brewer
Eastern (R)   Regional brewer
Portland (M)   Micro-brewery
Century (HBP)   Home-brew pub
Brooklyn (C)   Contract brewers who have their
own brand-name products made
under contract at another brewer's
plant

Heileman (N) BOND   Name and type of brewer followed
by name of parent company

---

new immigration after the "Hungry Forties" in Europe. Immigrants from the German-speaking world (from Bohemia to Luxembourg; Switzerland to Pomerania) were very well represented in the new wave. They arrived at a time when lager-beer brewing was the new technology. As in Europe, the development of steam power and the spread of the railroads encouraged technologically-progressive brewers to produce on a larger scale and distribute farther afield. The first great German city had been Philadelphia, but soon the Midwest was being opened. Newer cities had bigger, and even more Germanic, breweries.

Philadelphia was the nation's beer capital for many years (it had 94 breweries in 1879), and Pennsylvania to this day retains a memory of that reputation. Sad to say, the last of the old Philadelphia breweries, Schmidt's, closed in 1987. A new brewing company has emerged in the city, but its ale-ish Dock Street Amber Beer has thus far been contract-brewed. The Pittsburgh Brewing Company is the biggest in Pennsylvania, though it is now owned by Bond, of Australia. Its most interesting products are its several contract-brews, like Pennsylvania Pilsner, Olde Heurich (produced for a company in Washington, D.C.) and XIII Colony (for an entrepreneur in Savannah, Georgia). In the old monastic brewing town of Latrobe, Pennsylvania, the company that produces Rolling Rock beer is now owned by Labatt, of Canada. Rolling Rock enjoys cult status among some drinkers in the East, though it is a mainstream American light lager, albeit very clean-tasting.

Pennsylvania still has vestiges of tradition, though some are half-forgotten curiosities, like the licorice-accented, bottom-fermented Stegmaier Porter, from

The Lion Brewery, of Wilkes-Barre. The lightish Old Shay Cream Ale and the rather sweet Stoney's Beer are made by the family-owned Jones brewery, in Smithton, Pennsylvania. A roasty Porter, again bottom-fermenting, and a flowery American-style ale are produced by Yuengling, in Pottsville, Pennsylvania.

This is America's oldest brewery, founded in 1829. Yuengling is nonetheless primarily a lager brewery, with its old maturation caves dug into the side of the Delaware Valley. Given its history, it is a shame that this family-owned brewery does not have a deeper commitment to traditional styles.

The smallest of the old-established American breweries is also in Pennsylvania, at St Mary's, a German settlement in the Allegheny Mountains. The family-owned Straub brewery has a capacity of only 40,000 barrels, and the proprietors have been quoted as saying that a greater production would impinge upon their hunting, fishing, and gardening. Straub Beer has a reputation for being dry and clean, but in recent years seems to have become sweeter. A very dry, high-gravity version is no longer produced. The brewery makes a point that it uses no corn syrups (only flaked maize), but this claim is less significant in the days of all-malt micro-brews.

The most Germanic lagers now being brewed in Pennsylvania are produced by a man whose family name has variously been Steud, Staud, Staudt, and, now, Stoudt (the penultimate "d" might just forestall any confusion about beer styles). He traces his family history to 1535 in Germany and 1733 in the United States.

His micro-brewery began in 1987, with a range that included a malty, pale Munich Gold; a firm-bodied Dortmunder; and a tawny, toasty

Above: Beware appearances: no Stout is brewed here. The intervening "d" is German, and this new brewery makes lagers. The tower is a brew-house, not a church. A restaurant and an antiques market share the premises. *Far left:* The breweries of the far West. *Top:* From the Rockies to the Atlantic.

Kulmbacher Dark. The brewery adjoins a beer hall and garden and the Black Angus restaurant, on Route 272, at Adamstown, between Reading and Lancaster. There is also an adjoining Sunday antiques market. Eclectic though this combination may sound, these are Stoudt family businesses that have grown organically. With the development of the brew-pub notion, there will be many more bizarre enterprises. A good example is the Oldenberg Brewery and Entertainment Complex, just across the Ohio River from Cincinnati.

THE LAGER-BREWERS OF THE MIDWEST

Even Middle America is rediscovering its traditions. As the Midwest was settled, the city of St Louis, Missouri, was a propitious place in which to start a brewery. Even today, St Louis maintains a landmark arch to symbolize its role as a "gateway" city. It stands half way between the East Coast and the Rockies, with the Great Lakes to the north, and the Mississippi flowing south to New Orleans and the Gulf. It is in the middle of the United States, with easy communications to all the biggest cities east of the Rockies.

Despite these advantages, St Louis was still a small city when it gave birth to the brewing company that is today the world's biggest (making more than 70 million barrels a year, in a dozen breweries throughout the United States). The original

brewery, described later as "a hole in the ground," was founded by a man named Schneider in 1850-2, but soon faced collapse. Loans were provided by a wealthy businessman, Eberhard Anheuser, who had already made a fortune in soap manufacturing. (Hence, perhaps, the undignified American habit of calling beer "suds"?) Anheuser reluctantly took ownership of the brewery in 1860. His daughter subsequently married a brewers' supplier, Adolphus Busch, who had emigrated to the United States from Mainz. Busch became president of the brewery and a father of mass-marketing. A fourth-generation Busch is now chairman of the board.

At first it was described as a "Bavarian Brewery." The name Busch Bavarian was used until relatively recent times for a lager in the malty, South German style that was brewed as the local beer for St Louis.

This eventually evolved into the lighter, more typically American beer that is today sold under the Busch trademark as a competitively-priced brand.

At a time when the brewing style of Pilsen, Bohemia, was regarded as being highly sophisticated in many parts of Europe, a slightly different inspiration struck Adolphus Busch. He looked to Bohemia's other famous brewing city, known in German as Budweis.

Whereas the fame of Pilsen was more current, Budweis had once housed the royal court brewery of Bohemia; whereas the term "Pilsener" was by now commonplace, at least in Europe, "Budweiser" could still be protected. In 1876, Busch launched a "premium" beer, under the brand-name Budweiser, with a view to its being nationally marketed, by railroad. The idea of nationally marketing any product was still very new, and beer was known to be perishable. Busch even had an answer for that: he pioneered the use of refrigerated railroad wagons.

While the golden lagers of Pilsen have always been known for their dry aromatic hoppiness, those of Budweis have traditionally been sweeter, and perhaps very faintly fruity. It is not clear whether the actual beer, as well as the name, captured the imagination of Adolphus Busch, but that thought

Far left: Women and children first? Femininity and idyllic rusticity in early US beer advertising. "Suds" (*left*) is a more recent US slang term for beer. Small wonder the product sometimes gets no respect. Opposite this street-corner bar in Milwaukee the anonymous-looking building that once housed a bakery is now home to the Lakefront microbrewery. Better-known Midwest micros include Capital, Sprecher, Summit and James Page.

The old name Anheuser was used on a revivalist Märzenbier test-marketed by A-B. Much of the original Busch brewery (*below*), in St Louis, Missouri, survives unchanged. The company is now best known for its Budweiser and Michelob.

Below: Rhömberg was the original name, recently revived, of the Star brewery in Dubuque, Iowa. The regular Rhömberg (*right*) is in the Vienna style. There is also a lager called Classic Pale. The brewery has been used as a location in several movies.

should not be discounted.

Despite changes in the varieties of barley and hop cultivated over the decades, and refinements (but not fundamental changes) to the brewing process, it could still be argued that there is a distant family resemblance between the beers of Budweis (now known as České Budějovice) and St Louis. Budweiser is, indeed, slightly sweet and faintly fruity for a lager beer, with the tiniest hint of apple esters. However, it is a typically light-bodied American lager, and by far the best-known example. There were even other American brewers who imitatively marketed their beers under the designation Budweiser, but they have long been vanquished.

Unlike the beers brewed in Bohemia, American Budweiser is lightened by the use of rice as an adjunct to the barley malt. Most mass-market American beers have corn as their adjunct. Although Budweiser is by no means a hoppy beer, it does contain eight or nine varieties, European and American, all added in the form of blossoms.

During maturation, the beer rests for 18-21 days on a bed of beechwood chips. This is an old method still used by some Bavarian brewers to clarify beer, but it is very unusual. The beechwood attracts yeast particles. The chips are about a foot long and one or two inches wide, and look like leather straps. They are transported around the Busch breweries in specially-designed, torpedo-shaped trolleys. The ritual is the same in the elegant, original brewery in St Louis and the Busch plants across the nation.

Similar, but slightly more elaborate, methods are used in the production of the company's "super-premium" brand, Michelob, launched in 1896 and likewise named after a brewing town in Bohemia. Michelob has a higher malt content, and therefore a little more body. If the two are tasted side by side, that is quite clear, although Michelob is still very much a light-tasting, American-style lager. Michelob also has a little more hoppy dryness, albeit very slight, in the finish. The company claims that its use of rice makes for a "snappiness," but this characteristic seems less evident in today's Budweiser than it is in

the maltier Michelob, which is perhaps a better-balanced beer.

The company's three original beers, Busch, Budweiser, and Michelob, are all in the American style of light-tasting lager, but they are categorized in the industry as being respectively a "price" brand, a "premium," and a "super-premium."

These terms have come to be widely used by brewers in the United States. They have nothing to do with style, and merely indicate a brand's intended price-position in the market. These differences in price are usually based on the amount of malt used (anything from 60 to 100 per cent) and the time taken to mature the beer (most American brewers regard a total of 21 days as very respectable).

Perhaps Budweiser's sales offer reason enough to pursue troublesome methods in the production of very light-tasting beers. The procedures used in the case of Budweiser and Michelob arise also from the company's corporate culture. So long as a brewery, however large, is run by someone who has grown up in the industry, rather than a journeyman cost-accountant or a marketing sorcerer, it is likely to have some such rules of procedure. In other breweries, they may focus on quite different aspects of production. They sometimes seem idiosyncratic, and often selective. (Why not make an all-malt beer, and lager it for three months?) If nothing else, they insure that the beer is a specific product, not merely a name.

Not that Budweiser was an overnight success. It took about 80 years to achieve its pre-eminence in the American market, and has now been available for more than a century. That is not generally realized in a country where mass-marketing is taken for granted.

Few products in any category have been in the market as long as Bud. It is customary to describe long-dead entrepreneurs as "men of vision," but how many of today's generation are as far-sighted as Adolphus Busch was? And, in a world that demands instant gratification, how many companies would proceed with the patience and tenacity of Anheuser-Busch (AB)? Nor does the company rest on its laurels. In recent years, AB has test-marketed beers in credible interpretations of the true, traditional Pilsener and Märzen styles, and experimented with an ale. More distractingly, it has also diversified into snacks, the entertainment industry, and other fields.

Bud reached the top by overtaking Schlitz. Anyone who believes that beer-lovers "buy the advertising" and are wholly insensitive to quality might consider the case of Schlitz. It took short-cuts in production, and lost sales. The product's former qualities were restored, and perhaps exceeded, but the customers did not return. Schlitz sought a buyer for the company, which was eventually acquired by Stroh. Schlitz beer is still brewed, and has some loyalty, especially in the South, but Stroh's first concern is its own brand.

The Stroh family originated in Kirn, in the Rhineland Palatinate. At least as early as the 1700s, a

Stroh was an innkeeper there. His grandson arrived in Detroit in 1850, and shortly afterwards pioneered the Bohemian (ie Pilsener) style of lager there. The family still controls the company, although it no longer brews in Detroit. The city is still its headquarters, but its breweries are scattered around the country.

Wherever the Stroh's brand is brewed, the company uses kettles heated by direct flames. That is its particular tenet of brewing tradition. Once, all brewers heated their kettles in this way, then steam coils were introduced. Stroh restored direct flame in 1912, after a member of the family had seen "fire-brewing" in Europe and decided it was better. Direct flame is felt by some brewers to insure a vigorous, rolling boil. It also can cause a very slight caramelization of the boiling wort. This very faint caramel note has traditionally been a characteristic of Stroh's beer. It is more noticeable in the super-premium brand, Signature. Schlitz has a firm-bodied, drier super-premium named Erlanger, though this is hardly the Märzenbier suggested on the label. Like its parent, Schlitz has left its home town. It is no longer the beer that makes Milwaukee famous.

Milwaukee is today fighting for its title as the most-breweried city in the United States (against an unlikely rival: Portland, Oregon). Milwaukee still has two sizable breweries, with famous names and a linked history. An immigrant called Jacob Best, from Rheinhessen, founded a brewery in 1844, and his family subsequently became linked with that of Frederick Pabst, from Leipzig. The Pabst brewery became a national giant, and its sweetish, slightly chewy Blue Ribbon was until recently the classic blue-collar beer of America. As the product began to

Beyond Milwaukee, the state of Wisconsin has several small breweries. A Milwaukee contract brewer has the classic American Vienna-style lager beer, called Ambier, produced by Huber, at Monroe, Wisconsin. Huber's own best-known product is Augsburger, a hoppy, Pilsener-style lager which is marketed nationally. The last of the truly family-owned old breweries in Wisconsin is at Stevens Point. It produces Point Special, one of the tastier of the mainstream American lagers.

Almost all small breweries in the United States have courted extinction for years by trying to compete with the giants in the production of light-bodied lagers. One of the first to switch its focus to a range of specialty beers was the former Walter's brewery, called Hibernia since it was acquired by an American-Irish owner, in Eau Claire, Wisconsin. As an Irish-sounding brewery in a town with a French name, it has concentrated on producing classic German seasonal beers. Its excellent Dunkelweizen, with chocolate and vanilla notes, was the first dark Wheat Beer in the United States since Prohibition. Its Bock is the richest and spiciest of the several produced in Wisconsin. It is to be hoped that this revivalist brewery does not lose its early enthusiasm. The state capital, Madison, also has a small brewery, a new micro, with its own beer garden. This brewery, called Capital, produces an appetizing range of German-style specialties. Its basic lager is reminiscent of a Munich Pale. There are also German-accented specialties at the Brewmasters brew-pub in Kenosha, Wisconsin.

Wisconsin is very much the brew-house for the tri-state metropolitan area centered on Chicago, which recently spent several years with no brewery of its own. It now has the Sieben brew-pub, on West Ontario Street, in the River North area. There is a malt-extract brew-pub in Greektown, and more ventures are planned.

No other Midwestern state equals Wisconsin for its tally of breweries, old or new. No other cities in the Midwest approach Milwaukee and Chicago in their sense of beer tradition. Chicago's Blacks and Irish may be more visible, but the city has large German and Bohemian communities (and even a

look tired, the company stumbled into a tangle of takeover struggles and asset-stripping during the early 1980s. It is now in the same grouping as Falstaff and General Brewing, two other once-great names. Pabst's super-premium, Andeker, has at times been an excellent, hoppy beer, but it has undergone several changes of character.

The Best family also founded the Plank Road Brewery, which later became Miller. This was acquired in the 1970s by Philip Morris Inc., better known for cigarettes. Under their ownership, Miller popularized light beer. Miller Lite was not the first low-calorie beer in the United States, but it became by far the most successful. Inflated by its success, Miller mounted a challenge for the number one position in volume brewing, but failed to take the title. One problem was that the watery-tasting Lite took sales from the company's premium beer, the dryish Miller High Life.

Ironically, the success of Miller Lite probably did more than anything to persuade the big American brewers that they could no longer invest almost all of their effort in a single, premium brand. They began to understand that there was more than one type of consumer for beer, as for other products. Moreover, individual consumers have different needs from one moment, or mood, to another.

Miller went on to experiment with several different specialties — one unpasteurized, another unusually hoppy, a third containing wheat. None of these established a substantial market. In 1987, the company took a different tack, acquiring another brewery in its home state, the small, family-owned concern of Leinenkugel, in Chippewa Falls, Wisconsin. Leinenkugel is principally known for a very light, clean, dry American-style lager which has a cult following in the Midwest. No doubt Miller will seek to benefit from this following, perhaps with the launch of further Leinenkugel products.

Another famous Milwaukee name, Val Blatz, was for some years represented in the city only by its magnificent, 19th-century former brewery building. Blatz, a national giant in the 1940s and 1950s, had long been merely a brand owned by Heileman. Then, in 1986, in a purpose-built new small brewery, Val Blatz beers were again made in Milwaukee. The new brewery's several products include the all-malt Culmbacher Imperial, a Dark Lager, and Heileman Milwaukee Weiss, a Wheat Beer in the style of southern Germany.

The new Blatz brewery was conceived to produce specialty beers for Heileman, which is based not far away at La Crosse, Wisconsin. Heileman is a national giant but hardly a household word. Much of its growth has been by acquisition, and its own principal products have rather anonymous names. Its premium beer is the corny-tasting Old Style. Its super-premium is the spritzy Special Export. Heileman lays a great deal of emphasis on *kräusening*, though it is by no means the only major American brewer to use this technique.

Although Blatz is a small brewery, it is not a micro. Milwaukee had already gained its first micro-brewery in 1985, when two former Pabst employees opened Sprecher, producing a range of very hearty, German-style lagers and Wheat Beers. Most notable of the early products was the intense Sprecher Bavarian Black. Since then, the tiny Lakefront micro-brewery has been established. More micros and brew-pubs are set to emerge.

Left: Open for business: the gift-shop brewery in the Amana "Colonies". *Below*: Tourists in the Southwest might consider a visit to the Good Old Boys of the Spoetzl brewery in Shiner, Texas. The brewery produces Shiner Beer, not Lone Star, but has every right to fly the state flag. The original Spoetzl was Bavarian. The Spanish Mission style of the brewery buildings seems more congruous with the landscape. *Right*: A Southern selection. *Far right*: The feminine face of the rocky Southwest.

neighborhood still called Pilsen). Milwaukee has remained a much more German city than is perhaps realized elsewhere. In these two cities, as nowhere else in the United States, some of the older drinkers just about kept the torch alight for today's new generation of beer-lovers. Just as the survival of British tradition provided a starting point for its Real Ale movement, so Germanic heritage has helped the new brewers of Wheat Beers and classic lager styles in the tri-state area. That is less evident in the other Midwestern states, despite German, Dutch, and Scandinavian influence all the way from Michigan to Minnesota.

In Michigan, there are plans to restore production at the former Geyer brewery in the touristy Bavarian settlement of Frankenmuth — and some tasty, fruity, ales are being made by the tiny, new Kalamazoo Brewing Company, in the town of the same name. In Iowa, the handsome old riverside brewery at Dubuque has produced an excellent Vienna-style lager under the name Rhömberg All Malt — and there is more revivalism at touristy Amana, a religious community near Cedar Rapids. Members of the Church of True Inspiration, who trace their origins from Hesse, make German-style lagers and a seasonal Wheat Beer in the new Millstream Brewery.

Without losing their religious faith, the Amana people of Iowa metamorphosed from communalists into capitalists. Across the border in Minnesota, the Swabians who settled the elm-lined town of New Ulm believed that spiritual purity required hard work and exercise. Because of their devotion to gymnastics, they were known as Turners. New Ulm's August Schell brewery, founded in 1860 and still in the same Swiss-Bavarian family, has the prettiest location of any in America. It even has its own little deer park. The brewery makes a revivalist Pilsener which is one of the best in the United States: aromatic, with a hoppy palate and a lightly dry finish. It also has a fruity, liqueurish Wheat Beer in the style of southern Germany: August Schell Weiss. Another old brewery, at Cold Spring, Minnesota, has close links with Heileman.

Minnesota's state capital, St Paul, which interlocks with Minneapolis, has Heileman and Stroh branch-breweries. It also has the new Summit micro-brewery, making a notably dry ale and a smooth, roasty Porter, both of very high quality. In the shadow of the magnificent, but disused, Grain Belt brewery, Minneapolis has a new micro, called James Page, producing pleasantly tasty lagers.

From the Twin Cities, should the beer-hunter head back south down the Mississippi or cross the Rockies to the west? The South is the less promising option. The ultimate destination there, albeit more than a thousand miles away, might be New Orleans, the most colorful city in which to drink in America, but better known for its cocktails than for its beer.

New Orleans was once a beer town, too. Now, it has only one brewery. The wonderfully antique Dixie produces a pleasant Amber Light, and works hard to maintain civic pride. Across Lake Pontchartrain, the old spa town of Abita Springs has a new micro-brewery making lagers and a Wheat Beer in a lightish, Southern-accented interpretation of the German styles. The Jax brewery, by the river, on Jackson Square, has suffered the indignity of being turned into a shopping center. Jax is now one of the light, sweetish brands made in San Antonio, Texas, by Pearl, itself part of the Pabst grouping.

San Antonio also has the Lone Star brewery, producing drier and very slightly more characterful lagers. Lone Star belongs to Heileman. Between San

Antonio and Austin, the state capital, Texas has the small Spoetzl brewery, in Shiner. The brewery is in an astonishing "Spanish mission" building, in the middle of flat countryside. It was built at the turn of the century to service a scatter of seemingly incongruous Bohemian settlements. There are still communities in this area that hold Oktoberfests. Shiner's beers were once Bavarian in style, but today they are at least as light and sweet as their principal Southern competitors.

The nearest thing to German beer made in Texas today emanates from the Reinheitsgebot Brewing Company, in Plano, a suburban community in Collin County, on the edge of Dallas. Collin County Pure Gold is an all-malt Pilsener, with a nicely herbal hop character. Black Gold is a dry, coffeeish, Munich-style dark beer. The German accent is there, even if these are quite clearly American beers. The brewery has thus far not carried out its threat to produce a light beer, to be called Fool's Gold.

THE WEST: AMERICAN BEER'S NEW FRONTIER

The Southwest is of greater interest to the beer-lover if it is taken to include Colorado. That state has several features to attract the devotee. One, though not for the most obvious reason, is the Coors brewery. Coors is often thought to be a funky little brewery in the Rockies. It is, indeed, in an isolated, Rocky Mountain location at Golden, Colorado, but it is the world's biggest single brewery plant, capable of producing 20 million barrels a year. From the outside, it looks like an atomic power station. Inside, it is surely the world's most beautiful example of a large, modern brewery. Its pristine, tiled brewing halls are lined with rows of traditional copper vessels, a tub of blossom hops by every kettle. The conservatism of the Coors family, in brewing matters, extends to a dislike of pasteurization, instead of which the beer is sterile-filtered.

For a time, bumper-stickers reading "Coors — no pasteurization, no unions" were common. The critics were absurdly misguided to complain on the first count. Pasteurization of beer is not a health precaution; it is carried out to extend shelf-life. Not everyone will concede that pasteurization flattens the taste of beer, but many brewmasters would prefer to do without it. One area of hesitation is over the effectiveness of the alternative, sterile-filtration, and the fact that it, in its own way, removes some taste. Coors believes that its products have a fresher taste without pasteurization. The evidence is all in favour.

The second complaint on the bumper sticker has now been met; Coors settled its differences with the unions, though family members' conservatism on other political issues continues to alienate some consumers. There is an irony to this, since there were some notable liberals among the fashionable Californians who first helped Coors' principal product become chic beyond the mountain states.

The chic depended in part upon the beer's being in those days less common than it now is. That kind of success has its own limitation, but there was plenty of space for growth in the West, with its lack of the loyalties found in the older parts of the country. Coors, in the West since 1873, has a site in the East, but has yet to brew there. If it did, it could no longer point out in its advertising that its beers are made with Rocky Mountain spring water.

No doubt the Rocky Mountain spring water helps, but Coors also malts its own barley and grows it own hops. Some other breweries do this, too, but Coors has the most deeply vertical integration. The specifications of the raw materials, their particular formulation — and the intensity of filtration and lack of pasteurization — all contribute to the remarkable cleanness that defines Coors. Only a hint of malty dryness reminds the drinker that this is not just Rocky Mountain spring water. It is the cleanest and lightest of the mainstream American lagers. That is the point about Coors. It therefore sometimes disappoints consumers who had been led by the mystique to expect something more characterful.

Rocky Mountain Highs. What to do with all that malt during Prohibition? Coors nimbly made an innocent malted milk. Even for a brewing company, that was a fate better than death. In the years since, Coors became known as a one-beer company, but it now has a considerable range.

The lunar landscape of the Front Range on a snowy afternoon provides a dramatic backdrop for the futuristic architecture of the Boulder Brewery (*far left*). This pioneering micro moved into its purpose-built premises after being born in a goat-shed.

At one stage the company placed all of its effort behind the one brand, always known simply as Coors, though it has the small-print description "Banquet Beer." More recently Coors has produced a number of specialties: the super-premium Herman Joseph's is more aromatic, and slightly fuller-bodied. Winterfest, offered from Thanksgiving to New Year, is a very enjoyable beer broadly in the Vienna style. George Killian's, produced under license from the defunct brewery in Wexford, is loosely in the style of an Irish Ale. Although it has lost some of its early character, it offers a little variety.

Colorado also has one of the earliest micro-breweries, which released its first beer in 1980. The Boulder Brewery, in the town of the same name, produces a light but fruity Extra Pale Ale; a complex, roasty Porter; and an intense, medium-dry Stout.

Boulder, a college town in the mountains, is a haven of alternative lifestyles. One of the less curious local preoccupations is home-brewing. An association of home-brewers established there in the late 1970s became a clearing house for advice and information as interest spread. Over the decade that followed, home-brewing was legalized in one state after another, and the association became national. Many of today's home-brewers in the United States began because they wished to produce beer in classic styles that were not readily available. Some went on to become micro-brewers. The association set up a separate organization to cater to their needs. An annual festival was organized, at first in Boulder, then in Denver, around Memorial Day weekend, so that the public could sample beers from all over the United States. Although there have been regional festivals, this one is uniquely national. In 1987 the beers — more than 100 of them — were also placed before a panel of professional judges. In future, it is planned that the Great American Beer Festival will be in a different city each year, but the Association of Brewers remains headquartered in Boulder.

Several other mountain states now have breweries, all micros. An outstanding example, producing a wide variety of styles, is Kessler, in Helena, Montana. The same state has the interesting Bayern Gasthaus Bräuerei, in Missoula. The Schirf brewery produces an ale and a Wheat Beer in the

Fritz Maytag (*inset*) has become a familiar face in the business journals since this photograph was taken in 1976, and his Anchor brewery has been the inspiration of many others. His brewery is impeccable, with beers to match.

unlikely location of Park City, Utah. Snake River makes lagers in Caldwell, Idaho. Coeur D'Alene, Idaho, has a brew-pub . . . No doubt the Rockies and the West as a whole will have many more.

The rediscovery of American beer began in the West, in California. Not in trend-addicted Los Angeles, where it has been slow to emerge, but in and around San Francisco, a city that is gastronomically less fickle. Southern California is easily distracted. Northern California takes its pleasure more earthily.

Northern California is progressive and open-minded, though the unwitting prophet of its beer revival, Fritz Maytag, is amiably conservative. Maytag's story is related as a parable, not only among beer-lovers but also in business journals. He is a member of the family that made Maytag washing machines a household word, in both senses, in the United States. He spent his student days in Northern California, and encountered Anchor Steam Beer in a restaurant bar in San Francisco. He was attracted by the idea of what was obviously a very old, local product. One day in 1965, he was told that his next glass would be his last: the brewery was set to close.

Maytag called the brewery to check the story, asked whether there was any way in which he could help, and became involved in the company. By 1969, he had become the owner. In order to do so, he sold his shares in the family company. Cynics see Maytag as a wealthy savior, but he took a huge risk at a time when investment in a small brewery was unthinkable in the United States. The brewery was no plaything: it demanded great faith and dedication. It was another decade before Maytag was able to move out of the tumbledown Anchor plant in San Francisco and build his own brewery. Today, gleaming in copper, with brass trim, his is the most beautiful small brew-house in the world.

Romantic stories and beautiful brew-houses do not necessarily make fine beer, but the quality and distinctiveness of Anchor's products represent the company's truest claim to fame.

Many consumers, if they have heard of the company at all, know only its principal product, Anchor Steam Beer. In character, this Steam Beer is by no means Anchor's most assertive product, but it is a world classic in that it represents the only true beer-style to have emerged from the United States. (Malt Liquor is a questionable notion; and Cream Ale and American Light Lagers are variations on classic styles.)

No other brewer makes a beer in quite this style. Others could if they wished, but they would not be able to call it Steam Beer, since that name has been protected in the United States by Anchor. The company's litigious inclination in this respect is understandable from its commercial viewpoint, but regrettable in that it limits the designation.

Steam Beer dates from the time when lager was replacing ale as the conventional beer-style in the United States. The lager method's requirement for temperate temperatures was easier to meet in the

Great Lakes states than it was in San Francisco, and artificial refrigeration was not readily available during the Gold Rush years of the late 1800s, the growth period of Northern California.

A technique was evolved in which lager yeasts were used, but at warm temperatures more suitable for ale. In the absence of a more favorable temperature, these bottom-fermenting yeasts were encouraged to settle by the use of unusually shallow fermentation vessels. This hybrid fermentation method may well have produced a particularly lively beer. Legend has it that the release of carbon dioxide when the casks were tapped gave rise to the name "steam beer."

Perhaps bar-keepers in the area did, indeed, identify the local style in this way. There were several "Steam Beer Breweries" in Northern California in the late 1800s, but it seems more likely that they took the name for another reason. In the early days of steam power, brewers — like laundries — would boast that they were using this most modern technology. Not that the use of steam power had anything to do with this process of brewing.

Anchor Steam Beer is still fermented at ale temperatures of 16-21°C (60-70°F) but with a bottom yeast, in the traditional shallow vessels. It is then warm-conditioned, and *kräusened*. It does have a very powerful, all natural, carbonation (2.85-3.0 volumes of CO_2). The Steam Beer process marries some of the roundness of a lager with the fruitiness of an ale. Anchor Steam Beer is made to a gravity of 12-plus Balling (1048-52; 4.0 per cent alcohol by weight) with a proportion of crystal malt, and hopped three times. The varietal character is Northern Brewer, and blossoms are used. It is a firm-bodied, very clean beer, with plenty of hop character in both the aroma and the finish.

The Anchor Steam Beer brewery also makes a rich, creamy, strong (5.0 per cent by weight) Porter; an outstandingly intense, dry-hopped Liberty Ale (5.0); and a magnificent Barley Wine, called Old Foghorn. This is surprisingly lively for its weight, with a beautiful balance of malt, hop, and fruit. It is brewed only from first running, without sparging, hopped with Cascades, and aged for several months, emerging with an alcohol content of 7.0 per cent. The brewery has also a clean, dry Wheat Beer, very delicate, but with light honey and apple notes. In the 1970s, Anchor began to produce "vintage-dated" Christmas ales, to a different specification each year. Each "vintage" is keenly awaited by beer-lovers, and many micro-brewers have taken up the custom.

Anchor Steam is an old-established brewery (founded 1896), and can today produce a good 40,000 barrels a year. It is not regarded as a micro-brewer, even if it did encourage others to be such. The term "micro" implies membership of the new generation of companies, born since the mid-1970s. For a time, this generation were all well under 10,000 barrels in capacity, though some have since increased their capacity.

Above: Open fermenters are inclined to look like bathtubs at the best of times, but brew-pub pioneer "Buffalo Bill" Owens relishes the down-home style. He often wears tee-shirts advertising "rival" breweries. His brew-pub is a constant source of offbeat beers, with even odder names. They vary greatly, but all are hearty. *Left*: Owens produces a cinnamon-tasting Pumpkin Beer when the mighty gourd is harvested.

By whatever standard (and not just because it produces vintage-dated ales), this is a "Premier Cru" brewery, and would be judged as such in any world ranking, were anything so difficult to be attempted.

The notion of a "Premier Cru" brewery should not be altogether foreign in this context. Although his brewery is his first love, Maytag also owns vineyards. His York Creek Cabernet Sauvignon, Petite Syrah, and Zinfandel are well respected. When some of the finest Northern Californian wines were set against their counterparts from Bordeaux in a celebrated blind tasting in the late 1970s, there were some shocks. The same would be true if some West Coast ales, Porters and Stouts were tasted against their English inspirations. Of course, each country has its own character, in both wines and beers. In the latter, the Northwest of the United States is especially notable for the perfumy floweriness of the Cascade hop, grown in Washington State.

There is in Northern California a winery called Hop Kiln, and the two varieties of vine intertwine in this part of the United States. Northern California is famous for its wine grapes, but once also grew hops. Farther north, the states of Oregon and Washington make good wines, but are a greater force in hop cultivation. The precedent of wine has helped the boutique brewers of the Northwest. It is thirsty work in a vineyard, where they say it takes a lot of beer to make a good wine. In the Northwest, discussion of aroma, palate, and finish would not necessarily lead a beer-drinker to be thrown out of a bar. A bank manager who had funded a boutique winery might not instantly dismiss a micro-brewery, and the same

company might make the fermentation tanks for both.

If the designation "Premier Cru" were awarded to breweries, it would probably appear on the labels of not only Anchor Steam but also Sierra Nevada, the oldest surviving micro in Northern California. Sierra Nevada, in the college town of Chico, released its first beer in 1980. It has been growing ever since, but with the greatest caution and care for its products. Its

Pale Ale is fresh, flowery-fruity, clean and lightly sweet. Its Porter, firm, dry and coffeeish, is among the best produced anywhere in the world. Its Stout is smooth, powerful and complex. Its Big Foot Barley Wine, earthy and chewy, is the strongest beer in America, 8.48 per cent alcohol by weight, from a gravity of 1095.

Branch-plants of the national giants render California the biggest beer state in volume, but the

Above: An old car could die of thirst in remote eastern Washington, but its driver could be refreshed. Behind the utilitarian façade, a micro-brewery turns out some excellent British-style ales. *Left*: The US and German flags hang alongside each other in the Widmer family's micro-brewery in Portland, Oregon. Even the equipment is labeled in both English and German. A fine Altbier is among a range of German-style specialties. The family has roots in Düsseldorf, Berlin and Switzerland.

217

Column left: A Western selection, from Alaska's Chinook Amber, in broadly the style of an Altbier, to St Stan's, from the Central Valley. City of Angels (*below*), in Santa Monica, California, has featured a pleasant "golden lager" and a Porter among its beers.

micros and brew-pubs make it the most breweried. There are more than a dozen, mainly in Northern California. Although there are several claimants to being the smallest micro in the United States, Thousand Oaks deserves a hearing. This commercial micro, making a range of lagers (including the award-winning Golden Bear), operates in the basement of a suburban home in Berkeley. One of the most unusual micro-breweries in terms of style is Stanislaus, making Altbier in the Düsseldorf style in Modesto, California.

The first micro in the United States was New Albion, founded in 1976, in Sonoma, California. It closed in the early 1980s, but its equipment was used for a time by the Mendocino Brewing Company, based in a frontier saloon in Hopland, 100 miles north of San Francisco. Eventually, Mendocino — known for bottling its fruity ales in Champagne magnums — grew out of the equipment and expanded. This brew-pub was founded in 1983, the year when pioneer "Buffalo Bill" Owens opened his, at Hayward, east of San Francisco Bay. Bill Owens, a distinguished photo-journalist, runs the magazine *American Brewer*. He has become a spokesman for the brew-pub movement. San Francisco itself gained its first brew-pub in 1986, when a landmark saloon on Columbus Avenue changed owners and started making its own lagers. It is now known as the San Francisco Brewing Company, and additionally offers the products of other boutiques.

Having given birth to the first micro-breweries in the United States, California had for a time been losing ground to Oregon and Washington.

Oregon had drawn some attention to itself in the late 1970s, when a sizable independent, Blitz-Weinhard, in Portland, launched what was then perhaps the most distinctive lager in the United States. This beer, Henry Weinhard's Private Reserve, was especially notable for its hop aroma.

"Henry's" was also unusual in that its advertising discussed the use of Cascade hops and two-row barley. Most American beer advertising avoids discussing the product unless terms can be found that are wholly meaningless ("An upstream beer," "More gusto," "All you want from a beer, and less"). Distinguished voices praised "Henry's," and it retains a following. In the years since, the brewery has ceased to be independent, and is now owned by Heileman.

The city of Portland, the biggest in Oregon, has since become known for its three micro-breweries. Widmer produces an excellent range of German-style beers, including a splendidly hoppy Altbier. Wine-maker Dick Ponzi founded the Columbia River brewing company, with a range including the Scottish-accented BridgePort ale. The brewery's adjoining BridgePort pub, at 1313 NW Marshall, serves cask-conditioned ales. Portland Brewing (which has links with Grant's, of Yakima, Washington) makes fruity ales with an excellent hop character. They, too, are available at the brewery, at 1339 NW Flanders. All four Portland breweries are in the same part of the city. During the period when the three micros were being established, a similar number of brew-pubs grew up around the metro area.

At least for a time, and pending future developments, the Portland area of Oregon has more breweries than Milwaukee. Thus far, though, no one has started a brewery in the community of Milwaukie, Oregon. If anyone did, perhaps they

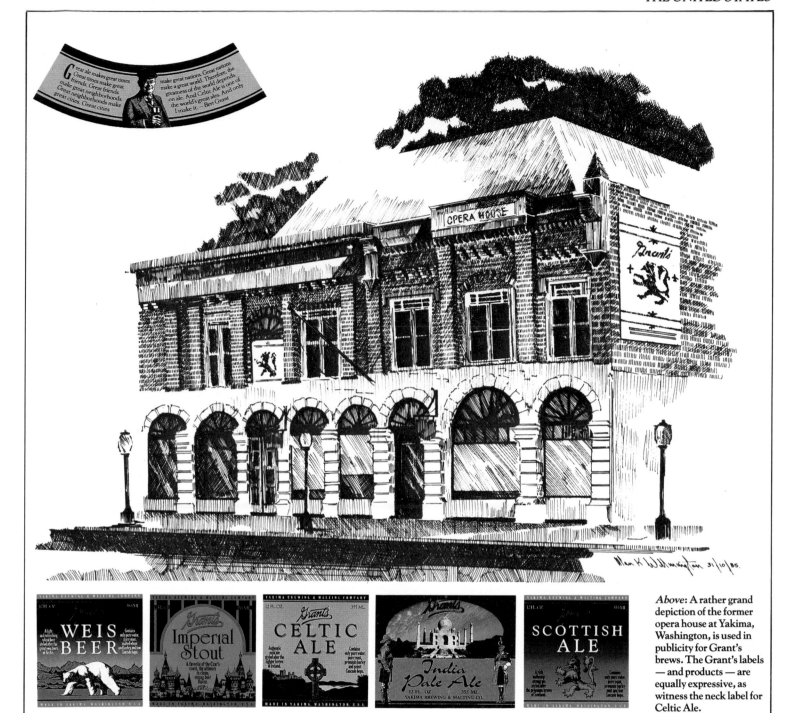

Great ale makes great times. Great times make great friends. Great friends make great neighborhoods. Great neighborhoods make great cities. Great cities make great nations. Great nations make a great world. Therefore, the greatness of the world depends on ale. And Celtic Ale is one of the world's great ales. And only I make it. — Bert Grant

WEIS BEER

Grant's Imperial Stout

Grant's CELTIC ALE

India Pale Ale

SCOTTISH ALE

Above: A rather grand depiction of the former opera house at Yakima, Washington, is used in publicity for Grant's brews. The Grant's labels — and products — are equally expressive, as witness the neck label for Celtic Ale.

would brew a beer to make *Milwaukie* famous.

Not far across the state line into Washington, in the small town of Kalama, the Hart micro-brewery makes several interesting products. Its Pyramid Ale, big bodied, soft, and with a powerful Cascade hop character, is a definitively New Western brew. Its Snow Cap Ale is a Barley Wine, beautifully balanced, but especially notable for its fruitiness. Wheaten Ale is a very dry Weizenbier.

Across the mountains, the Grant's brewery is in the heart of hop country, in Yakima, something of a Wild West town. Hop expert Bert Grant installed his kettles and pioneering brew-pub in the one-time opera house. The Yakima Valley is one of the world's biggest hop-growing regions, and Grant's beers have a fine local character. His Celtic Ale is the nearest America has to an English Dark Mild (original gravity 1034) — but much hoppier. His Scottish-style Grant's Ale is suitably malty — but hoppy, too.

His India Pale Ale is the hoppiest brew in America. His Imperial Stout (1068) has all the "Christmas pudding" character that defines the style — and is not altogether innocent of hops. Only his Wheat Beer, appropriately, is lightly hopped.

Washington State has six or seven micro-breweries. Two — Thomas Kemper and Küfner, both near Seattle — produce extraordinarily fruity lagers. The rest make ales. Washington gave birth to the first twin micro-brewery, Hale's. This has one brew-house in a Seattle suburb called Kirkland and another in the distant east of the state, at Colville. Hale's has made some very British-tasting brews, including a hoppy, tasty Special Bitter, and a Scottish Wee Heavy.

Seattle itself had one of the earliest micro-breweries, Red Hook, whose management includes a former executive with a winery, and the founder of a gourmet coffee company. The initial product, Red

Hook Ale, was so fruity as to be reminiscent of some Belgian specialties (De Koninck, perhaps?). Blackhook is a dry, but soft and soothing, Porter. Ballard Bitter (named after a district of Seattle) is nutty and well-balanced. With its great range of local brews, and a catchment area that stretches from Oregon to Canada, this is a splendidly wet city. Americans say it always rains in Seattle. It doesn't, but the weather is sufficiently temperate to encourage people to savor beer in bars, cafés, and restaurants instead of spending their entire drinking lives cracking cans at barbecues and beaches. Beer is talked about, and written about, in Portland and Seattle. There are no finer cities in the United States in which to drink it.

THE CARIBBEAN

Action must wait for the cool of the night. In the heat of the day a cool, crisp Caribbean beer is provided by Red Stripe, from Jamaica (*right*), or by Banks, from Barbados (*far right*). Alternative possibilities are Heineken's Amstel brand and several Stouts, including Guinness.

RED STRIPE LAGER, from Jamaica, has helped spread the reputation of beers from the Caribbean. Red Stripe is a very light-tasting, soft-bodied lager, with some fruity, aromatic notes that result from a short lagering period. It has a gravity of 11.8 (1047-8), 3.7 per cent alcohol by weight; 4.6 by volume. It is brewed from 70 per cent barley malt and 30 per cent corn, and has only 14 units of bitterness. It is an easy beer with which to wash down a fish snack at a cold-supper shop in Kingston.

Red Stripe is a conventional lager beer, but it has benefited greatly from the vivacious manner in which Jamaican people promote their country and social culture. It has its own following in the United States, and is brewed under license in Britain by Charles Wells.

In 1986, Wells launched a high-gravity (1085; around 6.8; 8.5) lager under the name Red Stripe Crucial Brew. The word "Crucial" was in vogue in Afro-Caribbean argot at the time, and heavily used on television by Lenny Henry, one of Britain's most popular comedians. Crucial Brew has a candyish fruitiness imparted by its esters. It is in broadly the style of Carlsberg Special Brew.

In Jamaica, Red Stripe is produced by Desnoes and Geddes, a company that was founded in 1918 and grew to be the biggest wholly locally-owned enterprise of any kind. There are still a Mr Desnoes and a Mr Geddes in the management, though Heineken now has a stake in the company.

The original Red Stripe was an ale-like dark beer. Today's style dates from 1934. The company also produces a strong (17; 1068; 6; 7) Sweet Stout, with a malty character. This bottom-fermented product is called Dragon Stout. Its classic slogan, "Dragon Puts It Back," refers to virility.

Light, well-attenuated lagers and strong, sweetish Stouts are widely produced in the Caribbean. This is not the only part of the world where Stout is regarded as having aphrodisiac properties, but that belief has helped these black brews become a part of West Indian tradition. Although the British and Irish brought them here during the colonial period, Stouts are not restricted to the English-speaking islands. A good example, very dry and fruity, is Prestige Stout, from the unlikely location of Haiti.

Beers from the British Isles were sent to the Caribbean in the earliest days of settlement, in the late 1600s, and Guinness had a product called West Indies Porter in the early 1800s. This was noted for its quality, and especially for its fresh hop character. West Indies Porter gave rise to a beer called Foreign Double Stout. This developed into the version of Guinness that is known within the company by the quaint name Foreign Extra Stout and either exported to or produced locally in the Caribbean, West Africa, and Asia. With its slight sourness, intended to make it quenching, and its high gravity (1073), this classic beer is ideally suited to the West Indies. It is produced in a Guinness brewery at Spanish Town, the old capital of Jamaica, and by the Carib company in Trinidad. Carib Lager is malty, dry, well-balanced and thoroughly attenuated. It is a very good example of a Caribbean lager. Banks Lager, from Barbados, has a touch of hop aroma and a lightly fruity character.

In addition to their lagers and Stouts, many Caribbean breweries also produce a non-alcoholic malt-extract drink. This type of product is known in Germany as Mälzbier. In the Caribbean and the Hispanic world it is called Malta.

There are between a dozen and 20 breweries on the islands of the Caribbean, and more on the mainland of Central America. Among international brewers, Heineken and Guinness are both notably active in this part of the world. Most of the breweries are small, and some, like the one on Montserrat, are almost cottage industries. Several new, small breweries are being built, or planned. St Thomas, in the US Virgin Islands, has the world's biggest malt-extract brewery, capable of producing 13,000 barrels a year of a product called Spinnaker Lager.

In some of these sunny islands water is in short supply. There are instances where desalinated seawater is used in brewing.

Banks, today known for its regular lager and a Stout, has at times made a lime-flavored light beer and a very strong dark lager called Ebony. Carib produced Allsopp's Light Lager under license from Allied, of Britain, but such colonial links are fading.

LATIN AMERICA

Right: The Peruvian harp serenades drinkers in the Andes. Their choice of beer is the Pilsener-style brew produced in Callao. When Pizarro conquered the region, the Incas had a brew made from fermented corn.

THE BEST KNOWN BEERS from Latin America are those produced in Mexico and marketed across the border in the United States.

Corona beer, from Mexico, for a time enjoyed a cult following north of the border, and challenged Heineken as the biggest import to the United States. It did so initially with very little marketing support, and its success was a phenomenon much studied in the business pages.

Corona is a beer made as cheaply as possible, so that it can be sold inexpensively to manual workers in Mexico. Every Mexican brewery has at least one such product in its portfolio, among several more interesting beers.

These modestly-paid bean-pickers get what they can pay for, and their thirsts are quenched. Corona tastes like a beer made with a very high percentage of corn adjunct and a short lagering time. It is thin-bodied, with some apple notes. It is no worse, nor better, than several similar products. That it should command a high price in the United States reflects upon the judgment of its consumers.

The idealized Mexican worker, thirstily reaching for his Corona, presented a macho model for the well-heeled kids of Texas and California (and later New York). The plain-glass bottle and rudimentary, enameled label no doubt added to the inverted snobbery. The beer was consumed from the bottle, with a slice of lime jammed in the neck. The lime was an important part of the ritual, but it also improved the taste. If Chuck, Chip, and Scooter really wanted to look like macho working men, they could have affected the Pabst of an unemployed steel-worker from Bethlehem, Pa., but that might have been too close to home.

No one should begrudge Mexico the foreign exchange, but it is a shame that Corona proved such a conspicuous success where better beers had fared less well. Only after the success of Corona were Mexican beers taken seriously in the United States. Before Corona, they had suffered from the belief that they might be as well-made as the local water.

In fact, Mexico has a long tradition of producing beer, and some well-equipped breweries. It is said to have had the first commercial brewery in the New World, in the 1500s, during the period of Cortés, and has been making lager beers since the 1880s or 1890s.

The appeal of Corona has not encouraged Mexican brewers to emphasize their more characterful products.

Among those in broadly the Pilsener style, the lightly fragrant and spritzy Superior is a good example of a mainstream Mexican beer. In Mexico, it has a gravity of 11 Plato (3.5 per cent alcohol by weight; 4.4 by volume) and 18 units of bitterness. The version exported to the United States is fractionally bigger in body and less dry (11.5 Plato,

but only 16 units of bitterness). Bohemia has a little more character all round, at 13 Plato (4.2; 5.25), with 23 units of bitterness. There seems to be more aroma-hopping in an unpasteurized, micro-filtered beer called Kloster, but this can be hard to find.

The more interesting Mexican beers are the darker Vienna and Munich types. Outside Mexico, Dos Equis is the best known of the reddish-amber Vienna types. It has lost a little of its tastiness over the years, but still has some character. It has 12 Plato (3.6; 4.5), and about 20 units of bitterness. Dos Equis is made with a dash of crystal malt, a pinch of black malt, and some caramel. A similar beer called Tres Equis Oscura, with more character all round, has not been produced in recent years.

Rival products in broadly this bracket include the thinnish, dry Indio Oscura and the darker, more chocolaty Negra Modelo, the perfect accompaniment to chicken *molé*. The Modelo company has also a similar regional product called Negra

In the heat of Jalisco province (*left* and *far right*), even cold beer can do nothing to stop the paint peeling and the road cracking, but Mexico has some smart modern breweries. Toluca (*below*) was founded by a Swiss brewer in 1865, and eventually absorbed by Cuauhtémoc.

Leon, from its subsidiary in Mérida, Yucatán. These two Modelo beers are in style somewhere between the Vienna and Munich types.

The best example of a Munich-style beer in Mexico is Nochebuena (15 Plato; 4.3; 5.4). This has only 10 per cent corn adjunct (most Mexican beers have 30-plus), more than six weeks' lagering, 28 units of bitterness and a dark claret color. It has a full body, with maltiness, hints of roastiness, and some hop notes.

Because more attention is being given to light-bodied beers, Nochebuena is under threat of being discontinued. A thinner-bodied rival called Navidad and a pale, sweeter Christmas beer, Commemorativa, can both be hard to find.

In Mexico, beer is still sometimes served at room temperature. This hardly flatters the lighter-bodied brews, but does wonders for a product like Nochebuena. Served excessively chilled, the Vienna and Munich types lose all taste and texture.

Although Dark Lagers are made elsewhere in Latin America, brewers in Mexico have been notably loyal to these specialty styles. In its early days of brewing, Mexico dried its malt in the sun, and all beers had a notable depth of color. Twenty years after Dreher made the first Vienna lagers, Archduke Maximilian of Austria became Emperor of Mexico, and it is tempting to speculate as to that cultural influence. Four years later, Maximilian was shot dead, but Vienna-style beers have managed to stay alive. In modern times, the first brewers in Mexico were Swiss, Alsatian, and German. Today, Mexico has 16 brewery plants, but only three owning companies, and two of those are linked. Modelo, headquartered in Mexico City, is the biggest brewing company in terms of sales. Its various breweries produce Corona, Victoria, and Pacifico, among other beers.

Cuauhtémoc, of Monterrey, is second. Its brands include Tecate, Carta Blanca, Bohemia, Indio Oscura, and Commemorativa. Its products tend toward a dry, faintly tannic house character.

The holding company that owns Cuauhtémoc also controls the third concern, Moctezuma, of Guadalajara and Orizaba, Veracruz. Its products include Sol, Superior, and the Equis variations. Moctezuma's beers have the most rounded character, and the premium products are kräusened.

In volume production, both Mexico and Brazil are major brewing nations, though consumption per head is modest. Every country in Latin America has breweries, ranging from more than 120 in Brazil to three each in Paraguay and Uruguay. In most countries, ownership is concentrated, and real choice limited. In Brazil, drinkers tend to choose whichever beer is being offered coldest. In Chile, beer is ordered by the square meter, to fill the bar table.

Occasionally, a label from Central or South America will venture into export markets. (Was

Colombian Gold meant to taste of hops, which it did, or their cousin cannabis?) Most countries have difficulty servicing their own market. In general, Latin American beers tend to be slightly fuller in body than their northern counterparts, with a high level of corn adjunct and low hopping rates.

Resch's Refreshes!

RESCH'S

AUSTRALIA

AT FIRST it was taken to be fantasy — Australians tangling with crocodiles and living to tell the tale. Then it turned to reality. Crocodile Dundee, the most successful among the many money-spinning roues in Australian legend, was created by an actor who had already become a star by presenting beer commercials, for Foster's Lager. That seemed the definitive Australian fable, but there was more to come.

Foster's Lager, in the shape of Carlton and United Breweries, under the cloak of their parents the Elders group, went hunting for international acquisitions. First, Foster's/Carlton/Elders took Courage, one of the Big Six in Britain. Then they also swallowed Carling, the Canadian brewing group. Ironically, Carling had over-strained itself playing the same role in years past: the colonial company expanding internationally, and teaching the world how to make and market beer.

Foster's rival, Swan Lager, in the guise of Bond Brewing, then tangled with the real crocodiles by entering the American market. Bond snapped up Pittsburgh Brewing and Heileman in short order. Heileman, despite a low public profile, was one of the world's biggest brewers. Having swallowed

Heileman, Bond Brewing proclaimed itself fourth biggest in the world. Elders is smaller internationally, but bigger in Australia, with almost half of the local market.

Foster's and Swan had both been local brands, penned in their own states a dozen years earlier. Now, the whole of Australia was too small for them.

That Bond should claim to be fourth in the world gives some indication of its ambitions. Whether it occupies exactly that position in the "league table" is hardly the point. Different analysts of the industry arrive at varying figures. Several would put Stroh (United States) and Kirin (Japan) ahead of the Australian company. What cannot be denied is that Bond has, albeit by acquisition, become one of the world's biggest brewers.

Australia is a big country, but very thinly populated, with only 16 million people. Its market has never been large, but its people are famous for their consumption of beer. In an intensely hot country, dominated by a male, frontiersman ethic, there was for many years not a lot else to do. In an attempt to control beer-drinking, the pubs (or "hotels") used to close in early evening. Like most measures aimed at curbing drinking, this merely

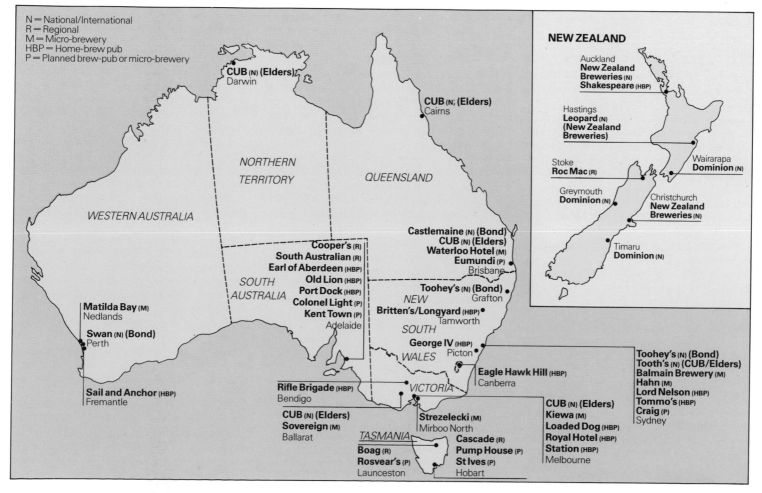

N = National/International
R = Regional
M = Micro-brewery
HBP = Home-brew pub
P = Planned brew-pub or micro-brewery

Western Australia

encouraged excess. Customers would drink against the clock, in what was known as "The Six O'Clock Swill." Australians may tire of hearing about this long-abandoned barbarity, but they have only themselves to blame. They told everybody about it in the first place. No nation has done more to sustain its stereotype than Australia. If he knew what it meant, the characteristically cheery Crocodile Dundee would no doubt describe himself as an iconoclast.

All of this is changing. At the moment when the beer-drinking Crocodile was winning international recognition for the Australian outback, his home country was developing more cosmopolitan and varied tastes. Consumption of beer (at least of the typically Australian kind) was falling. This development, on a par with the Pope turning to Buddhism, was kept quiet by the shamefaced Australians. They simply tried to sell more of their beer overseas.

The super-salesmen of Foster's and Swan had another motivation, too. Brewing is not a highly profitable business, but it has a quick cash-flow. Both companies are run by entrepreneurs with interests in other businesses — agriculture, land, mining — which are more profitable but very slow to produce the cash. Foster's was for many years just one brand among several produced by Carlton and United in the state of Victoria. Although the company opened two breweries in the state of Queensland and one in the Northern Territories, it did not become truly national until it entered New South Wales, the biggest beer market in Australia. It achieved that by acquiring one of the state's two brewing companies, Tooth's.

Swan was a local brand and brewery in the remote and thinly-populated state of Western Australia until it entered Queensland, by acquiring Castlemaine, and New South Wales, by taking over the other local brewery, Toohey's.

These mergers took brands across state lines, and in the short term appeared to offer the consumer a wider choice. In the long term, of course, brands selected for national exposure were developed at the expense of local products. Real choice was diminished, not expanded.

Among the breweries acquired, Castlemaine has retained a stronger image for its brands than Toohey's and Tooth's. In times past, they respectively serviced the Catholic and Protestant thirsts of Sydney, and were themselves the subject of fierce loyalties. The only old-established smaller breweries to survive are Cascade and Boag's, which operate under joint ownership in the island state of Tasmania, and two in South Australia. One of these is called simply the South Australian Brewing company. The other, Cooper's, is the country's most traditionalist brewery.

In all countries where the big brewers have concentrated the industry and limited real choice, there has been a reaction: the giants have found themselves developing one or two specialties; the most interesting independents have attracted new attention; and micro-breweries and brew-pubs have established themselves. Perhaps this would have happened even without the mergers. Beer as a commodity suffers when consumers become more sophisticated, but specialty brews benefit. In Australia, the number of frontiersmen may be diminishing, but the more cosmopolitan drinkers enjoy a Cooper's Sparkling Ale as much as an Adelaide Hills Cabernet.

A dozen years ago, only the most perceptive drew attention to the great character of Cooper's ale and Stout. Today, Cooper's is the most fashionable of the old-established breweries, and has further spread its range by supplying its wort or malt extract to micros and brew-pubs. This is an unusual idea, though a similar system is operated by some breweries in Britain, notably Whitbread.

The counterpoint between the big brewers and the small in Australia is personified in the story of Philip Sexton. As a brewer employed at Swan, he helped develop its low-alcohol beer, Special Light. He was later quoted as saying he admired this product, but did not enjoy it. "If I do not want to get intoxicated, I have a soft drink". Soon after working on Special Light, Sexton left Swan. He wanted to produce something with more character; his first idea had been to become a wine-maker. As a student of brewing at Birmingham University, in England, he had seen the success of the Campaign for Real Ale; that, too, was an inspiration. In 1984, at the age of 29, Sexton joined three friends in an enterprise that launched Australia's first micro-brewery, at Matilda Bay, Western Australia, as well as the country's first revivalist brew-pub, in Fremantle. Sexton has gone on to make beers of considerable sophistication.

By 1988, plans were well in hand to replace the original micro with a much bigger, 350,000-hectoliter brewery. An all-copper brew-house had been acquired from the defunct Brasserie De Clerck, in northern France. Meanwhile, Sexton's company has participated in the opening of another three or four brew-pubs in other Australian cities. His example had also been followed, to varying degrees, by many other micros and brew-pubs.

In international markets, most Australian beer is sweetish lager, usually about 70 per cent barley malt and 30 per cent cane sugar, with a short lagering time (one to two weeks) and a bitterness of 14-22. Alcohol content is usually in the classic Pilsener range of just under 4.0 per cent by weight, 5.0 by volume. Although lagers dominate the domestic market, some Australian brewers also have an ale and most have a Stout.

Sexton's breweries produce only all-malt beers, and the lagers have a maturation time of around a month. He makes a Wheat Beer, and seasonal specialties that have variously been spiced with juniper, cardamom, ginger or orange peel. It is a long way from the Six O'Clock Swill.

THE BLACK SWAN is the symbol of Western Australia, and its graceful figure appears on the label of the state's best-known beer, brewed in the city of Perth. When the British-born Australian entrepreneur Alan Bond acquired the company in the mid-1980s, he may have been attracted by another of its brand-names. The Swan Brewery company used to have a beer called Special Bond. That product is no longer featured.

The Swan name is still used on a variety of products. Swan Gold is a light, fresh lager with a low alcohol content (8 Plato; 1032; 2.8 per cent alcohol by weight; 3.5 by volume). Swan Draught has by Australian standards a light to medium body and bitterness (10-11; 1042-3; 3.8; 4.9; with 22 U.B.). Swan Lager is very similar, just fractionally higher in gravity and alcohol content. Swan Lager is the original beer from which Special Light is produced. Most of the alcohol is removed, by vacuum distillation. The idea is to retain insofar as possible the palate of the original beer in a low-alcohol (and low-calorie) brew. The end result is a dry, fruity product. It has an alcohol content of 0.7 by weight; 0.9 by volume, and is described in Australia as an "ultra-light" beer.

Swan Premium Export has a similar gravity and alcohol content to the regular Lager, but with a notably more aromatic hop character. Swan Stout, dry, top-fermented and bottle-conditioned, at just under 15 (1060; 5.4; 6.8), is produced to the company's specification by Cooper's. It has 35 units of bitterness.

Swan Lager and the same company's Emu Export Lager are birds of a feather, though the latter is perhaps marginally fuller in body. Emu Bitter is much hoppier (26 units of bitterness), but lower in gravity (10; 1040; 3.6; 4.6). The emu is also indigenous to Western Australia.

Down the road at Nedlands, the former Swan brewer Philip Sexton has his Maltilda Bay micro-brewery. Its biggest-selling product has proven to be its Wheat Beer, a style hitherto unknown in Australia. The beer is called RedBack, after a local spider.

RedBack is made from 65 per cent wheat, grown nearby in the Avon Valley. This local wheat has a medium protein level which provides a creamy palate without haze problems. The remainder of the mash is two-row barley malt. The beer is hopped with Saaz and Hersbrucker.

It's Perfect!

EMU BITTER

FROM THE NEW BREWERY

Left: The Emu name dates back at least to the first decade of this century. Originally, its Bitter was top-fermenting, and had a history of problems with wild yeast. The competitor Swan launched a bottom-fermenting Bitter in about 1923. The two companies had been locked in a long and often acrimonious rivalry, but in 1928 Emu was acquired by Swan. This advertisement dates from about 1937. The Emu brewery closed in 1979, but the product is still made.
Below: Traditional styles are revived by the state's micro-brewer.

It is available bottle-conditioned, or in a filtered version on draft. It has a gravity of 1045 and an alcohol content of 3.7; 4.8. RedBack is a very characterful brew, reminiscent of the Belgian "white" beers. It has a very pale golden color, a light, firm body, and a faintly acidic, honey-apple aroma and palate.

Matilda Bay also produces an all-Saaz Pils, with a hefty 40 units of bitterness; a Dark Lager; and a variety of specials, which are usually bottle-conditioned. The remainder of the beers are filtered but not pasteurized.

The same company's handsome Sail and Anchor brew-pub, in Fremantle, specializes in top-fermenting ales, served on hand-pump. These include a dry-hopped, English-style, Traditional Bitter (1038) and a strong ale called Dogbolter, in the tradition of David Bruce. A very interesting specialty is the Brass Monkey Stout (1055), which contains proportions of oats and lactose. This is an outstanding Stout, very fruity in the nose, with a good, rich head, medium-bodied and; with a long, full palate. It starts with sweetish, licorice notes, and dries toward the finish.

Various permutations of these two breweries' products are made at the associated brew-pubs elsewhere.

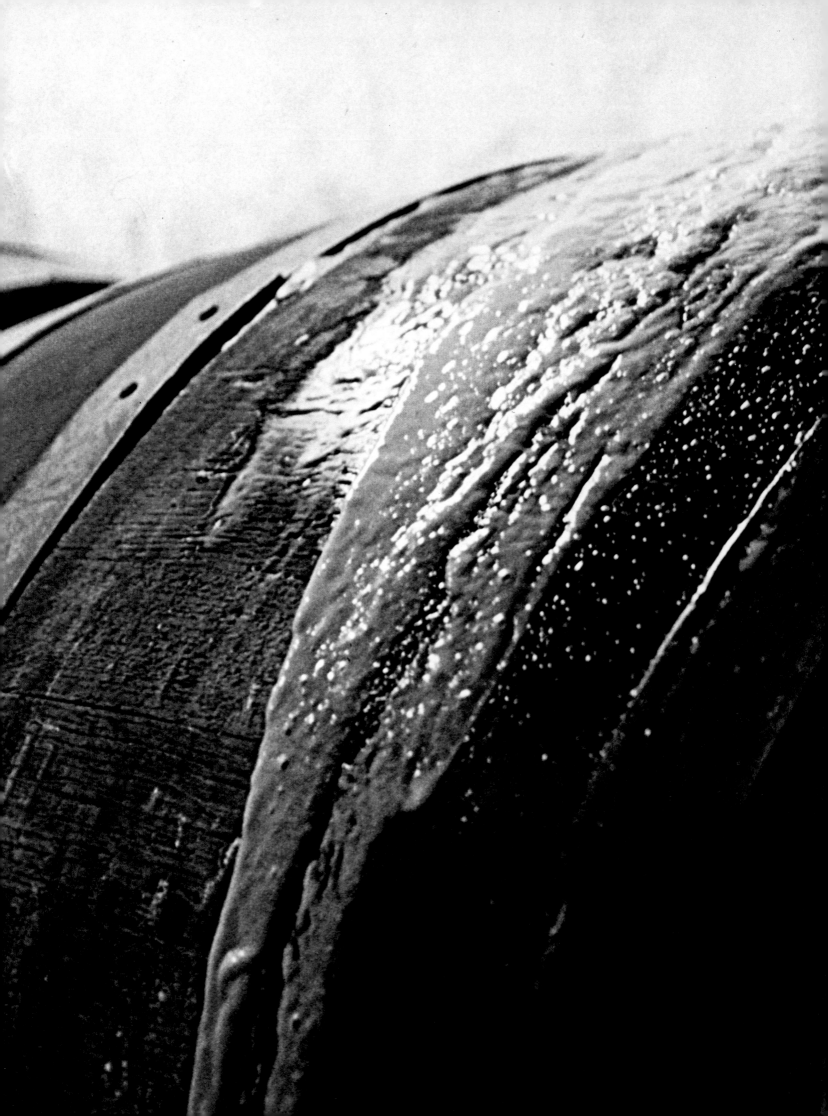

South Australia

PATRONS OF THE SYDNEY OPERA HOUSE often stop for a snack at the oyster bar in Circular Quay. The only beers served with the succulent bivalves are from Cooper's of Adelaide, South Australia. It would once have been unthinkable that anyone from Sydney, let alone an opera-goer, would drink a beer from South Australia. It would have been barely thinkable that anyone from Sydney had even heard of Cooper's.

An alleged beer-lover who grudgingly admitted to having tasted Cooper's was once heard to dismiss it on the grounds that "there are gisms in it." The "gisms" are yeast. Cooper's Sparkling Ale and Extra Stout are naturally-conditioned. Cooper's is heavily sedimented, and its sobriquet "sparkling" is regarded as an ironic joke by its producers and devotees alike.

The brewery was founded by a Yorkshireman in 1862, and is still run by his descendants. At the end of the 1970s, Cooper's was producing five brews a week, and seemed set to go the way of other, long-forgotten, independents in Australia. In the late 1980s, the brewery exceeded 30 batches a week and was still growing.

There have been casualties along the way. The brewery made the ale paler, and should now have the confidence to put some of the color back into its cheeks. It had a better balance when there was the faintest tinge of roastiness. The beer is still fermented in open wooden vessels but it no longer has its secondary in 108-gallon casks. These "puncheons" had to be retired. Instead, the beer has a longer period in the fermenters, is *kräusened* and given a dosage of yeast, and warm-conditioned for between four and six weeks in the bottle or keg. Perhaps the occasional puncheon of a "special" should be made. The draft version of Cooper's is dispensed by CO_2 but, because the beer is "alive," the keg must frequently be vented. The brewery tries to limit draft to pubs that can sell a fresh keg every day.

In a land of sweetish, rather bland beers, the joy of the Cooper's products is their antiquity of style, their heartiness and uncompromising honesty. The Ale, at 1046 (4.6; 5.75) is full of fruitiness, with a good dash of hop bitterness. The Stout (1054; 5.4; 6.8) is splendidly earthy and dry. The brewery also has two sweetish lagers, with a fairly full color for the style. The premium lager is called Adelaide Bitter, and the everyday beer Big Barrel.

The Port Dock regards itself as a pub and brasserie. Its early brews have included a lager, a Bitter, a Pale Ale and a Brown Ale. The Earl of Aberdeen began with a Light Ale, a Pale Ale and a Scotch Ale. Its ales are also available at the Duck Inn, at Coromandel Valley, in the southern hills of Adelaide.

Adelaide has also the South Australian Brewing Company, producing entirely bottom-fermenting beers. Its products include the dryish West End Draught (9.9; 1040; 3.6; 4.5); the perfumy, but maltier, Southwark Premium (12; 1048; 4.4; 5.5); and the medium-dry Old Southwark Stout (16.3; 1065; 5.9; 7.4). The company is headquartered in a neighborhood called Southwark, and formerly had a second brewery called West End. A lager recalling the old Broken Hill brewery has some hop in the nose, a firm body, and a spritzy finish.

There was long ago a brewery at the Old Lion Hotel in Melbourne Street, Adelaide, and this has now been restored. Philip Sexton's Brewtech company has installed kettles in the old tower brewery structure, and RedBack, Pils, and Dark Lager are being produced. There is an extract brewery at the Port Dock Hotel in Todd Street; and Cooper's wort is used at the Earl of Aberdeen, at 316 Pulteney Street.

Left: The yeasty swell of a top-fermented ale in a wooden cask at Cooper's, a brewery that time left behind and then rediscovered. Cooper's ales, Stout and lagers share their local market with the products of the South Australian Brewing Company.

Tasmania

Miner Sam Griffin used to walk into a hotel at Walsh's Creek, Victoria, every morning at 11.00 and demand a glass of Carlton. An artist painted him, and the brewery used the portrait on posters. There are several versions of the story, and considerable legend surrounds Sam Griffin.

THE ISLAND OF TASMANIA is a major producer of malting barley, and the most important hop-growing region in Australia. There is also a hop-growing region in the Ovens Valley of Victoria. Both regions primarily cultivate a local variety called Pride of Ringwood, which is a bittering hop with a high acidity. The name suggests that it may have been bred from a hop grown in Hampshire, England. Strongly held folklore has it that the cuttings were hidden in a traveler's suitcase, in contravention of quarantine regulations. Australia also grows the Cluster hop on a small scale. Although it is regarded as a bittering hop in its native Washington state, the Australian offspring is used for aroma. American Clusters and various German hops are also imported.

Tasmania has the brewing company with the longest unbroken history of operation in Australia: Cascade. Streams cascading down Mount Wellington originally supplied not only the water for brewing but also the power for the plant. They furthermore provided a name for the district where the brewery is to be found, in the town of Hobart, the state capital.

The Cascade Brewery was built in 1824. Nearly a century later, the company bought Boag's Brewery, in Launceston, at the other end of the island. Despite their having been under the same ownership for most of this century, the two companies still follow different procedures, even down to Cascade's use of a step infusion mash and Boag's loyalty to double decoction.

Both breweries have full ranges of products, all bottom-fermenting. Boag's Draught is a lager with quite a full color, and is very well attenuated (10.2; 1040-41; 3.6; 4.7). The beer called simply Boag's Lager (11.5; 1046; 4.3; 5.4) is quite hoppy by Australian standards (27 units of bitterness). Cascade's Sparkling Pale Ale turns out in reality to be a golden lager (11.7; 1047; 4.1; 5.2). Boag's Stout is slightly lighter in character than its Cascade counterpart.

Hobart has a Brewtech brew-pub, the St Ives, initially producing only its Traditional Bitter. A brew-pub has also been announced for Rosvear's, at Launceston.

Victoria

In addition to the legendary Foster's, the supposedly "amber nectar," there are well-known names like Carlton and Victoria Bitter in Elders' range in Victoria, its home state. Abbotsford is the Melbourne neighborhood where the brewery stands.

FOSTER'S LAGER, in a can, could be the Australian national icon. No matter that the original can looks big and butch enough to contain motor oil. Australians are perceived as being big and butch, too, and often see themselves that way, though not necessarily oiled with an automobile lubricant.

Like many overnight successes, Foster's Lager has been around a long time. Two brothers named Foster first brewed it, in the city of Melbourne, in the state of Victoria, a century ago, in 1888. Although Foster's Lager has spent most of its life as a local brand, it always seemed destined for a wider world.

It was one of the first lager beers to be successfully produced and marketed in Australia. At the time, the only way to obtain ice for lagering was to make it. The Foster brothers had an ice-making machine. The ice they made was not only used in lagering but also provided to bars, so that they could serve the beer cold. This was a new idea, and it proved popular. The renown of Foster's, the ice-cold lager, spread.

Long before any brewer had a plant in more than one state, Foster's had made forays as far north as Queensland. By 1901, there are records of its being sold outside Australia. In World War II, Australian beer was encountered by Allied troops fighting alongside Anzac forces. Not only the British, but also the Americans, on r-and-r from the Pacific War, came to know Foster's.

When the first post-war generation of young native Australians followed the hippie trail (in the "wrong" direction), heading in their Volkswagen minibuses to the old imperial capital, London, the beer that came with them was Foster's. An Australian comic character called Barry McKenzie featured in a cult strip in the satirical magazine *Private Eye* at the apogee of Swinging London.

The uncouthly provincial McKenzie long anticipated Crocodile Dundee, and among his obsessive desires was more Foster's Lager — in the familiar, stubby can, cold. "A stubby" . . . "A chilled tube" . . . "A frostie" . . . was his constant requirement. McKenzie's creator, Barry Humphries, went on to develop stage characters such as the Australian Minister for Culture and Dame Edna Everage. He should have been made a Knight of the Garter for his services to Australian brewing.

Foster's was already a symbol of Australia, but it was still not a national brand there. Even in its native state of Victoria, it shared billing with other brands. Only in the mid-1980s did mergers in Australia create the possibility of national brands, and Foster's was off to a head start. Very quickly, it also became international, at first thanks to a licensing deal with Watney's in Britain, then by the acquisition of Courage and, in Canada, Carling.

Foster's first encountered the world of mergers in 1907, when the original brewery was one of half a dozen that combined to form Carlton and United. Today, C.U.B. has two breweries in Victoria. One is at Abbotsford, Melbourne, the other at Ballarat.

In Victoria, C.U.B. still has eight or nine brands, most with an alcohol content of just under 4.0 per cent by weight, 5.0 by volume. Foster's is sweetish and fairly full-bodied, and Carlton Crown Lager is very similar. Carlton Draught is dryish and slightly fuller in color, while Abbots Lager is well-balanced. Victoria Bitter is a lager, light in flavor and slightly fuller in color. Melbourne Bitter is also a lager, with a dash more of the hoppiness its name suggests. The company has, in addition, two Stout brands, Double and Invalid, but these are barely promoted.

The company produces and markets not only Foster's but also Victoria Bitter as a national brand. As well as its breweries in Victoria and New South Wales, it has plants at Brisbane and Cairns, both in Queensland, and Darwin, in the Northern Territory. The latter is known, among other things, for its two-liter bottle of N.T. Draught. This mighty container is referred to as the "Darwin Stubby."

Meanwhile, Victoria is fast gaining some small beer. Kettles that formerly served a small brewery in Bavaria are now boiling and bubbling at the Royal Hotel, 75 Flemington Road, Melbourne, producing several beers from the Brewtech range. At the Loaded Dog pub, 324 St George's Road, North Fitzroy, an in-house brewery is producing a well-regarded range comprising exclusively top-fermenting ales. The Station Tavern and Brewery, at 96 Greville Street, Prahran, is producing ales in the Cooper's style.

A malting company in Ballarat owns a free-standing micro-brewery called Sovereign. This produces lager and Stout in the "European" style.

The Loaded Dog takes it name from a literary reference. The pub has produced five or six different styles of beer. Its Thunder Ale is claimed to have a hefty 8 per cent alcohol by volume.

New South Wales

This bizarre image of the man dropping in for a Foster's was drawn during the inter-war years. The brand has a history of wry and off-beat ads.

THE STATE OF NEW SOUTH WALES drinks more beer than any other, and has always boasted about the supremacy of its brews. It talked a good game, but let both of its local brewing companies fall to outsiders. It can reply that the headquarters of Bond Brewing are now in Sydney, but that is not quite the same thing.

Bond Brewing set a more important precedent by launching a new strong dark ale, Tall Ships, in New South Wales. Dark ales may not be on everyone's lips, but they are something of a local specialty in the state, and it is good to see this recognized. Tall Ships is a higher-gravity counterpart to Hunter Old, a well-known example of the style. Hunter Old is a top-fermenting, dark (E.B.C. 55) ale of a little over 10 Plato (1040; 3.6; 4.7), with some aromatic, estery fruitiness and roasted barley notes. This was originally produced in the Hunter Brewery, at Newcastle, New South Wales. That brewery no longer operates, but Bond still runs the Toohey's plants in Grafton and Sydney.

The survival of these dark "Old Ales" was in the past credited to the coal-miners of Newcastle. There may be an element of myth to this, but it is true that Newcastle, England, has a famous Brown Ale. Even old South Wales is quite keen on full-colored, malty ales.

New South Wales also had Tooth's Old, popularly known as "Three X." This product has been re-

Queensland

named Kent Old Brown now that the brewery is owned and operated by C.U.B. Such tinkering is beloved of marketing men, and irritating to their customers. Perhaps Toohey's and Tooth's did sound rather similar, but drinkers knew the difference. The former Tooth's plant is called Kent Brewery, hence the name. The founder, John Tooth, came from the hop-growing county of Kent, England, in the 1830s. For many years, the brewery's symbol was the white horse of Kent. This, in turn, was derived from the battle standard of two Saxon chiefs, Hengist (Stallion) and Horsa (Horse).

Kent Brewery also provided the initials K.B. for the dryish local lager which has traditionally been a big seller in the Sydney market. The company additionally has the brand Resch's, inherited in a takeover in 1929. The brewery's most characterful product is the dryish Sheaf Stout.

Although New South Wales has surrendered some of its identity in the battle of the giants, it is regaining ground with new micro-breweries. One micro-brewery is in Balmain. It is known simply as the Balmain Brewery, and its specialty is a tasty, strong Bock beer. Another micro, Hahn Brewing, has been announced for Camperdown. Early brew-pubs have included the Lord Nelson, at Kent and Argyle Street, in the Rocks neighborhood, and Britten's, in the country town of Tamworth. Several more are planned.

FAR AWAY IN THE UNITED STATES, an all-malt, aromatically hoppy, super-premium beer called Samuel Adams' Boston Lager began its life by being produced under contract at the Pittsburgh Brewery, owned by Alan Bond. Now Bond's brewery in Brisbane, Queensland, has a super-premium, all-malt, aromatically hoppy beer called John Boston Lager.

Any connection? Certainly not. For one thing, John Boston Lager is stronger, at 4.8; 6.0. For another, John Boston was the first recorded brewer in Australia, in 1794. The brew named after him was launched to mark the bicentennial of Australia, in 1988. John Boston made his mash from corn, and seasoned his brew with the leaves and stalks of the Cape gooseberry, which he mistakenly described as the "love apple" (an early name for the tomato).

John Boston brewed not in Queensland but in New South Wales. Queenslanders do not give a XXXX about that. Bond Brewing's Brisbane plant also produces Castlemaine XXXX, the principal beer of Queensland. In its Australian version, this has a gravity of 1043; 3.8; 4.8. It is a clean-tasting, firm-bodied lager which has perhaps the faintest dash more character than the country's other mainstream beers. Like all Australian lagers, it is on the sweet side, but it does have some hop notes, too.

The brewery, originally called Castlemaine Perkins, also has a fractionally stronger and slightly maltier beer called Gold Lager. Among Australian brewers, Castlemaine had in the past a particular reputation as a maker of Stout, and has had several famous products in this style, under a variety of names. The one that has survived is Carbine Stout, named after a famous racehorse. This is a tasty, full-bodied, bottom-fermenting Stout with a gravity of 1055; 4.03; 5.1.

Generally, Queensland beers are on the dry side, and this is also true of the local brands produced at the C.U.B. plants in Brisbane and Cairns.

Micros or brew-pubs have been slow in establishing themselves in Queensland, but several have been announced. In Brisbane itself, these include Eumundi Brewing and Power Brewing. Other addresses are: the Australian Beverage Company, 360 Lytton Road, Morningside; Sanctuary Cove, Discovery Bay, Southport; and the Waterloo Hotel, in Fortitude Valley.

Insignia like the four Xs of Castlemaine were originally brands in the literal sense. They were markings burned into wooden casks in breweries as a means of distinguishing one specification of beer from another. This was a simple system, especially in the days when many workers were illiterate. Today, the XXXX sign on Castlemaine's brewery (*top*) burns and flashes all night long.

Classic labels from New South Wales (*left*), and some of their modern counterparts (*above* and *right*). Stag is Bond's premium lager in this market. It is especially pale in color, but relatively full in aroma and palate.

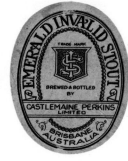

NEW ZEALAND

THE ACCOLADE of having launched the first new micro-brewery in the southern hemisphere goes to New Zealand. In 1982, hotelier Terry McCashin, an ex-All Black rugby player, established the Roc Mac Brewery, at Stoke, near Nelson, on the South Island. McCashin had visited Britain at the height of interest in "real ale" there, and returned with the notion of producing something similar in New Zealand. Soon afterward, he heard that the Rochdale Cider Brewery, at Stoke, was for sale. He bought it, and turned it to the production of "boutique" beers.

McCashin needed all the tenacity of his days as an All Black. Although barley is grown in New Zealand, he had difficulty persuading any maltster to take his venture seriously. Undaunted, he hired his own maltster. Together, they built a maltings. Of the several hundred micro-brewers elsewhere in the world, no other found that necessary.

Then he hired a brewer, a Briton who had previously worked in New Zealand. He was so far ahead of his time that his beers met with more curiosity than enthusiasm in New Zealand, though his venture was reported with interest not only in Britain but also in the United States.

Using local barley and seasoning his products with the flowers of New Zealand's small hop-growing industry, McCashin began with four products. His Mac's Real Ale is actually produced with a lager yeast and, in its bottled form, pasteurized. It is intended to have ale characteristics but is really a malty, full-flavoured bronze lager. Black Mac is a dark lager, with a deep copper color. Mac's Gold is a pale lager, well-hopped and smooth. Southtop is a sweet lager in the style typical of New Zealand. Predictably, the last has found the readiest market. Like pioneers of micro-brewing elsewhere, McCashin is now using his experience to help spread the movement. He is developing, and helping to establish, brew-pubs.

New Zealand's first brew-pub was the Shakespeare Tavern and Ale-House, at 61 Albert Street, Auckland. The Shakespeare's German-style, 12-hectoliter brew-house was constructed by the National Dairy Association of New Zealand. It began, in 1986, with a view to making two or three of its own products, including an ale and a Stout, under the Falstaff name, while also stocking seven or eight lagers from the national brewers.

Several other micros or brew-pubs have since been announced. These include: The Village Brewery, at Porirua, Wellington; Newbegin Brewery, Te Papapa, Auckland; the Stockan Brewing Company, at Henderson; and the Strongcroft Brewery, at Petone.

As elsewhere, there will undoubtedly be more, and not all will survive, but the opportunity for micros broadens as the mainstream industry concentrates yet further.

New Zealand has only two national groups. In the late 1980s the larger of these, called simply New Zealand Breweries, decided to close three of its plants. Wellington was scheduled to stop brewing in 1988, Hamilton and Dunedin the following year. This left all production at upgraded breweries in Auckland, Hastings, and Christchurch.

New Zealand Breweries has had considerable success in international markets with its premium product Steinlager. This is a mildly dry (22 units of bitterness) Pilsener-type, with a pleasantly hoppy aroma and a firm palate. It has a gravity of 11.25 Plato (1045) and 3.7 per cent alcohol by weight; 4.8 by volume. Whole hops, grown in New Zealand, are used, and fermentation is at very low temperatures. Steinlager was judged not only top of its class but also best overall entrant when 800 beers from all over the world were judged by a 33-member panel in the 1985 Brewing Industry Awards in Britain.

The company also has a sweetish everyday lager called Rheineck (9.8; 1040; 3.05; 3.85). Its Leopard Brewery, in Hastings, has its own product under that name. Leopard DeLuxe is a lightly-hopped, Pilsener-type beer with a slight, clean, spicy-fruity note reminiscent of Heineken. In 1984, Leopard DeLuxe came top out of 45 lagers in the *Los Angeles Times* Beer Olympics. Not only is there a Leopard, there are also two Lions, dating from a time when the company sought to make this its principal brand. New Zealand Breweries' parent company is Lion Corporation.

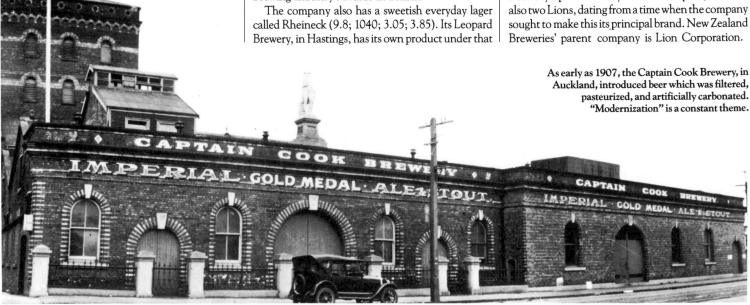

As early as 1907, the Captain Cook Brewery, in Auckland, introduced beer which was filtered, pasteurized, and artificially carbonated. "Modernization" is a constant theme.

The firm of Staples (*below*), in Wellington, was merged into the New Zealand Breweries group in 1923, along with Captain Cook and eight other companies. Some of New Zealand Breweries' current labels are shown here. Speights and Waikato originated as local brands.

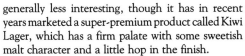

generally less interesting, though it has in recent years marketed a super-premium product called Kiwi Lager, which has a firm palate with some sweetish malt character and a little hop in the finish.

Considering that Captain Cook brewed New Zealand's first beer as early as 1773, from a decoction of spruce and tea plants, the time might be ripe for a return to something a little more exotic.

The regular lager in this range is Lion Red (9; 1036; 2.95; 3.7), which has a malty note and a full color (14 E.B.C.). There is also a Lion Brown, fermented at warm temperatures, and with high yeast levels. A distinctive esteriness is created by this method. When the beer is lagered in the normal way, it evinces a richly spicy-aromatic palate. Full-colored lagers with this ale-like character are a feature of brewing in New Zealand. Nothing quite like them is found elsewhere in the world.

The New Zealand brewers who make them are proud of this distinctive style. The continuous fermentation system was developed in New Zealand, and is not universally admired elsewhere.

The rival group, Dominion, has breweries at Wairarapa, Timaru and Greymouth. Its products are

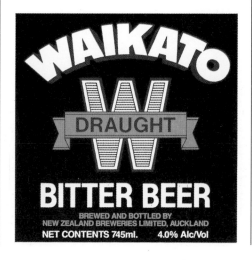

ASIA

The paintings on the left were originally reproduced as posters for the Sapporo Brewery during the 1920s and early 1930s, and later as postcards. The set shown here is part of a larger collection on show in the company's museum.

Over it all had brooded thirst, thirst for a warmish bottle of Tiger Beer. Or Anchor. Or Carlsberg.
— Anthony Burgess, *Time for a Tiger*, 1956

THERE ARE THE GOLDEN EAGLE of Himalayan India, the Kingfisher and Flying Horse of Bangalore, the Singha lion-legend and the Red-Tongued Wolf of Thailand, the Dog of Malaysia, the Tiger of Singapore, the Kirin dragon-horse of Japan . . .

The vivid images of Asia, the myths, the colors, the sounds, are indelible. There they are, even on the beer-labels, and in the daydreams of everyone who has ever set foot east of the Bosporus.

They are daydreams, rather than memories. None of the beers, or few, is as good as the best recollections. None is nearly as bad as the worst story about it. Contrary to rumor, none of these products is a "rice beer." Some may contain a proportion of rice as an adjunct, but so do a good few beers in other parts of the world. If it looks like a conventional beer, it is probably made from barley malt in a proportion of 60 per cent or more. There are much more primitive, turbid "traditional beers" made out of sweet potatoes, coconut sap or whatever is available, but they are a different matter.

Rumor has glycerine being added to Indian beers. Glycerol, which amounts to the same thing, can occur naturally in proportions of 0.1-0.3 per cent in the fermentation of barley malt, and contributes body and sweetness. To add more would be to risk destroying the head on the beer.

Muslim fundamentalism has closed breweries in some Asian countries, but the more cosmopolitan Islamic nations still permit beer to be produced, "for

Stopping for a Toddy

Almost every Third World country has a traditional fermented beverage described loosely as "beer." Several, including Sri Lanka, employ the sap of the coconut pod. Tapping the palm is an elaborate procedure, but the fermentation of the sap with wild yeasts takes only hours. The Sri Lankans call their "traditional beer" Toddy. It is sold from roadside huts, called Toddy Taverns; they announce themselves with a pictogram. Most sell an "ordinary" Toddy, fermented for a few hours, and a drier, stronger "special" (12 hours). The Toddy has a milky color and is viscous. It has a clammy aroma, a slight, sherberty carbonation, and a palate which seems at first salty, then soapy, and finally sweetish.

237

The Beers and Brewing Towns of Asia

Almost every capital city in Asia has its own brewery, and some have more than one. The labels shown here represent merely a selection, a sample from the vast number of beers which are available across this great continent. Each label is captioned with its city and brewery of origin. The world-famous names in Asian beer come from the nations of the Pacific and the South China Sea, but there are also brewing industries in the eastern Mediterranean and the Indian subcontinent.

THE MIDDLE EAST

The beer which links Europe and Asia is Efes, brewed in both Istanbul and Izmir (Smyrna), and thus straddling the Bosporus. Izmir has also a Tuborg brewery, and Ankara the Tekel Brewery. Pilsener-style and dark Münchener-style beers are both produced. Although it is in practice an Islamic country, Turkey has been nominally secular since the time of Ataturk. Its people are hardly great beer-drinkers, but it has few inhibitions about the existence of a brewing industry.

Beer is becoming more widely available in Syria. The Al-Chark Brewery, established there in 1954 and nationalized in 1965, produces a Pilsener-style beer (12 degrees Balling). Iraq has a government-owned brewery producing three lagers: Golden (11.5), Jawhara (12.5), and Kuhrmana (13.5), the latter in cans. The same country has also a joint-stock company producing Ferida Lager (12.1) and Amstel Gold (14.0)

In this part of the world not only Islamic fundamentalism but also war has exacted a toll. Iran had a brewing industry for more than 30 years, with lagers like Setarah (11.0) and Shams (11.5), both from the Sarkissian & Sahakians company, Tuborg (12.0), and the medium-palate dark-brown Majidieh (11.0) from a brewery backed by the Board for the Protection of Industries. The current status of these enterprises is uncertain.

Israel has a brewery which produces three lagers: Nesher (10.0), Abir (11.0), and Maccabee (12.0). It produces also a Pilsener-style beer called O.K. (11.5), a low-alcohol malt beverage, and an ale-type beer called Goldstar (12.0).

THE INDIAN SUBCONTINENT

Memories of the British Raj have survived fitfully in Pakistan at the Murree Brewery, Rawalpindi, where London Lager (10.4) has traditionally been labeled with an illustration of Nelson's Column. Murree is known also for an Export (11.4) and a bottom-fermented Medium Stout (14.2).

Although attitudes toward alcohol vary from state to state, India has a lively brewing industry, stretching from the Simla Hills in the north to Hyderabad and Bangalore in the south. At Solan, in the Simla Hills, the firm of Mohan Meakin produces five lagers: Baller (original gravity 1040), Gymkhana (1045), Lion (1046), Krown (1048), and Golden Eagle (1050). In Hyderabad the Vinedale Breweries produce three lagers with original gravities of 1046, two premium lagers under the names Flying Horse and Jubilee (both 1052), and two Bitter Stouts (1046) under the names London and Kingfisher.

Sri Lanka has two breweries, McCallum and Ceylon Breweries, which have continued to operate through war and peace.

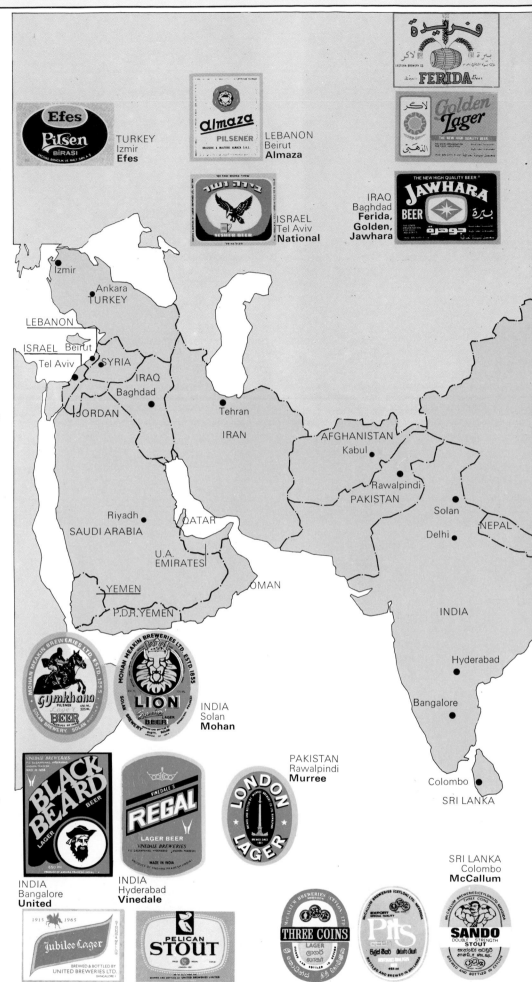

238

KOREA
Seoul
OB, Crown

JAPAN
Sapporo
Sapporo

JAPAN Tokyo **Kirin**

JAPAN
Osaka
Suntory

JAPAN Tokyo
Asahi

Okinawa
Orion

TAIWAN
Taipei
Taiwan

PHILIPPINES
Manila
San Miguel

THAILAND
Bangkok
Amarit, Singha

VIETNAM
Saigon
33

Singapore
Tiger

USSR

USSR

CHINA

Peking

Sapporo

JAPAN

Tokyo

KOREA

Seoul

Osaka

Taipei

TAIWAN

Hong Kong

BHUTAN

BANGLADESH

Dacca

BURMA

LAOS

Vientiane

THAILAND

Rangoon

Bangkok

Phnom
Penh

VIETNAM

CAMBODIA

Manila

PHILIPPINES

BRUNEI

SARAWAK

MALAYA

Kuala Lumpur

Singapore

BORNEO

Medan

SUMATRA

SUMATRA

Djakarta

JAVA

Surabaja

IRAN
Tehran
**Tuborg,
Sham,
Medjidieh**

SUMATRA
Medan
Galion

JAVA
Djakarta
Serimpi

JAVA
Surabaja
Bintang

MALAYA
Kuala Lumpur
ABC, Anchor

239

The graphic art of the brewer

このラベルは創製100年を記念して、明治9年発売当時の商標を再現したものです。

633ml ★ サッポロビール株式会社P

東京都中央区銀座7-9-20図1444

サッポロビール

Brewers all over the world have made lavish contributions to graphic art (in the United States, Pabst even gave its name to a typeface), but the Japanese have the most beautiful labels. Sad to say, the newer examples are far less decorative, and rely on English-language brand names in bold typographical styles. It would be sad if the splendor of Sapporo or the sacred symbol of Kirin were to be extinguished for the sake of corporate indentity.

members of other faiths, and visitors." India has its prohibitionist states, but it still supports more than 30 breweries, mainly producing dryish lagers in broadly the Pilsener style. Some also make Stout. In most states of India, beer labels carry a warning that suggests the consumption of alcohol is dangerous to the health.

There are breweries throughout the subcontinent. In Nepal, Star Beer stands out for its hoppy aroma. In Burma, Mandalay Beer is fruity and ale-like. This characteristic may be intentional, but it is often caused by yeast problems in breweries in hot countries, especially if they are in isolated regions where there may be difficulties in maintaining sufficient refrigeration.

In Sri Lanka, the roof of the malt silo at the McCallum "Three Coins" Brewery affords the best possible view of the 7,362ft mountain upon which is a depression variously argued to be the footprint of Adam, the Lord Buddha, or Shiva. The brewery makes a full-bodied, smooth chocolaty Dry Stout of 1060 called Sando. It is named after a Hungarian strong man who toured with circuses. That Stout, with a very English dash of invert sugar, is bottom-fermented.

Higher in the mountains, in the Buddhist holy city of Kandy, U.K.D. Silva's bar, in Colombo Street, serves a second Dry Stout, cask-conditioned, from the wood by hand-pump. Such a rare arrangement in such an absurdly unlikely place demands a celebratory drink. The Stout is soft and still, fresh, fruity, and delicious. Its odd companion, a cask-conditioned lager, is less stable in these conditions.

The same arrangement persists at the Beer Shop, in the mountain town of Nuwara Eliya, the tea-planting capital, where this cask-conditioned Stout is made by a company that still calls itself Ceylon Breweries. The Stout is served more yeastily at the Beer Shop. It is said that there has been brewing in Nuwara Eliya since 1860, though that does not appear to be well documented. The present brewery dates from the 1880s, and still carries out some of its fermentation in wooden vessels, of which there are a dozen. These are especially used for the Stout, which is top-fermenting. The brewery's several lagers are made with a rice adjunct, but the Stout (again, 1060) is all-malt.

Guinness began exporting to Asia in the late 1800s. Different shippers used to label the bottles with their own signs, usually animals. The original shippers to Thailand were called Blood, Wolfe and Company. Their emblem was a wolf with a red tongue. It became known as The Blood Wolf. In peninsular Malaya, there were Bulldog and Dog's Head brands competing with one another. Years later, when Guinness wanted to end this dogfight, peace was impeded by brand loyalties. Guinness settled for gradualism. The Bulldog's stance was subtly altered in successive redrawings, until only its head was visible. Had it been a cat, only the smile would have been left. Guinness is both imported and

Peak Pulling Power

For the lover of "real ale" the sight of hand-pumps in a remote corner of Asia is as welcome as it is astonishing. In the mountain towns of Nuwara Eliya and Kandy, Sri Lanka, The Beer Shop (*above*) go one further: they (*top left*) and U.K.D. Silva serve cask-conditioned Stout. This style in that form is no longer available even in its native Ireland. These two colorful establishments obtain their Stout from Ceylon Breweries - which still uses wooden fermenting vessels.

brewed locally in various parts of Asia, and is popular among ethnic Chinese communities. Demand rises at Chinese New Year and at the Eighth Moon (August/September). Stout is thought to benefit the complexion, and is sometimes poured into a newly-born baby's bath for this reason. According to yin-and-yang theory, Stout is "heaty," while lager is "cooling." That sounds reasonable enough. Some Chinese also believe that the finings in Guinness have especially aphrodisiac powers.

Thailand has an outstanding pale lager that would attract attention anywhere in the world. This beer is called Singha, after a lion-like creature of local mythology. It seems that Singha Lager may have originated as a pale Bock, with perhaps 16 degrees Plato. Today it has 13.8 (1055-plus), with 4.8 per cent alcohol by weight; 6 by volume. It contains 87 per cent barley malt, and sugar is used as an adjunct. Remarkably, it has 40 units of bitterness. The gravity, body, and hop character make for an unusual and excellent balance. Singha is a wonderfully hoppy, aromatic dry lager, full of flavor. This product was devised in the 1930s by a German brewmaster in Thailand, and it is to be hoped that its character is maintained. In the international market, there are scarcely any really distinctive lagers, and

every commercial pressure is to produce beers of mid-Atlantic blandness. The Thai beer Kloster is in this style. Thai Amarit, although a lager, has an ale-like fruitiness.

In Malaysia, as Anthony Burgess observed, Tiger Beer, Anchor and Carlsberg are the local brews. In his book *Little Wilson and Big God,* Burgess claims to have been "tight on draft cider" when he applied for a teaching post in what was then Malaya. While there, he wrote *Time for a Tiger,* set as the sun sank on the Empire.

Time for a Tiger had been a slogan for the beer since 1946, and the brewery's recollection is that Burgess approached them for clearance before using it as the title for his book. Burgess remembers that the slogan appeared on what he felt was a rather handsome clock, used as promotional material. He says he suggested that the brewery give him one of the clocks as a "thank you" for having featured their name. When they irritated him by asking to see the manuscript first, he responded by adding a favorable mention of Carlsberg to the text. Fourteen years later, Burgess and his wife were offered all the Tiger they cared to drink during a visit to Singapore — "But it was too late: I had become wholly a gin man."

Tiger and Anchor are both clean-tasting Pilsener-style beers of 12 Plato (1048; 4.1; 5.1) made by Malayan Breweries, of Kuala Lumpur and Singapore. The breweries are jointly owned by the local company Fraser and Neave, which also produces soft drinks, and by Heineken. The Dutch company has additional interests in Indonesia, as does Allied Breweries.

Tiger Beer was originally hoppier than Anchor, but the two are now very similar, with some Heineken family character. They are 75 per cent malt, with three to six weeks' lagering and 21 units of bitterness. The breweries also produce a creamy, caramelish, roasty, medium-dry Stout called ABC (18.2; 1073; 6.5; 8.1). This is bottom-fermented.

Tiger was a thirst-quencher for the British Forces during World War II and the colonial period, just as the dryish, lightly fruity, French-Vietnamese "33" became for the Americans. Today's armies of Britons are more familiar with San Miguel beer, albeit from its three breweries in sunny Spain. San Miguel, founded in 1890, is headquartered in the Philippines, where it has several breweries as well as extensive interests in food, agriculture and trade. After the fall of the Marcos government, there was a battle for control of the company.

San Miguel is a light, smooth, dry Pilsener-style beer of 12 Plato (1048; 4; 5), 80 per cent malt, with one month's lagering and about 20 units of bitterness. The company also has a dark lager, San Miguel Cerveza Negra, with an above-average gravity (13.5; 1054; 4.1; 5.2) and a good toasted-malt character. A pale lager called Red Horse has a higher gravity (14; 1056; 5.5; 6.8), and a soft, full, sweetish palate, with some fruity notes.

Manning levels seem to be quite high at this Chinese brewery but in fact modernization is today proceeding apace. The People's Republic has employed consultants ranging from Suntory to Ringwood. Its range of beers is more diverse than might be expected, but only its Pilsener types can easily be found in the West.

CHINA

The most populous nation on earth has brewed beer since the late 1800s, when the Germans occupied, then leased, the port of Tsingtao, on the Shantung peninsula, across the Yellow Sea from South Korea and Japan.

Even today, the town of Tsingtao (Qingdao, Shandong) has architectural reminders of a turn-of-the-century resort on the Baltic coast. It also has a sizable brewery. The beer made in Tsingtao, and bearing the name of the town, is China's super-premium brew. Since the post-Revolution blockade cut off supplies, China has grown its own hops. When tasted fresh, the regular beer of Tsingtao, a crisp Pilsener type, has a notably good hop character. It can be a little variable in malt character, though only slightly so. The brewery also makes a very sweet Porter which can be hard to find.

Tsingtao seems to have a plentiful supply of good hops, but this is not the case for all breweries. Some have even experienced problems with sand in supplies of hops grown near the Gobi Desert. China also grows barley, but a consistent supply of good malt has not been achieved yet.

Before the Revolution, there was only a scatter of breweries in China, but now every city has at least one, and some have two or three. There are at least 100 breweries of a significant size, but it is believed that the total number might be two or three times this figure. The brewing industry is not operated on a national scale but by provinces. As in several Third World or "intermediate" economies, the growth reflects an improvement in living standards, and a Westernization, of a country with a very large population. Consumption per head remains very low.

Nonetheless, demand cannot be met, and several international brewers are working on partnerships with the provinces. There is also at least one British-style micro-brewery, producing an ale. This was established at Changsha, in Hunan province, with the help of Ringwood. It seems incongruous that a small country brewery company from the New Forest of England should be helping mighty China meet its needs, but Ringwood is not alone in this. Very large brewing corporations from several Western countries, as well as from Japan, are likewise involved in China, variously in consulting roles or in partnerships of one sort or another. Having decided to enter the modern world, the republic seems determined to explore every possibility. It is to be hoped that this ultimately makes for true variety.

Ostensibly, all the established breweries produce pale lagers, though many of their products are murky and sweet, sometimes with a reddish tinge and a honeyish wortiness or an ale-like, yeasty fruitiness. A typical example is Wei Mei, from the tourist town of Kweilin (Guilin). Another is Mon-Lei, from Beijing. The same city's Tientan is a smooth, malty Pilsener type. There is the odd darkish lager (Guangminpai, from Shanghai, is an example). Apart from Tsingtao, few are hoppy, though Shenyang, from Manchuria, has a notably good bouquet.

Despite the shortage of beer in China, some local breweries export, as a means of earning hard currency. Their identities are often confused by trade-names devised by Western distributors. Names involving pandas are especially popular.

JAPAN

When the American Navy visited Japan in 1853, with a view to opening trade between the countries, there was more than an element of threat in its presence. Despite that, a glass of beer changed hands, and Japan has not been the same since.

One of Commodore Perry's smoky "Black Ships" was visited by a Japanese who was "an ardent student of all things foreign," and he was offered the beer. He later managed to find a textbook on brewing. This was in Dutch, but he was nonetheless able to use it, and to produce a brew for private consumption. He is credited with having first created interest in beer in Japan.

In 1869, the American company Wiegand and Copeland started an experimental brewery in Yokohama. Soon afterwards, the Japanese government sent a researcher to Germany to carry out a study with a view to establishing a local brewing industry. In the 1870s, a government mission that had been deputed to create industries on the undeveloped northern islands of Hokkaido established a brewery at Sapporo.

The first, American, brewery subsequently passed into Japanese hands and became Kirin. The first Japanese brewery took the name Sapporo. At one point, Sapporo also owned Tsingtao, in China, and two breweries in Korea. Today, both Koreas have brewing industries, making sweetish beers in broadly the Pilsener style.

Japan also has breweries owned by Asahi and Suntory. The country's beers are made to very high technical standards, with considerable use of Saaz hops. Except for the "light beer" type, they are generally lagered for about a month, and specialties may have eight or nine weeks. Although Japanese beers are thought in general to be very light-bodied, their more notable characteristic is their cleanness. They are often fuller in body than those of the United States.

Kirin takes its name from a creature in Chinese mythology. The Japanese joke about their propensity for borrowing other people's ideas, though they argue that they are really in the business of adaptation. The Japanese hiragana and katakana alphabets are adapted from the kanji characters of China. Japan's tea ceremony was modified from Chinese tradition. Japanese sake is a refinement of a cruder, ancient rice wine of China.

The Kirin is a mythical creature, half horse, half dragon, which features in a legend more than 2,500 years old. One evening, the story says, a Chinese woman called En Chen Tsai was strolling in her garden when she was confronted by the creature. "The Kirin enveloped her in its sacred breath. They both became attached to each other, and two nights passed before the Kirin reluctantly disappeared." Less than a year after this mysterious encounter, En Chen Tsai gave birth to Confucius. Thereafter, whenever a Chinese saint was born, legend maintains, the mother had previously been visited

Once their enthusiasm has been fired the Japanese are not given to half-measures. As with whiskey, so with beer. Among several types of drinking places that flourish in Japan, the rooftop beer-garden enjoys great popularity.

Today Detroit, Tomorrow Milwaukee...

The Americans, British and Dutch all had a hand in the popularization of beer in Japan, but the first beers to be sold on a wide scale were German imports; no doubt this was why researcher Nakawara (*above*) was sent to Germany in the 1870s. The first lithographic poster produced in Japan was for Kirin beer (*right*). Even in the early days, the same brewer took advantage of the Japanese flair for automative engineering (*top*).

by the Kirin. Thus the creature is regarded as the harbinger of happy and festive events, especially when it arrives with a beer.

Kirin is one of the world's largest brewers, making more than 30 million hectoliters of beer a year. Its headquarters are in Tokyo, and it has a very traditional, German-style old brewery there. There are a dozen others, some much newer, scattered around the country. The regular Kirin Lager Beer has the fullest body and palate among the Japanese Pilseners, with Hallertau and Saaz hops in both aroma and flavor. It has 11 degrees Plato (1044; 3.6; 4.9) and a bitterness of 27.5. The company claims to lager this beer for two months. In the Japanese market, the company has a stronger pale lager (14.5; 1058; 5.2; 6.5), again with a good hop character, called Mein Bräu. Kirin has traditionally also made what in Japan is known as a Black Beer, at 12.5 (1050; 4; 5). This is a dark lager with a color of 270 E.B.C. Japanese beers in this style seem originally to have been inspired by the dark lagers of Kulmbach, Bavaria. The product portfolio additionally includes a tasty, strong Kirin Stout (18; 1072; 6.4; 8), full of "treacle toffee" flavor. This is bottom-fermenting.

Sapporo now has two breweries in the city of its foundation, and eight elsewhere. Its older "Victorian" brewery in Sapporo has partly been turned into a large beer cellar and garden. Although this is the most interesting such establishment, most big cities have several. Rooftop gardens are also popular. Young businessmen meet for an after-work drink over a hearty noodle dish heated on a hotplate set into the table.

Sapporo, known for especially good sushi, is the only city in Japan built on the American grid system. It was designed by an American town-planner.

Nearby, in the small town of Yoichi, is one of Japan's prettiest whiskey distilleries. Sapporo's portfolio includes a distinctive, dryish Black Beer, with slight licorice notes. The brewery also has an unpasteurized, super-premium Pilsener-type called Yebisu, which is surprisingly fruity.

Asahi's beers tend to be dry and fruity, but with a weak finish. In 1987, the company launched a new style of very well attenuated beer called Super Dry, with which it has enjoyed considerable success.

Suntory, which began life as a wines-and-spirits merchant and now has the world's biggest malt-whiskey distillery, came late to brewing. Its state-of-the-art plants have brew-kettles in a modern rendition of the traditional shape, but with an iridescent finish, and the overall impression is of the flight deck aboard the Starship *Enterprise*.

Suntory produces a range of unpasteurized, micro-filtered beers that are notably clean-tasting and mild. They are lightly hopped, but have a malty

dryness. The company had an outstandingly fresh-tasting hoppy Märzenbier, but was unable to make it perform in the marketplace. It has been replaced by a paler all-malt beer that has less palate, especially in the finish. This has the elemental brand-name Malt's.

There have also been attempts among Japanese brewers to market a very light style of Wheat Beer. The industry has the inclination, the technical skills and the equipment to innovate, but the young consumer is more quickly and easily excited by packaging than by content. The older generation in Japan shakes its head over the new ways, and wonders whether it is really necessary for the country to have more than 100 variations on the shape and design of beer bottles, cans and kegs.

There has, indeed, been some very creative packaging from Japanese brewers. Who else would have devised a beercan that opens into a cup? Clever — but not the stuff of legend.

AFRICA

THE ANCIENT EGYPTIANS may have been the first brewers in Africa. They brewed with barley, had at least four different types of beer, and took the trouble to leave detailed and durable records of their habits. At the same time, brewing was probably going on elsewhere in Africa, and there is no reason to believe that it ever ceased. Indigenous beers are central to many African tribal cultures, and an 18th-century visitor recorded that he found "a hundred and a hundred" different brews. "Abundance of beer is the glory of a chief's court," reported another observer.

These indigenous brews, sometimes identified as "traditional beer," are typically made from millet, sorghum, cassava flour or palm sap. Maize is also widely used. This crop, the staple food for millions of Africans, is not indigenous; it was introduced from the Americas. Whatever their raw material, these brews "provide energy . . . contribute vitamin C . . . and several B vitamins in which the diet of the people may be lacking", according to British nutritionist Magnus Pyke, in his work *Food and Society*.

Most Third World countries have some form of traditional beer, but there are more in Africa than anywhere else. The beers are often home-brewed,

but are also produced on a commercial basis. In Central Africa, the trading company and conglomerate Lonrho developed a product of this type with the trade-name Chibuku. The commercially-brewed version is served at Chibuku bars and sold off-premises in milk cartons. It has only a slight carbonation, is turbid, and tastes like sharp, alcoholic malted milk.

Some of the indigenous fermentable materials are also used as an adjunct in more conventional beers. In Nigeria, the government stipulated in 1985 that at least 25 per cent of the mash of beers must comprise locally-grown cereals. Most brewers felt they could comply with this, but not with a longer-term plan to make beer exclusively from home-grown materials by 1990. Heineken and the United Africa Company, which jointly own Nigerian Breweries Limited, said that if this were enforced, they would have to withdraw their Gulder, a tasty pale lager which enjoys a very good reputation locally. Nigeria is Africa's biggest brewing country, with more than 30 plants.

In Burundi, cassava has been used as an adjunct in a pale lager. The end result was sticky and without much finish, but tolerable in the heat of East Africa,

Land of the Lion

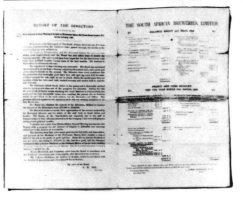

The two brands Lion and Castle share a long history as the best-known beers between the Zambezi and the Cape. In 1896 the first annual report of South African Breweries described "the experiment in lager-brewing" as "successful." The brewery (*above*) was built near Cape Town during the second Boer War.

Time for a Tusker

There was a pioneering spirit about the early days of East African Breweries. The setting-up of the original plant in 1922 was largely the work of a former gold-prospector who was then farming in Kenya. He and two partners imported their brewing equipment from Britain, and later hired a brewer from Burtonwood, England. Hops were imported from Kent, and the brewery's products were ales and Stout. The group picture (*inset*) shows the staff in 1929, and the photograph of the company's fleet in front of the brewery (*above*) was taken around the same time. Lager-brewing was introduced in 1930. In 1968, the company won two gold medals and one silver at the World Beer Competition in Nürnberg. When a new headquarters was built in 1970, the foundation stone was laid by President Kenyatta (*right*), who was later presented by the managing director with a bronze cast of a famous Kenyan Tusker called Ahmed.

The biggest-selling beers in West Africa are Gulder and Star, and the greatest beer-drinkers in all Africa are the Nigerians. Here, with a smile, Mrs Atinmo and her staff offer clients their two favourite brands — as well as Guinness.

The Nile rises among the lakes of East Africa. More than one nation can claim to be the home of its source. Uganda has been known to say it with beer (*above*). The same medium was used during the confrontation with Kenya in 1976 (*top*).

firm, clean palate, and a lightly dry finish. Tusker Premium is the top-of-the-line brand among five or six beers made by this company.

A beer called simply Pilsener Lager is very similar, but fractionally less hoppy. The regular Tusker and the slightly more fruity, aromatic White Cap are made at the lower gravity of 1038. In these products, the adjunct is unmalted barley. Versions called Tusker Export and White Cap Export likewise have a gravity of 1038, but are a little thinner in body; their adjunct is sugar.

The company was founded in 1922 by a former gold prospector and two farmer brothers, who were British settlers. One of the farmers was later killed by an elephant, and his brother named a beer Tusker in his memory. It seems odd that he named the beer after the killer and not the victim.

In a country that depends upon agriculture and tourism, a sizable, locally-owned brewing company is a very important enterprise. Its smart head office, in a suburb of Nairobi, is set in a valley, among jacaranda, wild fig, and banana trees. It looks over parkland which is being turned into a company golf course. A row of cream Mercedes stands in the executive parking lot. Outside the brewery, hefty "road train" trucks wait to shift loads of beer. The company employs 4,000 people. In Nairobi, there are two brewing lines, each in traditional copper, set into yellow tiling. The company also has another brewery in Mombasa, and one up country at Kisumu, near Lake Victoria. The parent company, East African Breweries, also owns a plant in Uganda.

Except for fundamentalist Muslim countries, every African nation has at least one brewery, usually making beers in the international interpretation of the Pilsener style. Several have a range of two or three products in this style, each with a different specification. Older styles like Bock beers and ales have largely vanished, but tropical Dry Stouts can still be found in some countries.

Zaire is one of Africa's major brewing nations, with about 20 plants. Consumption per head is not high, but it is a large country. To the casual observer, Zambia appears to drink a lot of beer, but statistically only wealthy South Africa is significant.

South of the Limpopo, South African Breweries has a virtual monopoly. Its only challengers are local micro-breweries. In 1984, a former S.A.B. employee, Lex Mitchell, founded a micro in Knysna, Cape Province. This operation, called simply the Knysna Brewery, has since expanded. It produces a lager, a Bitter and a Stout, all available unfiltered at the brewery. Two or three years later, a company called Our Brewery went into production at St George Street, Johannesburg. This is a Ringwood-style ale brewery, though its product is filtered. There have also been attempts to start a Wheat Beer brewery in South Africa. *Ex Africa semper aliquid novi.*

especially as nothing else was available. In difficult circumstances, most African countries produce creditable beers. None is consistently outstanding, but there will usually be one African beer or another among the award-winners at European competitions each year. From Togo to the Seychelles, breweries have produced clean-tasting Pilseners which have picked up prizes. Since colonial times, several major European brewers have been active in Africa. Most work in partnership with banks or trading companies or, most often, national governments.

Few African countries are sufficiently prosperous to take lightly the import of barley malt and hops, and in most the climate is too hot for their cultivation. Kenya, with its cool highlands, grows enough barley to use it, in unmalted form, as an adjunct in brewing. Kenya has also experimented with the cultivation of hops. Floodlights have been used to lengthen the days, but Africa can hardly afford such expensive effort. Kenya Breweries has its own barley-growing program with local farmers, cultivating a two-row strain of Australian origin. The company uses mainly Hallertau and Styrian hops.

Its Pilsener-style Tusker Premium is exported to the United States as a "Malt Lager." It is 90 per cent malt, with cane sugar as an adjunct, and a gravity of 11 Plato (1044). It has an excellent hop aroma, a

INDEX

ACKNOWLEDGEMENTS

Jacket photographs by John Heseltine and Paul Forrester; flap picture of author by Michael Lichter, Boulder, Colorado; **p2** Iain Macmillan; **p6** Helena Wilsonová; **p8** Ian Howes, Pavel Fošenbauer; **p10** Summit; **p11** Robert Micklewright; **p13** Licensed Victuallers' Gazette; **p15** Paul Forrester; **p17** Alan Austin; **p18** Licensed Victuallers' Gazette; **p19** Heineken, Alan Austin; **p23** Moretti; **p24, p27** (lagering tanks); **p30, p34** and **p35** Pavel Fosenbauer; **p25, p27** (Crystal), **p29** and **p31** (Krušovice) Roger Protz and **p31** (Beechwood) Ian Howes, all © Michael Jackson; **p28** and **p33** Helena Wilsonová; **p34** (Charles Bridge) Cedok; **p36** Jon Wyand; **p37** Michael Jackson ©; **p38** Quarto Library; **pp40-41** John Wyand and (nun at festival) Michael Jackson ©; **p43** Quarto Library; **pp44-45** Augustiner and Michael Jackson ©; **pp46-47** Michael Jackson © and Derek Walsh © Michael Jackson; **pp48-49** Landeshaupstadt München Fremdenverkehrsamt; **p50** Jon Wyand; **p51** Einbecker Brauerei; **p52** John Heseltine; **pp52-53** Jon Wyand; **pp56-57** Jon Wyand and Rauchenfels; **p60** Michael Jackson © and Jon Wyand; **p61** Jon Wyand, Alan Austin; **p62** Ian Howes © Michael Jackson; **p64** Brauhaus Bönnsch and Derek Walsh, © Michael Jackson; **p66** Trevor Wood; **p67** D.U.B.; **p68** Ian Howes, © Michael Jackson; **p69** Trevor Wood; **pp70-71** Zum Uerige; **pp72-73** Trevor Wood, Ian Howes © Michael Jackson and Derek Walsh © Michael Jackson; **p74** Trevor Wood; **p75** Jon Wyand; **p76** Ian Howes © Michael Jackson; **p77** Jon Wyand; **p78** Ian Howes © Michael Jackson, Jon Wyand and Trevor Wood; **p79** Peter Keen; **pp80-81** Trevor Wood (Rastal Collection); **p82** Deutscher Brauer-Bund; **p83** Trevor Wood; **pp84-85** Jon Wyand and Michael Jackson ©; **pp88-89** Trevor Wood; **pp90-91** Ian Howes © Michael Jackson; **pp92-95** Carlsberg; **p97** Ian Howes © Michael Jackson; **p100** Michael Jackson©; **p102** Michael Jackson ©; **p103** Lehtikuva; **p104** Michael Jackson ©; **p105** Liefmans; **p106** West Flanders Tourist Board (hop shoots), Michael Jackson ©; **p107** Ian Howes © Michael Jackson; **p108** Paul Forrester; **p109** Michael Jackson ©; **p110** Robert Morley; Kunsthistoriches Museum, Vienna; **pp116-117** Robert Morley; **p118** Michael Jackson © and Robert Morley; **p119** Liefmans; **pp120-121** Robert Morley/ Brouwerij Het Anker; **p122** De Kluis, Michael Jackson ©; **p123** Michael Jackson ©; **p124** Robert Morley, Liefmans; **p125** Michael Jackson ©, Derek Walsh © Michael Jackson; **p126** Ian Howes © Michael Jackson; **p127** Lamot; **p128** Michael Jackson ©; **pp129-131** Robert Morley; **pp132-133** Ian Howes © Michael Jackson; **p134** Heineken; **p135** Derek Walsh © Michael Jackson; **p136** Heineken; **p137** VVV Maastricht, Felix Jansen; **p138** Gulpener; **p139** Antiek Print, Brand, Michael Jackson ©; **p140** Richard Crouch; **p141** Derek Walsh © Michael Jackson, Grolsche; **p142** Schaapskooi, Michael Jackson ©; **p143** Mousel et Clausen; **p144** Trevor Wood; **p145** Caledonian Brewery; **p149** Samuel Smith; **pp150-151** Eldridge Pope; **pp152-153** Roger Daniels; **pp154-55** CAMRA; **p156** Ian Howes; **p157** Ridley's; **p158** Guinness; **p159** Michael Jackson ©; **pp160-161** Courtauld Institute, Bass; **p162** Marston's; **pp163-164** Samuel Smith; **p165** Iain Macmillan; **p166** Michael Jackson ©; **p167** Fuller's; **p168** Iain Macmillan, Ian Howes, Mary Evans; **p169** Michael Jackson ©; **pp170-171** Trevor Wood; **p173** Eldridge Pope, Doug Pratt; **p174** Whitbread; **p175** S. G. Sillem, Brewers' Society; **p176** Trevor Wood; **p177** Caledonian Brewery; **p178** Belhaven Brewery; **p179** Guinness; **p180** Michael Jackson ©, Trevor Wood; **p181** Lett's; **pp182-184** Jon Wyand; **p185** Kronenbourg; **p186** Jon Wyand, Laurence Orbach; **p187** John Heseltine; **p188** Feldschlösschen; **p189** Michael Jackson ©; **p190** Sibra; **p191** Michael Jackson ©; **pp192-193** Jon Wyand, Michael Jackson ©; **p195** Stefania Ciesielska; **pp196-197** Moretti, Farson's; **p199** Michael Jackson ©; **p200** Ontario Archives, Molson's, Labatt, Carling; **p201** Derek Walsh © Michael Jackson; **p202** Ian Howes; **pp205-207** Michael Jackson ©; **p208** Anheuser-Busch; **p209** Michael Jackson ©; **pp210-211** Anheuser-Busch, Michael Jackson ©, August Schell; **p212** Michael Jackson ©; **pp213-214** Coors; **p214** Boulder Brewery; **p215** Ian Howes; **pp216-217** Michael Jackson ©; **p218** Vince Cottone; **p219** Yakima Brewing; **pp220-221** Guinness; **pp222-223** Michael Freeman, Jerry Fox, Michael Jackson ©; **p224** David Brinson; **p227** Bond Brewing; **pp228-229** David Brinson; **pp230-232** C.U.B.; **p233** Bond Brewing; **pp234-235** New Zealand Breweries; **p236** Sapporo; **p237** Michael Jackson ©; **p240** Dai Nippon; **p241** Michael Jackson ©, Felix Greene; **p242** Guinness; **p243** Kirin; **pp244-245** South African Breweries, Kenya Breweries; **pp246-247** Guinness.